Best Practices in Psychosocial Rehabilitation

Ruth Hughes, Ph.D. and Diane Weinstein, M.S.W.

Editors

Contributing Authors

Richard Baron, M.A.

Laura Blankertz, Ph.D.

Barbara Caldwell, Ph.D.

Judith Cook, Ph.D.

Betty Dahlquist, M.S.W.

Laurene Finley. Ph.D.

Jessica Jonikas, M.A.

Ruth Hughes, Ph.D.

Sheree Neese-Todd, Ph.D.

Anita Pernell-Arnold, M.S.S.W.

Diane Weinstein, M.S.W.

John Woods, M. Div.

This document was supported by a contract from the
Center for Mental Health Services
Substance Abuse and Mental Health Services Administration
Order # 94MF11644401D

International Association of Psychosocial Rehabilitation Services
10025 Governor Warfield Parkway, #301
Columbia, Maryland 21044-3357

Voice (410) 730-7190   FAX (410) 730-5965   TTY (410) 730-1723
website: www.iapsrs.org

The International Association of Psychosocial Rehabilitation Services has worked to ensure that all information in this book is accurate as of the publication date and consistent with good industry practices. It is recommended, however, that readers evaluate the applicability of this information in light of particular situations and changing standards. It is sold with the understanding that the publisher is not engaged in rendering legal, accounting, or other professional service. If legal advice or other expert assistance is required, the services of a competent professional should be sought.

Library of Congress Cataloging-in-Publication Data

Best practices in psychosocial rehabilitation / Ruth Hughes and Diane Weinstein, editors ; contributing authors, Richard Baron ... [et al.].
    p. cm.
  ISBN 0-9655843-5-6
  1. Mentally ill--Rehabilitation. I. Hughes, Ruth Ann, 1949- II. Weinstein, Diane. III. Baron, Richard C.

  RC439.5 .B485 1999
  362.2'2--dc21

                                                          99-048345

ISBN 0-9655843-5-6

Design, composition and production management by ColburnHouse Publishing & Marketing

International Association of Psychosocial Rehabilitation Services
10025 Governor Warfield Parkway, #301
Columbia, MD 21044-3357

Printed in the United States of America

Table of Contents

Section III : Specialized Practices

Section IV : Psychosocial Rehabilitation Resources

Acknowledgements

The development of this manuscript was supported by a contract from the Center for Mental Health Services, Substance Abuse and Mental Health Services Administration. Our thanks go to the staff of the Center for their support and encouragement in this endeavor. Many thanks go to the authors of each chapter, who contributed their time, knowledge, expertise to this book. This manuscript would never have reached publication without the administrations of Heather McQuay and Karen Colburn, who were responsible for editing the manuscript and managing the publication process.

Ruth Hughes and Diane Weinstein

Introduction

Thirty five years ago, there was little hope that a person with a diagnosis of severe and persistent mental illness could lead a productive life. The symptoms of the illness were often considered intractable. Mental health treatments and medications could control the more troublesome symptoms, but few people were able to return to a normal life. Long-term institutionalization was the most common alternative.

With the deinstitutionalization movement, services were provided in the community and large numbers of people were discharged from state psychiatric institutions. But it became clear that traditional mental health treatment—in the community or in an institution—was not sufficient. Long-term institutionalization was replaced by the revolving door, as many persons were discharged and rehospitalized often. To address this problem, a small number of innovative and creative programs were developed to address the needs of persons with severe mental illness. These fledgling programs were the pioneers in the field of psychosocial rehabilitation.

Today we know that recovery is a real possibility, and many people with mental illness lead productive, independent lives in our communities. In 20 years, psychosocial rehabilitation has grown from a few experimental programs to an integral and essential component of the service system for people with severe and persistent mental illness. There is a rich diversity of program models, rehabilitation technologies, and service settings. Participation in psychosocial rehabilitation significantly reduces the number and length of psychiatric hospitalizations, increases the level of functioning and the likelihood of employment, and results in significantly higher consumer satisfaction and quality of life. Severe mental illness is no longer considered a hopeless disease.

While we have a rich literature of program models, the field of psychosocial rehabilitation has only recently begun to define the skills and knowledge base needed by every practitioner, no matter what the setting or the program model. We have had a fertile history of mentoring people with severe mental illness, of learning from people with mental illness, and of training them on the job. But few opportunities have existed for the psychosocial rehabilitation workforce to systematically learn the skills, abilities, and knowledge needed to be effective practitioners. Only a handful of colleges and universities provide preservice courses or degrees in psychosocial rehabilitation. The Training and Certification Committee of the International Association of Psychosocial Rehabilitation Services began 8 years ago to define best practices and to develop standards of practice, a code of ethics, and training curriculum.

One of the first steps in this process was to examine our current workforce. IAPSRS and Matrix Research Institute conducted a three-year study of the psychosocial rehabilitation workforce, which was funded by the National Institute of Disability and Rehabilitation Research. As part of the NIDRR project, Jessica Jonikas, from University of Illinois National Research and Training Center on Rehabilitation and Mental Illness (UICNRTC), reviewed the literature of psychosocial rehabilitation in order to describe the staff competencies which had previously been defined (Jonikas, 1993).

As the next step, IAPSRS brought together a group of psychosocial rehabilitation practitioners, who represented every major approach in the field, to help us define the common skills, abilities and knowledge needed by every practitioner. Judith Cook and Bill Trochim, from UICNRTC, facilitated the process by using a concept mapping approach. The group brainstormed ideas, prioritized plans, discussed options, and grouped competencies based on their importance to every aspect of psychosocial rehabilitation no matter what the setting or the program model. Two challenges faced this talented group: to define the commonalities across diverse program models and settings *and* to go beyond the values and principles of psychosocial rehabilitation to competencies and best practices for practitioners. Using a statistical mapping approach, they developed a map to display the major groupings.

The concept map and the defined competencies form the basis of this book. These competencies are reflected in the first two sections of this volume. While our original goal was to define the core competencies, we have also asked experts in a number of specialty areas to define practitioner competencies and best practices in vocational rehabilitation, residential treatment, housing, and rehabilitation of persons with multiple disabilities. These specialized practices are described in Section III. Finally, in Section IV, we have listed a number of resources for practitioners.

This volume is the result of more than 8 years of work by the Board, Committees, and Staff of the International Association of Psychosocial Rehabilitation Services (IAPSRS), and it is built on the foundation of the work of an extraordinary group of people in our field— consumers, practitioners, researchers, and family members—who have helped us to define the essential and important components of rehabilitation. This volume is designed for the psychosocial rehabilitation practitioner to use as a reference for particular skills, as a training guide, and as a text book.

A Word about Words

We often do not agree about the words describing the work we do, even if we *do* agree about the principles, values, and outcomes. The terminology you use is influenced by the country and region you live in, your role in mental health, and, most importantly, by your personal experiences. In this volume, psychosocial rehabilitation is used to describe the broad range of community services provided to people with serious and persistent mental illness. Psychiatric rehabilitation and community support services are often used to mean the same thing. Not one of these terms is specific to a particular model or approach, but all encompass the rehabilitation philosophy and values. The acronym PSR is sometimes used to refer to psychosocial rehabilitation.

We have chosen not to use the many terms referring to people with mental illness. Consumers, survivors, members, associates, clients, and patients have been replaced with the term "individuals with mental illness" or "persons with mental illness." IAPSRS is committed to people first language and people first values. If it is awkward sometimes, be reminded that the person *always* comes before their mental illness.

Concept Map of Key Competencies

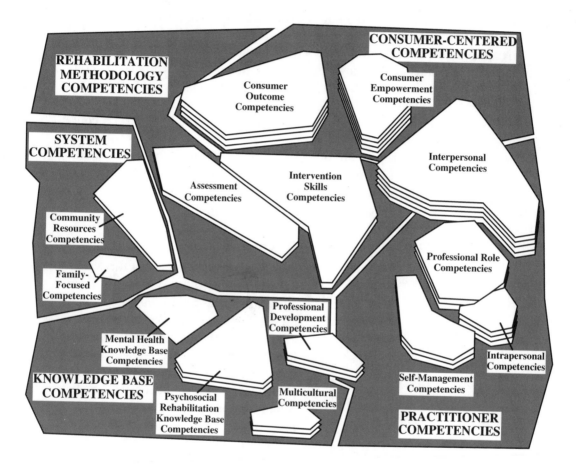

Best Practices in Psychosocial Rehabilitation
Summary of Competencies

Effective practitioners in psychosocial rehabilitation have developed the abilities, the skills and the knowledge to demonstrate each of the following:

Understanding Severe and Persistent Mental Illnesses

1. Recognize the population subset with a serious mental illness that is served by psychosocial rehabilitation services.
2. Learn the signs and symptoms of the most prevalent serious mental illnesses.
3. Understand the effects of stigma and discrimination.
4. Assess the effects of social factors in mental illness.
5. Understand the interaction of biological, social, and environmental factors in mental illness.
6. Understand the concept of recovery.
7. Know how legal issues impact the delivery of mental health services.

Knowledge of PsychosocialRehabilitation

1. Know the definition of psychosocial rehabilitation.
2. Know the history of psychosocial rehabilitation and community support.
3. Understand and believe in the principles of psychosocial rehabilitation.
4. Understand the distinction between the Medical Model and the Rehabilitation Model.
5. Describe the core components of psychosocial rehabilitation services.
6. Know the psychosocial rehabilitation models and technologies.
7. Stay current about research in the field of psychosocial rehabilitation, not only to shape practice, but also to share information with program participants and family members.

Person Centered Practices in Psychosocial Rehabilitation

1. View each individual as the director of his or her rehabilitation process.
2. Solicit and incorporate the preferences of the persons served in the rehabilitation process.
3. Believe in the value of self-help and facilitate an empowerment process.
4. Share information about mental illness and teach the skills to manage mental illness.
5. Facilitate the development of recreational pursuits.
6. Value the ability of each person with a mental illness to seek and sustain employment.
7. Help each person to choose, get, and keep a job.
8. Foster healthy interdependence.
9. Be able to facilitate the use of naturally occurring resources to replace the resources of the mental health system.

Practitioner Competencies

1. Listen effectively.
2. Motivate the person served to learn new behaviors.
3. Use the helping relationship to facilitate change.
4. Offer hope to others.
5. Believe in the recovery process.
6. Build on successes and minimizes failures.
7. Demonstrate connecting skills.
8. Normalize interactions and program practices.
9. Relate to others effectively.
10. Generate energy and enthusiasm.
11. Demonstrate an ability to nurture.
12. Demonstrate an ability to empathize.
13. Demonstrate an ability to interact and provide support in a non-judgmental fashion.
14. Work effectively with colleagues who have psychiatric disabilities.
15. Follow Code of Ethics.
16. Demonstrate a mastery of negotiation and mediation skills.
17. Work in cooperative and collaborative manner.
18. Assist in building positive relationships.
19. Be willing to have fun with others.
20. Demonstrate tenacity in work activities.
21. Demonstrate the ability to set limits.
22. Have the ability to let go.
23. Demonstrate the ability to use self as a role model.
24. Demonstrate the ability to overcome personal biases, attitudes, and prejudices when providing services.
25. Be willing to develop and grow.
26. Maintain self-awareness.
27. Demonstrate personal stability but is not egocentric.
28. Demonstrate the ability to handle personal stress.
29. Demonstrate the ability to be flexible.
30. Demonstrate patience.
31. Demonstrate a sense of humor.
32. Recognize the limits of the practitioner's ability to help.
33. Have the ability to be pragmatic and do hands-on work.
34. Demonstrate the ability to handle multiple tasks, prioritize and manage time, and partialize tasks.
35. Tolerate ambiguity.
36. Enjoy diversity.
37. Be willing to take risks.
38. Positively reframe potential stressors.
39. Demonstrate the ability to read and write effectively.

Assessment in Psychosocial Rehabilitation

1. Complete a functional assessment.
2. Complete a symptom assessment.
3. Complete a resource assessment
4. Assess and access appropriate housing.
5. Assess active addiction and co-dependency.
6. Assess the need for crisis interventions.
7. Assess the role of family support.

Interventions in Psychosocial Rehabilitation

1. Demonstrate crisis intervention strategies.
2. Demonstrate relapse prevention intervention strategies.
3. Demonstrate individual supportive counseling intervention strategies.
4. Demonstrate group intervention strategies.
5. Demonstrate skills training intervention strategies.
6. Demonstrate family intervention strategies.
7. Demonstrate community resource and environmental support intervention strategies.

Professional Standards of Multicultural Clinical Competence

1. Move from being culturally unaware to aware.
2. Value and celebrate differences of others.
3. Acquire knowledge regarding the socio-political systems operation and its treatment of ethnic group members.
4. Have a clear and explicit knowledge of traditional theories and principles concerning human behavior, development, psychopathology, therapy, rehabilitation, and community functions. The psychosocial rehabilitation practitioner can describe theoretical delimitations as they relate to cultural group members.
5. Describe current theories, processes, and practice models in the literature that have specific applicability and relevance to the treatment needs of ethnic/cultural group members.
6. Have knowledge of institutional, class, culture, and language barriers that prevent ethnic group members from using your mental health services.
7. Generate a wide variety of verbal and nonverbal responses, interventions, and strategies.
8. Demonstrate behaviors for enhancing the engagement with the culturally different person.
9. Conduct a multicultural assessment.
10. Assess cultural strengths, their impact on level of functioning, and integrate them into the ongoing treatment plan.
11. Conduct an accurate diagnostic assessment in which culturally deprived symptoms are differentiated from psychiatric symptoms.
12. Select appropriate assessment tools and diagnostic procedures that are properly normed and not used as methods of exclusion from service opportunities.

13. Spell out strategies in the rehabilitation plan to specifically engage individuals from different ethnic communities.
14. Select appropriate goals for each person served. Select appropriate methods for goal attainment which are compatible with the person's cultural background. Try to match services to the needs of the persons served.
15. Document attempts to integrate the person's natural support system (i.e., folk healers, family, friends, minister, church members, community organizations, and/or neighbors) into the rehabilitation program.
16. Design creative and motivational programming as structured methods to develop opportunities that will assist each person in growth and goal attainment.
17. Devise rehabilitation plans and refers to community resources when necessary.
18. Demonstrate advocacy and negotiating skills when coordinating agency and community services. Challenge service systems when appropriate and takes actions to correct identified issues.
19. Consult with supervisors, colleagues, same-cultural group representatives for feedback and monitoring of performance.
20. Recognize direct and indirect communication styles.
21. Demonstrate a sensitivity to nonverbal cues.
22. Recognize differences between cultural institutions and traditional institutions. Assist either the person served or institutions in making necessary adjustments in order to maximize the person's engagement in the agency setting.
23. Use language of each person's culture appropriately.
24. Identify features of personal professional style. Recognize limitations and strengths.

Vocational Rehabilitation

1. Engagement—Engage the individual with mental illness in the rehabilitation process.
2. Encouragement—Encourage each person to establish employment as a key goal in the overall rehabilitation process.
3. Empowerment—Assist the individual with mental illness in establishing the goals, nature, and pace of the rehabilitation process.
4. Education—Inform the individual with mental illness about the operations and options of available employment programs.
5. Assessment—Complete both initial and ongoing assessments of a person's employment-related strengths and deficits.
6. Financial Counseling—Assist the individual with mental illness in understanding the fiscal impact of employment.
7. Program Planning—Work together to develop a comprehensive vocational rehabilitation program plan.
8. Teaching—Be able to teach the technical and interpersonal skills needed at work.
9. Monitoring—Regularly monitor the individual's acquisition and ability to use both technical and interpersonal skills on the job.
10. Job Development—Be adept at finding welcoming job opportunities for persons with severe mental illness.

11. Job Finding—Be able to help the individual with mental illness to find a job independently.
12. Coordination of Services—Help to coordinate services through ongoing communication with other service providers.
13. Accommodations—Assist the individual with mental illness in shaping, negotiating for, and putting in place effective job accommodations that make continued work more feasible.
14. Transportation—Assist the individual with mental illness in assuring that transportation to and from the job is regularly available.
15. Stabilization—Help the individual with mental illness to become stabilized in the work environment.
16. Managing Crises—Assist the person with mental illness who is working to anticipate and to manage crises in ways that permit retention of employment.
17. Social Life—Assist the individual with mental illness in developing a social life that supports a career.
18. Career Mobility—Help the working individual to regularly examine job changes.
19. Job Loss—Help the individual to respond to job loss without a retreat from the labor force.
20. Vocational Independence—Assist the individual with mental illness in developing the supports needed for functioning more independently at work.

Residential Treatment Programs

1. Use the residential, normative setting as a primary treatment tool.
2. Use a diverse staff, including licensed and unlicensed professionals.
3. Be directly involved with each person, which is necessary in the operation of the program and in the determination of their service plans.
4. Be flexible in changing the program according to the needs of the persons who are currently living in the house and the demands of the treatment system.
5. Be committed to risk-taking and avoid over-control.
6. Use the residential environment and peers to enhance the acquisition or refinement of community living and interpersonal skills.
7. Assess a person's mental health needs, including the potential for injurious behavior to self or others.
8. Exhibit crisis intervention and stabilization skills including identification of precipitants to crises, focused problem solving, and use of non-pharmacological interventions.
9. Link, broker, and coordinate services among mental health and other community resources.
10. Shift in role and power and not experience such behavior as a diminution of status.
11. Support self-management of symptoms including knowledge of state-of-the-art medications, protocols, and side effects.
12. Facilitate the development of social skills that promote increased social and vocational performance.
13. Develop strategies to meet environmental demands including vocational and educational endeavors.

14. Identify and encourage the use of community resources for social and recreational activities.
15. Monitor and document progress related to goals.
16. Maintain ethical conduct and confidentiality.
17. Advocate for individual with mental illness and support protection of their civil rights.
18. Consult and support family members.
19. Conduct preference and needs assessment to implement discharge plans.

Housing

1. Collaborate with the person needing housing to learn his or her housing choices and the supports needed.
2. Learn to assess the personal, social and cultural factors that impact housing decisions.
3. Locate affordable and safe housing with public and private providers. Develop linkages with community resources regarding the availability of rental units, fair market values, rental subsidies, home ownership programs, and tenant , landlord, and homeowner responsibilities.
4. Coordinate, link, and broker access to supports and services to make housing livable and stable.
5. Develop strategies to meet environmental demands and instrumental activities of daily living that include vocational rehabilitation, employment, education and other age appropriate and normative activities.
6. Apply group dynamics in congregate living environments or other settings to facilitate and motivate participation in the activities of the home and in the community at large.
7. Facilitate problem solving and development of supportive relationships with roommates, other tenants, or neighbors.
8. Have general knowledge about all classifications of psychotropic medications. Know medication and treatment protocols for persons in the program.
9. Respond to psychiatric, medical and nonmedical emergency situations.
10. Employ advocacy skills to develop, retain, or access housing.

Multiple Disabilities

For all persons with dual disabilities:
1. Understand the reality of the person with dual disabilities through observation and empathy.
2. Develop rehabilitation plans that meet the current goals of the person.
3. Assess their behaviors to discover the strengths that can be built upon, and the deficits that need to be addressed by learning new skills or providing the appropriate supports.
4. Create an empowering environment by maximizing the decision making skill of the individual and supporting their decisions.
5. Individualize the interventions by presenting a range of services from which the person can choose.

6. Maximize the flexibility of the rehabilitation process by helping the individual with mental illness to choose new goals over time and constantly try to create new interventions and supports to meet individual needs.

Substance Abuse:
1. Provide assertive outreach.
2. Develop accurate assessments.
3. Provide holistic treatment.
4. Provide structure and opportunities to develop responsibility.
5. Provide opportunities to develop self esteem.
6. Provide interventions tailored to individualization of care.
7. Understand and demonstrate the stages of care.
   a. Engagement
   b. Persuasion
   c. Active Treatment
   d. Relapse Prevention
8. Understand the longitudinal nature of treatment.

Mental Illness and Mental Retardation:
1. Understand the individual is the essential core of the service plan.
2. Establish a working alliance.
3. Conduct a careful behavioral assessment.
4. Empower the person served.
5. Provide individualized rehabilitation interventions.
6. Interventions should be empirically proven.
7. Interventions should be holistic.

Mental Health and HIV:
1. Provide AIDS education and risk assessment.
2. Understand the care of individuals with AIDS.

Mental Illness and Deafness:
1. Develop knowledge of the deaf community.
2. Develop adequate supports and services.
3. Listen to the values of the individual being served.

References

Jonikas, J.A. (1993). *Staff competencies for service-delivery staff in psychosocial rehabilitation programs.* Chicago, IL: Thresholds National Research and Training Center on Rehabilitation and Mental Illness.

Trochim, W.M. & Cook, J. (1993). *Workforce competencies for psychosocial rehabilitation workers: A concept mapping project.* Final report for project conducted for the International Association of Psychosocial Rehabilitation Services: Columbia, MD.

1

Understanding Severe and Persistent Mental Illnesses

Diane Weinstein and Ruth Hughes

Most people with serious mental illness live in our communities. They are our family members, neighbors, co-workers, and friends. More than 5 million people in the United States are diagnosed with a serious and persistent mental illness. With treatment and rehabilitation, many people are on the road to recovery and are leading productive and satisfying lives. For practitioners, consumers and family members, understanding mental illness can be a fundamental step on the road back to a normal life.

Characteristics of serious and persistent mental illnesses in adults may include a diminished ability to function effectively in many life domains, such as the activities of daily living, and the performance of social, cultural, and occupational roles. These tasks are not only important for survival, but they also provide richness and meaning to our lives and provide a context for our relationship with other individuals, the community, and our spiritual belief system. Psychosocial rehabilitation services help people in the community compensate for, or eliminate, the functional deficits, interpersonal barriers, and environmental barriers that result from the disability of a serious mental illness (Hughes, 1994).

The understanding of mental illness is only one facet of the rehabilitation process. Each person has strengths, talents, personality, and life experiences which effect the experience of a mental illness and the rehabilitation process. This holistic understanding of each individual is one of the most fundamental underpinnings of psychosocial rehabilitation. This chapter will focus on the characteristics of the major mental illnesses and the effects of being diagnosed with a mental illness in our culture.

Knowledge of Mental Illness Competencies

Psychosocial rehabilitation practitioners need to have a fundamental understanding of serious mental illnesses in adults, and need to know how to apply this knowledge in their daily practice with consumers. At one time, there was a presumption that the onset of a serious mental illness, such as schizophrenia, would result in chronicity and with little hope of improvement. Longitudinal studies are now showing a wide range of long-term outcomes and considerable improvement and recovery for many people (Harding, Zubin et al, 1987; Harding, Brooks et al, 1987). "Mental illnesses should not be a limitation any more than diabetes" (Domenici, 1991). In fact, the treatment efficacy of many mental illnesses is comparable or better than many physical illnesses (NAMHC, 1993).

The education and application of best practices in psychosocial rehabilitation services is a dynamic process and includes significant contributions and collaboration with consumers, family members, researchers, and service providers. This chapter will review the basic knowledge about mental illnesses that is necessary for psychosocial rehabilitation practice:

- characteristics of the population using psychosocial rehabilitation services,
- the diagnostic categories and disability factors associated with a serious mental illness,
- the role of medications,
- relapse and relapse prevention,
- the concept of recovery, and
- legal issues and disability rights legislation.

Competency 1

Recognize the population subset with a serious mental illness that is served by psychosocial rehabilitation services.

Over 5 million Americans have a serious mental illness. Epidemiological studies identify between 2 and 3 percent of the American population are affected by a serious mental illness with 1.7% of the total population receiving treatment (NAMHC, 1993; Barker et al, 1992). These illnesses encompass a group of mental disorders with long-term or episodic behavioral, psychological, and biological features (APA, 1994). They include schizophrenia, manic depressive illness

(also known as bipolar disorder), major depression, panic disorder, and obsessive-compulsive disorder. There are other mental disorders that can also reach a level of severity and functional impairments that indicate a serious mental illness.

Prevalence Rates for Serious Mental Illness

Diagnosis	% of U.S. Adult Population
Schizophrenia	1.5
Manic Depression (Bipolar)	1.0
Major Depression	1.1
Panic	0.4
Obsessive Compulsive	0.6
Any of Above	2.8

Source: NIMH MECA, Unpublished Data in "Health Care Reform for Americans with Severe Mental Illnesses: Report of the National Advisory Mental Health Council" (NAMHC, 1993)

Psychosocial rehabilitation is a major component of a comprehensive community support system of long-term care for people with a serious and persistent mental illness. It is employed when there is a severe psychiatric illness, a disability that hinders a person's ability to carry out normative tasks and roles, and when the duration of symptomatology is persistent (Flexer & Solomon, 1993; Lawn & Meyerson, 1993). These are sometimes referred to as the diagnosis, duration, and disability factors that indicate a serious mental illness. The appropriateness of psychosocial rehabilitation services is particularly dependent upon the level of disability and functional limitations that a person experiences. A functional assessment of self care and of social and vocational deficits is helpful in determining the need for psychosocial rehabilitation. PSR services provide a person with the skills and environmental supports and resources to become competent and productive in order to participate more fully in the life of their communities.

There are diagnostic criteria that distinguish the characteristics and behaviors associated with each mental disorder. But the symptoms, or impairments, of a mental illness are also unique for each individual. A mental disorder is composed of multiple psychiatric symptoms and cognitive/emotional deficits. These deficits can impair the processing of information and lead to deficiencies in cognitive, attentive, and independent functioning. Functional limitations in areas of self-care, social relationships, work, or school, may result (Anthony & Liberman, 1994). The symptoms associated with a diagnosis, their duration, the degree of disability, the response and effectiveness of specific medications, treatment and rehabilitation modalities, and community supports vary from person to person.

Some of the more prevalent characteristics of serious mental illnesses may include: a feeling of worthlessness, a limited tolerance for stress, lack of assertiveness in routine interactions, lack of spontaneity, withdrawn and avoidant social behavior, inability to form and sustain intimate relationships, vulnerability to exploitation, and poor judgment (Bond, 1992). A person with a serious mental illness often has difficulty in sustaining goal-directed behaviors. Although the person may be engaged in a high level of activity, he does not necessarily complete the task or achieve the performance level needed on the job, at school, or at home. This may leave a person dependent on others to monitor, cue, or assist them in the completion of everyday tasks. Learning that one has a serious mental illness can be devastating, but for most people it is a treatable disorder. One of the first steps in rehabilitation is understanding the impact of the disorder on a person. This knowledge affects development of interventions, supports, and skills that assist an individual in the recovery process.

Competency 2

Learn the signs and symptoms of the most prevalent serious mental illnesses.

There are a recognizable set of defining features that have been associated with each of the five most prevalent serious mental illnesses: schizophrenia, manic depressive disorder, major depression, panic disorder, and obsessive compulsive disorder. Direct service workers must understand and recognize the significant features of each of these serious mental illnesses in order to be effective allies in the development of individualized treatment and rehabilitation strategies. While these are the most prevalent mental illnesses that affect consumers receiving psychosocial rehabilitation, other mental illnesses can result in marked distress and serious impairments in functioning. A competent worker must initiate further study in whatever diagnostic categories are relevant to the populations they serve.

It is important to emphasize that the PSR practitioner must not discount a person's subjective experience of serious mental illness. While the PSR practitioner should recognize clinical features of a disorder that a person presents, it is meaningless if the worker cannot engage consumers in effective coping and adaptation strategies. Manifestations of illness may become barriers to achieving a greater sense of control, competence, and mastery in self-determined activities and relationships (Hatfield & Lefley, 1993). Strauss (1993) notes that "Whenever we forget to listen carefully or lose cognizance of observer bias, the ways we shape what we see and record—forgetting, for example, to note the feelings and the competence as well as the problems of people with disorders—we push ourselves that much farther from finding the answer."

The *DSM-IV Diagnostic and Statistical Manual of Mental Disorders Fourth Edition,* published by the American Psychiatric Association (1994), is most often used in the United States to determine the diagnosis of a serious mental illness. It is the reference source for most of the information on symptomatology in this section and also includes diagnostic information on other mental illnesses. According to the DSM-IV (APA, 1994), the serious mental illnesses that will be discussed fall under three classification categories: schizophrenia, mood disorders, and anxiety disorders. Persons with schizophrenia and mood disorders comprise the majority of persons that are served by psychosocial rehabilitation programs, but the severity of disability and functional limitations that can be experienced by persons with anxiety disorders also warrants their inclusion in this discussion.

Schizophrenia

Schizophrenia is a disturbance that typically begins in late adolescence or early adulthood and is unlikely to begin after age 45. It is considered a thought disorder, characterized by a "loosening of association" where the logical progression between words and phrases is lost. Schizophrenia refers to this "splitting of associations." It does not mean "split

personality," which is a slang phrase that refers to dissociative states that occur in multiple personality disorder.

The DSM-IV (APA, 1994) describes schizophrenia as a constellation of signs and symptoms that involve a range of cognitive and emotional dysfunctions. It is associated with an individual's marked decline in interpersonal relationships, work, education, or self-care. Impairments in perception, inferential thought, language, communication, and behavioral monitoring affect fluency, productivity of thought and speech, capacity to enjoy oneself, attention, volition, and drive. There is a 10% risk of suicide among individuals diagnosed with schizophrenia.

There are two major categories of symptoms in schizophrenia: positive and negative. The positive or acute symptoms represent an excess or distortion of normal functioning, while the negative or residual symptoms reflect a loss of functioning or deficits. Cognitive impairments are significant features of schizophrenia, with some of these deficits also being classified as negative symptoms. The onset of schizophrenia may be gradual or abrupt. When onset is gradual, the early signs are often negative symptoms which appear to mimic normative phases of adolescence and young adulthood: social withdrawal, loss of interest in educational or occupational pursuits, poor hygiene and grooming, and unusual behavior or angry outbursts (APA, 1994). Family are more inclined to recognize the serious nature of their family member's disorder when positive symptoms become apparent.

The positive symptoms, particularly delusions and hallucinations, are characterized as the psychotic features of the disorder. Acute exacerbation of the illness, or a relapse, is associated with the return of psychotic symptoms. Antipsychotic medications are often effective interventions in the treatment of the positive symptoms. The negative symptoms and cognitive impairments are considered more insidious because they are less likely to respond to pharmacological interventions and diminish participation in occupational and social spheres. When psychotic symptoms are not prominent but negative symptoms remain, a person is considered to be in a residual phase of the disorder.

Premorbid functioning, which means functioning prior to the onset of illness,

Symptoms of Schizophrenia

Positive Symptoms

Delusions—erroneous beliefs; distortions or exaggerations of inferential thinking; delusions are deemed "bizarre" when they are clearly implausible, not understandable, or do not derive from ordinary life experiences.

Hallucinations—false perceptions that have a compelling sense of reality; auditory hallucinations where people perceive voices are the most common; hallucinations that are visual, tactile (touch), olfactory (odors), gustatory (taste), and somatic (perceptions of physical experiences within the body) also may occur.

Disorganized speech—formal thought disorder that describes grossly impaired language, communication and thinking; this is considered the most prominent feature of schizophrenia; it encompasses the "loosening of associations" among ideas that otherwise would be logical.

Grossly disorganized or catatonic behavior—problems in goal directed behavior that exacerbate performance of instrumental activities of daily living; marked motor abnormalities including a state of immobility; purposeless unstimulated excessive motor activity, extreme negativism etc.

Negative Symptoms

Affective flattening—the face appears immobile and unresponsive; poor eye contact; reduced body language; range of emotional expressiveness diminished.

Poverty of speech (alogia)—decreased fluency and productivity of speech that appears to be from a diminution of thoughts; replies may be brief and/or concrete; if amount of speech is adequate, it conveys little information.

Avolition—inability to initiate and persist in goal directed activities; lack of motivation; little interest in, or completion of, work, school, intellectual, social activities, or self care.

Anhedonia—diminished ability to experience pleasure; a loss of interest or sense of emptiness.

Social isolation or withdrawal—remains aloof, avoidant or unable to pursue and sustain interpersonal relationships.

Vulnerability to stress

Source: DSM-IV Diagnostic and Statistical Manual of Mental Disorders Fourth Edition *(APA, 1994)*

and the age of illness onset have been studied for their relationship to long-term prognosis. Having a good premorbid functioning in social, educational, and occupational spheres and onset at a later age are some of the factors associated with a better prognosis (APA, 1994; Haas & Sweeney, 1992). Most people who experience remissions or recovery do not return to full premorbid functioning; however, they can pursue normal, social, and vocational activities in the community with the adjunct of medications, mental health treatment, psychosocial rehabilitation services, and peer, family, and community supports.

While the causes of schizophrenia remain undetermined, researchers are exploring several possibilities. One of the hypotheses suggests that schizophrenia is a biochemical disorder and that an excess of the neurotransmitter dopamine is a significant factor. Neurotransmitters are essential chemicals for the transmission of nerve impulses in the brain and central nervous system. Schizophrenia researchers have become very sophisticated in their investigation of dopamine subtype receptors in different areas of the brain and are investigating whether the positive symptoms of schizophrenia are consequences of abnormally high levels of dopamine in the mesolimbic system, while negative symptoms may be attributed to diminished dopamine activity in the mesocortical tract (Judd & Rapaport, 1994). Structural abnormalities in the large ventricle of the hippocampal region of the brain is another theory being investigated to explain cognitive deficiencies. Weinberger and Lipska (1995) suggests that schizophrenia may be a neurodevelopmental insult to the brain that is a result of maldevelopment before birth. This does not become significant until early adult life, when intracortical circuitry in the brain matures.

Medications that block dopamine receptors have been used since the 1950s when chlorpromazine (Thorazine) was first given to patients in psychiatric hospitals (Davis & Gierl, 1984). This breakthrough medication was responsible for the discharge of large numbers of long-term patients in psychiatric hospitals in the 1950s and 60s. New generations of antipsychotic medications have since been developed that are similarly based on their ability to inhibit dopam-

Associated Features of Schizophrenia

Cognitive impairments—impaired attention and memory, confusion, difficulty concentrating, and distractibility; inability to transfer information from one situation to another; impairment of logic, problem solving, and ability to do abstract thinking; lack of insight.

Inappropriate affect—smiling, laughing, or other facial expression displayed in the absence of an appropriate stimulus.

Dysphoric mood—depression, anxiety, anger.

Psychomotor activity abnormalities—pacing, rocking, apathetic immobility.

Grimacing, posturing, odd mannerisms, ritualistic or stereotyped behaviors

Disturbances in sleep

Source: DSM-IV Diagnostic and Statistical Manual of Mental Disorders Fourth Edition *(APA, 1994)*

ine. Some are more effective in their relief of psychotic symptoms such as haloperidol (Haldol) and fluphenazine (Prolixin), while others are more useful to some individuals because of their sedating quality, such as thioridazine (Mellaril). Medications which have dopamine antagonistic properties are called neuroleptics. Neuroleptics are associated with a number of side effects, some of which include: low blood pressure, weight gain, cognitive problems, sexual dysfunction, and the anticholinergic effects—dry mouth, blurred vision, constipation, urinary slowness or retention.

Extrapyramidal side effects (EPS) are also potentially induced from the suppression of dopamine. EPS mimic the symptoms of Parkinson's Disease, which is a consequence of too little dopamine. Characteristics of EPS include tremors in the hands and/or feet, muscular rigidity, and akinesia—which is a state of decreased motor activity or slow movement often observed by problems in walking (APA, 1994). When antipsychotic medications are prescribed, doctors often prescribe anticholinergic medications, such as benztropine (Cogentin), to prevent or reduce the EPS symptoms.

People who have a history of neuroleptic use are also at risk for Tardive Dyskinesia. Features of this disorder include abnormal involuntary movements of the tongue, jaw, trunk or extremities. These movements may be rapid, jerky, slow, sinuous, continual, rhythmic and stereotypical (APA, 1994). Symptoms may vary during the day and disappear during sleep. They become worse with stress and when using anticholinergic medications or psychomotor stimulants (Davis & Gierl, 1984). While younger individuals generally tend to improve when neuroleptic medications are discontinued or lowered, Tardive Dyskine-

sia remission rates are lower among the elderly.

Researchers are also investigating dysfunctions in serotonin neurotransmitter receptors among people with schizophrenia. This work has propelled the introduction of medications that not only block dopamine but also serotonin receptors. Clozapine (Clozaril) and risperidone (Risperdal) are some of the newer atypical antipsychotic medications in this category. Both have had success with people who have been poor responders to other drugs. Extrapyramidal side effects appear to be absent when taking these drugs. However, clozapine is associated with a number of other serious side effects that include seizures and agranulocytosis (a significant disruption in the production of white blood cells). While the incidence of agranulocytosis is rare (under 2% of Clozapine users), it is potentially fatal. Agranulocytosis is a reversible condition when caught in a timely fashion, which has led to the requirement clozapine users have mandatory weekly blood tests. Risperidone, while similar to clozapine, binds differently to synapse receptors and is not associated with a risk of agranulocytosis. Researchers are continuing to develop other atypical antipsychotic agents that successfully reduce symptoms but have fewer side effects.

Manic Depression

Mood disorders are disturbances in affect or emotion that are characterized by extreme or prolonged states of sadness, apathy, or elation. Energy level, participation in daily activities, appetite, self-esteem, thinking, speech, sex drive, and interpersonal relations can be impaired (OTA, 1992; APA, 1994). Not all mood disorders fall into the category of a serious mental illness. Manic depression, also known as bipolar affective disorder, and major depression are considered serious mental illnesses when the individual has functional impairments in multiple life domains, such as going to work or school, participating in normal social interactions, eating properly, maintaining personal hygiene, taking prescribed medications, etc. There is a 10%-15% risk of suicide among the population with a serious affective disorder that usually occurs when an individual is in a depressed state (APA, 1994). It is estimated that about 50% of all suicides are committed by people who have a mood disorder.

Manic depression, or bipolar affective disorder, is characterized by mood swings. The onset of this disorder typically occurs prior to age 35, and usually begins in adolescence or young adulthood. Prevalence rates among men and women are equal, about 1% of the total population. An individual will have episodes of mania where their mood is overly "high," recognized by an increased state of excitement, expansiveness and/or irritability, then shifts to a cycle of depression where the person feels unusually "low" and experiences a deepened state of sadness, melancholy, or hopelessness. In between the highs

Mood Disorder Symptoms of Mania

Inflated self-esteem or grandiosity—an inflated appraisal of one's worth, power, knowledge, importance or identity; when extreme grandiosity may be of delusional proportions.

Diminished need for sleep—feels rested after only 3 hours of sleep.

Severe insomnia—difficulty falling asleep, awakening in the middle of the night or earlier than usual and unable to return to sleep.

Pressured speech—speech that is increased in amount, accelerated, and difficult to interrupt, usually loud and emphatic; frequently the person is talking without any social stimulation and may continue when no one else is listening or present.

Flight of ideas or subjective experience that thoughts are racing—a nearly continuous flow of accelerated speech with abrupt changes in topics usually based on understandable associations, distracting stimuli, or plays on words; when severe, speech may be disorganized and incoherent.

Distractibility—attention too easily drawn to unimportant or irrelevant external stimuli.

Increase in goal-directed activity—Excessive planning and participation in multiple activities such as social, work, school, political, religious or sexual activities.

Increase in psychomotor agitation—excessive motor activity that is usually non-productive and repetitious such as pacing, fidgeting, hand wringing, inability to sit still, pulling clothes.

Excessive involvement in pleasurable activities without considering potential for painful consequences—engaging in unrestrained buying sprees, sexual indiscretions, or foolish business investments that do not represent typical behavior.

Poor judgment, inappropriate irritability, impulsiveness, and inappropriate social behaviors that may be intrusive and demanding

Source: DSM-IV Diagnostic and Statistical Manual of Mental Disorders Fourth Edition *(APA, 1994)*

and lows are periods of normal or near normal recovery, but a person may continue to experience ongoing functional deficits that have serious consequences during episodic remissions. While most mood shifts are gradual, these cycles can recur within days, months, or years (NAMHC, 1993; NIMH, 1993).

During a manic episode, an individual can be unusually cheerful, euphoric or expansive, but still fail to recognize the atypical qualities of their behaviors or consider their consequences. Behaviors may be impulsive, dramatic, or flamboyant; energy level is increased; self-esteem can be inflated and marked by grandiosity or have a delusional quality. Grandiose delusions are marked by a person's belief that they have a special relationship to another person of great importance or notoriety, perhaps to God, or they believe that they can perform tasks without the prerequisite training or talent typically associated with them. When mood is marked by an irritable quality, a person may engage in atypical hostile comments, complaints, and angry tirades. It is not unusual for people to feel embarrassment or regret their actions after a manic episode. However, manic states are also associated with sensory acuity: colors are more vivid and smell, hearing, and taste are sharper. With the adjunct of an increased energy level and potential for greater productivity, in some people, these states contribute to periods of exceptional productivity, creativity, and genius (Andreasen & Glick, 1988). This can reduce the desire for some people to take drugs that modulate the highs and lows in order to maintain functioning and mood within a "normal" range. The depressive features of manic depression replicate those of a major depression and will be discussed in the next section.

Lithium, a naturally occurring mineral in the form of a carbonate or citrate, has been effective in the management of manic depression. What lithium exactly does, or why it is successful, is unclear. It is hypothesized that its broad range of action on several neurotransmitters has a therapeutic effect—calming the highs of a manic episode and diminishing the lows of a depression (APA, 1994; NIH January 1993). Lithium medications such as Eskalith, Lithobid, and Lithane may prevent or dampen future illness episodes. Side effects associated with lithium may include: thirst, nausea, cramps, diarrhea, muscle weakness, hand tremors, weight gain, and fatigue. Lithium users may drink more fluids than usual—sometimes without being aware of it—and urinate more frequently. It is important to regularly monitor lithium levels in the bloodstream to prevent lithium toxicity. Conditions that lower sodium in the body or decrease body fluids, such as fever, dieting, strenuous exercise, warm weather, vomiting, etc., are potential precipitants for toxicity. Slurred speech, blurred vision, confusion or stupor, loss of balance, seizures, and appearing as if intoxicated are some of the signs of toxicity. With immediate medical treatment, lithium levels can be returned to an appropriate therapeutic range.

Major Depression

Major depression is a serious mood disorder. Eating, sleeping, activity level and how one feels about oneself are affected. Major depression is more serious than the occasional blue moods that most people experience. It can begin in childhood or not appear until one is elderly. Most cases emerge in the late 20s, and more than 50% of those experiencing a major depression are likely to have recurrent bouts (OTA, 1992). Thoughts about death, suicidal ideation and suicide attempts, whether or not the person succeeds in suicide, are common features of the illness.

There is a pervasive feeling of sadness, hopelessness, worthlessness and guilt, with a pronounced decrease in the ability to enjoy activities that previously were enjoyed. Judgment, thinking, and concentration may be impaired (APA, 1994). Other people may notice this when they see signs of social withdrawal, a person's neglect of previously important activities, or an inability to adequately attend to self-care, occupational, and social endeavors. Disturbances in sleep are prevalent—inability to fall asleep, waking up frequently during the night with difficulty returning to sleep, or excessive sleeping. A person experiencing a major depression may be unusually irritable and hostile, tearful for no apparent reason, fatigued with a dramatic loss of energy, and experience psychomotor retardation where responses to environmental stimuli are slowed.

Biochemical research on depression has focused on a group of neurotransmitters that are called monamines, which include dopamine, epinephrine, norepinephrine and serotonin, and has lead to the development of a category of antidepressant medications called monoamine oxidase inhibitors (MAOIs). MAOIs are considered to be effective in the alleviation of tiredness, increased appetite, elevated anxiety levels and phobic characteristics during depressed states. Phenelzine (Nardil), isocarboxazid

Mood Disorder Symptoms of Depression

Depressed mood most of the day and nearly every day—Persistent sad, anxious or empty mood; appears tearful.

Feelings of hopelessness, pessimism, guilt, worthlessness, helplessness nearly every day—such feelings are excessive, inappropriate, and may have delusional features.

Thoughts of death, attempted suicide, or suicidal ideation with or without a specific plan

Diminished interest or pleasure in almost all activities—e.g. work, school, hobbies and activities that were once enjoyed, including sex.

Fatigue or loss of energy nearly every day

Psychomotor agitation or retardation almost daily—extreme restlessness, irritability or slowed response to environmental stimuli.

Insomnia or hypersomnia—difficulty sleeping or oversleeping nearly every day.

Difficulty thinking, remembering, concentrating, making decisions nearly every day

Significant appetite loss, weight loss or weight gain—a change of more than 5% of body weight in one month.

Persistent physical symptoms that do not respond to treatment, such as headaches, digestive disorders and chronic pain

Source: DSM-IV Diagnostic and Statistical Manual of Mental Disorders Fourth Edition *(APA, 1994)*

(Marplan), and tranylcypromine (Parnate) are classified as MAOIs. Individuals who use MAOIs should avoid foods or other medications containing tyramine, such as red wine, cheeses, fermented foods, and also avoid certain medications that can cause a hypertensive crisis resulting in a sudden and dangerous rise in blood pressure.

Tricylic antidepressants are another classification of antipsychotic medications that block the reuptake of neurotransmitters (NAMHC, 1988). Amitriptyline (Elavil) and imipramine (Tofranil) are two of the tricyclic antidepressants commonly used. Tricylic antidepressants are neuroleptics, and their side effects were previously addressed in the discussion of antipsychotic medications for schizophrenia.

Researchers have been investigating a decreased concentration in the neurotransmitter, serotonin, in people with depression (OTA, 1992). This has propelled the development of medications that only act on serotonin and are called serotonin reuptake inhibitors (SRIs). Fluoxetine (Prozac) and sertraline (Zoloft) are classified as SRIs. Bupropion (Welbutrin) is another type of SRI antidepressant. Mood disorders research is also exploring abnormal levels of the neurotransmitter norepinephrine. In some instances, it appears that genetic or inheritant factors predispose some persons to develop affective disorders. However, not all people who have a family history of mood disorders will develop them. Some researchers are investigating immune and viral factors that are related to the onset of depression (OTA, 1992). As in schizophrenia, it appears that a combination of genetic, biochemical, psychological, and environmental factors are involved in the onset, course, and treatment response of mood disorders.

Panic Disorders

Anxiety disorders are disturbances that are characterized by the apprehensive anticipation of future danger or misfortune. They are accompanied by symptoms of tension which can have psychological or physiological manifestations, or a state of dysphoria—unhappiness that is difficult to bear. Panic disorder and obsessive compulsive disorders are two of the anxiety disorders that are considered serious mental illnesses when their symptoms severely impair functioning in the performance of the necessary activities of daily living. While individuals with a severe anxiety disorder may be referred to psychosocial rehabilitation programs, cognitive and other behavioral interventions with medications are considered state-of-the-art treatment for these disorders. Often a practitioner will recognize symptoms associated with an anxiety disorder being exhibited by a person with schizophrenia or a mood disorder. When a practitioner or program does not have the expertise to appropriately respond to all or some of a person's clinical needs, a timely referral to another practitioner or agency with the indicated skills is necessary.

Panic disorders are characterized by brief episodes of intense fear that are called panic attacks and are accompanied by multiple physical symptoms. These discrete periods of intense fear or discomfort appear suddenly and most often without apparent precipitants (APA, 1994). The age of onset varies but is typically between late adolescence and the mid-30s. Over 20% of the individuals with a panic disorder will attempt suicide, but the actual number who succeed is unknown (OTA, 1992).

Panic attacks have been described as episodes of terror, a feeling of imminent danger, or the fear of losing control or becoming psychotic. Some of the physical symptoms that accompany them include heart palpitations, chest pains, a numbness or tingling sensation, dizziness, blurred vision, hot flashes and a cold sweat. This constellation of symptoms could lead someone to believe that they were having a heart attack or other life threatening illness, although medical tests do not substantiate an underlying physical disorder (APA, 1994; NIH & NIMH, 1993; NIMH, 1993 ; OTA, 1992).

Although panic attacks do not represent an imminent physiological danger, they can trigger phobias or irrational fears about social or environmental situations where a panic attack may occur. This fear of the next panic attack, or anticipatory anxiety, can be as debilitating as the symptoms that are experienced during the panic attack. Phobias can lead the individual to severely restrict their lifestyle in order to avoid circumstances where escape would be difficult or embarrassing, or the individual fears that no help would be available should a panic attack occur. A person who experiences panic attacks and also develops pervasive avoidance strategies is diagnosed as having a panic disorder with agoraphobia, which is prevalent in about one-third of the population with a panic disorder (APA, 1994; NIMH, 1993).

Phobias exacerbate the level of impairment already experienced from

Panic Attack Symptoms of Panic Disorders

Panic Attack—A panic attack is a discrete period of intense fear where the individual experiences multiple somatic or cognitive symptoms that develop abruptly and reach a peak within 10 minutes. At least 4 of the following symptoms must be present:

Palpitations, racing or pounding heartbeat

Chest pains

Numbness or tingling sensation

Trembling or shaking

Difficulty breathing, shortness of breath or smothering

Choking

Nausea or abdominal distress

Dizziness, unsteady, lightheaded

Chills or hot flashes

Sweating

Derealization—altered sensations or perceptions where people seem unfamiliar or mechanical.

Depersonalization—dreamlike sensations or perceptual distortions where the person feels detached from their body or mental processes.

Fear of losing control, becoming psychotic, doing something embarrassing

Fear of dying

Source: DSM-IV Diagnostic and Statistical Manual of Mental Disorders Fourth Edition *(APA, 1994)*

panic attacks. They further diminish the ability to maintain or initiate activities of daily living, such as the timing of an activity, being able to leave one's home to go shopping, or accomplish other significant tasks like using transportation, being in social or occupational environments, or even preclude visiting with friends or family at one's own residence. A person with a panic disorder can develop an extreme dependence on other people to either perform necessary tasks, or be available to accompany them when they complete tasks to prevent an anxiety attack (NIMH, 1993).

Researchers are investigating several biological and psychological responses in individuals who have panic disorders. Some neuroscientists are exploring increased activity in the portions of the brain that monitor external and internal stimuli and control the brain's responses to them (OTA, 1992). Others are focusing on increased activity in the system which regulates the physiological functions of heart rate and body temperature. Researchers are also examining abnormalities in brain receptors for benzodiazepines to determine if there is a dysfunction in these neural receptors that makes them unable to bind with the body's own naturally producing anxiety reducing substance.

Another area of panic disorder research includes investigation of the receptor activity for the neurotransmitters serotonin and dopamine. Some researchers hypothesize that people with a panic disorder have a low tolerance for normal physiological and psychological responses to stress. This means that the individual misperceives normal events as dangerous, which then unnecessarily triggers a set of physical and mental responses that are manifested in a panic attack. Another theory suggests that

when people, who are predisposed to a panic disorder, experience repeated life stressors, they develop disturbances in coping mechanisms (NIH & NIMH, 1993),(NIMH, 1993).

Medications are an important component of an intervention strategy to prevent panic attacks, reduce their frequency or severity, diminish anxiety, and diminish the disabling symptoms of phobia. Drugs used for panic disorders include medications that are currently used to treat depression: tricyclic antidepressants and monamine oxidase inhibitors. Benzodiazepines are a class of medications that are also known as anti-anxiety medications, which act as central nervous system depressants and are helpful in the control of panic disorder symptoms. Antianxiety medications take rapid effect, which is different from other antipsychotic medications that need to reach a therapeutic level in the bloodstream over several days or weeks before they work. Some of the anti-anxiety medications that are benzodiazepines include diazepam (Valium), alprazolam (Xanax), and chlordiazepoxide (Librium). Buspirone (BuSpar) is another commonly used antianxiety medication.

Side effects of benzodiazepines include drowsiness, involuntary muscle movements, confusion, memory loss, slurred speech, headache, nausea and becoming overexcited. People may become dependent on their usage and experience severe withdrawal symptoms when they are discontinued or reduced without medical supervision. Stopping them abruptly can result in a rebound effect whereby the individual becomes extremely irritable, nervous, or depressed and is at risk of suicide. When using benzodiazepines, it is important to avoid using alcohol to prevent dangerous interactions.

Obsessive Compulsive Disorder

Features of obsessive compulsive disorder include obsessions, which are recurrent thoughts and impulses that are time consuming each day, and compulsions, which are involuntary repetitive and dysfunctional behaviors that are initiated in order to prevent or reduce anxiety (APA, 1994). Functional impairments from this disorder can be severely disabling and render a person unable to carry out normally expected daily living skills to live successfully in the community. The typical age of onset for obsessive compulsive disorder is adolescence through early adulthood. Onset begins earlier in men, between ages 6–15, and in women, between ages 20–29. The onset is typically gradual, and symptoms seem to wax and wane. Acute exacerbation of symptoms may be related to stress (APA, 1994).

People with this disorder are characterized by their "idiosyncratic daily rituals and odd personal behaviors" (OTA, 1992). While most people understand that these recurrent thoughts and repetitive behaviors are excessive and unreasonable, they are unable to suppress them without treatment. Drug therapy with a behavioral therapy approach called "exposure and response prevention" have been found to be effective (NIMH, 1991). Exposure and response prevention therapy deliberately exposes a person to objects or ideas that are feared, directly or through imagery, while discouraging or preventing the usual compulsive response. Practitioners should seek specialized training, consult with experts, and/or make timely referrals to ensure that consumers who have an obsessive compulsive disorder receive the optimal treatment relevant to individual circumstances.

One of the more common obsessions are anxiety provoking thoughts about being unclean, or fear of germ contamination. This may lead to an avoidance of situations where the individual may be exposed to dirt or germs, not shaking hands with people or touching door knobs, not using public restrooms, as well as the performance of compulsive behaviors such as excessive hand washing, showering, or house cleaning, in order to gain momentary relief from an obsessive thought.

Performing compulsive behaviors does not provide satisfaction, and some of them are physically harmful: washing one's hands until they are raw, insisting on unnecessary surgeries to perfect

---

Obsessive Symptoms of Obsessive Compulsive Disorder

Recurrent and persistent thoughts, impulses or images that cause marked anxiety or distress

At some point are recognized as intrusive and inappropriate

Excessive worries about real-life problems

There is an attempt to ignore, suppress, or neutralize them with other thoughts or actions

They are recognized as coming from the individual (different than "thought insertions")

Source: DSM-IV Diagnostic and Statistical Manual of Mental Disorders Fourth Edition *(APA, 1994)*

Compulsive Symptoms of Obsessive Compulsive Disorder

Repetitive behaviors that the individual is driven to perform as a response to an obsessive thought

May have rigid or stereotypical requirements, as in a ritual

Performed in order to reduce or prevent distress, a dreaded event or situation

The performed acts are not connected in a realistic way with the event they are to neutralize or prevent, or the acts are performed excessively

Source: DSM-IV Diagnostic and Statistical Manual of Mental Disorders Fourth Edition *(APA, 1994)*

---

one's body, or weight training for too many hours. Compulsive behaviors are called rituals when they are performed in stereotypical fashion, such as arranging items in a special way, or performing behaviors routinely, or in a particular sequence. Sometimes rituals are performed to prevent something bad from happening, and eventually the individual becomes unable to distinguish "what is possible, what is probable, and what is unlikely"(NAMI-MIS).

Some people with the disorder know that their obsessions and compulsions make other people uncomfortable, and they try to conceal them. Their sense of shame and secrecy can further exacerbate the illness, when it causes a delay in seeking treatment.

Researchers are exploring the interaction of neurobiological factors and environmental influences in obsessive compulsive disorders. As in other mental illnesses, it is believed that certain individuals have a biological predisposition for this disorder and react strongly to stress. Researchers on obsessive compulsive have been investigating the abnormal functioning of the neurotransmitter serotonin. Tricylic antidepressants, such as clomipramine (Anafranil), which acts on serontonin, as well as the antidepressant fluoxetine (Prozac), have been successful providing symptom relief for some people.

Competency 3

Understand the effects of stigma and discrimination.

Simply being labeled with a serious mental illness can lead to stigma and discrimination. Stigma can create barriers to mental health treatment, employment, and housing as well as educational, recreational, and social opportunities (Anthony & Liberman, 1994). Discrimination is typically based on false beliefs or myths that the general public has about an individual with a mental illness. People presume the person is untrustworthy, unclean, worthless, dangerous, unpredictable or frightening (Mansouri & Dowell, 1989). The media perpetuates these prejudicial characterizations with an emphasis on portraying people with a mental illness as violent or aggressive in their behaviors. Stigma is a consequence of the lack of opportunities for self-determination, unemployment, crushed dreams, and the harmful effects of some treatment and treatment settings (Crossroads, IPRT, 1994).

When a poll was taken to rank categories of people on a ladder of social acceptance, "former mental patients" ranked below ex-convicts (Curtis, 1992). These negative attributes result in stigma where a person with a mental illness is characterized by a prejudicial stereotype. Once the mental illness label is given to a person, other people avoid them or see only those personality traits, problematic behaviors, and functional deficits that reinforce the stereotype. The person loses the opportunity to have an accurate or total representation of their personality strengths and abilities recognized. Curtis (1992) notes that the problems associated with stigma have been exacerbated by mental health practitioners who make derogatory comments about consumers to other workers, do not treat consumers with respect, engage in segregating practices such as separate agency bathrooms or dining areas, stereotype consumers, and limit vocational referrals to menial jobs that can diminish a person's sense of competence and mastery.

Internalized Stigma

Howie the Harp, a leading consumer advocate and founder of the Oakland Independent Support Center, gave the following testimony on "internalized stigma" in response to one of the survey questions from the Well-Being Project:

Having been in a mental hospital, having been diagnosed as mentally ill, often causes a lowering of your self-image. The way that you're treated gets internalized if you're treated like an incompetent. Eventually you begin to believe you're incompetent, you're not worth anything. It's also very easy to feel like you're a failure when you're out on the streets with nowhere to go and to feel like your whole being is a failure. It becomes very depressing. People often come in here to the Oakland Independent Support Center very, very depressed—suicidally depressed because they're homeless. (Campbell & Schraiber, 1989, page 42)

Unfortunately, negative stereotypes often become internalized. When people have endured minimal standards of living for extended periods, they have lowered expectations and "internalized a devalued status (and) may be satisfied with a lower quality of life or accept deprivation of certain factors" (Campbell & Schraiber, 1989). The person with a mental illness begins to feel he has disgraced his family and lives with an encompassing sense of shame. Cultural factors can exacerbate stigma, shame, and under utilization of psychiatric services (NMHA, 1995). A person with a mental illness can believe that he deserves the inferior status that has been relegated to him. This internalized stigma erodes into a state of loneliness, hopelessness and helplessness. Richard Weingarten described the effect in this way. "In my case, learned helplessness grew out of the despair I experienced in the initial years of my illness. The combination of the illness and stigma had me anti-social and reclusive. I unlearned some of the social skills I'd previously been adept at...Once I'd worked through the helplessness and despair, I was ready to move to a new stage of my recovery where I took a proactive stance to working on my problems and needs" (Weingarten, 1994).

Anthony and Liberman (1994) further emphasize the important role of rehabilitation services to compensate for "handicaps" that occur when "disabilities place the individual at a disadvantage relative to others in society" as exemplified when consumers experience stigma and discrimination. Stigma and discrimination are often the greatest barriers to autonomy, integration, and inclusion. They necessitate practitioner and consumer collaboration on "societal rehabilitation" strategies that will implement macrosystem changes, such as advocating for federal, state, and local statutes, to prohibit employment and housing discrimination, overturn health insurance practices that preclude coverage for psychiatric disabilities, and statutory language in the Social Security Act that acts as a disincentive to employment when people are receiving disability income benefits.

Competency 4

Assess the effects of social factors in mental illness.

People with a serious mental illness have little economic or political power and most often live in poverty. Even when the primary symptoms of the illness do not interfere with normalizing activities, poverty as a societal factor becomes an impediment for integration and full participation. About 23% of the adults with a serious mental illness (more than one million people) collect disability payments from a government program (Barker et al, 1992). Over 9% of Veteran's Administration (VA) benefits are for adults with a serious mental illness. Among all disabled workers receiving Supplemental Security Income (SSI), 24% were eligible as a result of a severe mental disorder, as were 27% of the beneficiaries receiving Social Security Disability Income (SSDI) (NAMHC, 1993).

SSI payments range between $4,000 to $5,000 per year and meet only 24% of the median income for a one person household (McCabe et al, 1991; Curtis et al, 1992). For people on SSI who can afford housing, it often means living in substandard dwellings or in dangerous neighborhoods. People must survive with little or no money available for the basic necessities of food, clothing, and transportation. Their stringent budgets frequently leave them without personal care items or any discretionary resources to participate in social and recreational activities.

The "Well-Being Project" in California conducted a survey in which mental health clients had the opportunity to speak for themselves and identify factors that are essential for well-being. When these factors are missing from one's life you may "lack well-being"(Campbell & Schraiber, 1989). The following factors were identified as essential for well-being:

- Health
- Good food/decent place to live
- Adequate income
- Happiness
- Meaningful work/achievement
- Privacy
- Safety
- Basic human freedoms
- Satisfying social life
- Warmth/intimacy
- Comfort
- Adequate resources
- Satisfying spiritual life
- Creativity
- Satisfying sexual life

These are the same well-being factors that everyone minimally needs to have a standard of living where satisfying personal relationships can thrive, and the supports to make meaningful choices about one's environment and productivity. As a result of the loss or erosion of these essential factors, people with a serious mental illness often live "in the margins of normal society." Disability from a serious mental illness and the ensuing poverty when a person cannot pursue substantial gainful activity to afford basic material necessities is difficult, but stigma and discrimination are often the greatest impediments to obtain these essential factors of well-being.

People with a psychiatric disability are less likely to receive health and dental services. Anthony and Blanch (1989) reviewed research studies that show higher rates of physical illness in psychiatric patients; however, they were unlikely to receive routine medical and dental care check-ups that would provide early detection of physical conditions.

Immigrants and their offspring from other cultures, such as the Hispanic population in the United States, experience additional barriers to accessing mental health services and health insurance coverage related to low wages, cultural norms, language barriers, fewer human service agencies in their communities, and a loss of familial support systems to pursue services and benefits (NMHA, 1993). Minority populations are being hospitalized at a three times greater rate than other populations, according to the chief office of consumer affairs from the Ohio Department of Mental Health, and there are high rates of misdiagnosis, which has led Ohio to make improvements in the training of mental health professionals, and in particular, targeting an increase in minority practitioners. Daniels (1994) has noted that when African Americans and Hispanics do receive services, they are more likely to be misdiagnosed as having schizophrenia when they have a bipolar affective disorder, and when receiving a diagnosis of a psychotic or affective disorder, minority clients are more likely to be labeled as having a chronic syndrome rather than an acute episode.

Other cultural influences appear to affect the treatment and rehabilitation process for women. Women with serious mental illnesses are more likely to be victims of sexual abuse and survivors of trauma; however, few programs employ recovery and survivor intervention strategies for women that uniquely focus on victimization, powerlessness, self-esteem, and intimacy issues (Harris, 1995; Cook & Jonikas, 1995). Programs have also languished in their capacity to address the issues of sexual abuse among men who are victims and/or abusers, and the issues of parents with psychiatric disabilities who want to maintain or resume parenting roles (Jonikas & Zeitz, 1995; Cook & Jonikas, 1995). Nicholson (1995) cites a survey of state mental health authorities showing only 16 states routinely collecting data on the parental status of women, and few programs target services to parents with children, although there is some indication that women clients actively caring for their children function better than women who do not have caretaking roles.

Gender differences impact the vocational rehabilitation services that men and women receive. There are indications that fewer women are receiving vocational rehabilitation services, their program discharges are slower than male counterparts, and women are placed in gender, stereotypical positions regardless of education. This perpetuates lower status and lower pay, with women earning 56% of the wages earned by men with similar rehabilitation experiences (Mowbray, 1995; Razzano & Cook, 1994).

Competency 5

Understand the interaction of biological, social and environmental factors in mental illness.

The vulnerability, stress, coping, and competence model put forth by Anthony and Liberman (1994) suggests there is a biological predisposition for a serious mental illness. However, onset and relapse of the illness are likely to occur when stressors are overwhelming and the individual is without adequate coping skills. Coping and problem solving skills have often been diminished as a result of a serious mental illness. Studies have documented that stressful life events can trigger the onset of episodes of schizophrenia, even when individuals are taking antipsychotic medications (Lukoff et al, 1984).

Socioenvironmental stressors can include problems with the primary support group, the social, educational, occupational, or residential environment, economic problems, problems accessing health care, interactions with the legal system, etc.(APA, 1994). Hatfield and Lefley (1993) emphasize how negative societal reactions to a person with a serious mental disorder can become significant stressors. These stressors not only shape an individual's response to a biologically based mental disorder, but also require the individual to develop coping strategies to survive the personal experience of having a serious mental illness.

An individual's biological predisposition for a serious mental illness and socioenvironmental stressors can be modulated by protective factors that facilitate coping and competence. Protective factors might include the utilization of employment and housing programs, case management services, and pharmacological strategies (Anthony & Liberman, 1994). Through the rehabilitation process, consumers learn "how to solve problems, select goals and acquire the competencies required by community living" (Liberman et al, 1993). In conjunction with antipsychotic medications, the development of skills and introduction of environmental resources are effective ways to reduce symptoms and increase periods between relapse. Psychosocial rehabilitation empowers consumers to develop protective coping skills and competence which extends into their interpersonal life, school, work, family, and self-care domains.

Competency 6

Understand the concept of recovery.

Recovery encompasses the belief that people with serious mental illness may regain control of their disability and lead satisfying, productive lives. The role of psychosocial rehabilitation is to create an environment that nurtures recovery so people can "experience themselves as recovering a new sense of self and of purpose within and beyond the limits of the disability" (Deegan, 1988). Recovery from a mental illness is not synonymous with cure.

Anthony (1992) describes the importance of having a "recovery vision" in which consumers, family members, and direct service workers open themselves to a person's potential. This vision asks the mental health system to discard the old prophecy that a mental illness is a chronic disease that always follows a deleterious course. The task of the direct service worker is to facilitate the recovery process, but the actual task of recovery belongs to the consumer. People who have experienced recovery observe that the "presence of people who are supportive and trustworthy and [who] believe that recovery is possible, are a common denominator" (Crossroads IPRT Program, 1994). Mental health practitioners who have "negative expectations and stereotyping, are among the greatest obstacles to recovery and keep many mentally ill persons immobilized by defeat and despair" (Lovejoy, 1982). While there is a progression towards growth in the recovery process, there are also setbacks. Periods of setbacks are the most critical times when the direct service worker's support needs to remain constant. With the help of the PSR practitioner, the person with a mental illness combats the negative self-fulfilling prophecies that are barriers to recovery.

Other observations, from people who have experienced a mental illness, give us insight into the recovery process. Recovery occurs in people independent of their belief system about the etiology of a mental disorder. The episodic nature of mental illness does not prevent recovery. People who experience an exacerbation of symptoms find that as one recovers, symptoms are less intrusive and their duration is for a briefer period. The recovery process is not linear. While the overall trend is towards improvement, there are also periods of no movement, or regression. One moment there is great hope and, in another, despair (Crossroads, IPRT, 1994; Deegan, 1988). Recovery encompasses an understanding that people with a disability "must be willing to try and fail, and try again" (Deegan, 1988). Psychosocial rehabilitation practitioners facilitate the recovery process by helping people appreciate each successful step, no matter how small it seems. The initial task for some practitioners will be assisting people in the accomplishment of instrumental activities of daily living that are essential for well being. Successful completion of these primary tasks becomes the building block necessary to achieve more complex and long-term goals.

The dilemma facing the psychosocial rehabilitation direct service practitioner is to know how to promote, facilitate, and provide optimism about recovery and simultaneously "maintain realistic expectations based on careful assessments of patients' ability to handle various kinds of stress" (Lamb, 1994). The creative and supportive role of the psychosocial rehabilitation worker is to help partialize goals in ways that people can make progress. Direct service workers and the people they serve can collaborate on the development of the incremental steps that are best tolerated. However, this does not mean prescribing the location, timing and sequence of steps. Direct service workers need to be flexible in their application of rehabilitation intervention strategies, if the real objective is for consumer empowerment, success, and an internalization of the recovery process, rather than program efficiency.

There is concern by some that using the word "recovery" will "lead to a denial of illness" and the consumer will inappropriately reject treatment and rehabilitation interventions when they are still appropriate. It has been suggested that the practitioner should rephrase periods of stability as "remission" or acknowledge that a person is "recovering—but never recovered" (Lamb, 1994). Facilitating recovery entails the engagement of the consumer in a dialogue to better understand the symptoms or stressors that are warning signs of decompensation and to promote the development of strategies to reduce their frequency and duration. This is not the same as colluding with a person to deny their illness and disability. One consumer has noted that reasserting control and implementing coping strategies that decrease a vulnerability to stress and anxiety are important factors to prevent relapse (Leete, 1987). Promoting a consumer's reassertion of control means the direct service worker needs to let go of control. Letting go of control does not mean eliminating contact with people on a regular or consistent basis, but instead requires respect for consumers as they learn how to define the physical and emotional space that is needed for them to take on the responsibility and risks to improve.

Recovery: The Lived Experience of Rehabilitation

"The recovery process is the foundation upon which rehabilitation services build. This is most evident in the simple observation that we can make the finest and most advanced rehabilitation services available to the psychiatrically disabled and still fail to help them. Something more than just 'good services' is needed (e.g., the person must get out of bed, shake off the mind-numbing exhaustion of the neuroleptics, get dressed, overcome the fear of the crowded and unfriendly bus to arrive at the program and face the fear of failure in the rehabilitation program). In essence, disabled persons must be active and courageous participants in their own rehabilitation project or that project will fail. It is through the process of recovery that disabled persons become active and courageous participants in their own rehabilitation project" (Deegan, 1988).

People who have had a history of a serious mental illness and have experienced recovery are sometimes challenged by mental health professionals about the accuracy of their previous diagnosis. These unconstructive efforts discount the knowledge that a person has learned about the recovery process. It is vital that rehabilitation programs seek out people who have experienced recovery and have them serve as mentors for people who are currently in the program, as well as hiring consumers who have experienced recovery as direct service practitioners and mental health administrators. Lovejoy (1982) writes that the "one single fact that offered me hope" was that staff persons in a residential program where she was briefly residing had previously been program clients. "For the first time I saw proof that a program could help someone, that it was possible to regain control over one's life" (Ibid.).

Advanced Directives

Advance directives are legal documents that consumers can prepare to express their choice of treatment, treatment settings, and persons to make "proxy" decisions in their behalf, should they be unable to do so in the future. They provide psychosocial rehabilitation practi-

tioners with an opportunity to engage consumers in informed decision making about interventions that should be implemented when symptoms are acute. Often the practitioner is collaborating with the consumer on treatment decisions when symptoms are moderate or in remission. However, discussing cycles of illness relapse and developing intervention strategies when there is a psychiatric emergency are important.

Instructive directives such as living wills and proxy directives that designate a third party to act as the decision maker are two types of advance directives that individuals with a mental illness have found helpful and empowering (Appelbaum, 1991). Persons with a mental illness use living wills in situations where they are incapacitated but have expectations that they will recover (Lefley, 1992). They can provide very specific information in a prescriptive will that identifies preferred treatments to use during a psychiatric emergency, or proscriptive wills to prevent treatments that are adversive to use when consumers are incapacitated by a mental disorder. Alternatively, living wills can have more general instructions regarding acceptable care and allow the treatment provider to determine the optimal intervention strategy during an acute illness episode.

A health care proxy or surrogate is someone legally appointed by a consumer to make medical decisions if the consumer loses the ability to independently make decisions. Proxies are typically family members, close friends, or a respected practitioner who knows the consumer well (Cross, Fleischner & Elder, 1992). A proxy is expected to act upon the consumer's wishes that were previously discussed. When it is unclear what the wishes of the consumer would have been in the current situation, a proxy will act in the consumer's "best interest" by weighing the risks and benefits of various treatment interventions and make a decision on behalf of the consumer.

Helping people develop advanced directives can be empowering. Instead of assuming a relapse will return the person to a prolonged state of helplessness or hopelessness or assuming prodromal symptoms, the advance directive can promote an opportunity to reassert some control over the direction one's life will take, even though a person is experiencing a cycle where judgment, or mental acuity, is severely impaired. It can offer consumers, practitioners, and the designated proxy an opportunity to have a clear and detailed understanding of the consumer's values and desires. It also furthers a relationship of trust with the designated proxy, who will reduce the risk of conflict among supportive network members if there is a period of incapacitation and treatment decisions must be made (Lefley, 1992).

In order to assist consumers in their preparation of advanced directives, reviewing past intervention successes as well as failures during relapse and identifying the prodromal symptoms typically experienced prior to the onset of an acute illness flare-up are important. For example, a consumer may indicate that problems getting to sleep or waking up, becoming suspicious about the actions of roommates or others normally trusted, not changing clothes, writing letters to the newspaper, or drawing pictures about a world inhabited by scary creatures may be predictors that a decompensation cycle will begin shortly.

When prodromal symptoms are present, an advance directive can indicate an intervention strategy to try to circumvent an acute illness stage or allow a designated proxy to assist in the selection of an intervention. For example, the advance directive may advise the practitioner or proxy to review compliance with the current medication, and if there are no signs of noncompliance, ask the physician to increase or decrease the medication by a pre-agreed upon dosage, recommend an additional medication to be prescribed or discontinued until the prodromal symptoms abate. An advanced directive may advise the practitioner to contact a consumer support network when particular prodromal symptoms occur and to contact a crisis stabilization program when other symptoms are present. The direct practitioner who has collaborated with the consumer on the development and periodic updates of an advanced directive will have information about a consumer preferred treatment when informed decision making is not possible.

Informed Consent and Ascertaining Competence

The role of the individual with a mental illness in decision-making regarding treatment and the right to refuse treatment are critical concepts that require an understanding of the legal standards of informed consent and competence (Beck, 1987; Callahan, 1983; Frese, 1994; Parry & Beck, 1990, Reisner, 1985). Informed consent for psychiatric and medical treatment is predicated on the following elements: the competence of the individual to make a rational decision, the individual having received all of the relevant information about the proposed intervention(s), knowledge of alternative treatment choices, and the consumer's voluntary consent to implement the intervention.

In the American legal system, an individual is presumed competent unless found incompetent through a judicial hearing. There are two central factors that are required to determine competency regarding psychiatric interventions. The first is the individual's capacity to assimilate relevant facts about the treatment intervention. This involves the direct service practitioner educating the individual about various aspects of the intervention. These aspects include: the risks, which should consider any harmful effects of the procedure, and any harm that might occur if the intervention was delayed; the benefits, which should detail particular symptoms to be relieved or diminished and overall benefits like increased confidence, independence etc.; the procedure for implementation, which should include the nature of the intervention, its expected duration and purpose, and any inconveniences that might be experienced.

In order for a consumer to understand the critical aspects of the intervention, the educative presentation of the relevant factors must be complete. Practitioners must be honest and thorough. While delineating every side effect that has ever been attributed to a particular intervention is unnecessary, the information presented must meet a standard of what the "reasonable practitioner" would be expected to disclose. Harmful side effects that have been well-documented, irreversible, or toxic should be discussed.

This psychoeducative process must be communicated in a format that is understandable by the individual. Handing a person with severely limited cognitive abilities or poor reading skills a textbook on the proposed treatment intervention and the alternatives is not appropriate. A one-on-one discussion, psychoeducation in a group context, or the provision of written or audio materials commensurate with a person's intellectual abilities are some of the informational approaches frequently used. After receiving information about the treatment intervention, competency is dependent upon the person assimilating the material. Although the information and educational presentation may have been thorough, if the consumer is unable to explain to the practitioner what the proposed treatment is, how it will be implemented, and its expected duration, risks, and benefits, then competence has not been ascertained. In this scenario, the worker cannot ask the consumer for a signature on an informed consent form or treatment plan in order to implement the proposed intervention.

The second factor to assess competence requires the individual to have a rationale understanding or acknowledgment that they have a mental illness, or at a minimum, an agreement that they are affected by symptoms associated with a mental disorder which require treatment. For example, an individual states that they are at a psychiatric treatment setting because they are nervous all the time, overwhelmed when trying to do simple tasks, and bothered by disturbing voices that other people do not hear. Although the person does not agree with any of the diagnostic labels that the practitioners states are associated with these symptoms, the person still wants treatment. That individual is competent to sign an informed consent form. However, if an individual denies having a mental illness, any disabling symptoms associated with a mental disorder, or adamantly disagrees with the impairments and symptoms that the practitioner has brought to that person's attention, the practitioner would be unable to ascertain competence and receive informed consent.

A person with a history of a mental illness who is experiencing a relapse is presumed able to make an informed decision about a treatment intervention. If a person with schizophrenia is delusional and experiencing hallucinations but can assimilate the relevant facts about a proposed treatment, such as the injection of a psychotropic medication, and describes severe side effects experienced when this medication was previously administered, this person has a rational reason to refuse the proposed treatment. While the direct practitioner may recommend a particular treatment modality, empowering people to make informed choices means providing people with information about alternative interventions. Informed consent must also be premised on the voluntary consent of the consumer. The practitioner cannot coerce informed consent by threats of force, or suggest that release from a program or treatment setting will be denied unless the proposed intervention is implemented, or, as a result of signing the informed consent form or treatment plan, the person will receive favored treatment or other benefits.

Direct practitioners, as advocates for consumers, have an obligation to see that informed consent is ascertained in an agency where they are employed, as well as in other locations where consumers are receiving psychiatric or medical treatments. Psychosocial rehabilitation practitioners often have ongoing roles as educators about psychotropic medications and other intervention modalities that consumers use on a regular basis. It is important to provide psychoeducational updates to consumers about the treatment interventions they are receiving. Not only do impaired cognitive abilities associated with a serious mental illness often impede retention of knowledge, but critical information about medication interventions fades over time in people who do not have a mental illness.

The philosophy behind informed consent and consumer participation in the decision making works in tandem with the collaborative process that direct practitioners of psychosocial rehabilitation apply in their daily work. Practitioners must be honest and thorough, sharing information about intervention strategies in formats that are understandable. Practitioners must present intervention choices that are real in order to empower consumers and help people maximize their independence and achieve personal goals. The engagement of someone in the community rehabilitation process must be voluntary. Coercing someone to sign a rehabilitation treatment plan that the individual does not want to do is the antithesis of the rehabilitation process and is unethical.

Involuntary Interventions

Involuntary treatment is an area of great controversy for people with serious mental illnesses. The Community Support Program in 1990 initiated a project to look at the use of involuntary interventions and encourage discussion on alternatives, such as the development of advance directives (Parrish, 1993). Some of the arguments supporting its use include:

- alleviating suffering, pain and embarrassment

- expediting recovery

- a belief that consumers are unable to make informed decisions when experiencing an acute stage of illness

- when access to an inpatient treatment setting would otherwise be denied if there was a voluntary request for admission (Parrish, 1993).

Arguments countering the use of involuntary interventions include:

- its usage deprives an individual of liberty and the abridgment of civil rights

- the capacity for self-determination should not be presumed lost when a person is experiencing an acute illness stage

- the person that is involuntarily committed to an institution or forced to undergo a treatment could be harmed

- forced treatment is dehumanizing, it leads to hopelessness, despair, chronicity, and suicidal behaviors

- use of "benevolent coercion" reinforces stigma and discrimination that people with a mental illness are dangerous, unpredictable, and incompetent.

In some situations, states and professional codes of ethics require practitioners to implement an intervention that prevents harm to the individual with the mental disorder, other persons, or the environment. There are many community based programs that effectively respond to psychiatric emergencies, but in certain situations, inpatient care is the most appropriate treatment intervention. Direct service practitioners are often successful at working with individuals in crisis who need inpatient care, helping them voluntarily access hospitalization. However, when it is clear that alternative community based interventions are not appropriate or available, and the consumer does not agree to a voluntary hospitalization, involuntary commitment to a psychiatric hospital may be the course of treatment that is indicated (Appelbaum & Roth, 1988).

Involuntary Hospitalization Commitment Standards

Involuntary commitment standards for psychiatric treatment are determined by state law. These standards are typically restricted to use when persons with a mental illness are reasonably expected at the time of their commitment to injure other persons or themselves if they were allowed liberty, and this danger is a result of a mental illness (Reisner, 1985). States differ on which mental disorders would be subject to commitment, as well as criteria that would be deemed dangerous or imply the probability of a dangerous event occurring. The time period that would establish an imminent danger or who must witness evidence of danger varies, as well as the credentials necessary for particular mental health professionals to have legal status to sign commitment orders. Some states include harm that results from self-neglect as a danger, but others do not.

After an authorized person, often a licensed psychiatrist or psychologist, documents the necessity for an involuntary hospitalization, the individual is admitted to a psychiatric hospital. Some communities require the assessment for any inpatient care that is covered by public funds be at a designated location that acts as a gatekeeping system. This can be a way to redirect people to less restrictive levels of care when the initial assessment for inpatient care is incorrect, or the crisis is resolved without the need for a hospital admission.

Because involuntary hospital admissions are initiated during a psychiatric emergency situation, they begin prior to a formal civil commitment process. If an individual no longer meets the criteria for commitment before the hearing or as a result of a decision rendered at the hearing, the individual must be discharged. Some patients initially admitted on an involuntarily basis have reevaluated their need for hospitalization and convert their stay to a voluntary hospitalization, which circumvents a civil commitment hearing.

Standards for informed consent apply to treatment interventions during an involuntary hospitalization, and advance directives remain applicable in most hospitals, although the laws and practices vary in communities. In general, if a patient is competent during the involuntary hospitalization and refuses treatment, such as medication, he cannot be compelled to accept treatment. However, hospital staff can override a refusal for treatment if it is considered an emergency situation and the individual is not competent or if the person is considered a danger to self or others (Callahan & Longmire, 1983).

Treatment preferences or information about previous adverse reactions not documented in old records or difficult to locate quickly during an emergency can be garnered from an advance directive when an immediate decision about a treatment intervention is required. Complying with advance directives can reduce some of the coercive aspects of an involuntary treatment placement. Respecting advance directives can expedite recompensation efforts and reduce the length of stay in an involuntary setting.

Federal Legislation and Civil Rights

Today there are several pieces of federal legislation that are instrumental in the funding and delivery of benefits and services for people with a serious mental illness. Prior to World War II, there were few federal statutes that directly or indirectly pertained to persons with disabilities.

The two largest disability benefits programs that provide people with a serious mental illness monthly cash benefits are the **Social Security Disability Insurance (SSDI)** program and the **Supplemental Security Income (SSI)** program which are administered by the federal Social Security Administration (Dinitto & Dye, 1983). Eligibility and the amount of money received under the SSDI program are dependent upon a person's work history or the work history of a parent if a person becomes disabled while still a minor child. A person on SSDI who is under the age of 65 becomes eligible for the Medicare federal health insurance program after being disabled for two years.

The SSI program is restricted to people who are elderly or disabled and who have no other income or a very limited income from other sources. In 1972, the federal government standardized the SSI eligibility criteria requirements and established a minimum payment level, but allowed states the discretion to supplement the minimum monthly payment. SSI recipients receive Medicaid, a federal/state health insurance program that is restricted to people with limited financial means.

Under the auspices of the **Rehabilitation Act**, the federal government provides matching funds to states for **vocational rehabilitation** services for people with disabilities. Supported employment, transitional employment (only for people with mental illness), job training, and job placement are some of the services provided by state vocational rehabilitation authorities.

In 1990, Congress passed the **Americans with Disabilities Act (ADA),** landmark legislation prohibiting discrimination against persons with disabilities. The act affects all businesses with more than 15 workers, public accommodations, public services, transportation, and telecommunication services. Employers cannot discriminate against a qualified person with a disability who, with or without reasonable accommodations, can perform the essential functions of the job. Employers are responsible for the provision of reasonable accommodations unless they would cause them undue hardship. With unemployment figures estimated to be as high as 85% among persons with a serious mental illness, the ADA offers civil rights protections to people with mental illness.

The **Fair Housing Amendments Act** of 1988, which extends the Civil Rights Act of 1986, also provides persons with disabilities protection that has been afforded other minority populations (Huggins & IAPSRS). This Act makes it unlawful for public and private entities to discriminate against persons with disabilities in the sale, rental, or advertising of dwellings, provision of services, availability of residential real estate transactions, implementation of land use and zoning laws, and enforcement of restrictive covenants and deeds.

In 1986, the federal government expanded its role in funding advocacy services for a disadvantaged population in the enactment of the **Protection and Advocacy for Mentally Ill Individuals Act (PAMI).** Persons with a mental illness living in or recently discharged from psychiatric hospitals, nursing homes, group homes, board and care homes, homeless shelters, and jails have access to advocacy services in their state that protect them under existing statutes and help consumers obtain the services that they are entitled to receive (NMHA).

The National Voter Registration Act of 1993, also known as the motor-voter bill, has had important ramifications to increase the numbers of constituents with disabilities, by requiring public agencies that serve poor people and people with disabilities to offer voter registration, an action that could otherwise be difficult for someone with limited resources.

Summary

Proficiency in the understanding of severe and persistent mental illness is an exciting challenge for practitioners in psychosocial rehabilitation. It seems that every day there are breakthrough discoveries generated from the scientific community studying the brain and mental disorders. New medications are constantly being developed. Demonstration projects and services research further define effective practice. The potential for maximum growth and change in individuals with psychiatric disabilities is enhanced by practitioners developing a basic knowledge about the diagnostic categories and disability factors that are associated with a serious mental illness.

It is important to understand how a variety of biological, psychological, and societal factors can effect the onset, course, treatment, and recovery of individuals with psychiatric disabilities.

References

Amaranth, E. (1994). Personal accounts: On alleged "remission" from severe bipolar disorder. *Hospital and Community Psychiatry, 45* (10), 967-8.

American Psychiatric Association. (1994). *DSM-IV Diagnostic and Statistical Manual of Mental Disorders Fourth Edition.* Washington DC: American Psychiatric Association.

Andreasen, N. C. & Carpenter, W. T. (1993). Diagnosis and classification of schizophrenia. *Special Report: Schizophrenia 1993:* 25-4; reprinted from *Schizophrenia Bulletin, 19*(2). Rockville, MD: National Institute of Mental Health.

Andreasen, N.C. & Glick, I. D. (1988). Bipolar affective disorder and creativity: Implications and clinical management. *Comprehensive Psychiatry, 29,* (3), 207-17.

Anthony, W. A. (1991). Recovery from mental illness: The new vision of services researchers. *Innovations and Research, 1,* (1), 13-14.

Anthony, W. A. & Liberman, R. P. (1994). The practice of psychosocial rehabilitation: Historical, conceptual, and research base. *In An Introduction To Psychosocial Rehabilitation: 18-41*; reprinted from *Schizophrenia Bulletin, 1986, 12*(4), 542-559. Columbia, MD: International Association of Psychosocial Rehabilitation Services.

Appelbaum, P. S. (1991). Advance directives for psychiatric treatment. *Hospital and Community Psychiatry, 42,* (10), 983-84.

Appelbaum, P. S. & Roth, L. H. (1988). Assessing the NCSC guidelines for involuntary civil commitment from the clinician's point of view. *Hospital and Community Psychiatry, 39*(4), 407-09.

Barker, P. R., Manderscheid, R. W., Hendershot, G. E., Jack, S., & Schoenborn, C.A. (1992). Serious mental illness and disability in the adult household population: United States, 1989. *Advance Data, 218.* Centers for Disease Control National Center for Health Statistics.

Beck, J. C. (1987. Right to refuse antipsychotic medication: Psychiatric assessment and legal decision-making. *Mental and Physical Disability Law Reporter, 11,* (5), 368-72.

Bond, G. R. (1993). Psychiatric disabilities. In M. G. Eisenberg, R. L. Glueckauf, & H. Zaretsky (Eds.), *Medical Aspects Of Disability: A Handbook For The Rehabilitation Professional*: 307-24. New York: Springer.

Callahan, L. A. (1983). Psychiatric patients' right to refuse psychotic medication: A national survey. *Mental and Physical Disability Law Reporter, 7,* (6), 494-99.

Campbell, J. & Schraiber, R. (1989). *In Pursuit Of Wellness.* Sacramento, California: The California Network of Mental Health Clients.

Christison, G. W., Kirch, D. G., & Wyatt, R. J. (1991). When symptoms persist: Choosing among alternative somatic treatments for schizophrenia. *Schizophrenia Bulletin, 17,* 2, 217-45.

Cohen, C. I. (1993). Poverty and the course of schizophrenia: Implications for research and policy. *Hospital and Community Psychiatry, 44*(10), 951-57.

Cook, J. A. & Jonikas, M. A. (1995). Addressing the needs of women consumers who are survivors of sexual abuse. *Community Support Network News, 10* (3).

Cross, J. H., Fleischner, R. D., & Elder, J. S. J. (1992). *Guardianship and con-*

servatorship in Massachusetts. Butterworth Legal Publishers.

Crossroads IPRT. (1994). Recovery and empowerment: A guiding vision for mental health services. NY Office of Mental Health 1994 IPRT Conference.

Curtis, L.C., Tanzman, B. H., & McCabe, S. S. (1992). *Orientation Manual For Local Level Supported Housing Staff.* Burlington, Vermont: University of Vermont, Center for Community Change through Housing and Support.

Dain, N. (1994). Reflections on anti-psychiatry and stigma in the history of American psychiatry. *Hospital and Community Psychiatry, 45*(10), 1010-14.

Davis, J. M. & Gierl, B. (1984). Pharmacological treatment in the care of schizophrenic patients. In Grune & Stratton (Eds.), *Schizophrenia,* (Chapter 5), 133-159.

Deegan, P. E. (1988). Recovery: The lived experience of rehabilitation. *Psychosocial Rehabilitation Journal, 11* (4), 11-19.

Dincin, J. (1989). *Looking backward and forward in psychosocial rehabilitation.* Keynote speech IAPSRS national conference, June 1989.

Dinitto, D. M. & Dye, T. R. (1983). *Social Welfare: Politics And Public Policy.* Englewood Cliffs, New Jersey: Prentice-Hall.

Domenici, P. V. (1991). The decade of the brain. *Innovations & Research, 1,* (1): 3.

Frese, F. J. (1994). Informed consent and the right to refuse or participate. *Journal of the California Alliance of the Mentally Ill, 5*(1), 56-7.

Fuller Torrey, E., Stieber, J., Ezekiel, J., Wolfe, S. M., Sharfstein, J., Noble, J. H., & Flynn, L. M. (1993). Criminalizing the seriously mentally ill: The abuse of jails as mental hospitals. *Innovations and Research, 2,* (1), 11-14.

Fisher D. B. (1991). Speaking out. *Psy-chosocial Rehabilitation Journal 14* (4): 69-70.

Flexer, R. W. & Solomon, P. L. (1993). Introduction. In R. W. Flexer & P. L. Solomon (Eds.) *Psychosocial rehabilitation in practice.* Stoneham, MA: Butterworth-Heinemann.

Garrett, B. & Posey T. (1993). Involuntary commitment: A consumer perspective. *Innovations and Research, 2* (1), 39-41.

Geller, J. L. (1993). On being "committed" to treatment in the community. *Innovations and Research, 2*(1), 23-27.

Haas, G. L. & Sweeney, J.A. (1992). Premorbid and onset features of first-episode schizophrenia. *Schizophrenia Bulletin, 18*(3), 373-86.

Harding, C. M., Zubin, J., & Strauss, J. S. (1987). Chronicity in schizophrenia: Fact, partial fact, or artifact? *Hospital and Community Psychiatry, 38*(5), 477-86.

Harding, C. M., Brooks, G. W., Takamura, A., Strauss, J. S., & Breier, A. (1987). The Vermont longitudinal study of persons with severe mental illness, I: Methodology, study sample, and overall status 32 years later. *American Journal of Psychiatry, 144*(6), 718-35.

Harris, M. (1995). Trauma recovery skills: Development and enhancement. *Community Support Network News, 10* (3).

Hatfield, A. B. & Lefley, H.P. (1993). A conceptual basis for understanding patients' behavior: The case of schizophrenia. In A. B. Hatfield & H. P. Lefley (Eds) *Surviving mental illness.* New York: The Guilford Press.

High, J. R. Recovery's role in the treatment of traumatic stress. (1994). *Recovery, Inc. Reports, 3*(2), 1-2.

Honberg, R. (1993). Editorial. *Innovations and Research, 2*(1), 3-5.

Huggins, M. & International Association of Psychosocial Rehabilitation Services (IAPSRS). The Fair Housing Amendments Act of 1988 extending the protections of the Civil Rights Act of 1968, Title VIII Fair Housing to Persons with Handicaps and Families with Children. Columbia, MD: International Association of Psychosocial Rehabilitation Services.

Hughes, R. H. (1994). Psychiatric rehabilitation : An essential health service for people with serious and persistent mental illness. *In An Introduction To Psychosocial Rehabilitation*: 9-17. Columbia, MD: International Association of Psychosocial Rehabilitation Services.

Jonikas, J. J. & Zeitz, M. A. (1995). Thresholds' mothers project's family support program and parenting wards program. *Community Support Network News, 10*(3), 8.

Judd, L. L. & Rapaport, M. (1994). A new antipsychotic medication for the treatment of schizophrenia. *Innovation & Research, 3*(1), 1-7.

Lamb, H.R. (1994). A century and a half of psychosocial rehabilitation in the United States. *Hospital and Community Psychiatry, 45*(10), 1015-20.

LaPlante, M. P. (1992). How many Americans have a disability? *Disability Statistics Abstract, 5.* University of California, San Francisco Disability Statistics Program.

LaPlante, M. P., Miller, S., & Miller, K. (1992). People with work disability in the US *Disability Statistics Abstract, 4.* University of California, San Francisco Disability Statistics Program.

Lawn, B & Meyerson, A. T. (1993). A modern perspective on psychiatry in rehabilitation. In R. W. Flexer & P. L. Solomon (Eds.) *Psychosocial rehabilitation in practice.* Stoneham, MA: Butterworth-Heinemann.

Leete, E. (1987). The treatment of schizophrenia: A patient's perspective.

Hospital and Community Psychiatry, 38, (5), 486-91.

Lefley, H. (1992). Developing living wills for the seriously mentally ill: An important aid when addressing psychiatric emergencies. *The Psychiatric Times: Medicine and Behavior, May 1992.*

Lefley, H. (1993). Involuntary treatment: Concerns of consumers, families and society. *Innovations and Research, 2,* (1), 7-9.

Liberman, R. P., Wallace, C. J., Blackwell, G., Eckman, T. A., Vaccaro, J. V., & Kuehnel, T. G. (1993). Innovations in skill training for the seriously mentally ill: The UCLA social and independent living skills modules. *Innovations and Research, 2*(3), 43-59.

Lovejoy, M. (1982). Expectations and the recovery process. *Schizophrenia Bulletin, 8,* (4).

Lukoff, D., Snyder, D., Ventura, J., & Nuechterlein, K. H. (1984). Life events, familial stress, and coping in the developmental course of schizophrenia. *Schizophrenia Bulletin, 10*(2), 258-292.

Manderscheid, R. & Sonnenstein, N. (Eds.) (1992). *Mental Health, United States 1992.* Washington DC: US Department of Health and Human Services and National Institute of Mental Health.

McCabe, S., Edgar, E. R., King, D. A., Mancuso, L., & Emery, B. (1991). *Holes in the housing safety net...why SSI is not enough: A national comparison study of Supplemental Security Income & HUD fair market rents.* Burlington, Vermont: University of Vermont, Center for Community Change through Housing and Support.

Mowbray, C. T. (1995). Women with severe mental illness: The ignored majority. *Community Support Network News, 10* (3).

National Action Commission on the Mental Health of Rural Americans

(NACMHRA). (1988). *Report of the National Action Commission on the Mental Health of Rural Americans.* Alexandria, VA: National Mental Health Association.

National Advisory Mental Health Council (NAMHC). (1988). *Approaching the 21st century: Opportunities for NIMH neuroscience research.* The National Advisory Mental Health Council Report to Congress on the Decade of the Brain. Rockville, MD: National Institute of Mental Health.

National Advisory Mental Health Council(NAMHC). (1993). *Health care reform for Americans with severe mental illnesses: Report of the National Advisory Mental Health Council.* Rockville, MD: National Institute of Mental Health

National Advisory Mental Health Council(NAMHC). (1988). *A national plan for schizophrenia research: Report of the National Advisory Mental Health Council.* Rockville, MD: National Institute of Mental Health.

National Alliance for the Mentally Ill, Medical Information Series (NAMI-MIS). *Obsessive compulsive disorder.* Arlington, VA: National Alliance for the Mentally Ill,

National Institute of Health (NIH) & National Institute of Mental Health (NIMH). (1993). Panic disorder: Pamphlet No. 93-3508. Rockville, MD: Panic Disorder Education Program, National Institute of Mental Health.

National Institute of Mental Health (NIMH). (1993). Bipolar Disorder: PAT 00-0019. Rockville, MD: Information Resources and Inquiries Branch, National Institute of Mental Health.

National Institute of Mental Health (NIMH). (1991). *Caring for people with severe mental disorders: A national plan of research to improve services.* Rockville, MD: National Institute of Mental Health.

National Institute of Mental Health (NIMH). (1993). Nontechnical summaries of articles. *Special Report: Schizophrenia 1993: 1-24; reprinted from Schizophrenia Bulletin, 19*(2). Rockville, MD: National Institute of Mental Health.

National Institute of Mental Health (NIMH). (1993). Number of US adults (in millions) with mental disorders, 1990: Based on five epidemiological catch area sites. *National Institute of Mental Health UPDATE,* July 1993.

National Institute of Mental Health (NIMH). (1991). Obsessive-compulsive disorder. Rockville, MD: Office of Scientific Information, National Institute of Mental Health.

National Institute of Mental Health (NIMH). (1993). Plain talk about depression. *Plain Talk Series,* Rockville, MD: Office of Scientific Information, National Institute of Mental Health.

National Institute of Mental Health (NIMH). (1993). Understanding panic disorder:Pamphlet No. 93-3509. Rockville, MD: Panic Disorder Education Program, National Institute of Mental Health.

National Institute of Mental Health(NIMH) & National Advisory Mental Health Council(NAMHC). (1988). *A national plan for schizophrenia research: Panel recommendations; reprinted from Schizophrenia Bulletin, 14*(3). National Institute of Mental Health.

National Mental Health Association (NMHA). (1995). Depression and mental health in the Hispanic community. *Depression Campaign Network News,* May/June Issue: 4. Alexandria, VA: National Mental Health Association.

National Mental Health Association (NMHA). *Protection and Advocacy for Mentally Ill Individuals Act: As amended through 1992; Legislative Summary Se-*

ries (13). Alexandria, VA: National Mental Health Association

Nicholson, J. (1995). Parents with psychiatric disabilities and their families: A consumer-based program of research. *Community Support Network News, 10* (3).

Office of Special Education and Rehabilitation Services. (1992). *Summary of existing legislation affecting people with disabilities.* Washington, D C: Office of Special Education and Rehabilitation Services, U.S. Department of Education.

Office of Technology Assessment (OTA), US Congress. (1992). *The biology of mental disorders.* Washington DC: US Government Printing Office.

Parrish, J. (1991). CSP: Program of firsts. *Innovations & Research, 1,* (1), 8-9.

Parrish, J. (1993). Involuntary intervention: Doing the right thing the wrong way. *Innovations and Research, 2,* (1), 15-22.

Parry, J. W. (1987). Psychiatric care and the law of substitute decision-making. *Mental and Physical Disability Law Reporter, 11*(3), 152-59.

Parry, J. W. & Beck, J. C. (1990). Revisiting the civil commitment/involuntary treatment stalemate using limited guardianship, substituted judgment and different due process considerations: A work in progress. *Mental and Physical Disability Law Reporter, 14,* (2), 102-07).

Post, R. M. (1993). Issues in the long-term management of bipolar affective illness. *Psychiatric Annals, 23*(2), 86-93.

Prien, R. F. & Potter, W. Z. (1990). NIMH workshop report on treatment of bipolar disorder. *Psychopharmacology Bulletin, 26*(4): 409-28. Recovery, Inc. (1994). *Recovery, Inc. Reports, 3,* (2), 4.

Reisner, R. (1985). *Law and the mental health system: Civil and criminal aspects.* St. Paul, Minnesota: West Publishing Company.

Rice, D. P., Kelman, S., Miller, L. S., & Dunmeyer, S. (1990). *The economic costs of alcohol and drug abuse and mental illness*: 1985. San Francisco: Institute for Health & Aging, University of California. Roche Laboratories. Frontiers of psychiatry. *Roche Report,* 5(16).

Segal, S. P. & Vandervoort, D. J. (1993). Daily hassles of persons with severe mental illness. *Hospital and Community Psychiatry, 44,* (3), 276-78.

Social Security Administration. (1993). Trends in types of mental impairment allowances for adults, 1986-1983. Office of the Actuary, Social Security Administration.

Social Security Administration. (1993). Mental impairment and DI and SSI. Office of the Actuary, Social Security Administration.

Stroul, B. A. (1994). Community support systems for persons with long-term mental illness: A conceptual framework. *In An Introduction To Psychosocial Rehabilitation*: 75-88; reprinted from *Psychosocial Rehabilitation Journal 12*(3), 9-26, 1989. Columbia, MD: International Association of Psychosocial Rehabilitation Services.

Strauss, J. S. (1993). Foreword. In R. W. Flexer & P. L. Solomon (Eds.) *Psychosocial Rehabilitation In Practice.* Stoneham, MA: Butterworth-Heinemann.

Stroul, B. A. (1986). *Models of community support services: Approaches to helping persons with long-term mental illness.* Community Support Program, National Institute of Mental Health.

Suppes, T., Baldessarini R. J., et al. (1993). Discontinuation of maintenance treatment on bipolar disorder: Risks and implications. *Harvard Review of Psychiatry, 1*(3), 131-144.

Weinberger, D.R. & Lipska, B. K. (1995). Cortical maldevelopment, anti-psychotic drugs, and schizophrenia: A search for common ground. *Schizophrenia Research 16,* 87-110.

Weingarten, R. (1994). Despair, learned helplessness and recovery. *Innovations & Research, 3*(2), 31-32.

Weinstein, D. (1993). *Rehabilitation Act Amendments of 1992: A resource manual.* Columbia, MD: International Association of Psychosocial Rehabilitation Services and the National Mental Health Association.

Wilson, W.H. & Claussen, A.M. (1993). New antipsychotic medications: Hope for the future. *Innovations & Research, 2*(2), 3-11.

Winokur, G., Coryell, W., Endicott, J., & Akisal, H. (1993). Further distinctions between manic-depressive illness (bipolar disorder) and primary depressive disorder (unipolar disorder). *American Journal of Psychiatry, 150* (8), 131-144.

2

What is Psychosocial Rehabilitation?

Diane Weinstein and Ruth Hughes

A rich and innovative range of services has developed to meet the needs of people with serious mental illness who are living in the community. In the last twenty years, psychosocial rehabilitation has expanded from a few isolated programs to become a major and integral part of the mental health service system. Practitioners who are well-versed in the history, the underlying principles, and the diversity of approaches are better prepared to provide effective rehabilitation services. This chapter will review:

- The Definition of PSR
- History of the Field
- Psychosocial Rehabilitation Principles
- Components of Services
- PSR Models and Technologies

Definition of PSR

The goal of all psychosocial rehabilitation is to restore each person's ability for independent living, socialization, and effective life management (Hughes, Woods, Brown, and Spaniol, 1994). It is a holistic approach that places the person—not the illness—at the center of all interventions. The wishes of the person being served direct the rehabilitation process through working partnerships

Competency I

Know the definition of psychosocial rehabilitation.

that are forged between the practitioner and the individual with mental illness. Effective rehabilitation builds on a person's strengths and helps the individual to compensate for the negative effects of the psychiatric disability.

Rehabilitation services are practical and empirical and are designed to make a real difference in the lives of people with mental illness. A home to live in, friends, a job, an income, and school are frequently the focus of rehabilitation services. Psychosocial rehabilitation services are usually provided in the community where these needs can best be addressed. A person with a mental illness is likely to be involved in a complex network of health and social services. Service management to coordinate the far flung and often unconnected services received by an individual with mental illness is an integral component of rehabilitation. Advocacy to redress the devastating effects of stigma, poverty, homelessness, and inadequate treatment is also important.

Psychosocial Rehabilitation Definition in 35 Words or Less

Psychosocial rehabilitation is a program for persons with long-term mental illnesses to explore and develop social, occupational, leisure, and living skills which will assist them in living as independently as possible in the community. *Submitted by:* Cindy Chambers, Ozark Center, Community Care Program, Joplin, Missouri.

Psychosocial rehabilitation means giving people with psychiatric disabilities the opportunity to work, live in the community, and enjoy a social life, at their own pace, through planned experiences in a respectful, supportive and realistic atmosphere. *Submitted by:* John Hilburgher, C.R.C., Chicago, Illinois.

Psychosocial rehabilitation means hope for the future. Hope for being a wanted member of society. Hope for again being accepted by loved ones and friends. Hope for self-esteem and self-worth. Hope for life. *Submitted by* Jennifer Conrardy, Harmony Center, Minot, North Dakota.

Psychosocial rehabilitation means that a person who was afraid to go into a store to order an ice cream soda before can now be an ice cream store manager. *Submitted by:* Martha Greene, Case Manager, Mental Health Case Management, West Hartford, Connecticut.

Source: I.D. Rutman. (1993). "Editorial: And Now the Envelope Please." Psychosocial Rehabilitation Journal, *16, (3): 1-3.*

Other practitioners have captured the programmatic elements and philosophy of psychosocial rehabilitation in more succinct definitions. The definitions above were contributed to the *Psychosocial Rehabilitation Journal* (Rutman, 1993) in response to a contest that asked readers to define psychosocial rehabilitation in 35 words or less.

Competency 2

Know the history of psychosocial rehabilitation and community support.

History of Psychosocial Rehabilitation

The concept for psychosocial modalities began with resocialization programs and social clubs that were formed in England and in the Soviet Republics in the 1930s (Rutman, 1981). The stigma of having a mental illness and a history of institutionalization were minimized in these environments, while opportunities for social acceptance were created. In the United States, psychosocial rehabilitation evolved during the 1940s, as mental health professionals and individuals with mental illness sought alternative treatment interventions and settings that were outside of psychiatric hospitals (Hughes, Lehman, & Arthur, 1996). A small number of innovative programs, sharing similar goals and principles, but with different rehabilitative approaches, began to emerge.

Fountain House, in New York City, was established in 1948 by a group of former psychiatric patients who had all "experienced discharge into the anomie of New York City to no friends, no jobs, often unwelcoming families, and isolation in marginal SRO hotels" (Propst,

1992). Fountain House went on to develop the club house model with the work oriented day and transitional employment program. Horizon House, in Philadelphia, developed a high expectancy approach that helped participants move through a series of training activities designed to promote community living and independence. Fellowship House, in Miami, modeled itself after "settlement houses", which were originally established as community centers to help immigrants improve their capacity to adapt and function in their neighborhoods (Stroul, 1986). George Fairweather developed the community lodge program, where individuals with mental illness typically reside in a communal setting and share the responsibility of operating the lodge, as well as a group business venture.

Some of the other pioneer psychosocial rehabilitation programs include Portals House in Los Angeles, Manning House in Dallas, The Corners in Massachusetts, Saints and Sinners Club in Phoenix, Forward House in Montreal, and Thresholds in Chicago. These early psychosocial programs were environments where people could make friends and know that people cared about their daily efforts to live and work in the community (Stroul, 1986). They provided social and recreational activities, training in practical skills like money management, cooking, shopping, laundering cloths, or offered education and employment opportunities for self-growth and development (Rutman, 1989).

The growth of psychosocial rehabilitation programs was spurred by the large number of individuals with mental illness discharged from state psychiatric hospitals. In 1955, there were approximately 560,000 people in public psychiatric hospitals. After the 1950s, hospital discharges escalated as individuals with

mental illness experienced dramatic improvements in functioning upon the widespread availability of antipsychotic medications. Tens of thousands of persons with mental illness returned to the community in the mid 1970s as a result of the deinstitutionalization movement and the growth of community mental health centers. By 1974, the number of people in state psychiatric hospitals was reduced to 216,000, and by 1990, there were fewer than 100,000 persons (Mechanic & Aiken, 1987; Ross, 1995).

The deinstitutionalization philosophy and mobilization for community care became embodied in the 1963 Community Mental Health Centers Act, and in 1965, federal funds were authorized for the construction of comprehensive mental health centers throughout the nation. By the mid 1970s, the locus of care for people with a serious mental illness shifted to the community. Unfortunately, there was a dearth of knowledge about psychosocial rehabilitation and community support programs. Not only do people in the community with a serious and persistent mental illness need mental health treatment and rehabilitation services, but they also need affordable and safe housing, a source of income, linkage to social, family and community network systems, overall medical care, and assistance to achieve employment and other goals to achieve growth and development.

While community mental health centers had been established to provide aftercare for people with mental illness who were discharged from state institutions, there was little, if any, system-wide planning as state psychiatric hospitals were emptied. Over time, it became increasingly evident that many of the community mental health centers had failed to respond to people with the most severe and persistent psychiatric problems

(Mechanic & Aiken, 1987). After the 1970's, it became evident that many people with serious and persistent mental illness in communities, particularly among younger adults, were experiencing multiple rehospitalizations in a short period of time, which became known as the "revolving door" phenomenon.

Many of the earlier psychosocial rehabilitation programs initially provided services in one area, usually social and recreational activities, but it soon became clear that "socialization activities alone left untouched the individual's need for either vocational training or for adequate living arrangements" (Rutman, 1989). Programs that singularly offered residential or vocation services also recognized the importance of programming to meet a person's social and recreational needs. Psychosocial rehabilitation practitioners quickly moved beyond a policy of deinstitutionalization to a broader concept of "noninstitutionalization," in order to holistically meet the multiple needs of people in the community. Interventions to divert hospitalizations or to decrease their duration and frequency during an acute illness episode became one of the primary objectives of psychosocial rehabilitation programs. Residential programs, housing supports, prevocational training, employment, and educational programs, case management services, crisis intervention, and crisis residential stabilization programs quickly expanded the range of psychosocial rehabilitation services being offered.

Community Support Program

In 1974, the National Institute of Mental Health began to officially address the systemic problems facing poorly prepared and ill equipped communities. One of its initiatives included the establishment of the ad hoc Community Support Work Group, charged with better ways to serve people with a serious mental illness in their communities. In 1977, the Government Accounting Office (GAO) issued a stinging report criticizing inadequate planning and program development efforts that were a consequence of hastily implemented deinstitutionalization policies in several states (Rutman, 1989). This report mobilized several efforts by government agencies to improve, expand, and coordinate services.

In 1978, the Community Support Program (CSP) was established by the National Institute of Mental Health to "stimulate pivotal system changes and a new service delivery concept based on rehabilitation principles," and to meet the needs of people with severe and persistent psychiatric disabilities (Parrish, 1991). The Community Support Program provided funding to states to help them plan systems of care and to develop innovative programs that support persons with serious mental illness in their own communities. After the nation's massive deinstitutionalization efforts, the lack of a comprehensive system of services which crossed many traditional borders made it evident that housing, work, education, and social supports were as important as mental health treatment. There are ten essential components of a comprehensive community support system that help people maximize their potential for growth, improvement, independence and integration:

- identification and outreach to persons with mental illness
- mental health treatment
- crisis response services
- health and dental care
- housing
- income support and entitlements
- peer support, family and community support

- rehabilitation services
- protection and advocacy, and
- case management (Stroul, 1994).

These services must be available if a community is to effectively meet the needs of people who are disabled as a result of a serious mental illness. The principles of community support encourage the mental health system and service providers to embrace a philosophy of self-determination, empowerment, and respect for each individual with mental illness and family members. Furthermore, programs and direct service workers must tailor services to meet individualized needs and ensure access, linkage, and coordination to all of the essential services and supports in a community that enable optimal functioning. The principles and essential components of community support services are embraced in the practice of psychosocial rehabilitation.

Psychosocial rehabilitation has become a preferred mode of services for persons with a serious and persistent mental illness (Stroul, 1986). Several programs employing psychosocial rehabilitation interventions were funded by the Community Support Program as demonstration projects and were replicated nationwide. As a direct result of the interest in and support of psychosocial rehabilitation by the National Institute of Mental Health, there has been a dramatic expansion in the number of agencies providing these services. Until 1977, there were only two clubhouse programs, but after Fountain House received a grant in 1976 to create a National Training Program, there were over 200 clubhouse programs by 1992. In 1971, there were thirteen agencies identified in the United States that offered a comprehensive program of psychosocial rehabilitation services. By 1990, *A National Directory: Or-*

ganizations Providing Psychosocial Rehabilitation and Related Community Support Service in the United States 1990 (IAPSRS, 1990) listed 1,334 programs having the capacity to serve over 121,000 people on a daily basis. Current estimates suggest that there are more than 2,000 agencies providing psychosocial rehabilitation services in the United States (Hughes, 1994).

Competency 3

Understand and believe in the principles of psychosocial rehabilitation.

Principles of Psychosocial Rehabilitation

There is a core set of principles and values that all psychosocial rehabilitation programs and practitioners ascribe to in their interactions with individuals with mental illness and in the delivery of services. First and foremost is the belief that all persons, no matter how disabled, have the capacity to learn and grow. Hope is a crucial and necessary ingredient of the rehabilitation process. Too often, a person with a serious mental illness has been discouraged from believing in his or her own ability to grow and to regain control over daily life. As this belief in one's own capacity is restored, real change can take place.

Self-determination is another key concept. The person with a mental illness needs to be an active partner in the rehabilitation process and assume increasing responsibility for making the decisions of every day life. This process of empowerment may evolve far beyond individual decision making through the inclusion of persons with serious mental illness providing input at every level—planning for systems of care, de-

Principles of Psychosocial Rehabilitation

- Hope is an essential ingredient in psychosocial rehabilitation. All people have an underutilized capacity to learn and grow that should be developed.

- All people should be treated with respect and dignity. No one should be labeled or discriminated against based upon their disability, dysfunction, illness or disease. The whole person, not the illness, is the focus of psychosocial rehabilitation.

- Psychosocial rehabilitation focuses on "real world" everyday activities and facilitates the development of skills and supports for people to participate as fully as possible in normal roles within family and community settings.

- Multicultural diversity among psychosocial rehabilitation program staff, participants and the community at large is appreciated as a source of strength and program enrichment. Programs take active measures to respond in ways that are considerate and respectful of diversity.

- Psychosocial rehabilitation is premised on self determination and empowerment. The individual served takes increasingly more responsibility for day to day decisions. The rehabilitation practitioner's role is to facilitate the decision making process, to help individuals with mental illness make informed choices, and to promote and recognize each individual's rights and responsibilities.

- An individualized approach to the development and provision of psychosocial rehabilitation services best meets the needs of people who choose to use these services. Assessments and interventions are individually tailored and flexible. Services are available whenever they are needed and for as long as they are needed.

- The psychosocial rehabilitation practitioner role is intentionally informal and participatory in activities that are designed to engage the person with mental illness in real world tasks and relationships.

- The prevention of unnecessary hospitalizations, and the stabilization of community tenure are primary goals of psychosocial rehabilitation.

livery of services, and the evaluation of them.

All approaches to psychosocial rehabilitation recognize the importance of community—the community one lives and works in, the community of one's peers, and the network of community supports that are essential to recovery. Too frequently, services have been provided in isolation, rather than coordinated with other services and integrated into the fabric of the community. It is not by accident that the federal program which spawned much of today's psychosocial rehabilitation programs was titled Community Support.

Since the inception of the field, there have been numerous articles discussing these fundamental principles that cut across all models and applications of rehabilitation technologies (Dincin, 1975; Anthony, 1978; Rutman, 1981; Anthony, 1982; Anthony, Cohen, & Cohen, 1983; Tanaka, 1983; Dincin and Pernell-Arnold,

1985; Anthony & Liberman, 1986; Anthony, Cohen, & Danley, 1988; Cnaan et al, 1988, 1989, 1990; Hughes, Lehman & Thomas, 1996; Curtis, Tanzman, & McCabe, 1992; Pernell-Arnold & Finley, 1992; IAPSRS, 1994). While programs, service delivery settings, and the job descriptions of practitioners may look different from program to program, the following principles are inherent in the delivery of all psychosocial rehabilitation, vocational rehabilitation, social rehabilitation, housing supports, residential programs, crisis intervention, and case management services that ascribe to the principles of psychosocial rehabilitation and community support.

There are other seminal figures in the field who have written about principles that are closely associated with one model of practice, but whose application have generalization across models. George Fairweather, the founder of the lodge model, articulated principles of group processes and the development of community life for persons with mental illness (Fairweather, 1980; Fairweather, Sanders, Cressler, & Maynard, 1969). Many of the lodge principles are similar to the fundamental concepts necessary for the operation of a clubhouse (Beard, Propst & Malamud, 1982). Both of these models recognize the importance of creating environments that provide hope for people. The dynamics for individual change and growth are mobilized by group processes in lodges, clubhouses, and other rehabilitation programs in the performance of normative activities.

Direct service workers in all rehabilitation settings value the restoration of natural support systems to advance independence, integration and inclusion in the community. Case management principles emphasize the importance of the relationship between the psychosocial rehabilitation practitioner and the person being served. Establishing linkages with community and family systems while employing individually determined environmental supports and skills training technologies in community settings are core principals of case management. (Rapp, 1989; Kanter, 1989). The value of supportive peer relationships have been further elevated in self help models that are run by people with mental illness, using or adapting rehabilitation principles. Empowering people, expanding choices and respecting self-determination are not dependent on the locus of services; they are endorsed by all psychosocial rehabilitation practitioners in all settings.

Tailoring assessments and intervention strategies according to individual strengths and needs is a core belief. While direct service workers in facility based settings utilize group dynamics to effect change, like their case manager counterparts in the community, they also value the establishment of genuine relationships with individual program participants. The formation of close egalitarian relationships serves as the foundation for a collaborative partnership that is critical in the rehabilitation process.

Competency 4

Understand the distinction between the Medical Model and the Rehabilitation Model.

Distinction Between Medical Model and Rehabilitation Model

One of the major contributions of psychosocial rehabilitation to mental health treatment, has been the shift from services based on the medical model to services incorporating rehabilitation principles. The medical model focuses on the removal of disease symptoms by medical professionals who are trained as expert authorities in the diagnosis and treatment of the disease. While mental health professionals ascribing to the medical model are an essential ingredient in the treatment of mental illness, particularly in the use of medications or need for inpatient care, the medical model is frequently not conducive to a comprehensive restoration of functioning.

The rehabilitation model focuses on the functioning of the individual in the normal, day-to-day environment, and looks at the strengths and skills people bring to the rehabilitation process and potential supports in the environment. Although an individual may still be symptomatic, the rehabilitation process helps a person learn ways to compensate for the effects of the mental illness through environmental supports and coping skills. The person with the mental illness becomes the expert in managing the disability. The medical model is intent upon minimizing sickness while the rehabilitation model is concerned with maximizing health (Anthony, Cohen, & Farkas, 1990). Regardless of the setting, rehabilitation practitioners promote the return of "personhood" that maximizes the individual's responsibility, control and feelings of self-worth, and encourage ownership of the rehabilitation process rather than "patienthood" with its emphasis on illness (Rutman,1989).

The rehabilitation practitioner collaborates with people in a pragmatic identification of their abilities, deficits, and environmental supports. Too often, learning about personal strengths and a person's capacity for normal functioning is overlooked once the diagnosis of a serious mental illness has been established. Psychosocial rehabilitation emphasizes the development of an individualized rehabilitation plan that articulates strategies to acquire deficient skills and supports to re-establish participation in everyday activities.

The rehabilitation model also helps people overcome the negative effects of "patienthood." During long periods of institutionalization, patients develop coping skills and behaviors which are counterproductive to independent functioning. Hospital patients may be expected to accept the direction and authority of the medical staff, to readily comply with all treatments that are ordered, and to make a minimum of fuss. Hospital staff often control every aspect of a person's daily life, leaving few decisions and little sense of control for the patient (Rutman, 1989). Consequently, long-term patients may develop the following kinds of behaviors:

- compliant and dependent behavior,
- apathy,
- loss of self-respect,
- depersonalization,
- feelings of powerlessness and helplessness,
- difficulty mastering the skills of daily living,
- problems maintaining social, family, and community networks,
- low motivation for seeking out and utilizing community resources,
- a high vulnerability to stress, and
- difficulty achieving educational and employment objectives commensurate with age and abilities.

Combined with the disabling effects of mental illness, these behaviors make it very difficult to leave the institutional setting and make a successful adjustment to community life. Detrimental "patient" experiences may also occur in some outpatient medical facilities. Psychosocial rehabilitation programs are specifically designed to minimize the likelihood of subsuming the patient identity as a personal identity. The rehabilitation model of treatment shifts its focus from the symptoms of psychopathology, even the establishment of a diagnostic label, to a focus on the behaviors, skills, and environmental modifications that people need to overcome their disabilities and become "psychiatrically able" (Anthony, 1980).

Psychosocial rehabilitation programs are purposefully designed to be informal settings where adults can participate in age-appropriate activities as they remediate or compensate for disability factors. Programs tend to avoid using clinical sounding names and often select ones that are uplifting such as Horizon House, Thresholds, or Independence Center (Rutman ,1989). Here, the practitioner works to empower people with mental illness to have ownership of the rehabilitation program and responsibility to perform tasks that operationalize and sustain it. Being a contributing member of a supportive group and relating to other peers has enormous benefits that cannot be duplicated in individual therapeutic models of treatment (Albee, 1986).

Competency 5

Describe the core components of psychosocial rehabilitation services.

CORE COMPONENTS OF PSR PROGRAMS

Community-based psychosocial rehabilitation programs are designed to be comprehensive and to meet the variety of needs of people with serious mental illness. Programs strive to provide each participant services that will prevent or reduce utilization of hospital care and that will promote the optimal level of functioning to achieve personal satisfac-

tion, growth, and productive citizenship within a program and the community at-large. All major aspects of living in the community are addressed, and while each program looks different, most of the following service components are provided (Rutman, 1989; Dincin & Pernell-Arnold, 1985; Pernell-Arnold & Finley, 1992; Cook & Hoffschmidt, 1993):

- social rehabilitation
- vocational rehabilitation
- residential and housing services
- educational supports
- education about mental illnesses and medications
- physical health
- intensive case management
- supportive counseling
- family support

The population using psychosocial rehabilitation services is heterogeneous. It is important that direct service workers remember not every program participant wants or needs assistance in each of these components. Practitioners must be knowledgeable about all of the core service components in order to assess the level of service need.

Social Rehabilitation Services

Social rehabilitation services are designed to promote social involvement while acquiring and strengthening the social skills that make possible meaningful relationships (Dincin & Pernell-Arnold, 1985). These services are delivered in activities where individuals with mental illness can learn attitudes, behaviors, and skills that ought to develop and retain normative relations with peers, mates, families of individuals with mental illness, associates and co-workers. (Pernell-Arnold & Finley, 1992). When these activities are mastered, they can contribute to a person's efficacy in a variety of contexts that will continue throughout a person's lifetime (Cook and Hoffschmidt, 1993). Furthermore, they are intended to help people overcome or compensate for the impaired interpersonal functioning and relationship to the external world, which often takes the form of social withdrawal and emotional detachment. "Isolation, inability to establish relationships, periodic regressions that alienate their friends, and an overwhelming sense of loneliness and failure often characterize the experiences of consumers" (Dincin, 1975). Social rehabilitation services include basic social skills, interpersonal skills, problem solving skills, and recreation and social interaction activities.

Basic social skills include performance of instrumental activities of daily living (i.e. personal hygiene, grooming, cooking, use of transportation, money management); listening skills, attending, following directions, conversational skills, etc. (Dincin & Pernell-Arnold, 1985: Pernell-Arnold & Finley, 1992). These skills promote a sense of accomplishment in endeavors that can be pursued throughout an individual's lifetime.

Interpersonal skills allow a person to relate to and care for oneself, to pay attention to the needs and feelings of others, to "get outside" of the problems in the personal world, and to participate in social groups, family situations, congregate living environments, and the community at-large (Dincin & Pernell-Arnold, 1985, Pernell-Arnold & Finley, 1992). They help people develop a positive self-image and empathic skills which facilitate relating and caring for others and teach them how to relax and enjoy interpersonal relationships in various contexts (Dincin & Pernell-Arnold, 1985).

Problem-solving skills help a person learn and practice adaptive behaviors. Individuals with mental illness often have deficient problem solving skills as a result of cognitive impairments associated with the psychiatric disorder. Problem-solving skills are used to handle everyday experiences, unusual situations, and crisis situations. They include the ability to identify a problem, generate alternative solutions, initiate new behaviors, maintain them and generalize them to other situations (Dincin & Pernell-Arnold, 1985; Pernell-Arnold and Finley, 1992).

Recreation and social interaction activities are designed to enhance participation in age appropriate activities in informal settings. Socializing and participating in leisure time activities are ways that people develop natural support systems among peers, family, co-workers and the community at-large. Learning how to participate in community activities, as well as with an individual's peers, promotes the formation of friendships, enhances self esteem, and builds reliable supports that a person can count on in daily interactions and at times of crisis. Recreation and social activities are promoted during the evening and weekend hours to parallel the times that abled peers pursue similar objectives (Cook & Hoffschmidt, 1993).

Vocational Rehabilitation

Work is the major vehicle for every person to become a productive and contributing member of the community (Dincin & Pernell-Arnold, 1985). While the unemployment figure for all people with disabilities is 68%, unemployment for people with a serious mental illness is much higher at 85% (Weinstein, 1993). Vocational rehabilitation activities include pre-vocational training, vocational training, career counseling, job placement and ongoing job support.

Pre-vocational work activities that are performed in order to operate the psychosocial rehabilitation program provide opportunities to improve work tolerance and enhance self-image (Dincin & Pernell-Arnold, 1985). PSR programs are often structured on a work-oriented day. Work is done in groups, teams, units, or crews. Pre-vocational training typically includes clerical work, preparing meals for program attendees, or performing daily maintenance tasks and other needed building repairs. Pre-vocational activities develop competence in following instructions, being accurate, learning to correct oneself, accepting criticism, getting along with co-workers and supervisors, taking initiative, improving concentration, and learning about symptoms that interfere with work. (Dincin, 1975).

Skills training in vocational rehabilitation programming involves the teaching of salable skills such as computer operations, general office skills, food preparation, or building maintenance. Salable skills can be learned within the program facility, through a community training program, or on the job. While most skills training is for entry-level positions, programs are beginning to recognize the need for a broad range of careers which require more sophisticated skills training.

Job placement and support is the cornerstone of vocational rehabilitation activities. There is a great variety in the way placements are made. Individuals can be placed alone or in groups. The ownership of the job can belong to a program or to the employed individual. Placements can be for part-time jobs or full time work. Strategies to achieve competitive employment include supported employment, transitional employment and permanent employment.

Individuals with mental illness in competitive employment are paid wages that are commensurate with abled workers at integrated work settings in the community. Supported employment and transitional employment utilize job coaches who help train and support the worker. These support services are provided on the job site or other appropriate locations in order to assist in the acquisition and retention of employment. While both models use job coaches, emphasize placements in entry-level positions, and develop group and individual placements, there are discrete differences (Bond, 1987). The "place-train" supported employment model quickly places a individual in a competitive and permanent job, and provides all of the training, skills, and supports necessary to do the job at the work site, without conducting an elongated assessment process. The "choose-get-keep" supported employment model emphasizes consumer choice in the identification of a career that is compatible with individual goals and aspirations. A careful career assessment process before job acquisition may counter the historic treatment of individuals with psychiatric disabilities as passive service recipients (Danley & Anthony, 1987).

The transitional employment (TE) model was initially developed by Fountain House and is usually associated with club house programs. Job placements are formal arrangements between a program and the employer (Bond, 1987). TE entails placing a person in a sequence of temporary transitional employment placements that typically last between six weeks and six months. Through participation in several TE experiences, a person develops critical work readiness skills and a work history in normative employment settings. After several transitional employment experiences, a person is ready for placement in a permanent employment position that reflects individual career objectives.

Residential Programs and Supportive Housing Services

Shelter is a fundamental need for all people. Psychosocial rehabilitation programs have developed a broad spectrum of housing options to provide people with meaningful choices. Residential programs, supervised housing, and supported housing services need to promote access to decent, stable, affordable, and safe homes in settings that maximize inclusion and the ability to function independently (IAPSRS, 1992). The array of options range from settings and services that address crisis and respite care needs in the least restrictive environment, to the provision of long-term flexible supports in commercially available integrated housing.

Local and state mental health delivery systems have frequently collaborated with psychosocial rehabilitation agencies to develop many styles of housing that meet consumer preferences and range of functioning. Residential programs and supervised housing have a supervision structure that is put in place by an agency or mental health authority, such as agency staff on site twenty-four hours to respond to people in crisis, housing units that are restricted to persons with disabilities, or the nature and timing of supports are predetermined by a program. The housing is available to members of the community at-large. Supported housing options shift the locus of control for supports to the individuals with mental illness to any environment they determine is optimal. The intensity of programming responds to acute care, transitional, or long-term needs, while the degree of supports and their structure reflect the nature, frequency and duration that are indicated and amenable to a person.

Style of housing, intensity of supports, duration of supports, and external factors related to housing decisions are some of the issues that direct service workers and the person with a psychiatric disability need to discuss when determining what residential environment and supports are optimal in the current circumstances.

Competency 6

Know the psychosocial rehabilitation models and technologies.

PSYCHOSOCIAL REHABILITATION MODELS AND TECHNOLOGIES

The Clubhouse Model

The clubhouse model was first developed at Fountain House in New York City. A group of people discharged from the state hospital began meeting on the steps of the New York City Library. A club called "We Are Not Alone" was born and eventually became Fountain House. This program and its first director, John Beard, were pioneers in the development of psychosocial rehabilitation services, and they have influenced the entire field with their profundity. The clubhouse model creates an intentional restorative environment where people with severe psychiatric disabilities can achieve or regain the confidence and skills to be socially and vocationally productive (Beard, Propst, & Malamud, 1982). A clubhouse belongs to its members who are voluntary participants in the clubhouse daily activities. Members is the term commonly used to describe everyone who participates in the clubhouse program. This term connotes the involvement, ownership, and role of each person in supporting the program, just as members in any other club do. Membership is not limited by time. You belong for as long as you choose to participate. All program elements are constructed with an intent to make persons with psychiatric disabilities feel welcome.

Work is central to the rehabilitation process and is the foundation for the work-oriented day that defines the structure of all clubhouses (Propst, 1988). Program participants develop ways to compensate for the psychiatric disability, while learning vocational and social skills. Pre-vocational programming is based on real activities which must be accomplished to support the program. Typically they include administrative tasks, research, intake and orientation procedures, education and training, clerical tasks, meal preparation, and maintenance in specialized units. The paid staff often includes persons who have a mental illness. No job is too menial for staff or too important to be done by a member. This philosophy of "mutual support" underlies the structure of the clubhouse which is in contrast to other kinds of "day programs," where professional staff provide all of the services that someone with mental illness needs.

Pre-vocational programming is designed to help each person develop the habit of coming to a place every day where they are expected to learn new work and social skills, to practice old skills that have often languished since the onset of a serious mental illness, or to find alternative ways to perform tasks to compensate for disability related impairments.

As staff and members work together, staff have opportunities to appreciate and respect the abilities and talents of each individual, learn about their social and vocational potential and recognize areas that need to be strengthened.

Clubhouse members "do not regard themselves as undergoing a formal rehabilitation process, in which something is being done to them" (Beard, Propst, & Malamud, 1982). The participation in clubhouse programming not only builds skills, but the "seeds of self-value and self-worth are sown" (Propst, 1988).

The transitional employment program is one of the major ingredients of the clubhouse model that has propelled people into real jobs in the community at competitive wages. Transitional employment programs make it possible for people who have previously experienced employment failures or who have no work history, to have access to time-limited job placements. Most of these jobs are designed to be part-time and at entry-level positions. They typically last between 3 to 9 months. The results of a 1988 survey of 120 clubhouses documented 708 employers supplying 1500 job placements that generated $56,308,132 in taxable revenue (Fountain House, 1988).

The Fairweather Lodge Model

George Fairweather developed the concept for the lodge program based upon his research in social learning theory. The lodge model is premised on the belief that people with serious mental illness are most likely to attain stability and residential and employment reintegration in small supportive group situations where they have a stake in the system. The creation of a social environment where everyone shares mutual responsibility for each other optimizes individual success. Lodges are typically community residences where 5 to 15 people live and often work together. However, today some are being developed as community-based training lodges (Onaga, 1993). Training lodges may be transitional in nature and act as referral sources to other lodges that have long-term membership or act as vocational training centers that teach people how to enter the workforce through participation in lodge entrepreneurial ventures or integrated competitive employment that is available in the community at large. In some lodges, members live together but may work elsewhere or reside at other locations but come to the lodge in order to participate in a work program. What is replicated at each lodge program is the philosophy that every person has a meaningful role within the lodge and that the demands and functions of the lodge role are not overwhelming.

Lodge participants are responsible for its upkeep. This facilitates the development of a cohesive group that is task-oriented and maintains the integrity and smooth operation of the lodge. This self-regulatory peer support group helps everyone become sensitive to the norms of the community, while internal norms are tolerant of symptoms that people experience. The group decision making process is a vehicle to improve self-confidence, to help people regain a sense of control and move towards independence, and to experience the positive rewards of decision making, as well as consequences when poor judgment is exercised. Lodges do not have live-in staff, but they do have relationships with rehabilitation and mental health practitioners. PSR practitioners provide guidance, skills training, consultation, informal support, and crisis intervention.

In its basic form, a Fairweather Lodge consists of a group of people with mental illness, living and working together in a community setting. However, it is much more than a group living situation. A home organized according to Dr. Fairweather's principles is a *unique* kind of social organization. It differs from other kinds of programs such as family care homes, boarding homes, group homes or half way houses which are established to operate under the supervision of paid staff. In a Fairweather lodge, the *group members* themselves, rather than staff are *responsible* for maintaining the integrity and functioning of the organization (Fairweather Implementation Project, MSU).

Fairweather Lodges were pioneers in the development of entrepreneurial business ventures operated by people with mental illness. While not all lodges operate their own businesses, the role of work is elevated in every lodge. In some lodges, everyone works in crews or enclaves doing lawn care, custodial work, laundry services, printing, furniture repair, shoe repair, catering etc. Jobs that

The Role of Staff in Lodges

"The role of staff can be tenuous and uncertain because staff needs to pull back when members are able to carry out their responsibilities, yet assert themselves to do whatever is necessary when the members are struggling or unable to carry out their tasks." (Onaga, 1993).

According to Fairweather, the role of staff is "to push, cajole, shape, and urge the group" towards autonomy (Fair-weather, 1980). Staff must have a willingness to allow each person the freedom to fail as they grapple with the social world around them.

While staff retain a veto power, their role is to gradually wean the Lodge society away from staff intervention or direction (MSU, 1978).

The Healing Power of Self-Help Groups

"Peer fellowship in self-help groups is premised on unconditional acceptance and respect for each person. Self-disclosure allows people to be accepted for who they are without the expectation that they must change to experience healing or recovery. These are environments where people can heal the wounds of alienation, stigma, abuse, and neglect that may accompany mental illness. Within the mental health system, sometimes the cure was worse than the disease. Participants can discover ways for symptom management that come from within. They do not have to come from the "professional" system. Real healing is casting off the role of patient and viewing oneself as OK. It is getting the unique support of peers and having a place to be a helper versus a helpee. Being elevated to a peer who can give and who can get allows a person to cast off limitations that were previously internalized."

"Self-help groups encourage people to take back power and to be advocates for themselves and for their peers. Advocacy is an empowering tool that helps people work through shame, move away from a paternal mental health system and become a valued player. It is also an important vehicle for advocates with a mental illness to join together with other players in the mental health system. This includes mental health and rehabilitation agencies, direct service workers, family organizations, and other local, state and national parties who want to ensure that people have access to all of the supports and tools they need for their recovery" (Rosenthal, 1995).

Harvey Rosenthal

belong to the group rather than to an individual build group cohesion and allows for worker substitution should someone be unable to work. When lodges do not develop their own businesses, individuals work for other community employers by themselves or in work crews.

Michigan's Fairweather Programs have described lodges as psychosocial programs which put social learning principles to work, rehabilitation programs based on empirical evidence, and community support programs for persons with serious mental illness. They are mental health services that are directed by the participants. The lodge programs are cost effective residential and work programs, vehicles for social empowerment and a proven means to teach community survival through decision making and problem-solving skills (Fairweather Implementation Project, MSU).

Self-Help Programs

There are several other models of programs which are run directly by people with mental illness. Within these programs, participants may identify themselves as survivors, expatients, consumers, or people in recovery. While the functions of particular programs and their beliefs about the role of the mental health system vary, there are important unifying elements among most self-help programs.

There are many different self-help environments where direct service practitioners employ psychosocial rehabilitation interventions. Peer case management teams and club houses where all staff have been recipients of mental health services, peer-operated respite care and crisis intervention programs, drop in centers, programs that locate or provide employment or housing, and entrepreneurial ventures are some examples. Some of the initial drop in centers primarily functioned as settings for socialization and recreation, but many today have taken on educational and vocational training, ownership of businesses, provision of information and referral services on the electronic communications highway, operations of hotlines or warmlines, consultations to academic mental health programs, and leadership in advocacy for changes in local, state, federal health, and mental health policy (Sullivan, 1995).

Just as there is heterogeneity among the backgrounds of practitioners in other psychosocial rehabilitation models, the same is true in self-help programs. People are employed in their professional and paraprofessional capacities in self-help programs and use their academic training and licensure in psychiatry, psychology, social work, nursing, the allied health profession, counseling, teaching, business, law, and diverse occupational trades. Many of these programs have helped people return to careers that were interrupted by the onset of a serious mental illness or persistence of symptoms and resulting disabilities. Other people have been inspired to acquire academic degrees or vocational training to pursue employment in "alternative" programs. Self-help programs pioneered the promotion of individuals with mental illness into administrative and supervisory positions.

The Independent Living Center movement has done an enormous amount of the groundwork to advance peer support, self-help, self-determination, equal access, and individual and system advocacy for individuals with severe impairments (Weinstein, 1994). The National Empowerment Center developed out of this movement. It provides information, technical assistance, and a national directory of mutual support groups, drop in centers, and statewide organizations in accordance with its objective to promote recovery, empowerment, hope and healing. The National Mental Health Consumers Self-Help Clearinghouse is another organization that provides education, resource materials, and training for persons with mental illness nationwide. Both of these organizations are instrumental in the planning of the yearly "Alternatives Conference" where people with psychiatric disabilities from across the country gather to support and expand the self-help movement.

Intensive Case Management Models

Intensive case management services are targeted to those people who are at high risk of :

- requiring intensive services
- high frequency of psychiatric hospitalizations or crisis intervention services
- lengthy inpatient stays
- difficulties finding treatment in a less restrictive environment
- high drop out rates at facility based programs (Stroul, 1986)
- homelessness
- co-occurring disorders (substance abuse, HIV, tuberculosis, etc.)

The practitioner in this model is also referred to as a "'full service case manager" who provides most of the ongoing assessment, treatment, rehabilitation, and supports in the community (Curtis, 1992). Case managers are the "glue" of all the systems people interface, empowered to access services across system lines and to intervene when there are problems, gaps, or barriers (Pernell-

Arnold & Finley, 1992). The functions of the psychosocial rehabilitation practitioner providing intensive case management exceeds the case coordination services that are more typically associated with case management for other populations.

The following activities are common to all intensive case management services models:

- Services are invivo, or in the individual's natural settings.

- There is aggressive outreach to engage and sustain the case management relationship with people who are considered by the mental health system as "difficult to serve."

- A small worker-to-person-served ratio is necessary in order for the direct service worker to have the amount of time necessary to engage and maintain people in a relationship that stabilizes or improves their situations.

- Services must be available 24 hours to respond to emergencies and divert inpatient care whenever treatment in a less restrictive setting is appropriate.

- There is a respect for the individual with mental illness in the process of defining goals and delivering services that represent what both the individual with mental illness and worker can realistically commit to working on together.

- Services are not time limited, and there is an expectation that the individual with mental illness will utilize case management services for an extended period.

The invivo nature of intensive case management services means meeting with people in their homes, shelters for the homeless, living space on the streets, jail, neighborhood restaurants, or locations where resources such as food stamps, disability income, clothing, housing vouchers, employment, education or training programs can be accessed. Learning skills "invivo"—or in the natural environment—circumvents the inability for many with a severe psychiatric disability to generalize learning from one setting to another, or their failure to negotiate complicated social and bureaucratic systems to receive critical services and supports (Stroul, 1986; Stein & Diamond, 1985).

While practitioners in these models, have most frequently been called "case managers," there is a growing recognition that people receiving services or assistance do not want to be considered "cases" nor, as people, do they want to be "managed" (Everett et al., 1990). Programs are not only rethinking their nomenclature, but also the structure of the relationship between the practitioner and the individual served. Some case management models are elevating the development of "partnerships" in place of case management language, while others are redefining their services into a "helping framework with counselors" (Everett et al., 1990). Mind Empowered, in Portland, Oregon, is a peer-operated case management program, where the recipients of services are identified as program participants. Participants and staff have the opportunity to share their experience of a mental illness and allow this aspect of their lives to "emerge as an asset, rather than a hidden liability." The modeling of competence and seeing a peer lead a satisfying life and provide support to others further enhances the relationship that develops between staff and program participants (Nikkel et al., 1992).

Leonard Stein, one of the originators of this model of community care sums up this intervention strategy as "not a case management program, treatment program, or rehabilitation program; rather, it is a care program that makes use of well-trained professionals and paraprofessionals who together provide treatment, rehabilitation, and services" (Stein, 1990).

Rehabilitation Technologies

Skill deficits may be the cause of psychiatric symptoms, the consequence of symptoms, or any combination of these factors; however, the direct service worker is not focused on symptom etiology, but on pragmatic approaches to improve functioning with the minimum amount of support necessary from professional and paraprofessional helpees (Farkas, Cohen & Nemec, 1988; Anthony, 1980). Impaired cognitive functioning in the areas of memory, attention, processing speed and capacity, reaction time, problem solving, concept formation, integrating diverse sensory stimuli, distractibility, etc., have been implicated as significant factors associated with behavioral dysfunctions and other impediments to the acquisition and use of coping skills (Lamb, 1994). Skills are defined as observable, measurable, and teachable behaviors. Rehabilitation technology provides the practitioner a structure that helps the person with mental illness "perform the physical, intellectual and emotional skills needed to live, learn and work" (Anthony, 1980). The application of skill development technologies are premised on the assumption that the individual with mental illness freely chooses to be involved in the process.

There are several skill development rehabilitation technologies. Direct skills teaching and social skills training are the most frequent technologies employed by psychosocial rehabilitation practitioners. Direct skills teaching is based on education constructs, or a "teaching as treatment" model, and uses some of the behavioral and social learning principles. Social skills training, also based on behavioral learning theory, incorporates principles from the education, or classroom, model (Nemec, McNamara & Walsh, 1992). Both of these technologies are used to develop and expand a person's skill repertoire. Skills programming is another skill development strategy that uses teaching methods, as well as behavioral and social learning principles, to help individuals use skills that they already have (Anthony, Cohen & Danley, 1988). Skill development technologies develop and improve the individual's skill performance abilities and establish competencies in skill areas necessary to cope in real world situations, such as school, work, relationships, housing, etc., that achieve self-determined goals.

William Anthony and his associates at The Center for Psychosocial Rehabilitation have developed a comprehensive rehabilitation approach that emphasizes the use of direct skills teaching technologies and skills programming in diverse contexts such as vocational rehabilitation, case management, supported education, supported housing programs, etc. There are three distinct phases that practitioners systematically employ in this comprehensive rehabilitation approach. Phase one is determining a rehabilitation diagnosis; phase two is developing a rehabilitation plan, and phase three is providing rehabilitation interventions. These three phases of psychosocial rehabilitation have foundations in physical rehabilitation constructs which have been integrated with elements of Carkhuff's psychotherapeutic approach (Cohen & Anthony, 1984).

The application of direct skills teaching not only requires practitioner knowledge about the skill development approach, but also effective interpersonal skills. The practitioner must engage the individual with mental illness in a collaborative rehabilitation relationship; orient, instruct and encourage ongoing participation in the process; modify and adapt the approach according to individual dynamics; critique individual progress, listen and respond appropriately (Anthony, Cohen & Farkas, 1988; Nemec, McNamara & Walsh, 1992).

Cohen, Ridley, and Cohen (1983) identify seven skills-teaching issues for the practitioner to consider: teaching methods, feedback, motivation, amount of practice, whole skill versus partial skill learning, social facilitation, and skill generalization. Nemec, McNamara, and Walsh (1992) further elaborate on the principles and elements of direct skills teaching instructing practitioners that it is only indicated when very little or nothing about the necessary skill is known; it is an individualized and structured process; like school teachers, rehabilitation practitioners need to know individual learning styles; it requires the preparation of detailed work plans that outline the sequence of events to be implemented for the acquisition and maintenance of each intermediary skill; all necessary materials must be acquired or research-completed before the appropriate curriculum can be developed or initiated; preparatory arrangements for indicated experts, peers, family members, etc., to teach or participate in the skill activity must be performed; and upon completion of the direct skills instruction, the practitioner must evaluate a

person's skill mastery and have a plan for the provision of supplemental instructions to retain skill competence when it is indicated.

Not only does direct skills teaching take place in one-on-one interactions, but it can also be done in a group format. Some of the factors that practitioners need to consider in a group context include: certainty that all group members want and need similar skill instruction; the lesson plan accommodates the learning style of each member; the practitioner understands group dynamics and does not pressure participation upon individuals who do not tolerate group settings or do not choose learning in a group environment; after the group is terminated, there is appropriate follow-up on the progress of individual members that includes a plan to retain skill performance at individually needed levels (Nemec, McNamara & Walsh, 1992).

Social skills training approaches are systematic and organized approaches that direct practitioners employ to help restore or maintain independent living skills, interpersonal skills, social perception skills, problem solving skills, and vocational skills and have been developed and conducted in a manner that will compensate for cognitive deficits (Kuehnel et al., 1994). Some of the earliest social skills training approaches for individuals with schizophrenia in the 1970s emphasized the acquisition of basic motor skills (i.e. eye contact, hand and body gestures, voice volume etc.), that are important for normative social interactions. This motor skills model of social skills training employed a "behavioral overlearning" approach, in order to promote an automatic response when the targeted skill should be performed (PORT, 1994).

Problem solving and social skills training models also emerged in the

1970s. There are three primary interventions associated with problem solving paradigms: component skills interventions, social learning approaches, and self-instructional interventions. Component skills interventions focus on a person's sequential ability to identify the problem, specify the desired outcome or goal, generate solutions or options, understand the consequences of options, choose a solution, implement the selected problem solving strategy, and evaluate its success. Social learning approaches emphasize modeling techniques to mobilize change. Self-instructional interventions are frequently used by cognitive behavioral therapists to treat depression, addictive behaviors, and anxiety disorders (PORT,1994).

Social skills training modules have been developed to teach persons with mental illness effective behaviors and coping strategies in a variety of contexts. Previous studies have been conducted on practitioner trainer competence and indicate that module leaders from diverse backgrounds can learn the skills training procedures and deliver them with a high degree of fidelity (Eckman & Liberman, 1990). Liberman and Wallace with their colleagues at the UCLA Clinical Research Center for Schizophrenia and Psychiatric Rehabilitation have developed a series of modules for training social and independent living skills that are durable and can be generalized to other settings. Their module topics include: medication management, symptom management, recreation for leisure, grooming and personal hygiene. Modules for each targeted skill consist of seven learning activities designed to fit the "constraints of local programs, and ensure reliable replication by a wide array of paraprofessionals and professionals who are delivering clinical services" (Liberman et al., 1993; Kuehnel et al.1994).

Skill training modules have been used at a broad range of settings such as VA medical centers, public institutions, private psychiatric hospitals, forensic settings, and in community based rehabilitation programs. Other topics that have been effectively used in skills training modules include: psycho-education for family members, (Anderson, Reiss, & Hogarty, 1986), learning street skills (Corrigan & Holmes, 1994), HIV-risk assessment (Susser, Valencia, & Torres, 1994; Cook et al., 1994), and methods to prevent sexual assault and rape (Jonikas & Cook, 1993).

The modules designed by the UCLA Clinical Research Center for Schizophrenia and Psychiatric Rehabilitation have been used with diverse populations including a subset of difficult to serve individuals who are homeless or dually diagnosed with a substance abuse disorder. Standardized curriculums typically provide practitioners with a trainer's manual, demonstration videos, users guides, workbooks for participants, self monitoring tools, homework exercises and additional materials to master separate skill areas (Kuehnel et al., 1994; Alger, A., 1988; Susser, Valencia, & Torres, 1994). For example, the UCLA designed modules include a set of questions and a standardized sequence of interventions such as prompting, cueing, coaching, shadowing, reinforcing, modeling, and positive feedback activities to correspond with typically incorrect or incomplete participant responses that assist the practitioner in promoting competence among individual participants (Kuehnel et al., 1994).

Heterogeneity Among Programs and Models

The field of psychosocial rehabilitation has been enriched by the willingness of practitioners to build programs around the diverse needs of individuals with mental illness in their communities. Some agencies provide services under the configuration of one psychosocial rehabilitation model, such as services available only in a clubhouse setting or through case managers. As previously noted, while following model constructs, each lodge, clubhouse, case management program, and individual with mental illness operated program, etc., has a distinct presentation or personality that reflects community characteristics and often charismatic qualities of particular staff and program participants who demonstrate exemplary practices that enhance the performance of other workers and participants. Programs frequently combine aspects of several psychosocial rehabilitation and mental health service delivery models or implement most of the core psychosocial rehabilitation components and elements of a comprehensive community support system. This further elevates programmatic uniqueness and heterogeneity within the field. An agency may offer provocational programming and replicate several clubhouse elements, such as individuals with mental illness working in units, but not identify itself as a clubhouse because it utilizes paid work crews to perform the tasks necessary to operate the provocational program.

Many psychosocial rehabilitation programs employ skills training technology where direct service practitioners apply behavioral learning techniques in structured educational modules for individuals with mental illness to build a repertoire of skills (Kuehnel et al., 1994). In some programs, skills training takes place in time-limited learning modules which can be repeated, while other programs use these behavioral learning techniques in a looser format that adapts to the pace of the participants. The training centers that have developed these technologies recognize and value the unique ways that programs have applied them to fit individual strengths and needs, as well as modifications by local community planners, state mental health authorities, and key figures who influence national disability policy (Anthony, 1994).

There are myriad reasons why psychosocial rehabilitation programs vary. Some agencies consider it essential to maintain their programmatic separateness from medical practitioners, but make sure that individuals with mental illness have access to psychoeducation and advocacy services in order to respond to medication and other clinical issues. Another program may hire a psychiatrist to ensure each person has access to a physician who similarly endorses a holistic community based treatment and rehabilitation approach, which upholds the right of individuals to accept or reject the use of chemotherapy, and when psychotropic medications are prescribed, it is at the lowest possible therapeutic dosage (Barreira & Dion, 1991; IAPSRS Medication Position, 1994). Other agencies employ their own psychiatrists because the psychosocial rehabilitation program is one component of a larger comprehensive mental health center.

Lack of safe and affordable housing for individuals with mental illness is a common problem that most programs face. While one agency has done extensive development of housing units that could include scattered site housing, congregated living units, and crisis residential services operated by the agency, another agency may restrict direct service worker assistance to providing supports in generic community housing because of a philosophical belief that program services should be "uncoupled" from housing. Both programs may strictly adhere to principles that emphasize choice, self-determination, flexible supports, non-discriminatory housing, and increasing access to permanent and integrated housing and socialization in the community, but their implementation approach and assigned staff responsibilities are different. True choice is contingent upon an array of housing options and service options that suit individual needs and preferences (IAPSRS Housing Position, 1994). What brings these psychosocial rehabilitation agencies together is their shared recognition that programs and direct service staff must help individuals with mental illness meet their housing objectives, as well as other rehabilitation goals.

Programmatic differences may relate to demographic trends, such as a community having a high census of elderly persons with a serious mental illness, implement strategies that tailor residential services, day programming, linkages to health care providers and other community systems that are sensitive to this population's strengths and needs (Bernstein & Rose, 1991). Some programs have been innovative in the development or adoption of psychosocial rehabilitation programming to bridge service gaps experienced by persons who are deaf and mentally ill in their communities (Breakout, 1992). Thresholds, in Chicago, has a multifaceted service system that not only includes prevocational services, assertive case management teams, employment, education, and housing programs, but also highly specialized services for people who are deaf, school-age adolescents, mothers with children, and supportive services for people with HIV/AIDs.

The diversity of funding streams has also influenced the growth and shape of programs. Agencies that receive funds from Medicaid cannot use them for vocational or educational services, which means that supported education, supported employment, or transitional employment services must be clearly separated from other prevocational or invivo activities. These kinds of constraints may influence administrative decisions, such as the utilization of staff who act as psychosocial rehabilitation generalists versus staff who are specialists. For example, one program may have all staff perform vocational rehabilitation tasks, while another may have supported employment specialists, and an even higher degree of specialization with particular staff designated as job developers, job coaches, benefits counselors, etc.

Macro level economic, political, and social dynamics influence the design of particular programs, as well as having implications for programmatic change. Just as the deinstitutionalization and noninstitutionalization movement forced systems to change and expanded the growth of community based psychosocial rehabilitation services, new forces will continue to mobilize change within state mental health delivery systems and agencies. Treatment and rehabilitation services that have traditionally been provided only in the public mental health system are now being integrated with private behavioral health care systems under the rubric of managed care. Managed care can vastly expand the delivery of psychosocial rehabilitation services, but also adds a new gatekeeping system with standardized criteria on the number of days people are authorized to receive services. While there is concern that these external factors can negatively alter the field, they may also hold out new possibilities to create better psychosocial rehabilitation interventions for individuals with mental illness entering the 21st century. As psychosocial rehabilitation agencies or program models continue to diversify, the challenge for the field is to maintain integrity and adhere to key principles, and "manage innovation and change in a way that furthers the development of programs, direct practitioners, and individuals with mental illness" (Spaniol, Zipple, & Cohen, 1991).

Summary

Programs today have become increasingly adept at recognizing the cultural, social, political, and economic dynamics of their communities. New psychosocial rehabilitation interventions have been developed—or older ones modified—to target the needs of special populations such as homeless people with a serious mental illness, aging populations, individuals with co-occurring disorders such as substance abuse, HIV/AIDS, mental retardation, and development disabilities, hearing impairments, or other physical, sensory, and cognitive disabilities. Programs have continued to develop new ways to be effective advocates and collaborate with individuals with mental illness, their children, siblings, and parents to address problems or reflect unique individual family and community strengths. Practices in the field have become increasingly respectful of sexual orientation, race, ethnicity, and age factors. Programs continue to expand access to integrative and normative housing, employment, educational, and social settings.

Today, most agree that community-based care is more humane, more therapeutic and less stigmatizing. In the present climate of severe budgetary constraints for acute health care, as well as long-term care services for the elderly and individuals with disabilities, we must guard against the simplistic and false notion that banishing people with a severe and major mental illness from our communities is acceptable. Providing people with a life of hope and dignity within the community is the solution (Propst, 1988). These values are embodied in the principles of psychosocial rehabilitation and in the daily practices of direct care workers in diverse community settings throughout the United States, Canada, and other nations.

Being in the community requires the capacity to meet personal, emotional, social, vocational, and economic needs. Psychosocial rehabilitation practitioners assist people to not only meet their basic needs of food, clothing, and shelter, but to ensure that personal dignity, civil rights, and liberties are safeguarded, dysfunctional behaviors or relationships are replaced with successful and growth producing ones, normative and integrated opportunities to participate in age appropriate social, cultural, and occupational endeavors are accessed, and greater autonomy and a satisfying quality of life is achieved (Rutman, 1989). Symptom reduction interventions are important competencies for the rehabilitation practitioner to master, and collaboration with medical model interventions to diminish symptoms are actively pursued. However, community tenure, employment, and attainment of goals that increase functioning and autonomy are the primary rehabilitation objectives, which can be achieved by individuals with mental illness regardless of symptoms that are persistent or intermittent.

References

Albee, G. W. Psychosocial rehabilitation is not a medical procedure. Paper based on June 1986 presentation for IAPSRS annual meeting: Cleveland, Ohio.

Alger, I. (1988). Fresh approaches to psychoeducation. *Hospital and Community Psychiatry, 39*(3), 253-56.

Anderson, C.M., Reiss, D.J., & Hogarty, G.E. (1986). *Schizophrenia and the family: A practitioner's guide to psychoeducation and management.* New York: Guilford.

Anthony, W.A. (1980). *The principles of psychosocial rehabilitation.* Baltimore, MD: University Park Press.

_____. (1979). The rehabilitation approach to diagnosis. In L.I. Stein (Ed.) *New Directions for Mental Health Services: Community Support Systems for the Long-Term Patient.* San Francisco: Jossey-Bass.

_____. (1994). Whither the "Boston University Model"? *Psychosocial Rehabilitation Journal 17*(4), 169-70.

_____., Cohen, M.R. & Cohen, B.R. (1983). Philosophy, treatment process, and principles of the psychosocial rehabilitation approach. In I. Bachrack (Ed) *New Directions for Mental Health Services.* San Francisco: Jossey-Bass.

_____., Cohen, M.R., & Farkas, M. (1988). Professional pre-service training for working with long-term mentally ill. *Community Mental Health Journal, 124*(4).

_____., (1990). *Psychosocial rehabilitation.* Boston: Center for Psychosocial Rehabilitation; Boston University, Sargent College of Allied Health Professions.

Barreira, P.J. & Dion, G.L. (1991). Training psychiatrists in rehabilitation principles and practice for working with people with long-term mental illness. *Psychosocial Rehabilitation Journal 5,* (1): 47-53.

Beard, J.H., Propst, R.N., & Malamud, T.J. (1982). The Fountain House model of psychosocial rehabilitation. *Psychosocial Rehabilitation Journal 5*(1), 47-53.

Bernstein, M.A. & Rose, D. (1991). Psychosocial programming for the elderly who are mentally ill. *Psychosocial Rehabilitation Journal 14*(3), 3-13.

Breakout Conference 1992. Conference sponsored by Deaf-REACH: Washington, D. C. & Thresholds: Chicago.

Bond, G. (1987). Supported work as a modification of the transitional employment model for clients with psychiatric disabilities. *Psychosocial Rehabilitation Journal, 11*(2), 57-73.

Chamberlin, J. Concept paper: Ex-patient self-help groups. Prepared for the seventh CSP Learning Community Conference. Self-Help: How Can It be Part of a Community Support System.

Cohen, F.B. & Anthony, W.A. (1984). Functional assessment in psychosocial rehabilitation. In A.S. Halpern & M.J. Fuhrer (Eds.) *Functional Assessment In Rehabilitation*: 79-100. Baltimore MD: Paul Brooks.

Cohen, B.F., Ridley, D.E., & Cohen, M.R. (1983). Teaching skills to psychiatrically disabled persons. In H.A. Marlowe (Ed.) *Developing Competence.* Tampa: University of South Florida Press.

Cnaan, R.A., Blankertz, L., Messinger, K.W., & Gardner J.R. (1990). Experts' assessment of psychosocial rehabilitation principles. *Psychosocial Rehabilitation Journal 13*(3), 59-73.

Cnaan, R.A., Blankertz, L., Messinger, K.W., & Gardner J.R. (1988). Psychosocial rehabilitation: Toward a definition. *Psychosocial Rehabilitation Journal 11*(4), 2-18.

Cnaan, R.A., Blankertz, L., Messinger, K.W., & Gardner J.R. (1989). Psychosocial rehabilitation: Towards a theoretical base. *Psychosocial Rehabilitation Journal 13*(1), 33-55.

Cook, J.A. & Hoffschmidt, S.J. (1993). Comprehensive models of psychosocial rehabilitation. In R.W. Flexer & P.L.

Solomon (Eds.), *Psychosocial rehabilitation in practice*: 81-97. Boston, MA: Andover Medical Publishers.

Cook, J.A., Jonikas, J.A., and Solomon, P.L. (1992). Models of vocational rehabilitation for youths and adults with severe mental illness: Implications for America 2000. *American Rehabilitation*, Autumn Issue: 6-11.

Cook, J.A., Razzano, L., Jayaraj, A., Myers, M., Nathanson, F., Stott, M.A., & Stein, M. (1994). Hiv-risk assessment for psychiatric rehabilitation clientele: Implications for community-based services. *Psychosocial Rehabilitation Journal 17*(4), 105-15.

Corrigan, P.W. & Holmes, E.P. (1994). Patient identification of street skills for a psychosocial training module. *Hospital and Community Psychiatry, 45* (13), 273-277.

Curtis, L. (1992). Supported housing and case management. *In Community 2,* (4). Burlington, Vermont: Center for Community Change through Housing and Support; Trinity College of Vermont.

Curtis, L.C., Tanzman, B. H., & McCabe, S.S. (1992). Orientation manual for local level supported housing staff. Burlington, Vermont: Center for Community Change through Housing and Support; Trinity College of Vermont.

Danley, K. and Anthony, W.A. (1987). The choose-get-keep model: Serving severely psychiatrically disabled people. *American Rehabilitation, 13,* (9), 6-9.

Dincin, J. (1975). Psychosocial rehabilitation. *Schizophrenia Bulletin, 13* (Summer): 131-47.

Dincin, J. & Pernell-Arnold, A.(1985*). Psychosocial rehabilitation: Definition, principles and description.* Columbia, MD: International Association of Psychosocial Rehabilitation Services.

Eckman, T.A. & Liberman, R.P. (1990). A large-scale field test of a medication management skills training program for people with schizophrenia. *Psychosocial Rehabilitation Journal 13*(3), 31-35.

Emerick, R.E. (1990). Self -help groups for former patients: Relations with mental health professions. *Hospital and Community Psychiatry, 41*(4), 401-07.

Everett, B., Birkhoff J. R., Goring, C., Pritchard, J., Shephard, M., & Tindall, C. (1990). Re-thinking case management: Helping framework for counselors. Toronto, Ontario: Homeward Projects Special Task Force on Case Management.

Everett, B. & Nelson, A. (1992). We're not cases and you're not managers: An account of a client-professional partnership developed in response to the borderline diagnosis.*Psychosocial Rehabilitation Journal 15*(4).

Fairweather, G.W. (1980). The prototype lodge society: Instituting group process principles. In *New Directions For Mental Health Services—The Fairweather Lodge: A Twenty-Five Year Retrospective.* San Francisco, CA: Jossey -Bass.

Fairweather, G.W., Sanders, D., Cressler, D., & Maynard, H. (1969). *Community life for the mentally ill: An alternative to hospitalization.* Chicago: Aldine Co.

Fairweather Implementation Project, Michigan State University Michigan's Fairweather Programs. BPPST: SS 5/30/89. Brochure sponsored by the Michigan Department of Mental Health.

Farkas, M.D., Cohen, M.R. & Nemec, P B. (1988). Psychosocial rehabilitation programs: Putting concepts into practice. *Community Mental Health Journal, 20*(1), 7-21.

Fountain House. (1988). Results of January 1988 survey. Transitional Employment. Survey Memorandum 288. New York City: Fountain House Research Unit.

Harris, M. & Bergman, H.C. (1988). Clinical case management for the chronically mentally ill: A conceptual analysis. In M. Harris & L.L. Bachrach (eds.), *Clinical Case Management: Directions for Mental Health Services.* San Francisco: Jossey Bass, 40.

Hughes, R. A. (1994). Psychosocial rehabilitation: An essential health service for people with a serious and persistent mental illness. In *An Introduction To Psychosocial Rehabilitation*: Columbia, MD: International Association of Psychosocial Rehabilitation Services.

Hughes, R. A., Lehman A., & Arthur, T. A. (1996.) *Psychosocial Rehabilitation And Community Care Of Persons With Serious Mental Illness.* In Press.

Hughes, R.A., Woods, J., Brown, M.A., & Spaniol, L. (1994). Introduction. *In An Introduction To Psychosocial Rehabilitation*: Columbia, MD: International Association of Psychosocial Rehabilitation Services.

International Association of Psychosocial Rehabilitation Services (IAPSRS). (1994). Position on use of medications. Columbia, MD: International Association of Psychosocial Rehabilitation Services.

International Association of Psychosocial Rehabilitation Services (IAPSRS). (1994). Position statement on housing. Columbia, MD: International Association of Psychosocial Rehabilitation Services.

International Association of Psychosocial Rehabilitation Services (IAPSRS). (1990). *A National Directory: Organizations Providing Psychosocial Rehabilitation And Related Community Support Services In The United States, 1990:* 2nd ed. Columbia, MD: International Association of Psychosocial Rehabilitation Services.

Jonikas, J. A. & Cook, J.A. (1993). *Safe Secure And Street-Smart: Empowering Women With Mental Illness To Achieve Greater Independence In The Community.* Rehabilitation Training Curriculum. Chicago: Thresholds National Research and Training Center on Rehabilitation and Mental Illness.

Jonikas, J.A. and International Association of Psychosocial Rehabilitation Services (IAPSRS) Training and Certification Committee. (1994). Psychosocial rehabilitation: Models and services approaches. International Association of Psychosocial Rehabilitation Services: Columbia, MD.

Kanter, J. (1989). Clinical case management: Definition, principles, components. *Hospital and Community Psychiatry 90*(4), 361-68.

Keith, S.J. & Turner, J.C. (1978). Foreword to W.A. Anthony's (author) *The Principles of Psychosocial Rehabilitation.* Baltimore, MD: University Park Press,

Kisthardt, W.E. (1992). A strengths model of case management: The principles and functions of a helping partnership with persons with persistent mental illness. In *Practice, Ideology, Principles, And Methods*: Chapter 6. Longman Publishing Group.

Knisley, M.B. Case management: The big picture. Columbus, OH: Ohio Department of Mental Health.

Kuehnel, T.G., Howard, E., Backer, T.E., & Liberman, R.P. (1994). *Psychosocial Rehabilitation: Competencies For Mental Health Workers* (Draft: October, 1994). Los Angeles: Center for Improving Mental Health Systems, Human Interaction Research Institute.

Kuehnel, T.G., Liberman, R.P., Storzbach, D., & Rose, G. (1990). *Resource Book For Psychiatric Rehabilitation: Elements Of Service For The Mentallly Ill.* Baltimore, MD: Williams & Wilkins.

Lamb, H.R. (1994). A century and a half of psychosocial rehabilitation in the United States. *Hospital and Community Psychiatry, 45*(10), 1015-20.

Liberman, R.P., Mueser, K.T., Wallace, C.J., Jacobs, H.E., Eckman, T.A., & Massel, H.K. (1986). Training skills in the psychiatrically disabled: Learning coping and competence. *Schizophrenia Bulletin, 12*(4), 631-46.

Liberman, R.P., Wallace, C.J., Blackwell, G., Eckman, T.A., Vaccaro, J.V., & Kuehnel, T.G. (1993). Innovations in skills training for the seriously mentally ill: The UCLA social and independent living skills modules. *Innovations and Research, 2*(2), 43-59.

Mechanic, D. Aiken, .H. (1987J. Improving the care of patients with chronic mental illness. *The New England Journal of Medicine 357*(26), 1634-38.

Michigan State University (MSU). (1978). What is the lodge. In The Small Group Ward Program. East Lansing, Michigan: Michigan State University-NIMH Innovation Diffusion Project.

National Alliance for the Mentally Ill (NAMI). (1992). Survey of members in 1992. National Alliance for the Mentally Ill: Arlington, VA.

Nemec, P.B., McNamara, S., & Walsh, D. (1992). Direct skills teaching. *Psychosocial Rehabilitation Journal 16*(1): 12-25.

Nikkel, R.E., Smith, G., & Edwards, D. (1992). A consumer operated case management project. *Hospital and Community Psychiatry 43*(6), 577-79.

Noren, L. and Gantenbein, A.J. (1990). Career planning and job development: Book III. In *Beth De Point (Ed) Tools of The Trade: A Hands-On Training Program For Supported Employment Personnel.* Spring Lake Park, MN: Rise Inc.

Onaga, E.E. (1994). The Fairweather Lodge as a psychosocial program in the 1990s. In *An Introduction To Psychosocial Rehabilitation.* Columbia, MD: International Association of Psychosocial Rehabilitation Services.

Parrish, J. (1991). CSP: Program of firsts. *Innovations & Research, 1*(1), 8-9.

Pernell-Arnold, A. & Finley,L. (1992). *Psychosocial Rehabilitation Curriculum.* South Carolina Department of Mental Health.

PORT. (1994). *Phase I-A Literature Review Treatment Approaches For Schizophrenia. Schizophrenia Patient Outcomes Research Team* (draft). Center for Mental Health Services. Baltimore: University of Maryland.

Posey, T. (1990). Guest editorial: A home, not housing. *Psychosocial Rehabilitation Journal, 53*(9), 3-9.

Propst, R.N. (1992). Introduction special issue: The clubhouse model. *Psychosocial Rehabilitation Journal 16*(2), 3-4.

Propst, R. N. (1988). The clubhouse model and the world of work. *Tie Lines, 5*(2).

Rapp, C. Case management: Research findings. Kansas Mental Health Laboratory: University of Kansas.

Rosenthal, H. (1995). Conversation with D. R. Weinstein on Self-Help Programs, April 1995.

Ross, E.C. (1995). State mental health agencies: Statistical overview. 1/5/95 report prepared for the National Association of State Mental Health Program Directors, Alexandria, VA.

Rutman, I.D. (1981). Community based services: Characteristics, principles and program models. In I. Rutman (Ed), *Planning for Deinstitutionalization.* Human Services Monograph Series, Department of Health and Human Services.

_____. (1993). Editorial: And now the envelope please. *Psychosocial Rehabilitation Journal 16*(3): 1-3.

_____. (1989). The psychosocial rehabilitation movement in the United

States. In A. Myerson & T. Fine (Eds.), *Psychiatric Disability: Clinical, Administrative And Legal Dimensions.* Washington, DC: American Psychiatric Press.

Scallet, L.J. (1994). A message from the executive director. *Policy in Perspective,* October. Washington, DC: Mental Health Policy Resource Center.

Spaniol, L., Zipple, A., & Cohen, B. (1991). Managing innovation and change in psychosocial rehabilitation: Key principles and guidelines. *Psychosocial Rehabilitation Journal, 54*(3): 27-38.

Stein, L.I. (1990). Comments by Leonard Stein. *Hospital and Community Psychiatry, 45*(6): 649-51.

Stein, L.I. & Diamond, R.#. (1985). A program for difficult-to treat patients. In L.I. Stein and M.A. Test (Eds.) *The Training In Community Living Model: A Decade of Experience.* New Directions for Mental Health Services, 26. San Francisco: Jossey-Bass.

Stratoudakis, J.P. (1986). Rehabilitation of the mentally ill: Psychosocial, vocational, and community support perspectives. In E.L. Pan, S.S. Newman, T. E. Backer, C. L. Vash (Eds.), *Annual Review of Rehabilitation, Vol. 5.* New York: Springer Publishing Co.

Stroul, B. (1986). Models of community support services: Approaches to helping persons with long term mental illness. Boston: Center for Psychosocial Rehabilitation; Boston University, Sargent College of Allied Health Professions.

Sullivan, P. (1995). Conversation with D. R. Weinstein on Self-Help Programs, April 1995.

Susser, E., Valencia, E., & Torres, J. (1994). Sex, games, and videotapes: An HIV-prevention intervention or men who are homeless and mentally ill. (1994). *Psychosocial Rehabilitation Journal 17*(4), 31-49.

Tanaka, H. T. (1983). Psychosocial rehabilitation: Future trends and directions. *Psychosocial Rehabilitation Journal 6*(4), 7-12.

Test, M.A. and Stein, L.F. (1977). Special living arrangements: A model for decision-making. *Hospital and Community Psychiatry, 8*: 608-10.

Vorspan, R. (1985). Staff/member relationships in the clubhouse model. *The Fountain House Annual, 3.* New York City: Fountain House Inc.

_____. (1992). Why work works. *Psychosocial Rehabilitation Journal, 16,* (2), 49-54. Originally presented at the Fifth International Seminar on the Clubhouse Model: St. Louis, MO., 1989.

Wallace, C. Psychiatric rehabilitation. Unpublished manuscript.

Weinstein, D.R. (1993). *Rehabilitation Act Amendments of 1992: A Resource Manual.* International Association of Psychosocial Rehabilitation Services: Columbia, MD

Williams, M.L., Forster, P., McCarthy, G.D., & Hargreaves, W.A. (1990). Managing case management: What makes it work? *Psychosocial Rehabilitation Journal 18*(1), 49-59.

Zipple, A. and Anzer, T.C. (1995). Building code enforcement: New obstacles in siting community residences. *Psychosocial Rehabilitation Journal, 18* (1), 5-11.

3

Research in Psychosocial Rehabilitation

Jessica Jonikas and Judith Cook

The importance of measuring outcomes of mental health services, including psychosocial rehabilitation services, has gained increasing attention in recent years. Outcome assessment is critical in the field of psychosocial rehabilitation (PSR), because widespread use of this service-delivery approach is relatively new and a number of components have not been well-evaluated. At this point in time, a review of outcomes in PSR research can have many benefits: refining service-delivery models, tailoring approaches for specific individuals, enhancing quality of care, improving policies and future research, incorporating the viewpoints of people receiving services, and preparing for policies of health care cost containment and mental health care reform.

Competency I

Psychosocial rehabilitation practitioners need to stay current about research findings in the field of psychosocial rehabilitation, not only to shape practice, but also to share information with program participants and family members.

During the past two decades, a number of researchers have provided comprehensive reviews of the research literature regarding the effectiveness of psychosocial rehabilitation (e.g., Anthony, Cohen, & Vitalo, 1978; Anthony & Liberman, 1986; Dion & Anthony, 1987; Jacobs, Donahoe, & Falloon, 1985). Others have provided reviews of selected areas of research within the field, including assertive community treatment approaches (Olfson, 1990; Taube, Morlock, Burns, & Santos, 1990), case management services (Chamberlain & Rapp, 1991; Solomon, 1992), vocational rehabilitation models (Anthony & Jansen, 1984; Bond, 1992; Bond & Boyer, 1988; Spooner, Algozzine, & Saxon, 1980), and social skills training programs (Benton and Schroeder, 1990; Donahoe & Driesenga, 1988; Halford & Hayes, 1991).

Much of this literature has provided largely descriptive information about programs and desired outcomes with fairly limited data from empirical analyses. Such descriptive studies have been useful to providers, individuals with mental illness, families, researchers, and administrators as they have sought to replicate a variety of PSR services. Overall, there has been a relative lack of empirical research about the effectiveness of a number of PSR services, in spite of the recognition that the model as a whole has received (Cook, 1993; Research Committee of IAPSRS, 1995). There has been growing recognition that the field must commit to overcoming these research shortcomings by increasing the number of empirical studies conducted about a variety of outcomes in psychosocial rehabilitation (Cook, 1993; Research Committee of IAPSRS, 1995).

In spite of some of the gaps in PSR research to date, many existing studies do provide useful findings about the effectiveness of certain PSR interventions. The studies summarized below can be used to guide future rehabilitation programming and research endeavors while helping the field to further strengthen its standing among other community-based mental health service approaches. This chapter presents research findings published from the mid-1980s through 1996 in a number of key areas of psychosocial rehabilitation:

- prevention of rehospitalization,
- skills training and socialization,
- needs assessments and satisfaction with services,
- residential treatment and support services,
- vocational training and support services,
- preparation for higher/ postsecondary educational settings,
- hiring of persons with mental illness to be service-providers, and
- quality of life.

This chapter is not an exhaustive review of the recent literature on PSR outcomes. Rather, it presents a picture of trends and programmatic directions in the field based on recent program evaluation and research studies.

Prevention of Rehospitalization

Prevention of unnecessary hospitalizations and reduction in the lengths of stay in psychiatric institutions have long been central components of the psychosocial rehabilitation approach (Beard, Propst, & Malamud, 1982; Cook & Hoffschmidt, 1993; Dincin, 1975). Reducing recidivism has been a particularly important outcome for programs which use intensive case management or an assertive community treatment approach with individuals at high-risk for rehospitalization, a model first developed in Madison, Wisconsin (Marx, Test, & Stein, 1973; Stein & Test, 1980) and later adapted for use in urban settings and rural areas in the south (Santos, Deci, Lachance, Dias, Sloop, Hiers, & Bevilacqua, 1993; Witheridge & Dincin, 1985). The following is a summary of the current research regarding the effectiveness of methods and approaches to reducing recidivism.

Reducing Recidivism

Research regarding recidivism among persons with mental illness has focused on strategies for reducing the number of hospitalizations and lengths of stay in psychiatric institutions (Chang, Brenner, & Bryant, 1991; Conning & Brownlow, 1992; Tucker & Brems, 1993). The large bulk of this research has replicated earlier findings (Stein & Test, 1980) that intensive case management and assertive outreach significantly reduce the need for hospitalization, over study periods of six months (Bond, Miller, Krumied, & Ward, 1988), one year (Bush, Langford, Rosen, & Gott, 1990), two years (Jerrell & Hu, 1989), three years (Dincin, Wasmer, Witheridge, Sobeck, Cook, & Razzano, 1993), and five years (Borland, McRae, & Lycan, 1989). A decrease in hospital utilization in many of these studies was accompanied by an increase in the use of crisis intervention and residential services (Borland, McRae, & Lycan, 1989; Jerrell & Hu, 1989). Whether or not this reliance on alternatives to hospitalization leads to "cost-shifting" between mental health settings is an important, yet largely unanswered research question and has been suggested by some as a new direction for future evaluations (Taube, et al., 1990).

Importantly, several recent evaluations of assertive community treatment and intensive case management have demonstrated some mixed results regarding reduced readmissions to psychiatric institutions. For example, a study by Goering and her colleagues (1988) revealed that at follow-up at both 6 months and 2 years, case management did not reduce the need for hospitalization. Franklin and his associates (1987) and Curtis and his collaborators (1992) found that those persons who used intensive case management services actually experienced an increase in psychiatric hospitalizations after 1 year and 18 to 52 months respectively.

A number of methodological problems (e.g., differing interventions, lack of matched control groups, etc.) in these recent studies make findings difficult to compare (Hornstra, Bruce-Wolfe, Sagduyu, & Riffle, 1993). Further, mixed results regarding reduced hospitalization may be due to a lack of crisis intervention and residential treatment alternatives in the communities in which programs are located (Borland, McRae, & Lycan, 1989; Hornstra, et al., 1993). Finally, as Olfson (1990) points out, the wide-spread adoption of assertive community treatment principles into mainstream mental health programs has narrowed differences between the two types of care, and may have contributed to the mixed results shown in these studies.

There has been somewhat less research conducted recently on recidivism among other PSR program models. At one psychosocial program in Chicago (Dincin & Witheridge, 1982), people were randomly assigned to the psychosocial program or to a support group. The proportion of PSR participants who were rehospitalized (14%) was significantly lower than the proportion of readmitted control group individuals (44%). A study of VA inpatients randomly assigned to receive rehabilitation services or treatment as usual (Ryan & Bell, 1985, cited in Dion & Anthony, 1987) found that a significantly lower percentage (26%) of the rehabilitation clients were rehospitalized than were the control group participants (62%). A longitudinal study of the Fountain House program (Beard, Malamud, & Rossman, 1978) found that only 37% of those receiving peer outreach services were rehospitalized, while the corresponding recidivism rate for those persons who did not receive peer outreach was significantly higher at 77%.

Other PSR models demonstrate similar results. The original Fairweather Lodge model evaluation (Fairweather, Sanders, Maynard, Cressler, & Bleck, 1969) revealed a significant difference in recidivism between Lodge and control group participants over a 40 month follow-up period. During the study period, people participating in the Lodge program spent an average of 80 to 100% of their time in the community compared to those in the control condition who spent 20 to 30% of their time out of the hospital. A more recent study of the Lodge model demonstrated that the Lodge significantly reduces the number of post-lodge hospitalization days as compared to prior hospitalization days (Fergus, Bryant, & Balzell, 1989). Several studies have found that social skills training approaches to psychosocial rehabilitation reduce relapse, as defined by symptom exacerbation (Hogarty, et al., 1986; Wallace & Liberman, 1985). However, this model does not appear to reduce hospital admission and utilization (Bellack, Turner, Hersen, & Luber, 1984; Goldsmith & McFall, 1975; Wallace & Liberman, 1985).

Skills Training and Socialization

Skills training interventions have assumed increasing importance in psychosocial rehabilitation programs over the past two decades (Corrigan, Schade, & Liberman, 1992; Mueser, Levine, Bellack, Douglas, & Brady, 1990; Shepherd, 1990). Skills training interventions emphasize helping persons with psychiatric disabilities (often those with a diagnosis of schizophrenia) to acquire skills that are associated with major societal roles and/or modifying their environments to accommodate their disabilities (Corrigan, Schade, & Liberman, 1992; Liberman, Wallace, Blackwell, Eckman, Vaccaro, & Kuehnel, 1993). Skills are taught with relatively simple instructional techniques such as explanation, modeling, rehearsal (e.g., role playing and homework assignments), and corrective feedback. Interventions in this area increasingly are emphasizing not only behavioral deficits/skills, but also cognitive deficits/skills among persons with psychiatric disabilities (Stuve, Erickson, & Spaulding, 1991; Strauss, 1993).

To date, the value of certain aspects of skills training programs has been documented in more than fifty research studies (for recent reviews of these studies, see Atkisson, Cook, Karno, Lehman, McGlashan, Meltzer, O'Connor, Richardson, Rosenblatt, Wells, & Williams, 1992; Corrigan, Schade, & Liberman, 1992; Donahoe & Driesenga, 1988; Halford &

Hayes, 1991; Liberman, Mueser, Wallace, Jacobs, Eckman, & Massel, 1986). For instance, psychoeducational and social skills training techniques have been shown to be associated with reduced relapse, improved social functioning, and diminished family stress and burden in a number of controlled clinical trials (Hogarty, Anderson, Reiss, et al., 1986; Liberman et al., 1993; Tarrier, Barrowclough, Vaughn, et al., 1988). At the same time, recent research suggests that cognitive and behavioral skills and impairments among those with schizophrenia appear to be unevenly distributed across persons and within the *same* person over time (Mueser, Bellack, Douglas, & Morrison, 1991), an important issue in program design and evaluation. Three areas are thought to be among the most important in studies of skills training programs: skill acquisition, generalizability of skills, and durability of skills.

Skill acquisition

Recent reviews of this research support the conviction that social skills training does lead to the acquisition of targeted skills (Benton & Schroeder, 1990; Donahoe & Driesenga, 1988; Halford & Hayes, 1991). In one recent study, 41 outpatient male veterans with schizophrenia were randomly assigned to either a skills training group regarding medication and symptom management based on the *UCLA Social and Independent Living Skills Modules* (developed by Wallace, Liberman, and their associates at the UCLA Clinical Research Center for Schizophrenia and Psychiatric Rehabilitation) or a supportive therapy group (Eckman, Wirshing, Marder, Liberman, Johnston-Cronk, Zimmerman, & Mintz, 1992). Individuals in the medication and symptom management group demonstrated a significantly greater increase in their knowledge and skills from pre- to post-test than did the individuals in the supportive therapy group. In a recent field test involving 160 individuals with mental illness who received skills training in medication management, again based on the *UCLA Social and Independent Living Skills Modules,* the modules led to significant gains in cognitive mastery, skills attainment, skill utilization, and medication compliance (Eckman & Liberman, 1990). Finally, in a study of 16 persons who were hospitalized and randomly assigned either to a coping skills group (e.g., structured cognitive restructuring techniques, social skills training to manage stress, etc.) or a problem-solving group (e.g., identifying situation-specific difficulties, generating and implementing solutions, etc.), those in the coping skills group were significantly more likely to reach their goals, an implied indicator of the effectiveness of the skills training approach (Bradshaw, 1993).

Generalizability of acquired skills

A widely-shared concern in this area has been the generalizability of skills to environments outside of institutional settings (Atkisson, et al., 1992; Corrigan & Storzbach, 1993; Liberman, Jacobs, Boone, Foy, Donahoe, Falloon, Blackwell, & Wallace, 1987; Shepherd, 1990; 1988). While many researchers acknowledge that skills training is effective in reducing targeted social deficits, others point out that research in this area has not adequately evaluated or demonstrated the use of skills outside of inpatient or program settings or in trainees' environments of choice (Atkisson, et al., 1992; Dion & Anthony, 1987; Donahoe & Driesenga, 1988; Morrison & Bellack, 1987).

At least two recent controlled studies have addressed this concern by testing the ability of persons with mental illness to use the skills learned in the *UCLA Social and Independent Living Skills* program in more natural settings (Liberman, et al., 1993). The first is the study of skills training for the 41 male veterans described earlier (Eckman, et al., 1992). In the second study, 200 persons with schizophrenia or schizoaffective disorders, who were either in a day hospital or in residential treatment settings, received training modules regarding leisure time activities, grooming and personal hygiene, and medication management (Vaccaro, Liberman, Blackwell, & Wallace, 1992).

For the persons in the hospital, the control group consisted of the persons put on a waiting list; for those in the residential settings, a one-group, pre/post-test design was used. Results from these two studies indicate that a wide variety of participants were indeed able to utilize acquired skills, such as medication and symptom management, food preparation, money management, and job finding, in their daily lives (Eckman, et al., 1992; Liberman, et al., 1993; Vaccaro, et al., 1992). Those persons who used these skills also were more likely to report improved personal well-being and quality of life. However, caution should be exercised in interpreting these results, since one of the studies did not include any women and used role plays to assess the transfer of skills, which may not be predictive of actual behaviors. Moreover, these findings are limited by a small sample size (Eckman, et al., 1992) and inpatient or treatment facility settings rather than naturalistic settings (Vaccaro et al., 1992).

In general, most researchers agree that further controlled studies must be conducted before conclusive statements can be made about the generalizability of social skills acquired in structured programs (Donahoe & Driesenga, 1988; Halford & Hayes, 1991). Naturalistic observations of participants' ability to use acquired skills in their daily lives would enhance what is known about the generalizability of acquired skills as well.

Durability of acquired skills

Another important question for research in this area is the durability or maintenance of acquired skills over time (Atkisson, et al., 1992), with some suggesting that skills should last at least 6 months if not supported, and 1year if the environment provides positive feedback and support for use of the given skills (Liberman et al., 1993). In their research reviews, both Donahoe and Driesenga (1988) and Halford and Hayes (1991) found support for the conclusion that acquired skills appear to be durable over time. Further, in the two controlled studies described above, individuals were shown to have increased their skills levels and to have maintained these skills at 1 year follow-up (Eckman, et al., 1992; Liberman, et al., 1993; Vaccaro, et al., 1992).

In another controlled study in which 43 persons with schizophrenia were randomly assigned either to an experimental skills training group or to one of two comparison groups that did not use skills training, the persons in the experimental group exhibited acquired skills at 18 month follow-up. As Liberman and his associates (1993) point out, however, durability of skills depends upon a variety of factors, including the opportunity to use the skills, and encouragement and support for their use within one's natural environment. This is especially important because there are some skills that may prove to be durable, even though they are not necessarily generalizable. For example, an individual in a PSR program may be able to regularly respond to a caseworker's prompt in a socially appropriate manner while in the program, yet not be able to use that same response with co-workers while on the job. Therefore, future evaluations will need to take these factors into account when assessing maintenance of skills over time.

New trends in skills training

Finally, it is important to note that there are a number of important skills training strategies used in rehabilitation programs that have not been captured in the skills training literature. Most of the research reviews in this area have purposefully excluded skills that are not necessarily related to interpersonal difficulties associated with psychiatric impairments (although they certainly might be compromised by the presence of disability) for a number of reasons, including that they complicate analyses and comparisons.

Nevertheless, many programs are developing skills training approaches in a number of important areas such as HIV/AIDS prevention (Cook, Razzano, Jayaraj, Myers, Nathanson, Stott, & Stein, 1994; Lauer-Listhaus & Watterson, 1988; Sladyk, 1990; Susser, Valencia, & Torres, 1994), personal and neighborhood safety (Corrigan & Holmes, 1994; Jonikas & Cook, 1993), sexual assault and rape prevention (Jonikas & Cook, 1993), exercise and physical well-being (Pelham, Campagna, Ritvo, & Birnie, 1993; Unger, Skrinar, Hutchinson, & Yelmokas, 1992), and avoidance of substance abuse (Nikkel, 1994; Ryglewicz, 1991). Although limited outcomes data exist regarding these training programs, they indicate an important move in the field to helping individuals learn life skills that are generally thought to be integral to personal well-being regardless of the presence of disability.

In general, although recent research has demonstrated that some structured social skills training programs do help individuals with mental illness acquire moderately durable skills, there is a need for more rigorous, randomized studies before definite conclusions can be drawn about the benefits of these interventions. More controlled studies with persons who are receiving services in the community and reports that include descriptions of the demographic features of individuals who benefit from skills training programs (e.g., gender, age, and ethnicity) would strengthen findings about these services. Finally, as a number of researchers and service providers have pointed out, skills training interventions also must build upon people's strengths and individualized needs, assisting them in identifying skills that they themselves deem necessary in their environments of choice (Nemec, McNamara, & Walsh, 1991; Shepherd, 1990).

Needs Assessments and Satisfaction with Services

An important, recent trend in mental health services and rehabilitation is assessment of the ways in which individuals with mental illness identify their own needs and their satisfaction with current mental health services. Including service recipients' perspectives in the evaluation of programs and systems is increasingly being seen not only as desirable but essential to ensure accuracy and integrity (Elbeck & Fecteau, 1990). Although many more programs and states are initiating needs and satisfaction assessment surveys, outcomes data still are relatively

sparse, partially due to the fact that such measures are program- or system-specific, making findings difficult to compare (Elbeck & Fecteau, 1990). Further, few surveys that report needs within or satisfaction with PSR programs have been published. Nevertheless, a look at some of the recent surveys in this area, though none specific to PSR settings, will highlight possible future directions for improving rehabilitation services and evaluation efforts.

Needs Assessment Surveys

Needs assessments that are based on the views of individuals with mental illness are gaining popularity at the program and systems levels in mental health (Uttaro & Mechanic, 1994). Historically, the opinions of people receiving services have been disregarded due to the misguided perception that they are unable to identify their own needs accurately due to their disability. Thus, asking individuals with mental illness to identify their own needs and goals, especially in more formalized surveys and interviews, is a relatively new occurrence in the field (Ridgway, 1988).

In their fairly well-known study comparing differences in perceptions of individuals with psychiatric disabilities versus mental health professionals, Lynch and Kruzich (1986) found that while individuals with mental illness were very concerned with financial constraints (including the ways in which such constraints limited access to needed services), lack of transportation, and unavailability of services, professionals were more concerned with the provision of individual therapy, medication checks, and client "resistance" to therapy. These authors note that while there are difficulties inherent in evaluating needs assessment data due to the lack of standardized measures, the need to develop more responsive and beneficial services might outweigh these methodological limitations.

From their interviews with 522 individuals with psychiatric disabilities, Uttaro and Mechanic (1994) found that surveyed persons identified needs to keep busy, to recognize and control symptoms, to maintain friendships and intimate relationships, and to control anger as of highest priority. The authors also report that unmet needs related to "role restoration" (e.g., maintaining social networks, intimate relationships, employment, and productive activities, etc.) were found among individuals with mental illness who were *currently* receiving services. This finding is important due to the assumption that these needs typically go unmet for people who "fall through the cracks of services," not for those who are well-integrated into the service system, as were the participants in this study.

Two recent needs assessment surveys are notable because they were developed, implemented, and evaluated by individuals with psychiatric disabilities themselves (Beall, 1992; Campbell, Schraiber, Temkin, & ten Tusscher, 1989). Campbell and her associates (1989) conducted a systematic, comprehensive survey of a sample of diverse individuals with psychiatric disabilities (N=331), family members (N=53), and mental health providers (N=150) to assess perceptions of the overall well-being, needs, and satisfaction with mental health services of the persons served. Some of the key points are relevant to the other outcomes reported here.

For example, surveyed individuals with psychiatric disabilities cited their top three needs as having enough money, satisfying relationships, and having decent housing. By contrast, none of the surveyed professionals and only two of the family members identified financial security as critical for individuals with psychiatric disabilities, and none of the professionals or family members cited romantic or sexual relationships as essential to well-being. Surprisingly, neither professionals nor family members identified housing as a top priority for individuals with psychiatric disabilities. Seventy-four percent of the respondents with psychiatric disabilities stated that meaningful work or achievement was essential to their well-being, yet nearly half of them lacked such activities. Ninety-one percent of the individuals with psychiatric disabilities and 100% of the family members cited the need for greater funding and opportunities for vocational pursuits. Less than 5% of the professionals listed education or vocational training as significant in improving the lives of persons with psychiatric disabilities.

Beall (1992) also conducted a consumer-driven survey of both the needs and satisfaction of persons with psychiatric disabilities throughout the state of Virginia. Again, although the findings are too comprehensive to report here, some of the highlights bear noting. Although survey respondents identified a wide variety of needs (differing from region to region), one of the most important was for meaningful employment that might lead to a career, rather than dead-end, minimum wage jobs. Here, too, people expressed tremendous financial difficulties, as well as problems due to lack of rehabilitation and/or case management services, inaccessible transportation, and long waiting lists for housing.

As Ridgway (1988) notes, there still is much to be learned about appropriate research methods that are reliable and valid and represent the needs of persons with mental illness from their own perspectives. In the future, researchers and administrators should work to create standardized needs assessment surveys to gather the opinions of individuals with psychiatric disabilities, family members, and professionals. Such a goal is paramount not only to facilitate involvement and empowerment, but to develop rehabilitation services that are truly responsive and helpful to individuals with mental illness and their families.

Satisfaction Surveys

Satisfaction surveys also are gaining importance in rehabilitation and mental health services. As is true of consumer-driven needs assessments, there is a shortage of such studies in the literature, especially in PSR settings, partially because individuals with psychiatric disabilities continue to experience the stereotype that they are unable to identify elements of services that are beneficial to them (Ridgway, 1988). However, as a number of recent surveys have demonstrated, persons with psychiatric disabilities are willing and able to provide thoughtful, clear, and comprehensive descriptions of the ways in which services meet and do not meet their needs (Beall, 1992; Campbell, et al., 1989; Lynch & Kruzich, 1986).

A number of satisfaction surveys have indicated that individuals with psychiatric disabilities generally have positive feelings about mental health services, typically defined as traditional clinical services such as case management and medication management (Elbeck & Fecteau, 1990; Polowczyk, Brutus, Orvieto, Vidal, & Cipriani, 1993; Slater, Linn, & Harris, 1982). In a recent study of the perspectives of individuals with mental illness, family members, and case managers, Massey and Wu (1993) found that the majority of persons receiving mental health services (63%) and family members (63%) were satisfied with these services. Their results also indicated that some of the dissatisfaction with services was related to the infrequent scheduled contacts between those receiving services and case managers (monthly rather than weekly or bi-weekly).

In their study of five consumer-run drop-in centers, Mowbray and Tan (1993) found that levels of satisfaction with these peer-run programs were uniformly high. Greater satisfaction was expressed by persons who also reported that they benefited from group support and mutual learning, as well as those who believed that their center helped them to enhance decision-making abilities and to stay out of the hospital. In their evaluation of nine consumer-run drop-in centers, Kaufmann and her colleagues (Kaufmann, Ward-Colasante, & Farmer, 1993) also found that program participants were highly satisfied with the services, yet they desired improvements in the number of paid staff, hours of operation, and transportation.

Some have suggested that the uniformly positive results published to date about satisfaction with mental health services raise the question of whether these data are valid, especially given inattention to the connections between people's symptoms, functioning, and general life satisfaction and their feelings of satisfaction with programs (Elbeck & Fecteau, 1990). Further, researchers have been concerned that evaluations may be biased due to acquiescent or social-desirability response sets (i.e., research participants feel that they must express satisfaction with services to please the interviewers or to continue to receive treatment; Elbeck & Fecteau, 1990). In response to the potential for response biases, some researchers have explored whether individuals with mental illness would respond differently to surveyors who have psychiatric disabilities versus interviewers who do not.

In a recent study by Polowczyk and her colleagues (1993), individuals with psychiatric disabilities interviewed by their peers, although generally satisfied with mental health services, were significantly more likely to have less positive responses about whether or not they would return to the program, whether services have helped them to deal more effectively with their problems, whether they got the services they desired, and whether they would recommend the program to a friend when compared to those persons who were interviewed by staff of the program. The authors speculate that the interviewers with mental illness either may have elicited more honest responses or may have unwittingly encouraged socially desirable responses of *dissatisfaction* with services. Either way, it appears that participants responded differently when interviewed by peers as compared to staff.

Along these lines, other studies that have been conducted by individuals with psychiatric disabilities have indicated less overall satisfaction with current services. For example, in the previously described survey by Campbell and her associates (1989), almost 25% of surveyed individuals reported that professionals "seldom" or "never" listen to them or find what they have to say as valid or important, although 90% of the providers felt that they listen to and value each individual's input. In her statewide survey, Beall (1992) found general consensus that not only do current clubhouses need significant expansion, but that such programs would be much improved by more collaboration between individuals with mental illness and staff.

Others stated that residential services were sorely lacking and were not tailored to meet people's needs and preferences.

Finally, in a recent controlled study, Solomon and Draine (1994) assigned 91 persons to receive case management services either from a staff team that included people with psychiatric disabilities or a staff team that did not. This study revealed that at 1 year follow-up those persons who perceived their case managers as possessing certain "personal" characteristics (e.g., is empathic, provides comfort, listens, is a friend, etc.) were more satisfied with mental health services than individuals who thought that their case managers did not possess such characteristics. Participants appeared to be less satisfied with services provided by the team which included staff with mental illness, as compared to the team that did not include such staff, even though clinical and psychosocial outcomes for service recipients did *not* differ at 1 year follow-up (these results are discussed further later; Solomon & Draine, 1995a; 1995b). This finding indicates that case managers who have a psychiatric disability themselves might need assistance in developing the emotional and supportive elements of the working alliance which either they never were taught or are possibly masked by medication side effects or psychiatric impairments. In general, this study emphasizes the importance of the alliance between practitioners and clients, regardless of whether or not the provider has a psychiatric disability.

Residential Treatment and Support Services

Residential treatment and provision of housing supports have been concerns of community mental health providers and clients since deinstitutionalization, although mental health systems took at least a decade to respond adequately to the need for housing for persons who had formerly been institutionalized (Randolph, Ridgway, & Carling, 1991). Despite the fact that policy changes during the late 1970s stimulated the development of housing and supports across the United States, most would agree that a lack of adequate, affordable housing remains one of the largest barriers to social integration for persons with a psychiatric disability (Fields, 1990; Randolph, Ridgway, & Carling, 1991; Tanzman, 1993). Therefore, the issues surrounding housing are some of the most important to consider when helping people with psychiatric disabilities to achieve higher quality of life. A look at the outcomes research regarding housing conditions, some specific person-level influences on residential outcomes, and the housing preferences of persons with psychiatric disabilities will shed light on current issues in this area.

Space limitations do not permit an exploration of housing concerns for persons who are homeless, but several sources will guide the interested reader (see, for instance, Asmussen, Romano, Beatty, Gasarch, Shaughnessey, 1994; Culhane, 1992; Drake, Wallach, & Hoffman, 1989; First, Rife, & Kraus, 1990; Lipton, Nutt, & Sabatini, 1988). Additionally, as Tanzman (1993) notes, although the need for more housing options for individuals with psychiatric disabilities is rarely challenged, the best strategies for providing these options are decidedly less clear. Nevertheless, the important debate regarding the benefits and drawbacks of "supported" versus "transitional" housing options will not be discussed here, both because limited outcomes data are available and the largely imprecise definitions and descriptions of

housing services/models in the available evaluation literature make such findings difficult to compare. Many resources are available for interested readers (see, for example, Blanch, Carling, & Ridgway, 1988; Carling, 1993; Fields, 1990; Geller & Fisher, 1993; Ridgway & Zipple, 1990a; 1990b).

Housing Conditions

Several recent studies regarding residential treatment/support have evaluated or controlled for specific attributes of the housing conditions in which individuals with psychiatric disabilities typically live (Levstek & Bond, 1993; McCabe, Edgar, Mancuso, King, Ross, & Emery, 1993; Newman, 1994). Such characteristics include the affordability and physical condition of the housing, as well as the presence of serious neighborhood problems (Levstek & Bond, 1993; Newman, 1994). One such study compared housing conditions for 307 persons with psychiatric disabilities (data from the Community Care Survey conducted by the Robert Wood Johnson Foundation) versus those for the general population (data from the well-known American Housing Survey) in Baltimore, Columbus, and Cincinnati (Newman, 1994). Renters with psychiatric disabilities generally had housing cost burdens (housing guidelines typically set this amount at 30% of one's gross income) that were significantly higher than the general population: between 39% and 54% of the income of persons with mental illness was devoted to rent (these differences were not significant in Columbus). Another nationwide study in this area revealed that in 1990, on average, 66% of an individual's monthly SSI check was required to pay rent for an efficiency apartment, and 80% for a one-bedroom apartment (McCabe, et al., 1993).

During that same year, in 61 counties or standard metropolitan statistical areas (SMSAs) the cost of renting an efficiency apartment exceeded the SSI payment, while in 259 counties/SMSAs, rent for a one-bedroom apartment was more than one and a half times greater than the monthly SSI payment. It would appear that either federal and state entitlements must be raised or more affordable housing must be made available if persons with psychiatric disabilities are to be fully integrated into their communities (McCabe, et al., 1993).

Survey data also reveal that persons with mental illness typically have worse housing and neighborhood conditions than the general population (Newman, 1994). Physical housing conditions typically were substandard, with more heating, window, plumbing, and rodent problems than the general population. Finally, reports of neighborhood crime as a problem were significantly more likely for individuals with psychiatric disabilities than for those without in Columbus (55% higher) and Cincinnati [70% higher (differences in Baltimore were nonsignificant)].

Overall, there is a growing recognition that while the issues that arise when housing persons with psychiatric histories can be related to their disabilities, they have been affected more frequently by economic and social factors, such as low income levels and lack of affordable, decent housing (Anthony & Blanch, 1988; Cournos, 1987; Levstek & Bond, 1993; McCabe, et al., 1993; Newman, 1994; Rubenstein & James, 1990; Tanzman, 1993). Research must begin to take these factors, as well as others related to the general housing market, into account when conducting outcomes research regarding residential services/supports for persons with psychiatric disabilities.

Individual Level Influences on Residential Outcomes

Outcomes research in the area of residential rehabilitation offers other clues about factors that might affect an individual's ability to maintain independent living in commercially available housing over time. As is true with predictors of success in vocational settings, such findings should not be used as reasons to exclude certain individuals from attempting to live independently, but rather, can be used to guide future program design and evaluations.

Prior research indicates that women tend to have better residential outcomes than do men. In one study of housing situations for 187 persons following release from an urban state psychiatric hospital, women were significantly more likely to be in stable housing and less likely to be homeless than were men (Drake, Wallach, & Hoffman, 1989). A study of 122 young adults with schizophrenia and schizophrenia-related disorders who were receiving assertive community treatment services found that young women spent significantly more time than young men residing in apartments and houses, while the men spent more time than the women living in rooming houses (Test, Burke, & Wallisch, 1990). A review of 320 records of individuals in seven psychiatric institutions found that women were more likely to live independently (but also more likely to live in nursing homes), while men were more likely to reside in group or foster homes, in jail, or with family (Mowbray & Chamberlain, 1986).

Importantly, Cook's (1994) multivariate analysis of the residential outcomes of 650 PSR participants revealed that gender itself was not a significant predictor of independent living when the effects of functioning level, parental status, program tenure, community participation, and ongoing support were controlled. As Cook notes, future directions for research would be the ways in which females and males experience these five important correlates of residential independence, as well as an examination of their implications for service-delivery.

Level of functional impairment also appears to be a client-level influence on residential outcomes. For example, in one study of board-and-care homes, those persons with lower Global Assessment Scale (Endicott, Spitzer, Fleiss, & Cohen, 1976) scores had more difficulty fitting in with housemates and needed more practical support from residence operators than did higher functioning individuals (Davies, Bromer, Schulz, Dunn, & Morgenstern, 1989). A study of deaf persons with mental illness in a PSR setting found that level of functioning remained significant in a multivariate model predicting who was able to live in commercial housing (Cook, Graham, & Razzano, 1993). In the study by Cook (1994) mentioned above, one of the most powerful predictors of residential success at the individual level was the person's level of functioning. Those with better functioning at the time of closing from a PSR program were more likely to be living on their own at 6 month follow-up than those with poorer functioning. In this same study, persons with longer program tenure also were more likely to be living in commercial housing at 6 month follow-up (Cook, 1994).

A person's age also has been found to be related to independent living outcomes. In one study of board-and-care residents, younger persons were less likely to reside in structured, non-normal community housing (Davies, et al., 1989) and, in another, were more socially involved in residence and community ac-

tivities than older individuals with mental illness (Grusky, Tierney, Manderscheid, & Grusky, 1985).

Individual Housing Preferences

Residential researchers and advocates also have called for more studies that explore the preferences of people with psychiatric disabilities for housing and supports (Carling, 1993; Massey & Wu, 1993; Salem, 1990). In spite of the "client-centered" approach to PSR services, researchers in this area typically have relied upon the perspectives of service providers regarding preferences/needs in housing, and only recently have incorporated the views of individuals with psychiatric disabilities and their families into evaluations (Tanzman, 1993; Ridgway, 1988). This is particularly striking since there has been only moderate agreement between service providers, individuals with psychiatric disabilities, and family members about the needs of persons with psychiatric disabilities (Grusky, Tierney, & Spanish, 1989; Lynch & Kruzich, 1986). For example, in one random survey of the preferences for and satisfaction with services among 38 persons with psychiatric disabilities, participants chose normal, commercially available living settings 80% of the time, while their families and case managers chose these settings for them 60% of the time (Massey & Wu, 1993).

In her analysis of 26 survey studies of housing and support preferences among individuals with psychiatric disabilities, Tanzman (1993) found that despite the diversity of target populations, sampling strategies, implementation methods, and geographic regions represented in the studies, housing preferences were largely analogous. She notes that the most preferred housing arrangement in every study was independent living in a house or an apartment. The second most cited preference (in 11 of 26 studies) was living with family members. In 21 of the 26 studies, group homes were among the least popular options, named by 0 to 7 percent of those surveyed. Not surprisingly, the least preferred options across all settings were hospitals and being homeless. In terms of staff support, the most frequently requested services were the availability of staff to conduct home visits night or day and help with finances. Importantly, the least cited support in each study was live-in staff, chosen by between 0 and 26 percent of the survey participants. As Tanzman points out, these findings indicate that although they prefer independent living options, most persons would still request help from mental health providers on an ongoing, as-needed basis.

In a more recent look at the differing perspectives between persons with psychiatric disabilities and families regarding residential needs, family members again more often cited congregate living situations and more staff supports than did persons with psychiatric disabilities themselves (Rogers, Danley, Anthony, Martin, & Walsh, 1994). As was true in Tanzman's (1993) analysis, the majority of persons with psychiatric disabilities in this survey stated that they did not want to live with either staff or other persons who experience psychiatric disorders. Importantly, this study and the majority of those cited by Tanzman successfully used researchers with psychiatric disabilities not only as key informants but as data collectors and interpreters, a strategy that is gaining increasing popularity in mental health services research (Campbell, 1989; Everett & Steven, 1989; Kaufmann, 1993; Rapp, Shera, & Kisthardt, 1993).

Vocational Training and Support Services

Vocational training and supports have been central to psychosocial rehabilitation since its inception (Beard, Propst, & Malamud, 1982; Dincin, 1975). Transitional employment (TE) services were the hallmark of the early psychosocial rehabilitation agencies such as Fountain House in New York, Thresholds in Chicago, and Horizon House in Philadelphia, and recently have come to be offered even in traditional mental health programs (Cook & Hoffschmidt, 1993). At the same time, vocational services utilizing a supported employment (SE) approach, which advocates for minimal pre-vocational training and the provision of ongoing, unlimited support (Wehman & Moon, 1988), are gaining increasing attention in the field of psychosocial rehabilitation (Cook, Jonikas, & Solomon, 1992; Trottner, Minkoff, Harrison, & Hoops, 1988).

Effectiveness of Vocational Interventions

Analysis of recent controlled or quasi-controlled research studies regarding the effectiveness of vocational rehabilitation reveals that vocational interventions have been moderately to strongly successful in helping individuals with psychiatric disabilities to find and maintain paid jobs in the community (Cook & Pickett, 1995). This has been shown in studies of services delivered at psychosocial rehabilitation agencies and clubhouses (Cook & Rosenberg, 1994; Fountain House, 1985; Laird & Krown, 1991; Rogers, Anthony, Toole, & Brown, 1991), Fairweather Lodges (Fairweather, et al., 1969; Fergus, Bryant, & Balzell, 1989), supported employment programs (Drake, Becker, Biesanz, Torrey, McHugo,

& Wyzik, 1994; Fabian, 1992a), job skills training programs (Sherman & Porter, 1991), and job clubs (Jacobs, Wissusik, Collier, Stackman, & Burkeman, 1992).

Recent program developments and evaluations offer additional information about the effectiveness of current vocational services in helping individuals with mental illness to obtain and maintain competitive community employment. A review of recently published literature suggests that, in addition to implementation of individualized, ongoing supports, there are a number of new trends in the development of employment services, including but not limited to linkages between psychiatric symptoms, diagnosis, and employment outcomes, the effects of employment on workers' self-esteem and quality of life, and job satisfaction (Cook & Pickett, 1995). A brief overview of each of these trends is given below.

Linkages Between Psychiatric Symptoms, Diagnosis, and Employment Outcomes

One of the major features of PSR programming is the provision of assistance with symptom and medication management to assist with a variety of life goals, including community employment (Cook & Hoffschmidt, 1993). Prior reviews of vocational literature have suggested no significant relationship between psychiatric symptoms, diagnosis, and work performance (Anthony & Jansen, 1984; Dion, Tohen, Anthony, & Waternaux, 1988; Moller, von Zerssen, Werner-Eilert, & Wuschenr-Stockheim, 1982). Yet recent work suggests that hospitalization histories, a diagnosis of "schizophrenia" or "psychosis" (versus other broadly defined categories such as "non-schizophrenic" or "neurotic"), and/or the severity of one's symptoms (and related work-

place behaviors) may be associated with poorer vocational outcomes (Anthony, 1994; Jacobs, et al., 1992; Liberman, 1989; Marshak, Bostick, & Turton, 1990; Trottner, et al., 1988; Wehman, Revell, Kregel, Kreutzer, Callahan, & Banks, 1990). Results from a recent study of longitudinal employment outcomes suggest that the persons most likely to be unemployed at 12 months follow-up were those with schizophrenia versus all other types of diagnoses (Fabian, 1992a). As these recent findings indicate, there is still much to be learned about the interaction of diagnosis, symptoms, skills, and job environment. Because the severity of symptoms does not necessarily correspond with an individual's functional limitations, it is important to develop a better understanding of how psychiatric symptoms and diagnosis affect vocational outcomes (Cook & Pickett, 1995). Ultimately, as Anthony (1994) points out, predictors of poor vocational performance may very well be mitigated by being goal-oriented and by receiving effective vocational rehabilitation interventions.

The Effects of Employment on Workers' Self-Esteem

Another hallmark of the PSR approach is the creation of hopefulness and enhanced self-esteem among persons with psychiatric disabilities (Cnaan, Blankertz, Messinger, & Gardner, 1988). The consumer empowerment movement has helped to extend this approach to the aspects of employment that are found to be esteem-enhancing, dignifying, and rewarding as well as financially remunerative (Fisher, 1994; Harp, 1994). This shift has turned attention to outcomes such as life satisfaction, quality of life, and job satisfaction, and how these are influenced by work experiences.

Several studies have explored the connection between self-esteem and the employment of persons with psychiatric disabilities. In one naturalistic follow-up study of the connection between self-esteem and employment for 88 persons with psychiatric disabilities, feelings of self-esteem, life satisfaction, and coping mastery were significantly higher among those who had experienced positive changes in employment such as becoming employed or moving to better jobs (Arns & Linney, 1993). The theoretical model derived from this research was that improvement in vocational status increases feelings of self-efficacy thereby improving self-esteem which, in turn, improves life satisfaction. This research indicates the importance of studying not only static indicators of employment success (e.g., employed/not employed), but *changes* in employment status as well. In another study, those expressing the most dissatisfaction with their unemployment were those living in the community with friends or family (Hatfield, Huxley, & Mohamad, 1992). The authors argue that this suggests the important role of social context in defining what individuals will find satisfying in the employment realm.

In a recent study of employment status on quality of life among 110 persons with mental illness, Fabian (1992b) found that having a supported employment job was associated with higher satisfaction on dimensions such as work and finances but not areas such as family, safety, or health. Noting the specificity of effects on some life domains but not others, the author warns service providers about the dangers of using work as a panacea for all of a person's problems. In a separate analysis, employed men but not women with psychiatric disabilities were more satisfied than were their non-working counterparts (Fabian, 1989). This may be due to the fact that life satisfaction for working women is mediated by a number of factors, such as quality of home life and child care, which may lower satisfaction for employed versus non-employed women with psychiatric disorders.

Job Satisfaction

A focus on job satisfaction among workers with psychiatric disabilities is long overdue given its importance to vocational outcomes in the general population (Cook & Pickett, 1995). For instance, persons with psychiatric disabilities in one supported employment program had especially low levels of job satisfaction, which the authors suggested was possibly due to their *under*employment at jobs below their skill levels (Danley, Rogers, MacDonald-Wilson, & Anthony, 1994). Bond and his colleagues (1995) showed that individuals in a supported employment program who received job placements within a month had higher job satisfaction (especially when paid) than those who participated in unpaid, pre-vocational crews for four months. These studies noted that satisfaction was higher among those persons who were placed more quickly. While this relationship may be causal, with quicker placement leading to job satisfaction, it also is possible that both outcomes (higher satisfaction and quicker placement) are associated with higher functioning. This bears further investigation, especially to determine whether *any* individuals with mental illness need lengthy pre-vocational assessment and preparation periods and, if so, which persons and how to target them.

Growth of Individualized Models Providing Ongoing Vocational Support

The literature contains many examples of new models designed to take specific account of the nature of psychiatric disability and to be more sensitive to people's preferences regarding when they are placed and at what types of jobs. Two common features shared by many of these models are their individualized nature and the availability of ongoing supports. These characteristics respond to the desire for employment that is non-stigmatizing, with natural supports rather than obtrusive professional job coaching. Also apparent is the movement away from work in groups, which may draw unnecessary attention to workers' disabilities, to individualized models which are more natural and less stigmatizing (Cook, Jonikas, & Solomon, 1992; Cook & Pickett, 1995).

The availability of ongoing supports is echoed in many of these models, stimulated perhaps by the importance of supported employment (Cook & Razzano, 1992) as well as a tradition within PSR programs of offering lifelong "membership"(Cook & Hoffschmidt, 1993). Research suggests that the availability of ongoing assistance is critical (Bond & Boyer, 1988). In one study of 550 persons in a PSR program who received vocational services, a logistic regression analysis predicting employment status six months after program exit found that ongoing support was a significant factor in a model including education, ethnicity, and types of job supports received (Cook & Rosenberg, 1994).

In another study of a model program at the same agency (Cook & Razzano, 1992), providing as-needed, workplace-based employment support to those who held at least one paid job raised the em-ployment rate from 50% to above 80% throughout the 36-month program period. A comparative study of two day programs providing sheltered work to individuals with psychiatric disabilities found that the one converting to a supported employment approach had superior vocational outcomes compared to the program that continued its original sheltered work model (Drake, et al., 1994). It would seem that the twin services of community job placement and ongoing supports have advantages over sheltered workshop and time-limited models. However, much more information is needed before we can understand the meaning of some of these findings as principles of service design.

Another principle embodied by many model programs is the importance of rapid placement of persons who are seeking employment. For example, one randomized study found that supported employment participants who were immediately placed in jobs reported superior outcomes (e.g., higher employment rate, higher job satisfaction, etc.) than those who received pre-vocational services prior to their first jobs (Bond, Dietzen, McGrew, & Miller, 1995). Despite high levels of satisfaction in one small supported employment program, participants were most dissatisfied with the amount of time it took to obtain employment (Danley, Rogers, MacDonald-Wilson, & Anthony, 1994). Based on their study of a transitional employment program for people with psychiatric disabilities, Schultheis and Bond (1993) speculate that individuals who perform unpaid work in rehabilitation program settings, especially if they have participated in *paid* employment training in the past, experience a "demoralization" effect that leads to poorer work behavior ratings by vocational staff. These studies suggest that the prevocational phases of most models should be examined to determine for which persons, if any, this type of job preparation is useful.

The field of vocational rehabilitation for persons with psychiatric disabilities is characterized by tremendous potential. Yet, to date, the growth of new approaches has been hindered by a lack of valid, reliable knowledge about effective vocational practices and how to encourage them. Vocational research also has been limited by a lack of both multiple outcome measures (Bond & Boyer, 1988) and attention to the effects that the labor market may have on vocational services. Nevertheless, the most recent research offers many promising and suggestive avenues for vocational program development and further study.

Preparation for Higher/Post-secondary Educational Settings

Along with normalization of work as a goal for persons with mental illness has come a growing acceptance of post-secondary education and training for persons with psychiatric disabilities. Given the age of onset of severe mental disorders in the late teens and young adult years, education is an appropriate developmental goal (Cook, Solomon, Farrell, Koziel, & Jonikas, in press). But beyond this has come the recognition that many persons are forced into entry-level employment because more satisfying career changes are not possible without re-education and support (Cook, Jonikas, & Solomon, 1992).Yet postsecondary education is a service seldom suggested for persons with psychiatric disabilities, even though it is commonly used in the rehabilitation of persons with physical and communication disabilities (Unger, 1994).

In one study of people with schizophrenia, over a third (35%) had attempted formal education while less than a tenth (9%) had completed their course of study (Navin, Lewis, & Higson, 1989). There is evidence that a number of adults with psychiatric disabilities need remedial work in reading and mathematics, along with ongoing supports for attempting mainstream college or vocational/technical training. For example, screening of one group of students with psychiatric disabilities entering a supported education program in a large psychosocial rehabilitation agency indicated that over half had reading and mathematical computation skills below the 12th grade level (Cook & Solomon, 1993).

Outcome studies have confirmed the usefulness of postsecondary education, or "supported education" approaches (Unger, 1994), that include academic supports along with mental health services (Jacobs & Glater, 1993; Ryglewicz & Glynn, 1993). These programs typically offer remedial and preparatory education, counseling and advocacy, and ongoing support for a variety of educational and case management needs. In one study of 68 supported education students and a group of matched individuals receiving identical clinical but no educational services, supported education participants were significantly more likely than the comparison group to return to college and to do so full-time (Hoffman & Mastrianni, 1993). In a followup study of 52 supported education participants, significant increases over baseline were found in college class enrollment, competitive employment, and self-esteem (Unger, Anthony, Sciarappa, & Rogers, 1991). A third outcome study of 102 supported education students at a psychosocial rehabilitation agency found that 78% of the participants were employed during the program and showed significant increases in both hourly wages and number of hours worked per week (Cook & Solomon, 1993). Compared to their scores at pre-test, these individuals also had significantly higher self-esteem and coping mastery after participating in the program.

As with employment, postsecondary education involves the cooperation of silent partners such as faculty, administrators, and other students. Several programs have explored the role of faculty in-service training for integrating students into college and vocational education settings (Jacobs & Glater, 1993; Wolf & DiPietro, 1992). Results of one field-test of a faculty in-service training for working with students with psychiatric disabilities revealed that the training significantly improved knowledge levels and attitudes toward these students (Cook, Yamaguchi, & Solomon, 1993).

As the field begins to look beyond entry-level employment for persons with psychiatric disabilities, the role of supported education services will become increasingly important. Past experience has indicated that many persons with psychiatric disabilities need assistance to succeed at college or technical training. Now that the techniques for providing this support have been developed, it remains to be seen whether or not they will become readily available to individuals who need them.

Persons with Mental Illness as Service Providers

During the past five to ten years, PSR programs have been expanding employment options for individuals with psychiatric disabilities by hiring them as service delivery staff (Besio & Mahler, 1993; Chamberlin, 1990; McGill & Patterson, 1990; Nikkel, Smith, & Edwards, 1992; Sherman & Porter, 1991; Solomon,

Jonikas, Cook, & Kerouac, 1998; Solomon & Draine, 1995a; 1995b). Available information about this important and encouraging trend in service delivery is largely descriptive, focusing on such overlapping considerations as approaches to consumer-run programs (Curtis, 1993), guiding principles of peer service provision (Stephens & Belisle, 1993), unique qualities of, and contributions by, service providers who have had personal experience within the mental health system (Van Tosh, 1993), the benefits and challenges of hiring persons with psychiatric disabilities (Besio & Mahler, 1993; Deegan, 1988; Solomon, Jonikas, Cook, & Kerouac, 1998), issues that arise between staff with psychiatric disabilities and nondisabled staff when working together (Maccauley, 1993; Solomon, Jonikas, Cook, & Kerouac, 1998), and accommodations that individuals with mental illness may need when working in clinical/ rehabilitation settings (Fisher, 1994; Harp, 1991).

A number of researchers also have explored the benefits of consumer-run programs (see, for example, Kaufmann, Ward-Colasante, & Farmer, 1993; Mowbray, Chamberlain, Jennings, & Reed, 1988; Mowbray & Tan, 1993). Although two recent projects have integrated staff with psychiatric disabilities into traditional mental health settings, evaluative data are not yet available (McGill & Patterson, 1990; Nikkel, Smith, & Edwards, 1992). In fact, there have been only a few studies providing data about the impact of individuals with psychiatric disabilities as service providers in more mainstream mental health or rehabilitation settings (Sherman & Porter, 1991; Solomon & Draine, 1995a; 1995b). Reporting the outcomes that result from service provision by those with psychiatric disabilities as though they somehow differ from other rehabilitation outcomes (e.g., rehospitalization rates, employment, quality of life, etc.) is rather artificial. At this stage in the consumer movement, however, it is important to highlight such findings separately so that they do not get lost in general analyses.

In their project to train individuals with psychiatric disabilities to become case management aides, Sherman and Porter (1991) found that 18 (72%) of the 25 persons who started the training program graduated. At the 2-year follow-up, the 15 participants (60%) who still were employed as aides had required a total of only 2 bed days in psychiatric institutions from the time they completed the training program. This program appears to have led to a higher employment rate for individuals with mental illness than that reported in previous studies and reviews (see, for example, Anthony & Liberman, 1986; Dion & Anthony, 1987) and these rates have been maintained over a 5-year period (Sherman, 1994). Controlled evaluations regarding the reactions *to* and outcomes *for* persons with mental illness who receive services from their peers as part of this program have not yet been reported.

In their controlled studies of outcomes for persons with mental illness receiving services from teams of staff with and without psychiatric disabilities at 1-year (N=91) and 2-year follow-ups (N=90), Solomon and Draine found that at both points in time there was *no difference* in symptomatology or in clinical and quality of life outcomes for persons who received services from teams of staff with or without psychiatric disabilities (Solomon & Draine, 1995a; 1995b). As the authors suggest, these data indicate that case management services offered by individuals with mental illness are as effective as those provided by nondisabled staff in terms of psychosocial and clinical outcomes.

Another recent trend in this area is the utilization of persons with psychiatric disabilities in delivering *employment* services. In this capacity, people with psychiatric disabilities have been hired as job coaches (Cook, Jonikas, & Solomon, 1992), as well as program staff and directors of vocational rehabilitation programs (Allen, 1994). Additionally, persons with mental illness have been involved in developing affirmative businesses (Warner & Polak, 1993). One report that describes the establishment of nine Pennsylvania Department of Mental Health-funded drop-in centers also details the vocational components of such programming (Kaufmann, Ward-Colasante, & Farmer, 1993). With quite minimal funding (the average center award totaled just $16,500 per year), each center helped its participants prepare resumes, obtain job leads, negotiate the job search process, and maintain jobs over time. Some offered supported work, training in word processing, or job placement services.

A follow-up report on the nine projects one year after startup (McCormack, 1992) found that 18% of all participants (N=123) had performed some type of unpaid work in the drop-in center, 7% (N=48) had received job-seeking skills training, and 4% (N=25) had received assistance following up job leads. Regarding employment outcomes, 4% (N=25) acquired full or part-time jobs outside their centers while another 5% (N=29) were employed within their centers. The follow-up study noted that scarce financial resources and limited vocational training of center staff and volunteers were impediments to development of more effective services. Also noted was an extremely high level of vocational interest among center participants coupled with frustration among staff with psychiatric disabilities because limited resources prevented them from providing higher quality employment services.

Another project based in Pittsburgh called The Self Help Employment Center uses a model combining peer supports in conjunction with professionally provided vocational services (Kaufmann, Roth, & Cook, 1992). Persons with mental illness in this project provide job skills training and counseling to program participants coupled with job development and ongoing supports from abled providers. In a randomized study comparing this model to "customary vocational services," preliminary results indicated that those in the experimental condition showed significant improvements in employment status over time in comparison with the control group (Kaufmann, 1994).

Clearly, the trend to hire people with psychiatric disabilities in psychosocial rehabilitation would be strengthened by more evaluation studies. Besides replicating the findings reported by Solomon and Draine (1995a; 1995b) in a variety of mental health settings, researchers will need to examine the long-term impact of hiring providers with psychiatric disabilities, focusing on variables such as the benefits of these services both to staff with psychiatric disabilities and service recipients, changes these services effect at the program and systems levels, and characterizations of persons who benefit from peer staff approaches as compared to those who gain more from traditional approaches to service delivery.

Quality of Life

An understanding of quality of life for persons with psychiatric disabilities has gained increasing attention in the field of mental health services in recent years

(Lehman, 1988; Lehman, Ward, & Linn, 1982). Although few quality of life studies have been conducted specifically in PSR settings, a review of some of the recent surveys in this area will highlight future directions for assisting individuals with mental illness in improving the quality of their lives.

In the previously described satisfaction survey conducted in California by Campbell and her colleagues (1989), those surveyed rated their general quality of life as very low, especially when compared to studies of the general population in California. In the survey, 21% of those questioned stated that "seldom" or "never" were things going well in their lives, while 45% described the general state of their psychological and emotional health as "only fair" or "poor." In terms of feeling as though they have control over their own lives, 15% reported that they had "a little control" or "no control," and about one-third reported that they had only "some control." Interestingly, when asked to rank factors essential to their well-being, respondents chose many of the same factors that are emphasized in PSR programming, including health and mental health, a decent place to live, adequate income, happiness, and meaningful work.

In their study involving 157 members in a clubhouse program, Rosenfield and Neese-Todd (1993) found that the perception of empowerment (measured by items regarding decision-making power, being heard and valued in the program, supportive interactions, etc.) within the program was significantly associated with most of the aspects of quality of life they measured, including living arrangements, social relations, family relations, pre-vocational activities, safety, health, and leisure activities. Importantly, neither level of functioning or depressed mood influenced these associations.

These authors speculate that empowering methods of service-delivery are as important to the individual's quality of life as the services themselves.

Conclusion

This chapter has summarized recent research on a number of different outcomes that constitute the goals of PSR programming. There is fairly convincing evidence that some types of PSR approaches result in decreased hospital utilization and increased vocational functioning. Although this research has a long tradition and is now fairly substantial, there remain many gaps in our understanding of whether and how PSR services help individuals with psychiatric disabilities achieve the kinds of lives they want to live in the community. There is a lack of information about PSR's effectiveness in establishing residential independence, acquiring generalizable social skills that lead to social integration, and providing higher education and training. In addition, more research is needed in order to understand the effects of PSR programming on other important dimensions such as people's perceived quality of life, their own assessment of their needs, and their degree of satisfaction and dissatisfaction with the services they receive. Finally, it is of critical importance that issues involved in the delivery of PSR services by staff with psychiatric disabilities be studied as this approach grows in popularity.

References

Allen, J. (1994). Personal communication. October 17, 1994.

Anthony, W.A. (1994). Characteristics of people with psychiatric disabilities that are predictive of entry into the rehabilitation process and successful employment. *Psychosocial Rehabilitation Journal, 17*(3), 3-13.

Anthony, W.A., Cohen, M.R., & Vitalo, R. (1978). The measurement of rehabilitation outcome. *Schizophrenia Bulletin, 4,* 365-383.

Anthony, W.A. & Blanch, A. (1988). Research on Community Support Services: What have we learned? *Psychosocial Rehabilitation Journal, 12,* 55-81.

Anthony, W.A. & Jansen, M.A. (1984). Predicting the vocational capacity of the chronically mentally ill. *American Psychologist, 39,* 537-544.

Anthony, W.A. & Liberman, R.P. (1986). The practice of psychosocial rehabilitation: Historical, conceptual, and research base. *Schizophrenia Bulletin, 12*(4), 542-559.

Arns, P., & Linney, J.A. (1993). Work, self, and life satisfaction for persons with severe and persistent mental disorders. *Psychosocial Rehabilitation Journal, 17,* 63-79.

Asmussen, S.M., Romano, J., Beatty, P., Gasarch, L., & Shaughnessey, S. (1994). Old answers for today's problems: Integrating individuals who are homeless with mental illness into existing community-based programs: A case study from Fountain House. *Psychosocial Rehabilitation Journal, 18* (1), 75-93

Atkisson, C., Cook, J.A., Karno, M., Lehman, A., McGlashan, T.H., Meltzer, H.Y., O'Connor, M., Richardson, D., Rosenblatt, A., Wells, K., & Williams, J. (1992). Clinical services research. *Schizophrenia Bulletin, 18*(4), 561-626.

Beall, M.A. (1992). *Virginia Mental Health Consumers Association Commissioners Guidance Questionnaire: Survey results.* Falls Church, VA: Virginia Mental Health Consumers Association.

Beard, J.H., Propst, R.N., & Malamud, T.J. (1982). The Fountain House model of psychosocial rehabilitation. *Psychosocial Rehabilitation Journal, 5,* 47-54.

Beard, J.H., Malamud, T.J., & Rossman, E. (1978). Psychosocial rehabilitation and long-term hospitalization rates: The findings of two research studies. *Schizophrenia Bulletin, 4*, 622-635.

Bellack, A.S., Turner, S.M., Hersen, M., & Luber, R.F. (1984). An examination of the efficacy of social skills training for chronic schizophrenic patients. *Hospital and Community Psychiatry, 35*, 1023-1028.

Benton, M.K. & Schroeder, H.E. (1990). Social skills training with schizophrenics: A meta-analytic evaluation. *Journal of Consulting and Clinical Psychology, 58*(6), 741-747.

Besio, S.W. & Mahler, J. (1993). Benefits and challenges of using consumer staff in supported housing services. *Hospital and Community Psychiatry, 44* (5), 490-491.

Blanch, A.K., Carling, P.J., & Ridway, P. (1988). Normal housing with specialized supports: A psychosocial rehabilitation approach to living in the community. *Rehabilitation Psychology, 33*(1), 47-55

Bond, G.R. (1992). Vocational rehabilitation. In R.P. Liberman (Ed.), *Handbook of Psychiatric Rehabilitation* (pp. 244-275). Boston, MA: Allyn and Bacon.

Bond, G.R. & Boyer, S.L. (1988). Rehabilitation programs and outcomes. In J.A. Ciardiello & M.D. Bell (Eds.), *Vocational Rehabilitation of Persons With Prolonged Psychiatric Disorders* (pp. 231-263). Baltimore, MD: The Johns Hopkins University Press.

Bond, G.R., Dietzen, L., McGrew, J.H., & Miller, L.D. (1995). Accelerating entry into supported employment for persons with severe psychiatric disabilities. *Rehabilitation Psychology, 40*, 75-94.

Bond, G.R., Miller, L.D., Krumied, R.D., & Ward, R.S. (1988). Assertive case management in three CMHCs: A controlled study. *Hospital and Community Psychiatry, 39*(4), 411-418.

Borland, A., McRae, J., & Lycan, C. (1989). Outcomes of five years of continuous intensive case management. *Hospital and Community Psychiatry, 40* (4), 369-376.

Bradshaw, W.H. (1993). Coping-skills training versus a problem-solving approach with schizophrenic patients. *Hospital and Community Psychiatry, 44* (11), 1102-1104.

Bush, C.T., Langford, M.W., Rosen, P., & Gott, W. (1990). Operation outreach: Intensive case management for severely psychiatrically disabled adults. *Hospital and Community Psychiatry, 41* (6), 647-649.

Campbell, J., Schraiber, R., Temkin, T., & ten Tusscher, T. (1989). *The Well-Being Project: Mental Health Clients Speak For Themselves.* San Francisco, CA: The California Department of Mental Health, Office of Prevention.

Carling, P.J. (1993). Housing and supports for persons with mental illness: Emerging approaches to research and practice. *Hospital and Community Psychiatry, 44*(5), 439-449.

Chamberlain, R. & Rapp, C. (1991). A decade of case management: A methodological review of outcome research. *Community Mental Health Journal, 27*(3), 171-188.

Chamberlin, J. (1990). The ex-patients' movement: Where we've been and where we're going. *The Journal of Mind and Behavior, 11*(3), 323-336.

Chang, G., Brenner, L., & Bryant, K. (1991). Factors predicting inpatient length of stay in a CMHC. *Hospital and Community Psychiatry, 42*(8), 853-855.

Cnaan, R., Blankertz, L., Messinger, K., & Gardner, J.R. (1988). Psychosocial rehabilitation: Towards a definition. *Psychosocial Rehabilitation Journal, 11*(4), 61-77.

Conning, A.M. & Brownlow, J.M. (1992). Determining suitability of placement for long-stay psychiatric inpatients. *Hospital and Community Psychiatry, 43*(7), 709-712.

Cook, J.A. (1994). Independent community living among women with severe mental illness: A comparison with outcomes among men. *The Journal of Mental Health Administration, 21*(4), 361-373.

_____. (1993). *Outcome Assessment In Psychosocial Rehabilitation Services For Persons With Severe And Persistent Mental Illness.* Washington, DC: National Institute of Mental Health.

Cook, J.A., Graham, K.K., & Razzano, L. (1993). Psychosocial rehabilitation of deaf persons with severe mental illness: A multivariate model of residential outcomes. *Rehabilitation Psychology, 38,* 265-278.

Cook, J.A. & Hoffschmidt, S.J. (1993). Comprehensive models of psychosocial rehabilitation. In R.W. Flexer & P.L. Solomon (Eds.), *Psychosocial rehabilitation in practice* (pp. 81-97). Boston, MA: Andover Medical Publishers.

Cook, J.A., Jonikas, J.A., & Solomon, M.L. (1992). Models of vocational rehabilitation for youths and adults with severe mental illness: Implications for AMERICA 2000 and ADA. *American Rehabilitation, 18*(3), 6-11.

Cook, J.A. & Pickett, S.A. (1995, Winter). Recent trends in vocational rehabilitation for persons with psychiatric disability. *American Rehabilitation, 2-12.*

Cook, J.A., & Razzano, L. (1992). Natural vocational supports for persons with severe mental illness: Thresholds supported competitive employment program. In L. Stein (Ed.), *New directions in mental health services: Innovations in mental health services, 56,* (pp. 23-42). San Francisco: Jossey-Bass.

Cook, J.A., Razzano, L., Jayaraj, A., Myers, M., Nathanson, F., Stott, M.A., & Stein, M. (1994). HIV-risk assessment for psychosocial rehabilitation clientele: Implications for community-based services. *Psychosocial Rehabilitation Journal, 17*(4), 105-115.

Cook, J.A., & Rosenberg, H. (1994). Predicting community employment among persons with psychiatric disability: A logistic regression analysis. *Journal of Rehabilitation Administration, 18,* 6-22.

Cook, J.A., & Solomon, M.L. (1993). The community scholar program: An outcome study of supported education for students with severe mental illness. *Psychosocial Rehabilitation Journal, 17,* 84-97.

Cook, J.A., Solomon, M.L., Farrell, D., Koziel, M., & Jonikas, J.A. (in press). Psychosocial rehabilitation for transition-age youth with severe mental illness: Program model and client outcomes. In S.H. Henggeler & A. Santos (Eds.), *Innovative Services For Difficult To Treat Populations.* New York: American Psychiatric Press.

Cook, J.A., Yamaguchi, J., & Solomon, M.L. (1993). Field-testing a post-secondary faculty in-service training for working with students who have psychiatric disabilities. *Psychosocial Rehabilitation Journal, 17,* 157-169.

Corrigan, P.W. & Holmes, E.P. (1994). Patient identification of street skills for a psychosocial training module. *Hospital and Community Psychiatry, 45*(3), 273-276

Corrigan, P.W., Schade, M.L., & Liberman, R.P. (1992). Social skills training. In R.P. Liberman (Ed.), *Handbook of Psychosocial Rehabilitation* (pp. 95-126). Boston, MA: Allyn and Bacon.

Corrigan, P.W. & Storzbach, M.A. (1993). Behavioral interventions for alleviating psychotic symptoms. *Hospital and Community Psychiatry, 44*(4), 341-347.

Cournos, F. (1987). The impact of environmental factors on outcome in residential programs. *Hospital and Community Psychiatry, 38*(8), 848-852.

Culhane, D.P. (1992). Ending homelessness among women with severe mental illness: A model program from Philadelphia. *Psychosocial Rehabilitation Journal, 16*(1), 63-76.

Curtis, J.L., Millman, E.J., Struening, E., & D'Ercole, A. (1992). Effect of case management on rehospitalization and utilization of ambulatory care services. *Hospital and Community Psychiatry, 43*(9), 895-899.

Curtis, L.C. (1993). Consumers as colleagues: Partnership in the workforce. *In Practice.* Newsletter by the Center for Community Change through Housing and Support, Institute for Program Development, Trinity College of Vermont, Burlington, Vermont.

Danley, K.S., Rogers, E.S., MacDonald-Wilson, K., & Anthony, W. (1994). *Supported Employment for Adults With Psychiatric Disability: Results of an Innovative Demonstration Project.* Boston: Center for Psychosocial rehabilitation, Boston University.

Davies, M.A., Bromer, E.J., Schultz, S.C., Dunn, L.O., & Morgenstern, M. (1989). Community adjustment of chronic schizophrenic patients in urban and rural settings. *Hospital and Community Psychiatry, 14,* 824-830.

Deegan, P.E. (1988). Recovery: The lived experience of rehabilitation. *Psychosocial Rehabilitation Journal, 11*(4), 11-19.

Dincin, J. (1975). Psychosocial rehabilitation. *Schizophrenia Bulletin, 1,* 131-148.

Dincin, J., Wasmer, D., Witheridge, T.F., Sobeck, L., Cook, J.A., & Razzano, L. (1993). Impact of assertive community treatment on the use of state hospital inpatient bed-days. *Hospital and Community Psychiatry, 44*(9), 833-838.

Dincin, J. & Witheridge, T.F. (1982). Psychosocial rehabilitation as a deterrent to recidivism. *Hospital & Community Psychiatry, 33,* 645-650.

Dion, G.L. & Anthony, W.A. (1987). Research in psychosocial rehabilitation: A review of experimental and quasi-experimental studies. *Rehabilitation Counseling Bulletin, 30,* 177-203.

Dion, G.L., Tohen, M., Anthony, W.A., & Waternaux, C.S. (1988). Symptoms and functioning of patients with bipolar disorder six months after hospitalization. *Hospital and Community Psychiatry, 39,* 652-657.

Donahoe, C.P. & Driesenga, S.A. (1988). A review of social skills training with chronic mental patients. In M. Hersen, R.M. Eisler, & P.M. Miller (Eds.), *Progress in Behavior Modification, 23,* Newbury Park: SAGE Publications.

Drake, R.E., Becker, D.R., Biesanz, J.C., Torrey, W.C., McHugo, G.J., & Wyzik, P.F. (1994). Rehabilitative day treatment vs. supported employment: I. Vocational outcomes. *Community Mental Health Journal, 30*(5), 519-532.

Drake, R.E., Wallach, M.A., & Hoffman, J.S. (1989). Housing instability and homelessness among aftercare patients of an urban state hospital. *Hospital and Community Psychiatry, 40*(1), 46-51.

Eckman, T.A. & Liberman, R.P. (1990). A large-scale field test of a medication management skills training program for people with schizophrenia. *Psychosocial Rehabilitation Journal, 13*(3), 31-35.

Eckman, T.A., Wirshing, W.C., Marder, S.R., Liberman, R.P., Johnston-Cronk, K., Zimmerman, K., & Mintz, J. (1992). Technique for training schizophrenic patients in illness self-management: A controlled trial. *American Journal of Psychiatry, 149,* 1549-1555.

Elbeck, M. & Fecteau, G. (1990). Improving the validity of measures of patient satisfaction with psychiatric care and treatment. Hospital and Community Psychiatry, 41(9), 998-1001.

Endicott, J., Sptizer, R.L., Fleiss, J.L., & Cohen, J. (1976). The Global Assessment Scale: A procedure for measuring overall severity of psychiatric disturbance. *Archives of General Psychiatry, 33,* 766-771.

Everett, B. & Steven, L.D. (1989). Working together: A consumer participation research project to develop a new model of high-support housing. *Canada's Mental Health,* June, 28-32.

Fabian, E.S. (1992a). Longitudinal outcomes in supported employment: A survival analysis. *Rehabilitation Psychology, 37,* 23-35.

Fabian, E.S. (1992b). Supported employment and the quality of life: Does a job make a difference? *Rehabilitation Counseling Journal, 36,* 84-87.

Fabian, E.S. (1989). Work and the quality of life. *Psychosocial Rehabilitation Journal, 12,* 39-49.

Fairweather, G.W., Sanders, D.H., Maynard, H., Cressler, D.L., & Bleck, D.S. (1969). *Community Life For The Mentally Ill: An Alternative To Institutional Care* (pp. 199-237). Chicago, IL: Aldine Publishing Company.

Fergus, E.O., Bryant, B., & Balzell, A. (1989). The Lodge society: An update on Michigan's outcomes. Unpublished manuscript. Lansing, Michigan: Michigan State University, Ecological Psychology Program.

Fields, S. (1990). The relationship between residential treatment and supported housing in a community system of services. *Psychosocial Rehabilitation Journal, 13*(4), 105-113.

First, R.J., Rife, J.C., & Kraus, S. (1990). Case management with people who are homeless and mentally ill: Preliminary findings from an NIMH Demonstration Project. *Psychosocial Rehabilitation Journal, 14*(2), 87-91.

Fisher, D. (1994). New vision of healing: A reasonable accommodation for consumers/survivors working as mental health service providers. *Psychosocial Rehabilitation Journal, 17*(3), 67-81.

Fountain House. (1985). Evaluation of clubhouse model community-based psychosocial rehabilitation: Final report to the National Institute of Handicapped Research [Contract No 300-84-0124]. Washington, DC: National Institute of Handicapped Research.

Franklin, J.L., Solovitz, B., Mason, M., Clemons, J.R., & Miller, G.E. (1987). *American Journal of Public Health, 77*(6), 674-678.

Geller, J.L. & Fisher, W.H. (1993). The linear continuum of transitional residences: Debunking the myth. *American Journal of Psychiatry, 150,* 1070-1076.

Goering, P.N., Wasylenki, D.A., Farkas, M., Lancee, W.J., & Ballantyne, R. (1988). What difference does case management make? *Hospital and Community Psychiatry, 39*(3), 272-276.

Goldsmith, J.B. & McFall, R.M. (1975). Development and evaluation of an interpersonal skills training program for psychiatric inpatients. *Journal of Abnormal Psychology, 84,* 51-58.

Grusky, O., Tierney, K., Manderscheid, R.W., & Grusky, D.B. (1985). Social bonding and community adjustment of chronically mentally ill adults. *Journal of Health and Social Behavior, 26,* 49-63.

Grusky, O., Tierney, K., & Spanish, M.T. (1989). Which community mental health services are most important? *Administration and Policy in Mental Health, 3-16.*

Halford, W.K. & Hayes, R. (1991). Psychological rehabilitation of chronic schizophrenic patients: Recent findings on social skills training and family psychoeducation. *Clinical Psychology Review, 11*(1), 23-44.

Harp, H. (1994). Empowerment of mental health consumers in vocational rehabilitation. *Psychosocial Rehabilitation Journal, 17*, 83-89.

_____. (1991). A Crazy Folks Guide to Reasonable Accommodation and "Psychiatric Disability."

Hatfield, B., Huxley, P., Mohamad, H. (1992). Accommodation and employment: A survey into the circumstances and expressed needs of users of mental health services in a northern town. *British Journal of Social Work, 22*, 61-73.

Hoffman, F.L., & Mastrianni, X. (1993). The role of supported education in the inpatient treatment of young adults: A two-site comparison. *Psychosocial Rehabilitation Journal, 17*, 109-119.

Hogarty, G.E., Anderson, C.M., Reiss, D.J., et al. (1986). Family psycho-education, social skills training, and maintenance of chemotherapy in the aftercare treatment of schizophrenia. *Archives of General Psychiatry, 25*, 470-480.

Hornstra, R.K., Bruce-Wolfe, V., Sagduyu, K., & Riffle, D.W. (1993). The effect of intensive case management on hospitalization of patients with schizophrenia. *Hospital and Community Psychiatry, 44*(9), 844-847.

Jacobs, E., & Glater, S. (1993). Students, staff, and community: A collaborative model of college services for students with psychological disabilities. *Psychosocial Rehabilitation Journal, 17*, 201-209.

Jacobs, H.E., Donahoe, C.P., & Falloon, I. (1985). Rehabilitation of the chronic schizophrenic: Areas of intervention. *Annual Review of Rehabilitation, 4*.

Jacobs, H.E., Wissusik, D., Collier, R., Stackman, D., & Burkeman, D. (1992). Correlates between psychiatric disabilities and vocational outcome. *Hospital and Community Psychiatry, 43*, 365-369.

Jerrell, J.M. & Hu, T.W. (1989). Cost-effectiveness of intensive clinical and case management compared with an existing system of care. *Inquiry, 26*, 224-234.

Jonikas, J.A. & Cook, J.A. (1993). *Safe, secure, and street-smart: Empowering women with mental illness to achieve greater independence in the community.* Rehabilitation Training Curriculum. Chicago, IL: National Research & Training Center.

Kaufmann, C.L. (1994, October). Long-term employment supports. Paper presented at the First Annual National Research Seminar on Work: Establishing an Ongoing Dialogue, Philadelphia, PA.

Kaufmann, C.L. (1993). Roles for mental health consumers in self-help group research. *The Journal of Applied Behavioral Science, 29*(2), 257-271.

Kaufmann, C.L., Roth, L.R., & Cook, M. (1992). *The self-help employment center project* (CSP Services Research Grant). Rockville, MD: Center for Mental Health Services.

Kaufmann, C.L., Ward-Colasante, C. & Farmer, J. (1993). Development and evaluation of drop-in centers operated by mental health consumers. *Hospital and Community Psychiatry, 44*, 675-678.

Laird, M. & Krown, S. (1991). Evaluation of a transitional employment program. *Psychosocial Rehabilitation Journal, 15*(1), 3-8.

Lauer-Listhaus, B. & Watterson, J. (1988). A psychoeducational groups for HIV-positive patients on a psychiatric service. *Hospital and Community Psychiatry, 39*, 776-777.

Lehman, A.F. (1988). A quality of life interview for the chronically mentally ill. *Evaluation and Program Planning, 11*, 51-62.

Lehman, A.F., Ward, N.C., & Linn, L.S. (1982). Chronic mental patients: The quality of life issue. *American Journal of Psychiatry, 139*(10), 1271-1276.

Levstek, D.A. & Bond, G.R. (1993). Housing cost, quality, and satisfaction among formerly homeless persons with serious mental illness in two cities. *Innovations and Research, 2*(3), 1-8.

Liberman, R.P. (1989). *Psychiatric symptoms and the functional capacity for work: Provisional final report.* Los Angeles, CA: Clinical Research Center for Schizophrenia & Psychosocial rehabilitation, UCLA School of Medicine.

Liberman, R.P., Jacobs, H.E., Boone, S.E., Foy, D.W., Donahoe, C.P., Falloon, I.R.H., Blackwell, G., & Wallace, C.J. (1987). Skills training for the community adaptation of schizophrenics. In J.S. Strauss, W. Boker, & H.D. Brenner (Eds.), *Psychosocial treatment of schizophrenia.* Toronto: Hans Huber.

Liberman, R.P., Mueser, K.T., Wallace, C.J., Jacobs, H., Eckman, T.A., & Massel, K. (1986). Training skills in the psychiatrically disabled: Learning coping and competence. *Schizophrenia Bulletin, 12*(4), 631-647.

Liberman, R.P., Wallace, C.J., Blackwell, G., Eckman, T.A., Vaccaro, J.V., & Kuehnel, T.G. (1993). Innovations in skills training for the seriously mentally ill: The UCLA social and independent living skills modules. *Innovations and Research, 2*(2), 43-59.

Lipton, F.R., Nutt, S., & Sabatini, A. (1988). Housing the homeless mentally ill: A longitudinal study of a treatment approach. *Hospital and Community Psychiatry, 39*(1), 40-45.

Lynch, M.M. & Kruzich, J.M. (1986). Needs assessment of the chronically mentally ill: Practitioner and client perspectives. *Administration in Mental Health, 4*, 237-248.

Macauley, R. (1993). Professionals need training to accept ex-patients as colleagues. *Resources, 5*(1), 18.

Marshak, L.E., Bostick, D., & Turton, L.J. (1990). Closure outcomes for clients with psychiatric disabilities served by the vocational rehabilitation system. *Rehabilitation Counseling Bulletin, 33*, 247-250.

Marx, A.J., Test, M.A., & Stein, L.I. (1973). Extrahospital management of severe mental illness. *Archives of General Psychiatry, 29*, 505-511.

Massey, O.T. & Wu, L. (1993). Service delivery and community housing: Perspectives of consumers, family members, and case managers. *Innovations and Research, 2*(3), 9-15.

McCabe, S., Edgar, E.R., Mancuso, L.L., King, D., Ross, E.C., & Emery, B.D. (1993). A national study of housing affordability for recipients of supplemental security income. *Hospital and Community Psychiatry, 44*(5), 494-495.

McCormack, J. (1992). *Interim report on consumer-operated projects: 1991-92.* Philadelphia, PA: Division of Continuing Education, Medical College of Pennsylvania.

McGill, C.W. & Patterson, C.J. (1990). Former patients as peer counselors on locked psychiatric units. *Hospital & Community Psychiatry, 41*(9), 1017-1019.

Moller, H., von Zerssen, D., Werner-Eilert, K., & Wuschenr-Stockheim, M. (1982). Outcome in schizophrenic and similar paranoid psychoses. *Schizophrenia Bulletin, 8*, 99-108.

Morrison, R. & Bellack, A. (1987). Social functioning of schizophrenic patients: Clinical research and issues. *Schizophrenia Bulletin, 13*(4), 715-725.

Mowbray, C.T. & Chamberlain, P. (1986). Sex differences among the long-term mentally disabled. *Psychology of Women Quarterly, 10*, 383-392.

Mowbray, C.T., Chamberlain, P., Jennings, M., & Reed, C. (1988). Consumer-run mental health services: Results from five demonstration projects. *Community Mental Health Journal, 24*(2), 151-156.

Mowbray, C.T. & Tan, C. (1993). Consumer-operated drop-in centers: Evaluation of outcomes and impact. *The Journal of Mental Health Administration, 20*(1), 8-19.

Mueser, K.T., Bellack, A.S., Douglas, M.S., & Morrison, R.L. (1991). Prevalence and stability of social skills deficits in schizophrenia. *Schizophrenia Research, 5,* 167-176.

Mueser, K.T., Levine, S., Bellack, A.S., Douglas, M.S., & Brady, E.U. (1990). Social skills training for acute psychiatric inpatients. *Hospital and Community Psychiatry, 41*(11), 1249-1251.

Navin, C., Lewis, K., & Higson, P. (1989). The role of formal education in the rehabilitation of persons with chronic schizophrenia. *Disability, Handicap and Society, 4,* 131-143.

Nemec, P.B., McNamara, S., & Walsh, D. (1992). Direct skills teaching. *Psychosocial Rehabilitation Journal, 16*(1), 13-25.

Newman, S.J. (1994). The housing and neighborhood conditions of persons with severe mental illness. *Hospital and Community Psychiatry, 45*(4), 338-343.

Nikkel, R.E. (1994). Areas of skill training for persons with mental illness and substance use disorders: Building skills for successful community living. *Community Mental Health Journal, 30*(1), 61-72.

Nikkel, R.E., Smith, G., & Edwards, D. (1992). A consumer-operated case management project. *Hospital and Community Psychiatry, 43*(6), 577-579.

Olfson, M. (1990). Assertive community treatment: An evaluation of the experimental evidence. *Hospital and Community Psychiatry, 41*(6), 634-641.

Pelham, T.W., Campagna, P.D., Ritvo, P.G., & Birnie, W.A. (1993). The effects of exercise therapy on clients in a psychosocial rehabilitation program. *Psychosocial Rehabilitation Journal, 16*(4), 75-84.

Polowczyk, D., Brutus, M., Orvieto, A.A., Vidal, J., & Cipriani, D. (1993). Comparison of patient and staff surveys of consumer satisfaction. *Hospital and Community Psychiatry, 44*(6), 589-591.

Pratt, C. & Gill, K. (1990). Sharing research knowledge to empower people who are chronically mentally ill. *Psychosocial Rehabilitation Journal, 13*(3), 75-79.

Randolph, F.L., Ridgway, P., & Carling, P.J. (1991). Residential programs for persons with severe mental illness: A nationwide survey of state-affiliated agencies. *Hospital and Community Psychiatry, 42*(11), 1111-1115.

Rapp, C.A., Shera, W., & Kisthardt, W. (1993). Research strategies for consumer empowerment of people with severe mental illness. *Social Work, 38*(6), 727-735.

Research Committee of the International Association of Psychosocial Rehabilitation Services. (1995). *Toolkit For Measuring Psychosocial Outcomes.* Prepared for the Evaluation Center at the Human Services Research Institute. Columbia, MD: International Association of Psychosocial Rehabilitation Services.

Ridgway, P. (1988). The voice of consumers in mental health systems: A call for change. Unpublished manuscript. Burlington, VA: Center for Community Change through Housing and Support.

Ridgway, P. & Zipple, A.M. (1990a). Challenges and strategies for implementing supported housing. *Psychosocial Rehabilitation Journal, 13*(4), 115-120.

Ridgway, P. & Zipple, A.M. (1990b). The paradigm shift in residential services: From the linear continuum to supported housing approaches. *Psychosocial Rehabilitation Journal, 13*(4), 11-31.

Rogers, E.S., Anthony, W.A., Toole, J., & Brown, M.A. (1991). Vocational outcomes following psychosocial rehabilitation: A longitudinal study of three programs. *Journal of Vocational Rehabilitation, 1*(3), 21-29.

Rogers, E.S., Danley, K.S., Anthony, W.A., Martin, R., & Walsh, D. (1994). The residential needs and preferences of persons with serious mental illness: A comparison of consumers and family members. *The Journal of Mental Health Administration, 21*(1), 42-51.

Rosenfield, S. & Neese-Todd, S. (1993). Elements of a psychosocial rehabilitation clubhouse program associated with a satisfying quality of life. *Hospital and Community Psychiatry, 44*(1), 76-78.

Rubenstein, L. & James, L. (1990). New funding strategy for housing people with mental disabilities. In A. Meyerson and P. Solomon (Eds.), *New developments in psychosocial rehabilitation* (pp. 65-73). San Francisco, CA: Jossey-Bass (*New directions for mental health services,* 45).

Ryan, E.R. & Bell, M.D. (1985, May). Rehabilitation of chronic psychiatric patients: A randomized clinical study. Paper presented at the meeting of the American Psychiatric Association. Los Angeles, CA.

Ryglewicz, H. (1991). Psychoeducation for clients and families: A way in, out, and through in working with people with dual disorders. *Psychosocial Rehabilitation Journal, 15*(2), 79-89.

Ryglewicz, H., & Glynn, L. (1993). Project Change revisited: An experiment in entry or reentry into college. *Psychosocial Rehabilitation Journal, 17,* 69-81.

Salem, D.A. (1990). Community-based services and resources: The significance of choice and diversity. *American Journal of Community Psychology, 18,* 909-915.

Santos, A.B., Deci, P.A., Lachance, K.R., Dias, J.K., Sloop, T.B., Hiers, T.G., & Bevilacqua, J.J. (1993). Providing assertive community treatment for severely mentally ill patients in a rural area. *Hospital and Community Psychiatry, 44*(1), 34-39.

Schultheis, A.M.M. & Bond, G.R. (1993). Situational assessment ratings of work behaviors: Changes across time and between settings. *Psychosocial Rehabilitation Journal, 17*(2), 107-119.

Shepherd, G. (1990). A criterion-oriented approach to skills training. *Psychosocial Rehabilitation Journal, 13*(3), 11-13.

_____. (1988). The contribution of psychological interventions to the treatment and management of schizophrenia. In P. Beggington & P. McGuffin (Eds.) *Schizophrenia: The major issues.* London: Heinemann/Mental Health Foundation.

Sherman, P.S. (1994). Personal communication.

Sherman, P.S. & Porter, R. (1991). Mental health consumers as case management aides. *Hospital and Community Psychiatry, 42*(5), 494-498.

Sladyk, K. (1990). Teaching safe sex practices to psychiatric patients. *American Journal of Occupational Therapy, 44,* 284-286.

Slater, V., Linn, M.W., & Harris, R. (1982). Satisfaction with mental health care scale. *Comprehensive Psychiatry, 23,* 68-74.

Solomon, P. (1992). The efficacy of case management services for severely mentally disabled clients. *Community Mental Health Journal, 28*(3), 163-180.

Solomon, M.L., Jonikas, J.A., Cook, J.A., & Kerouac, J. (1998). *Positive partnerships: How consumers and non-consumers can work together as service providers.* 2nd Edition. Chicago, IL: National Research and Training Center.

Solomon, P. & Draine, J. (1995a). One-year outcomes of a randomized trial of consumer case management. *Evaluation and Program Planning, 18*(2), 117-126.

Solomon, P. & Draine, J. (1995b). The efficacy of a consumer case management team: Two year outcomes of a randomized trial. *The Journal of Mental Health Administration, 22*(2), 135-146.

Solomon, P. & Draine, J. (1994). Satisfaction with mental health treatment in a randomized trial of consumer case management. *The Journal of Nervous and Mental Disease, 182*(8), 179-184.

Spooner, F., Algozzine, B., & Saxon, J.P. (1980). The efficacy of vocational rehabilitation with mentally ill persons. *Journal of Rehabilitation, 46*, 62-66.

Stein, L.I. & Test, M.A. (1980). Alternative to mental hospital treatment, I: Conceptual model, treatment program, and clinical evaluation. *Archives of General Psychiatry, 37*, 392-397.

Stephens, C.L. & Belisle, K.C. (1993). The "consumer-as-provider" initiative. *The Journal of Mental Health Administration, 20*(2), 178-182.

Strauss, M.W. (1993). Relations of symptoms to cognitive deficits in schizophrenia. *Schizophrenia Bulletin, 19*(2), 233-260.

Stuve, P., Erickson, R.C., & Spaulding, W. (1991). Cognitive rehabilitation: The next step in psychosocial rehabilitation. *Psychosocial Rehabilitation Journal, 15*(1), 9-26.

Susser, E., Valencia, E., & Torres, J. (1994). Sex, games, and videotapes: An HIV-prevention intervention for men who are homeless and mentally ill. *Psychosocial Rehabilitation Journal, 17*(4), 31-40.

Tanzman, B. (1993). An overview of surveys of mental health consumers' preferences for housing and support services. *Hospital and Community Psychiatry, 44*(5), 450-455.

Tarrier, N., Barrowclough, C., Vaughn, C.E., et al. (1988). The community management of schizophrenia: A controlled clinical trial of a behavioral intervention with families to reduce relapse. *British Journal of Psychiatry, 153*, 532-542.

Taube, C.A., Morlock, L., Burns, B.J., & Santos, A.B. 1990). New directions in research on assertive community treatment. *Hospital and Community Psychiatry, 41*(6), 642-647.

Test, M.A., Burke, S.S., & Wallisch, L.S. (1990). Gender differences of young adults with schizophrenic disorders in community care. *Schizophrenia Bulletin, 16*(2), 331-334.

Trottner, S., Minkoff, K., Harrison, K., & Hoops, J. (1988). Supported work: An innovative approach to the vocational rehabilitation of persons who are psychiatrically disabled. *Rehabilitation Psychology, 33*(1), 27-35.

Tucker, P. & Brems, C. (1993). Variables affecting length of psychiatric inpatient treatment. *The Journal of Mental Health Administration, 20*(1), 58-65.

Unger, K.V. (1994). Access to educational programs and its effect on employability. *Psychosocial Rehabilitation Journal, 17*, 117-126.

Unger, K.V., Anthony, W.A., Sciarappa, K., & Rogers, E.S. (1991). A supported education program for young adults with long-term mental illness. *Hospital and Community Psychiatry, 42*, 838-842.

Unger, K.V., Skrinar, G.S., Hutchinson, D.S., & Yelmokas, A.M. (1992). Fitness: A viable adjustment to treatment for young adults with psychiatric disabilities. *Psychosocial Rehabilitation Journal, 15*(3), 21-28.

Uttaro, R. & Mechanic, D. (1994). The NAMI consumer survey analysis of ummet needs. *Hospital and Community Psychiatry, 45*(4), 372-374.

Vaccaro, J.V., Liberman, R.P., Blackwell, G., & Wallace, C.J. (1992). Combining social skills training and assertive case management. In R.P. Liberman (Ed.), *Effective psychosocial rehabilitation* (pp. 33-42). San Francisco, CA: Jossey-Bass (*New Directions for Mental Health Services*).

Van Tosh, L. (1993). Working for a change: Employment of consumers/ survivors in the design and provision of services for persons who are homeless and mentally disabled. Baltimore, MD: The Center for Mental Health Services Research, University of Maryland.

Wallace, C.J. & Liberman, R.P. (1985). Social skills training for patients with schizophrenia: A controlled clinical trial. *Psychiatry Research, 15*, 239-247.

Warner, R. & Polak, P. (1993). An economic development approach to the mentally ill in the community. Boulder, CO: Mental Health Center for Boulder County.

Wehman, P., Revell, W.G., Kregel, J., Kreutzer, J., Callahan, M., & Banks, P.D. (1990). Supported employment: An alternative model for vocational rehabilitation of persons with severe neurologic, psychiatric, or physical disabilities. In J. Kregel, P. Wehman, & M.S. Shafer (Eds.), *Supported employment for persons with severe disabilities: From research to practice.* (Cooperative agreement No. H133B80052). Washington, DC: U.S. Department of Education.

Wehman, P. & Moon, M.S. (1988). *Vocational rehabilitation and supported employment.* Baltimore, MD: Brookes.

Witheridge, T.F. & Dincin, J. (1985). The Bridge: An assertive outreach program in an urban setting. In L.I. Stein & M.A. Test (Eds.), *The Training in community living model: A decade of experience* (pp. 65-76). San Francisco, CA: Jossey-Bass (*New directions for mental health services, 26*).

Wolf, J., & DiPietro, S. (1992). From patient to student: Supported education programs in southwest Connecticut. *Psychosocial Rehabilitation Journal, 15*, 61-68.

Person-Centered Practices in Psychosocial Rehabilitation

Sheree Neese-Todd and Fran Pavick

The general goals of psychosocial rehabilitation speak to community integration for persons whose lives have often been derailed by the disabling consequences of serious mental illness. In essence it is a service model that aspires to reinforce the independence and functional capabilities of persons with psychiatric disabilities. As well, it is a tradition framed by hope and acceptance. Certainly, we believe proficient psychosocial workers can enhance rehabilitation practice. However, in order for professionals to facilitate a rehabilitation effort that leads towards recovery and a self-determining and satisfying life, fundamental attitudes and values must be operating. Positive, non-stigmatizing attitudes about persons with mental illness, nested within an empowerment framework are central to the practice and organization of psychosocial rehabilitation (PSR). The concepts underlying an empowerment stance—respectful self-determination and choice—are ideas that take into account a service environment which is organized to promote individual preference and decision making. In the face of remarkable social deterrents, individuals deserve to bring to their rehabilitation experience an environment that is staffed by people who

have a deep respect for their courage and desire. These ideas are made explicit in the context of rehabilitation practice centered on the person rather than the illness.

Empowerment Values

The concept of social "empowerment" is liberally employed by social theorists when discussing disenfranchised groups. Scholars cite the converging lines of evidence which reveal the importance of self-determination for ameliorating the life circumstances of vulnerable and stigmatized populations (Rappaport, 1981, 1985; Rappaport, Swift, & Hess, 1984; Rosenfield, 1987, 1992; Rosenfield & Neese-Todd, 1993; Zimmerman, 1990; Zimmerman & Rappaport, 1988). Broadly speaking, social empowerment has been characterized as an individual perception of human agency, self-esteem, and mastery, or control over one's environment (Bandura, 1989; Pearlin, Menaghan, Lieberman, & Mullan, 1981). This vision suggests that although social empowerment operates through a self-efficacy mechanism it can only be promoted within particular social arrangements. Thus the important lesson of social empowerment is that it must embody a co-equal interaction between individuals and social environments.

This general discussion has prompted an assumption that social empowerment as a *technology* may be a critical tool in the campaign to enhance life quality among people subject to social inequities. In other words, human service organizations may contribute to the well-being of recipients of services if they consider the importance of empowerment principles. This viewpoint is especially salient in the mental health arena where the label of mental illness has long been associated with great social stigma, a deviant social identity, compromised life satisfaction, and poor social outcomes (Becker, 1963; Jones et al., 1982; Lehman, 1986; Link et al., 1987). Consequently, it is often presumed that a social empowerment perspective, imbedded within mental health service systems, promotes not only improved treatment outcomes but higher levels of satisfaction by service recipients (Rapp et al, 1993).

Mental health service systems that consider the social forces active in treatment and rehabilitation settings must explore the potential consequences of social empowerment practice. In this sense, empowerment theory taken to its logical conclusion insinuates a service system centered on the *person,* not the mental illness. In fact, for some time, the related therapeutic benefits of empowering the recipients of mental health services have been held up as a key component in mental health policy considerations and have even been mandated by law (Mental Health Act Amendments of 1990). For example, the National Institute of Mental Health (1991) specifically urges mental health professionals to re-examine service delivery and the importance of the preferences of the persons served.

Psychosocial Rehabilitation: The Tradition of Empowerment

Psychosocial rehabilitation (PSR) has historically boasted a commitment to practice which facilitates empowerment of people with mental illness. Early efforts in the field have demonstrated a rehabilitation process practiced in a milieu of collaboration and support (Anthony and Liberman, 1986). For example, a 1971 study of prototypical psychosocial centers bears evidence to this mission (Glasscote, et. al, 1971). Six of the earliest psychosocial programs, all described in some detail in this report, exhibited a deep respect for the initiative, participation, and choices of the people participating in the program, as well as demonstrating a caring attitude toward persons with psychiatric disabilities. PSR was initially conceived as an intervention designed to strengthen the role of the individual's participation in rehabilitation activities. In a large part, the development of a person-focused philosophy was a response to the intellectual currents of the earliest period of mental hospital deinstitutionalization.

Psychosocial rehabilitation was deliberately shaped as an alternative approach to traditional psychiatric treatment, which was at that time rooted in a hierarchical, medical model of care. Efforts were made to diminish the "patient role," restore constructive social roles, and provide opportunities for new, satisfying social roles. Many programs refer to the individual with mental illness of rehabilitation services as "members"[1] of a rehabilitation community making explicit an egalitarian social experience (Beard, 1978).

Individuals who encounter persistent role strain and discrimination are vulnerable to the loss of self-esteem and feelings of competence. It was reasoned that community mental health rehabilitation programs could essentially maintain a social organization that would reflect self-forming ideas and counteract the negative effects of stigma experienced by people struggling with serious mental illness. Supportive interpersonal relationships represent one normative method of coping with the hardships associated with serious mental illness.

The PSR pioneers had great hope that non-traditional interpersonal relationships between rehabilitation staff and individuals with mental illness could bolster community tenure. It was also assumed that people disabled by psychiatric disease could provide important insight into the process of their own recovery of function. Individuals with mental illness are best equipped to tell service providers what was needed to allow them to regain mastery in their lives. Thus, even at its inception, PSR sought to incorporate the person with mental illness into the service intervention as a full partner in rehabilitation (Anthony et al, 1990; Freedberg, S. 1989; Moxley and Freddolino, 1990).

Although the original intent of PSR programming theoretically embraced the application of a person-centered practice, over time actual services often failed to produce comprehensive participation of those in rehabilitation (Anthony, Cohen, & Kennard, 1990; Ansapach, 1979; Ferguson, 1994; Moxley & Freddolino, 1990; Rosenfield & Neese-Todd, 1993; Saleebey, 1992). More recent developments, driven to a large extent by the self-help consumer as survivor movement, have served to reorient PSR personnel toward the importance of the voice of those receiving services in rehabilitation practice. Briefly, advocates have called for individual "empowerment" opportunities as well as rehabilitation programs dedicated to pursuing rehabilitation outcomes that are "driven by the needs perceived by the people using the services" (Chamberlin, 1984).

Specifically, advocacy groups of persons with mental illness have demanded a participatory role in designing, implementing, and evaluating PSR services (Chamberlin, 1984; Mowbray et al., 1988; NIDRR, 1993). Contemporary thinkers, informed by the consumer movement, now call for a more scrupulous person-centered practice, one that relies upon individually-driven rehabilitation outcomes. This technique, espoused alternately as person "self-determination," "support and representation," "mutual empowerment," the "strengths" perspective, and "consumer-centered service" within community mental health service systems, seeks to incorporate the voice of persons with mental illness into the service intervention as a full partner in rehabilitation planning and decision making (Moxley & Freddolino, 1990). Today's PSR leaders listen carefully to service recipients and clearly recommend that collaboration with the person in rehabilitation be seen as an essential ingredient to successful rehabilitation.

As stated above, PSR person-centered service delivery has been applied in an uneven manner. In part, problems lie in the lack of clear consensus and directives for such practice. Rehabilitation services for people with serious mental illness are labor intensive and require specialized knowledge, yet appropriate preparatory training is rarely available to professionals working in PSR. Disciplines such as social work, nursing, education, occupational therapy, or psychology contribute to the PSR staff ranks but these systems of higher education do not adequately prepare professionals to treat the particular needs of people with serious mental illness (NIMH, 1990;

NIMH, 1991). Consequently, service professionals may not demonstrate adequate competency with respect to person-centered practice. In addition, organizational strategies designed to enhance the individual's participation in the rehabilitation process are necessary for service reform.

However, this past decade has newly emphasized person-centered practice as a salient component of effective rehabilitation services. More rehabilitation service systems now consider expanding the role every person with mental illness plays in rehabilitation settings and eagerly explores the potential consequences of person-centered practice. In this sense, PSR has identified and championed a service principle that is applicable to a range of mental health services and has provided pivotal leadership to the larger world of mental health practice (Anthony, 1994; Anthony, Cohen, & Kennard, 1990; Beard, 1978; Stein and Test, 1978; Rappaport, 1985).

Person-Centered Practice: Legitimate Social Roles and the Participation of Persons with Mental Illness

Person-centered practice begins essentially with a philosophical position. Simply put, this attitude is the belief that people who grapple with psychiatric disabilities deserve to be treated with respect and that they shall be "self-determining" (Deegan, 1992:10). This stance involves deliberately incorporating the social empowerment theory discussed above with an organizational commitment to the principle of individually-generated rehabilitation goals. In other words, effective PSR services must be structured so that they are individualized and flexible to account for personal differences and to reflect a "partnership"

approach to personal growth and recovery (Anthony & Liberman, 1986; Leete, 1988:51).

Rehabilitation must be facilitated in a caring and supportive manner. Person-centered practice specifically embodies the two concepts of perceptions of personal influence and recognition of emotional support and acceptance. It reflects a programming emphasis on the individual strengths in order to counteract the demoralization long associated with psychiatric disability (Lanoil, 1982; Saleebey, 1992). This approach addresses self-esteem and confidence through the formation of supportive relationships and satisfying social roles. For example, when individuals perceive themselves to have an active decision making role in a PSR collaboration, it enhances their sense of competence or mastery. When people perceive care and friendliness, they believe they are worthy of attention and this builds self-esteem. An overall milieu of acceptance and appreciation in implementing PSR strives to create a destigmatizing environment, (Neese-Todd, 1995).

Our culture equates specific social roles with specific social status, consequently the absence of acceptable social roles or even diminished roles can erode the self-concept (Beard 1978; Fairweather, 1972; Stein & Test, 1980). Individuals who repeatedly experience the patient role are vulnerable to the loss of self-esteem and feelings of competence. People who struggle with serious mental illness are especially affected in this manner because of the socially debilitating nature of this illness. One corrective approach to this problem is to provide people with alternative social roles. There are ample opportunities in person-centered PSR to adopt legitimate social roles. Recipients of rehabilitation services cite, for example, numerous functions that are pertinent and accessible within the structure of rehabilitation activities. To illustrate this point we provide a short list of examples: researcher, service provider, peer-counselor, supportive friend, community volunteer, co-worker, student, or consultant. Studies of citizen participation also link individual empowerment—a sense of causal importance, a sense of competence, and leadership—to social and organizational change (Kieffer, 1984; Levens, 1968; Zucher, 1970). In general, individuals who were more involved with their community organization showed higher corresponding empowerment scores. More recently Zimmerman & Rappaport (1988:746) found that "psychological empowerment is related to actual participation in the life of one's community." We reason that participation in one's own "community" of rehabilitation will encourage the empowerment process so central to person-centered services. By comparison the inverse viewpoint, non-participation, would suggest a mental health system that takes full responsibility and therefore, control of a rehabilitation process. However, this tradition, though well-intended, has served only to dehumanize the individual with mental illness.

Effects of Person-Centered Practice

Although the conceptualization of person-centered practice techniques have been elaborated in general within the context of a PSR and community psychology, little work has advanced comprehensive tools for measuring levels of practice and rehabilitation outcomes of this method of service delivery among those receiving services (Beard, Propst, and Malamud, 1982; Rappaport, 1981; Rosenfield, 1992). Program evaluation is

necessary if we are to understand the effects of approach. We propose that the structures in PSR service organizations can enhance the social mechanisms that foster empowerment processes for people with serious mental illness. Effective community mental health programs have capitalized on this lesson. For example, researchers of successful model community psychiatric treatment programs have suspected that non-traditional empowering relationships between staff and those persons receiving services may account for their success, particularly in the realm of life satisfaction (Fairweather, 1972; Modrcin, Rapp, & Poertner, 1988; Mosher and Menn, 1978). In other words, an "empowerment" method of service delivery, which is characteristic of exemplary rehabilitation programs, (Rosenfield, 1987; Stein & Test, 1976, 1978) assumes that particular kinds of social interactions will amend the internalized stigma and promote an improved identity for people who have mental illness (Becker, 1963).

Sarah Rosenfield (1992) has pursued this line of inquiry within one community PSR program. Rosenfield and colleagues proposed a theoretical model that would examine program elements and assess their impact on quality of life. Rosenfield's work supports a person-centered service hypothesis. This investigation found that the "empowerment" method of service delivery, which provides decision making power to people with a mental illness within a supportive rehabilitation environment, is critical for a range of quality of life outcomes (Rosenfield, 1992; Rosenfield and Neese-Todd, 1993). Individual empowerment was related to satisfaction with living arrangements, family relations, pre-vocational activity, personal health, and safety (Rosenfield & Neese-Todd, 1993). The empowerment technology was also found to improve social functioning indicators over time. Specifically, controlling for clinical characteristics and quality of life at baseline, greater empowerment resulted in more social relationships and more social contact. Empowerment, as well, increases the extent that individuals with mental illness engage in leisure activities (Rosenfield, 1995).

Services which are sponsored by people with a mental illness also offer support for the importance of an empowerment hypothesis (Kaufmann, et al., 1989). These services are generally characterized as collaborations between consumers of mental health services and professional service providers with the governing control and responsibility resting with the individual with mental illness. Self help service initiatives provide alternative PSR supports which feature a peer-based approach. One notable example is the consumer drop-in center. This model of service has been quickly embraced by many people with mental illness and is supported by mental health policy makers as well. Mowbray and Tan (1992) describe an evaluation of a consumer drop-in center. They found that participants were generally very satisfied with these services. Participants noted increased social activities, perceived that the drop-in center facilitated community tenure, and also credited the center with freeing them from time spent in hospital settings. This was by all accounts a satisfying person-centered PSR experience where "individuals with mental illness are encouraged to make their own decisions" (Mowbray and Tan, 1992:21).

Defining Staff Competencies

Professional competency is molded by attitudes, knowledge, and skills (NIMH, 1990). In order to shape rehabilitation practices to reflect a consumer-centered agenda, we suggest that PSR staff must both engender an empowerment stance and promote individual with mental illness driven outcomes. We believe this can be accomplished in any service setting and in step with any professional tradition. In other words, a nurse, a social worker, a physician, an occupational therapist, or a teacher working in the PSR setting can all successfully engage in person-centered practice. The Psychosocial Rehabilitation Practitioner will:

Competencies 1–9

View each individual as the director of his or her rehabilitation process.

Solicit and incorporate the preferences of the persons served in the rehabilitation process.

Believe in the value of self-help and facilitate an empowerment process.

Share information about mental illness and teach the skills to manage mental illness.

Facilitate the development of recreational pursuits.

Value the ability of each person with a mental illness to seek and sustain employment.

Help each person to choose, get and keep a job.

Foster healthy interdependence.

Be able to facilitate the use of naturally occurring resources to replace the resources of the mental health system.

An empowering milieu will thus promote natural community supports and take into account the therapeutic power of self-help and autonomy. Only in this context can mutual trust and inter-dependence thrive. Direct PSR practitioners must forge person-centered outcome based rehabilitation plans as well. They must demonstrate an ability to discuss mental illness with knowledge and humanity. Competent staff will assist each person with the establishment of measurable goals. Staff must value the ability of people with mental illness to pursue employment, education, and social relationships. In addition, practitioners must provide clear strategies to cope with the symptoms of serious mental illness. Clearly, rehabilitation planning is guided by a conviction that regards participation of the person with mental illness as the crucial ingredient of successful rehabilitation.

Revising PSR Environments Through Participation of People with Mental Illness

We cannot simply rely upon the continuity of philosophy in a PSR world fraught with dynamic, political change. Continuity of service delivery, in particular a specific method of service delivery, depends on solid organizational plans. Such a blueprint will be useful in developing standards of professional competency, it will aid in the development of a training curriculum conceived to restructure existing mental health programs in order to expand and enhance person centered services, and as well, it will provide a clear model of person-centered practice that is essential to evaluate the effects of this mode of service.

In order to gain a perspective on the specific structures that promote a person-centered practice, we have considered PSR through the framework of individual involvement in a rehabilitation organization. In view of the unique demands rehabilitation activities place on service organizations and the clear correspondence between citizen participation and empowerment, we suggest that rehabilitation programs can successfully incorporate these organizational strategies. We suggest ways individuals with mental illness can 1) participate in organizational goal planning, 2) structure program values, 3) assume leadership roles, 4) develop problem solving strategies and 5) consider the distribution of authority, power, and decision making. These five facets of organizations are thought critical to augmenting opportunities for worker empowerment as well as crucial to humanizing human service organizations (Toch & Grant, 1982; Zimmerman, 1990).

Organizational Goal Planning

The prevailing goal of the PSR model is to engage psychiatrically disabled individuals with mental illness as active participants in service planning, evaluation, and implementation of their rehabilitation in order to provide them with the skills they need to live successfully in the community (Bachrach, 1989; Anthony, 1982). As this volume illustrates, PSR is a multi-faceted service which is person-oriented and committed to a collaboration between the person served and the service provider. The resultant benefits of person-centered practice have been measured in terms of the improved quality of social relations, life satisfaction and enhanced self efficacy. These outcomes are major goals in the treatment of severe mental illness and we see that they are related to empowerment practices. In order for the participation of individuals with mental illness to flourish in a PSR environment, programs must provide a culture that is flexible, informal, and not bound by status differences and professional hierarchy. The interpersonal context of PSR organizations require effective communication and cooperative problem solving which may be thwarted by hierarchical management structures and rigid routine (Mechanic, 1976). Although empowerment strategies are specifically geared to enhance personal involvement in the rehabilitation process, this is more likely to happen in an agency where all workers, regardless of status, are viewed as an important part of the contributing work force.

Organizations must take steps to assure that "active involvement of consumers in their rehabilitation process" (Anthony, Cohen, & Farkas, 1990:65) is *routine*. It must be an organizational goal. Formal program structures may serve to enhance this goal in several ways:

- The program mission statement should express this intent and be made available to all staff and individuals with mental illness.

- Rehabilitation plans and progress reports can provide opportunities to emphasize this goal. Plan formats should require input and concordance in the form of comments and an approving signature from individuals with mental illness. Individuals with mental illness who plan and evaluate their own goals will reap the benefits of self-determination.

- In a PSR environment that is inclusive, relationships and roles of staff and individual with mental illness are viewed as egalitarian partnerships, status differences are minimized, and the individuals with mental illness is viewed as the director of the rehabilitation process.

This is realized in service communities, for example, in defining program space as communal, addressing all staff and participants in the rehabilitation process on a first name basis, providing the work unit groups with actual program responsibility, and defining a decision making process that integrates individuals with mental illness in a real way (Smith & Ford, 1986).

Clarification of PSR Values

If there is a conflict between the professional values and organizational goals, efficient and reliable service performance is jeopardized (Georgopoulos, 1986). Therefore, when PSR program personnel do not espouse the person-centered philosophy, rehabilitation programs can become vulnerable to this conflict. In fact, as stated above, many practitioners of PSR have not been trained *per se* in rehabilitation theory and often they fail to recognize the intrinsic rewards of working with this population (Anthony, Cohen, & Farkas, 1990; Minkoff, 1987). This deficit necessitates augmented training in the rehabilitation setting which must provide ample opportunity for values clarification and values adoption.

In particular, knowledge of empowerment theory, the mechanisms that foster participation of persons with mental illness, and related research findings may be foreign to uninitiated program staff and program participants. As well, clarifying individual attitudes about mental illness, disability, and people who are coping with mental illness are an integral part of training PSR personnel. Psychosocial rehabilitation programs must therefore structure continuous, in-service training for staff and those receiving services to counteract the social forces that conspire to diminish an empowering environment. Weekly in-service training sessions are routine in some programs and offer the opportunity to explore the implications of the empowerment method to service delivery as it applies to all aspects of programming. Staff and persons receiving services that are accustomed to empowerment practice are best equipped to facilitate training for empowerment methods. Those persons working as PSR professionals who also have a mental illness fill a critical gap in such training (Roberts, Rotteveel, & Manos, 1995). *Prosumers* offer service environments a unique opportunity to fix a vision of person-centered practice. These staff bring an uncommon wisdom to the act of rehabilitation. As well, they remain an essential role model, provide a most important link to understanding the experience of serious mental illness, and quite willingly keep professionals honest in the presently changing world of PSR (NIMH, 1990).

Staff turnover weakens person-centered practice because an influx of new staff will dilute the process of structuring this value. If, indeed, participatory rehabilitation impacts upon morale as well as efficiency, it may correct the persistent staff recruitment and retention problems within the delivery system. Recent findings suggest that PSR staff are committed to their agencies for emotional rather than profit factors. Specifically, organizational commitment experienced by PSR staff has been explained by their perceptions of the intrinsic rewards of emotional commitment to the job and career identification offered in PSR settings (Mowday, 1979; Walko et al, 1993). Since PSR personnel are less apt to leave this field if they are emotionally engaged in the rehabilitation process, program structures can capitalize on these results and utilize management styles that will emotionally engage staff

in the process of the PSR mission. However, staff commitment to the tenets of person-centered practice must be advanced by the organizational leadership.

Organizational Leadership

Participation made real for those receiving services and staff is ultimately a programming decision determined by those individuals in positions of program control. Charles Perrow (1986) consistently points out that in the real world of organizations, power relations are rarely counterbalanced; however, the nature of PSR charges that program participants and workers remain full participants. Participatory management spreads the decision making power across groups regardless of rank and this may require great philosophical and organizational challenges for some PSR programs. In some cases, management culture must be transformed.

Leaders rank high in organizational power; therefore, they prove critical to fostering a culture that empowers individuals with mental illness. Psychosocial rehabilitation program leaders must commit program resources to the empowerment strategy. Commitment amounts to actively sponsoring genuine and varied opportunities for empowerment on all levels. Said differently, leaders must do more than simply talk about person-centered practice. An empowering environment depends upon a creative, committed, knowledgeable, and responsive leadership; these leaders must be interested in capitalizing on diverse solutions. With these thoughts in mind, we recommend a *visible* leadership approach.

Individuals with mental illness and staff with the richest empowerment experience and best communication skills should supervise less experienced staff.

In this manner the leader/facilitator will model empowering interactions. They will listen to people, use praise and feedback, promote collegial teamwork and show empathy. Leaders should be evident and accessible in PSR programs. Supervision should not take place sitting at desks or behind closed doors, but rather must rely on the PSR milieu for inspiration.

For example, if the activity of PSR is incorporated into the process of group problem solving and linked to program objectives, then everyone involved with the program will know why they are vital to the program mission and goals. As well, the practice of PSR—helping each person problem solve with a posture of respect and trust—provides all workers ample opportunity to build participation skills and thus self-esteem. This strategy promotes visibility of the leadership and harnesses the social forces that facilitates an empowerment stance.

A style of *shared* or *collaborative* leadership is also essential to person-centered practice. This is to say that key decisions which influence rehabilitation must reflect broad decision making and democratic values; agencies must incorporate the voice of all staff and all persons receiving services into judgments that affect them. The simple habit of managers asking for help with program decisions encourages community involvement and self evaluation. The act of articulating a clear process of decision making will clarify programmatic roles and counter balance the communication difficulties experienced by many people with severe mental illness. Collaborative leadership thus fosters organizational pride and trains both program participants and staff to assume real partnership roles.

Models of Collaborative Problem Solving

Psychosocial rehabilitation settings are essentially problem solving systems (Ferguson, Howell, & Bataldin, 1993). Research examining problem solving in health care settings suggests that organizational structure reflects the "problem solving framework of the system" and that problem solving adequacy has been tied to clinical efficiency (Georgopoulos, 1986:15). PSR workers and rehabilitation participants generally operate in teams thus posing a small group framework for problem solution. Theoretically, this structure recommends that all persons should contribute to the problem solving effort, yet studies of *ad hoc* experimental small group situations suggest "strong associations between high external status and higher participation, leadership, and influence" (Feiger & Schmitt, 1979:218). Clearly status differences among those individuals with mental illness and staff must be evaluated and balanced if they are to proceed in an empowering manner.

Status inequalities have compromised teaming efforts in the health field particularly among professionals and paraprofessionals (Bloom, 1980). In order for the work groups to advance the empowerment processes they should be "collegial" (Feiger & Schmitt, 1979:221), or collaborative. Specifically, this means that participation rates among group members are on the whole equal among participants. A leadership hierarchy can develop in task oriented groups when individuals with higher status are expected to contribute and perform in the leadership role to the exclusion of lower status individuals. This will defeat the person-centered practice agenda. Jones et al note (1984) that when stigmatized people are in relationships where they share comparable status (e.g., in a collegial work group) they can develop satisfying relationships and by extension improve their self-esteem. Psychosocial rehabilitation programs must provide structures that correct the status differences inherent in organizational settings.

The concept of the quality circle[2] (QC) is one model of a problem solving work group that aims to diminish hierarchy and promote collaboration. The QC method of problem solving places the responsibility for a particular solution with *front line workers and individuals with mental illness* rather than traditional managers. Assigning line staff and program participants to internal management tasks can address the issue of status equality and incorporate person driven outcomes. This allows the whole PSR program to monitor its performance as a community. These work groups not only give instrumental control to workers and those receiving services, but they serve to highlight the group and bestow a special status upon the group (Maheshwari, 1987). In theory the QC problem solving teams can be more productive than any individual because the group as a whole is accorded more authority then any one person. However, in practice, the integration of individuals with mental illness and lower status employees might prove difficult unless participation is truly decentralized and the QC groups contribute to providing actual power and decision making to work group members.

In summary, the QC intervention provides a method for team building, serves as a motivational device, teaches problem solving skills, provides leadership opportunities at the program participant and line staff level, and serves as an instrument to promote empowerment processes. Organizational communication which contributes to problem solving is enhanced by this strategy (Blau & Scott, 1969). It is not, however, a quick fix toward opening up communication. Productive circles depend on a formal training process of all those involved and effective group leadership.[3]

Authority and Decision Making

Social empowerment implies actual power and self-determination; it intimates, as well, that problems of living are often best resolved in real life situations by the people who experience the problem (Rappaport, 1981). Indeed, PSR services provide a *real community* in which to practice empowerment. Yet a *genuine* collaboration, where each person is viewed as critical resource to the rehabilitation process, does not always exist among staff and persons with mental illness. If actual decision making and authority are not distributed organizations have failed in the goal of person-centered practice.

Many professionals represent a challenge to implementing this process because the empowerment method requires staff to alter their traditional approach to rehabilitation activity and change how they view their specialist role. Although some staff prize the collaboration of people with mental illness for humanitarian reasons, many argue that their professional training and experience forge an undisputable claim of authority. In other words, implementation of this method of service delivery depends upon the people who are ultimately responsible for the program, those individuals who have the power to make innovative changes and to institute collaborative authority.

As noted above, program leadership is of primary importance. Often PSR programs have an organized leadership group whose members are appointed to serve in a governance capacity backed by organizational authority. This management group usually includes program directors and supervisory staff. It should also include leaders who have a mental illness. Actual program authority would then rest with those who live with mental illness as well as professionals.

Secondary Problems in Assuring Person-Centered Practice

Leaders must also be alert to structural realities that temper and restrain the empowerment enterprise. We discussed earlier the obstacle personnel turnover represents for the PSR program. Other factors can also potentially threaten empowerment. Elderly persons who lived most of their adult lives in the mental hospital often have difficulty adjusting to the opportunity of self-determination and choice. It is imperative that empowerment opportunities be individualized so as not to threaten a person's ability to utilize the resources of PSR setting.

Due to the important role families play in the lives of individuals with mental illness, comprehensive PSR must include addressing the needs of families as well.[4] However, families may be concerned about the empowerment process. Some family members may question the wisdom of an empowerment strategy because they have lost confidence in a mental health system that has historically blamed relatives for treatment inadequacies. This problem arises most often when family members have insufficient information regarding rehabilitation. Workers who systematically educate families on the benefits of the empowerment model will circumvent notions that hinder this experience. Program based family groups or orientations have been found useful to families be-

cause they provide information that can foster a sense of competence and carve out an appropriate role for family involvement in the rehabilitation process (Hatfield, 1990). Family members can be a crucial resource to person-centered services if they understand the goals and consequences of this practice.

In order for everyone with a mental illness to be seen as equal members of problems solving teams, everyone must have confidence in their ability to contribute effectively to the group work. The empowerment management framework depends, in other words, upon fluency within group relations. Inadequate skill training of group participants has proved disastrous among industrial settings when traditional management attempted to utilize a quality circle strategy (Maheshwari, 1987). All group participants need skill training so that they have an array of interpersonal tools to promote problem solving. Social deficits, common among people experiencing serious mental illness, can compromise the social interaction necessary for full involvement in group activities. Social skill development is a standard goal of PSR and therefore building skills that enhance group involvement supplements the objectives of psychosocial rehabilitation.

Psychosocial rehabilitation practice may embody a vision of collective decision making because it is thought to improve rehabilitation outcomes. The benefits for persons with mental illness are obvious. Yet organizational restructuring that focuses on collaboration is not a simple remedy to promote empowerment. Organizations must also ask, "What are the professional rewards for fostering empowerment?" For although person-centered rehabilitation techniques can be energizing and contagious in PSR program setting, staff incentives must be considered if organizations are to maximize the potential of each person in the program. A partnership approach to PSR promises to empower staff as well as individuals with mental illness. This means staff, as well as those participating in the program, will have more control over their work, more influence over the organization they work for, and be partner to an ameliorated rehabilitation process (Rapp, 1993). As we noted earlier, person-centered services have been tied to improvements in social functioning for people challenged by serious mental illness. Improved rehabilitation outcomes will also motivate staff. Anthony (1994) candidly notes that re-framing empowerment concepts in terms of personal responsibility may be helpful to managing unreceptive staff. This goal is clearly recognized by the broadest sector of mental health workers and therefore appeals to even the most traditional rehabilitation reasoning.

Agencies require both efficient coordination and good problem solving techniques. Unfortunately, what hampers one process often promotes the other. Blau and Scott (1969) found that hierarchy is functional when coordinating activities are required and dysfunctional when problem solving action is needed. For example, open communication improves problem solving but it is detrimental to efficient coordination. This is a balancing act for organizational leaders who must continually weigh the advantages of democratic over authoritarian management.

Conclusion

The social processes that facilitate empowerment, and thus a person-centered practice, rely upon both the individual and the environment. Psychosocial rehabilitation has crafted an approach that takes into account the individual and the social milieu. Thought is shaped by the practices in which people are engaged Indeed our expectations and meanings of others change through the activities we share with them. Person-centered PSR practice, as such, can refine our definitions of disability and ultimately provide a method for improving PSR services.

We argue that to great magnitude, organizations have a life of their own that is defined by the structures that govern the business at hand. We cannot ignore the reasoning that the activities of PSR depend upon the involvement of persons with mental illness, nor can we disregard the structures that promote participation. Practitioner proficiency rests not only with the particular individual resources staff bring to the job, but competency in this area depends upon how organizations structure the rehabilitation experience. Therefore, we propose that the social forces which foster participation can be deliberately enhanced in order that person-driven services become routine.

Notes

1. This term will be employed subsequently in the discussion.

2. For detailed descriptions of implementing quality circles see American Society for Quality Control. *Quality Control Circles—Applications, Tools, and Theory*, Milwaukee, 1979 and Fitzgerald, L. and Murphy, J., *Installing Quality Circles: A Strategic Approach,* San Diego, California, University Associates, 1982.

3. Psychiatric disability often limits social competence which is important is group participation. In order to provide individuals with mental illness

with real "roles" in task oriented groups, training in particular skills is encouraged. This problem is discussed in detail in the section entitled "Secondary Problems in Assuring Empowerment."

4. "Families" is taken to mean a group of people related by kinship or similar close ties. There are variations in the form "family" takes and the authors acknowledge that it is often the nature of interpersonal relationships that defines family as well as blood ties.

References

Anthony, W.A. (1982). "Explaining 'Psychosocial rehabilitation' by an analogy to 'physical rehabilitation.'" *Psychosocial Rehabilitation Journal, 5*(1):61-65.

_____. (1994). Institute of Health, Health Care Policy and Aging Research. Rutgers University: Post-Doctoral seminar.

Anthony, W. A., Cohen, M. & Farkas, M. (1990). *Psychosocial Rehabilitation.* Center for Psychosocial rehabilitation: Boston.

Anthony, W.A., Cohen, M. & Kennard, W. (1990). Understanding the current facts and principles of mental health systems planning. *American Psychologist, 45*(11):1249-1252.

Anthony, W.A. & Liberman, R.P. (1986). The practice of psychosocial rehabilitation: Historical, conceptual, and research base. *Schizophrenia Bulletin, 12*(4), 542-559.

Ansapach, R.R. (1979). From stigma to identity politics: political activism among the physically disabled and former mental patients. *Social Science and Medicine,* (13A):765-773.

Bachrach, L.L. (1992). Psychosocial rehabilitation and psychiatry in the care of long-term patients. *American Journal of Psychiatry* 149:1455-1463.

_____. (1989).The legacy of model programs. *Hospital and Community Psychiatry, 40*: 234-235.

Bandura, A. (1989). Human agency in social cognitive theory. *American Psychologist, 44*:1175-1184.

Beard, J.H. (1978). The rehabilitation services of fountain house. In Stein, L.I., & Test, M.A. (eds.) *Alternatives to Mental Hospital Treatment*, New York: *Schizophrenia Bulletin.*

Beard, J.H., Propst, R.N. & Malamud, T.J. (1982).The fountain house model of psychosocial rehabilitation. *Psychosocial Rehabilitation Journal,* 47-54.

Becker, H.S. (1963). *Outsiders: Studies in the Sociology of Deviance.* New York: The Free Press.

Blau, P. & Scott, W.R. (1969). Dilemmas of formal organization. In Etzioni, A. (ed.) *Readings On Modern Organizations,* Prentice-Hall Readings in Modern Sociology Series, Prentice-hall, Inc., Englewood Cliffs, NJ, 1969.

Chamberlin, J. (1984). Speaking for ourselves: An overview of the ex-psychiatric inmates' movement. *Psychosocial Rehabilitation Journal, 8*(2):56-64.

Deegan, P. (1992). The independent living movement and people with psychiatric disabilities: Taking back control over our own lives. *Psychosocial Rehabilitation Journal, 15*(3): 3-19.

Fairweather, G. (1972). *Social Change: The Challenge to Survival.* Morristown, N.J.: General Learning Press.

Feiger, S. M. & Schmitt, M.H. (1979). Collegiality in interdisciplinary health teams: Its measurement and its effects. *Social Science and Medicine,* 13A :217-229.

Ferguson, S., Howell, T., & Batalden, P. (1993). Knowledge and skills needed for collaborative work. *Quality Management in Health Care, 1*(2):1-11.

Ferguson, T. (1994). Empowerment: The key to wellness. *Network: Newsletter of*

New Jersey Self-Help Clearinghouse, 15(1):1.

Freedberg, S. (1989). Self determination: Historical perspectives and effects on current practice. *Social Work, 1*:33-38.

Glasscote, R. M. (1971). *Rehabilitating the Mentally Ill in the Community: A Study of psychosocial Rehabilitation Centers.* American Psychiatric Association.

Georgopoulos, B.S. (1986). *Organizational Structure, Problem Solving, and Effectiveness: A Comparative Study of Hospital Emergency Services.* San Francisco: Jossey-Bass Publishers.

Hatfield, A. (1990). *Family Education in Mental Illness.* Washington, D.C.: American Psychiatric Press.

Jones, E., Farina, A., Hastorf, A., Markus, H., Miller, D., & Scott, R. (1984). *Social Stigma: The Psychology of Marked Relationships.* New York, New York: Freeman.

Kaufman, C., Freund, P. & Wilson, J. (1989). Self-help in the mental health system: A model for consumer-provider collaboration. *Psychosocial Rehabilitation Journal, 13*(1):5-21.

Kieffer, C.H. (1984). Citizen empowerment: A developmental perspective. In *Studies in Empowerment,* 9-35, Haworth Press, Inc.

Lanoil, J. (1982). An analysis of the psychiatric psychosocial rehabilitation center. *Psychosocial Rehabilitation Journal,* 1:55-59.

Leete, E. (1988). A consumer perspective on psychosocial treatment. *Psychosocial Rehabilitation Journal, 12*(2):45-52.

Lehman, A.F., Possidents, S., & Hawker, F. (1986). The quality of life of chronic patients in a state hospital and in community residences. *Hospital and Community Psychiatry, 37*:901-907.

Levens. (1968). Organizational affiliation and powerlessness: A case study of the welfare poor. *Social Problems, 16*:18-32.

Link, B., Cullen, F.T., Frank, J., & Wozniak, J.F. (1987). The social rejection of former mental patients: Understanding why labels matter. *American Journals of Sociology, 92*(6):1461-1500.

Maheshwari, B.L. (1987). *Quality Circles.* Oxford & IBH Publishing Co., PVT. Ltd., New Delhi.

Mechanic, D. (1976). *The Growth of Bureaucratic Medicine: An Inquiry into the Dynamics of Patient Behavior and the Organization of Medical Care.* John Wiley and Sons, Inc.

Minkoff, K. (1987). Resistance of mental health professionals to working with the chronic mentally ill. In Meyerson, A.T. (ed.) *Barriers to Treating the Chronic Mentally Ill, New Directions for Mental Health Services.* San Francisco: Jossey-Bass, 33:3-20.

Modrcin, M., Rapp, C., & Poertner, J. (1988). The evaluation of case management services with the chronically mentally ill. *Evaluation and Program Planning, 11*:301-314.

Mosher, L.R. & Menn, A.Z. (1978). Community residential treatment for schizophrenia: Two-year follow-up. *Hospital and Community Psychiatry, 29*(11):715-723.

Mowbray, C.T. & Tan, C. (1992). Evaluation of an innovative consumer-run service model: The drop-in center. *Innovations & Research, 1*(2):19-24, 1992.

Mowbray, C.T., Wellwood, R., & Chamberlain, P.(1988). Project stay: A consumer-run support service. *Psychosocial Rehabilitation Journal, 12*(1):33-42, 1988.

Mowday, R.T., Steers, R.M., & Porter, L.W. (1979). The measurement of organizational commitment. *Journal of Vocational Behavior, 14*:224-247.

Moxley, D. & Freddolino, P. (1990). A model of advocacy for promoting client self-determination in psychosocial rehabilitation. *Psychosocial Rehabilitation Journal, 14*(2):69-82.

National Institute on Disability and Rehabilitation Research. (1993). *CORD: Constituency-Oriented Research and Dissemination.* A Proposed Policy Statement for NIDRR, November.

National Institute of Mental Health. (1990). *Clinical Training in Serious Mental Illness.* Lefley, Harriet P. (ed.) DHHS Pub. No. (Adm)90-1679. Washington, D.C.; Supt. of Docs, U.S. Govt. Print. Off.

National Institute of Mental Health. (1991). *Caring for people with severe mental disorders: A national plan of research to improve services.* DHHS Pub. No. (ADM)91-1762. Washington, D.C.: Supt of Docs., U.S. Govt. Print. Off.

Neese-Todd, S. (1995). *Stigma awareness: The consequences of social empowerment in rehabilitation programs.* Unpublished manuscript.

Pearlin, L.I., Leiberman, M.A., Menaghan, E.G., & Mullan, J.T. (1981). The stress process. *Journal of Health and Social Behavior, 22*:337-356.

Perrow, C. (1986). *Complex organizations: A critical essay* (3rd ed.). New York: Random House.

Rapp, C.A., Shera, W., & Kisthardt, W. (1993). Research strategies for consumer empowerment of people with severe mental illness. *Social Work, 38*(6):727-735.

Rappaport, J. (1981). In praise of paradox: A social policy of empowerment over prevention. *American Journal of Community Psychology, 9*(1):1-24.

_____. (1985). The power of empowerment language. *Social Policy, 6*(2):15-21.

Rappaport, J., Swift, C. & Hess, R. (1984). (Eds.) *Studies in empowerment: steps toward understanding and action.* NY: Haworth Press.

Roberts, M., Rotteveel, J. & Manos, E. (1995). Mental health consumers as professionals: Disclosure in the workplace. *American Rehabilitation*, 20-23.

Rosenfield, S. (1987). Service organization and quality of life among the seriously mentally ill. In Mechanic, D. (ed.). *Improving Mental Health Services: What the Social Sciences Can Tell Us, New Directions for Mental Health Services,* 36:47-59.

_____. (1992). Factors contributing to the subjective quality of life of the chronic mentally ill. *Journal of Health and Social Behavior, 33*: 299-315.

Rosenfield, S., Mechanic, D., & Neese-Todd, S. (1995) Unpublished Manuscript.

Rosenfield, S. & Neese-Todd, S. (1993). Elements of a psychosocial clubhouse program associated with a satisfying quality of life. *Hospital and Community Psychiatry, 44*:76-78.

Saleebey, D. (1992). *The strengths perspective in social work practice.* Longman Publishing Group: New York.

Smith, M.K. & Ford, J.(1986). Client involvement: Practical advice for professionals. *Psychosocial Rehabilitation Journal, 9*(3):25-34.

Stein, L.I. & Test, M.A. (1978). Training in community living: Research design and results. In Stein, L.I. and Test, M.A. (eds.) *Alternatives to Mental Hospital Treatment.* New York: Plenum Press.

_____. (1980). Alternatives to mental hospital treatment. *Archives of General Psychiatry, 37*:392-397:1980.

Toch, H. & Grant, J.D. (1982). *Reforming human services: Change through participation,* V.142, Sage Library of Social Research, Sage Publication, Inc.

Walko, S.E., Pratt, C., Siiter, R., & Ellison, K. (1993). Predicting staff retention in psychosocial rehabilitation. *Psychosocial Rehabilitation Journal, 16*:30:150-153.

Zimmerman, M. (1990). Toward a theory of learned hopefulness: A structural model analysis of participation and empowerment. *Journal of Research in Personality, 24*:71-86.

Zimmerman, M. & Rappaport, J. (1988). Citizen participation, perceived control, and psychological empowerment. *American Journal of Community Psychology, 16*:725-750.

Zucher. (1970). The poverty board: Some consequences of "maximum feasible participation." *Journal of Social Issues, 26*:85-107.

5

Practitioner Competencies

Diane Weinstein

Introduction

The field of psychosocial rehabilitation is receiving increased attention as more people become aware of its efficacy in the treatment and rehabilitation of adults with a serious and persistent mental illness. With more than 2,000 agencies today providing psychosocial rehabilitation services (Hughes, 1994), there is a need for a competent workforce of practitioners who are committed to the highest standards of job performance. Psychosocial rehabilitation proudly encompasses a diverse workforce. A recent study by Matrix Research Institute and IAPSRS surveyed over 10,000 people and found that practitioners with mental illness comprised 12% of the total labor force (Blankertz et al.). The study further reported that more than 26% of the workforce identified themselves as either African-Americans, Hispanic, Asian or Native Americans, while academic backgrounds of personnel show that approximately 22% of the workforce are high school graduates, 13% have some college, 38% have bachelor degrees, and 26% have graduate level degrees.

This chapter presents the reader with an understanding of the knowledge, skills, values, attitudes, and outcomes that are central to practitioner competence and ethical conduct. It includes descriptions of the interpersonal, professional, intrapersonal, and self-management competencies that are relevant to all psychosocial rehabilitation models and technologies and applicable to the delivery of each service component within a comprehensive community support system. Authorities in the field often list the traits of quality staff and recommend that programs hire personnel who are ethical, empathic, flexible; who offer hope; who believe in recovery; who build on successes; who are willing to have fun; and who can tolerate ambiguity. This chapter describes the application of these characteristics in the practice of psychosocial rehabilitation. While the level of mastery may vary from practitioner to practitioner, these competencies are relevant to the work performed by practitioners with graduate level degrees, as well as their colleagues with high school diplomas.

In 1993, IAPSRS brought together a group of experts in the practice of psychosocial rehabilitation to participate in a concept mapping process to define psychosocial rehabilitation workforce competencies (Trochim and Cook, 1993). An extensive literature review of practitioner competencies was completed by

Jonikas (1993) in preparation for this seminal gathering, which represented all of the models and technologies of psychosocial rehabilitation. An earlier project of the Southern Regional Education Board in the 1980s addressed the characteristics of effective psychosocial rehabilitation workers (Friday & McPheeters, 1985) and case managers (Friday, 1986).

Agencies delivering community support services recognize the knowledge, values, attitudes, beliefs and skills that are components of competence in order to hire and train quality staff (Anthony, 1980; Anthony, Cohen, & Farkas, 1990; Friday & McPheeters, 1985; Friday, 1986; Trochim & Cook, 1993; Stroul, 1985; Curtis, 1993; Mosher & Burti, 1994; Curtis, Tanzman & McCabe, 1992; Jonikas, 1993; Stroul, 1993; Danley & Mellen; 1987; Spaulding, Harig, & Schwab, 1987). Training manuals that are premised on the principles of psychosocial rehabilitation are important tools that can be used to teach the practitioner the competencies they need to develop a comprehensive rehabilitation program (Finley, 1990; Pernell-Arnold & Finley, 1992; Hoeltzel & Finley, 1992; Kuehnel, Howard, Backer, & Liberman, 1994; Anthony, Pierce, Cohen, & Cannon, 1980).

The foundations of psychosocial rehabilitation practice are imbedded in theory espoused by practitioners from other helping professions. The seminal work of Carl Rogers (1959) describes the characteristics of a helping relationship. Robert Carkhuff (1972, 1973, 1976, 1977) has developed training techniques to develop interpersonal skills, problem solving, and training approaches for human service workers, and Irvin Yalom (1985) has described the methods to facilitate groups. Textbooks for students in the helping professions substantiate the need for practitioners to demon-strate competency based approaches that include a basic set of abilities required to solve problems (Gambrill, 1983; Compton & Galaway, 1983). Clearly, the competencies that qualified psychosocial rehabilitation practitioners must master are those shared by their colleagues in other human service organizations providing community based services (Human Services Research Institute, 1995).

The requisite interpersonal, professional, intrapersonal and self-management competencies allow practitioners to be positive agents of change in their work to help individuals with mental illness achieve goals that are self determined. Gambrill (1983) considers interpersonal skills "socio-political" in nature because they concern exchanges that involve the distribution and control of resources, authority, status, and power. The mastery of interpersonal skills promotes the development and maintenance of the rehabilitation relationship by learning to listen attentively, ask helpful questions, promote constructive behaviors and present useful interventions, through the performance of effective social behavior and coping skills (Gambrill, 1983). Having positive regard and displaying genuineness, empathy, and warmth are also enveloped in interpersonal competence (Friday & McPheeters, 1985).

Professional role competencies require the practitioner to know how and when to be an agent of change. Understanding the standards of ethical practice is a fundamental professional competency (IAPSRS, 1996). Just as important as acquiring the skills of particular intervention strategies is learning how to use oneself effectively during their implementation. Negotiation skills, a willingness to have fun, setting limits, overcoming prejudices, and asking for help are some of the critical professional role competencies (Trochim & Cook, 1993).

Intrapersonal competencies represent the personal values and beliefs of the practitioner that affect their relationships with other people (Friday & Mc-Pheeters, 1985). This includes a self-awareness of how one's own personality traits are perceived by others and their positive or negative influence on the rehabilitation relationship. Being enthusiastic, creative, flexible and patient, having a sense of humor and the capacity to handle stress are some of the practitioner qualities that constitute intrapersonal competence.

Self-management competencies encompass the attitudes and skills that practitioners need to perform all of the tasks and activities inherent in their job. Having language art skills to write comprehensive rehabilitation programs, read and understand materials about mental health treatment and rehabilitation, the ability to manage one's time and prioritize tasks, tolerate ambiguity, and enjoy diversity are some of the essential components for self-management competence (Trochim & Cook, 1993; Friday and McPheeter, 1985; Friday, 1986).

Competency I

Listen effectively.

Interpersonal Competencies for Direct Service Staff

Practitioners must learn how to accurately hear what persons with mental illness are saying, while they simultaneously convey a respect and understanding of the person and their message. Gambrill (1983) observes that people want to be understood without being given advice and acknowledged

that their message has been heard. Some of these communication techniques have been widely defined (Corey & Corey; Hoeltzel & Finley, 1992; Pernell-Arnold.& Finley, 1990; Gambrill, 1983; Compton & Galaway; 1984). They include:

- **Active Listening**—The practitioner absorbs the content, gestures, mannerisms, body movement, etc. of the individual and observes subtle changes or incongruences in any of these, employs intuition about what is not being said, and pays attention to any obstacles that are interfering with effective listening.

- **Reflecting**—The practitioner rephrases the affective elements of the person's message to convey an understanding of the feelings expressed in a genuine way.

- **Paraphrasing**—Without being mechanical, the practitioner closely mirrors the content of what has been said to indicate that the practitioner has accurately heard the message and to provide the individual an opportunity to hear back important issues.

- **Clarifying**—Clarifying summarizes the major issues and brings them into a sharper focus. This allows the individual to get a better picture of the communication and assists in understanding underlying issues and conflicting feelings.

- **Reframing**—From information that the person has labeled as negative, the practitioner finds some positive aspect to illuminate. Reframing is a way to provide an alternative interpretation of something that is seen as a problem.

- *Summarizing*—The practitioner condenses key issues that have been raised to help bring a dialogue to its close, identify a common theme, or provide an opportunity to review and further explore options and potential areas to target for rehabilitation strategies.

Finley (1990) notes that in interactions "facial expression far outweighs the power of words used in communication" and identifies the following key behaviors that should be observed by the practitioner: eye contact, head and facial movements, body posture, vocal quality, and distracting personal habits. Effective communication is complicated; it relies upon the sender and receiver recognizing and transcending differences in cultural backgrounds, social roles, knowledge base, internal frame of reference, value systems, personality factors, communication abilities, needs and goals. Finley (1990) illustrates this with examples of cultural variations that affect eye contact: Asian-Americans may avoid direct eye contact with an authority figure to show respect, while most Americans from a European descent will look directly at their communication partner. Not only do African-Americans tend to use indirect eye contact, but they are less likely to demonstrate physical cues of attentive listening that the speaker with a Eurocentric background may expect, such as nodding one's head intermittently during a dialogue.

multiple strategies. These include identifying the reasons behavioral changes are indicated and their potential consequences, the practitioner's willingness to serve as a role model for the desired change, and the worker's ability to reinforce constructive behavioral changes that have been made (Trochim & Cook, 1993).

Helping a person make intentional changes requires the practitioner to engage the person in goal-directed activities that are structured in an orderly problem solving process (Compton & Galaway, 1984). Motivating change requires practitioner skill in breaking down a problem into smaller components that can be sequentially addressed. Compton and Galaway (1984) observe that a "linear sequencing of tasks is an oversimplification of the process" and that sometimes clarity is not achieved until one embarks on the rehabilitation process. Furthermore, it may take a failed intervention to identify the optimal solution, or that the initial presenting problem is not the significant problem that needs to be worked on.

Motivation can be dependent upon the worker demonstrating timing skills that anticipate what needs to be done and "jumping in" when a person is prepared to act or risk losing the moment when critical opportunities for change are presented (Swayze, 1994). Learning to seize the moment is a way that practitioners use naturally occurring events as tools for change (Hodges, 1990).

Competency 2

Motivate the person served to learn new behaviors.

Competency 3

Use the helping relationship to facilitate change.

Mobilizing positive behavioral changes depends on practitioners employing

In order to facilitate change in the helping relationship, a practitioner needs to be seen as a "real person," which allows him to expose his own set of strengths and skills, as well as being honest about personal struggles (Curtis, Tanzman, & McCabe, 1992). Practitioners must learn to employ their own life experiences in ways that encourage and guide others to achieve their own self determined goals (Trochim & Cook, 1993).

Practitioners in the helping relationship simultaneously act as friends and advocates and "provide tangible proof that the client is cared about and belongs" (Hodges, 1990). Hodges notes that while friends are nonjudgmental, they also help people see their blind spots and overcome dysfunctional behaviors. When practitioners are acting as advocates, they aggressively pursue strategies that enable a person to receive any benefits and services that a person is entitled to receive, urge others to be understanding and supportive, and recognize positive efforts. According to Hodges, understanding the following four rules of thumb will provide a solid foundation for a helping relationship:

- People want control over their lives. Therefore, while practitioners should help a person obtain what they want and need, it is important to let individuals do for themselves all that they can.

- What a person can or cannot do is unknown until that person has had every opportunity to try.

- Optimism and hope are sometimes the most important qualities that practitioners bring to the relationship.

- It is not enough for the practitioner to reduce discomfort; he or she must also work to increase the individual's skills and resources.

In a helping relationship, practitioners must express their approval of every accomplishment (Trochim & Cook, 1993). While engaging in a helping or therapeutic relationship is serious work, it is important to communicate a joy in living and introduce an element of fun. Making positive changes in one's life should feel good.

Competency 4

Offer hope to others.

Practitioners offer hope by articulating a sincere belief that the person with a mental illness can lead a fulfilling life. When practitioners believe that individuals with mental illness can grow and make productive changes, they are motivated to corral all of their personal resources, as well as those of the agency and community to advance the rehabilitation process (Friday, 1986). Focusing on successes, helping individuals recognize personal growth, minimizing adversity, and introducing humor in situations that would benefit from levity all increase hopefulness (Trochim & Cook; 1993).

Hodges (1990) observes when there is optimism and an emphasis on the individual's strengths and assets, positive relationships are more likely to ensue. "Clear, consistent realistic and positive expectations offered by practitioners are powerful determinants of behavior and can help individuals with mental illness begin a remoralization process that will not only sustain them but also the worker" (Mosher & Burti, 1994). However, Mosher and Burti (1989) warn practitioners to not put forth unrealistic expectations or send flawed messages of being a "rescuer" and then proceed to label individuals with mental illness as "uncooperative" or "unmotivated" rescuees when they are unable to achieve inappropriate goals.

Persons with mental illness and their families often assume that mental health practitioners understand the importance of having someone believe in them, which becomes a catalyst for them to believe in themselves. Spaniol and Koehler (1994) write that hope is an important aspect of coping with a psychiatric disability and survival is barely possible without hope. Personal and familial devastation is experienced when a practitioner extinguishes hope. Stigma, discrimination, negative expectations, pejorative stereotypes, and pessimism about one's potential for well-being are barriers to recovery and occur when there is a loss of hope and discouragement from others, such as mental health professionals (Campbell et al., 1989; Lovejoy, 1982). People need dreams and aspirations that an improved quality of life is possible.

Competency 5

Believe in the recovery process.

"Recovery is what people with disabilities do" says Anthony (1993) in his essay "Recovery From Mental Illness: The Guiding Vision of the Mental Health Service System in the 1990s." The process and definition of recovery is unique and personal to each individual who experiences it. While recovery does not mean that a person is cured, in remission, or that all symptoms have ceased, it is typically synonymous with the ability to manage the psychiatric disability and to function effectively in daily life. Symptoms may interfere less frequently; the duration between acute illness episodes is lengthened; recompensation becomes easier; and the individual is actively participating in meaningful endeavors that are self-determined.

Recovery entails the development of coping strategies that are tailored to individual circumstances to modulate a person's vulnerabilities to stress. Anthony (1993) notes that recovery can occur without professional intervention. However, the role of psychosocial rehabilitation practitioners is to facilitate recovery. He emphasizes that the practitioner's task is more than delivering an array of specialized mental health services. It must entail a person's engagement in a variety of normative and integrative activities in the community at large and is facilitated by support from people that are valued by the individual, such as family, friends, co-workers, teachers, mental health practitioners, and peers who are participants in mutual support organizations.

Medication, community support services, willingness to manage symptoms, vocational activity, spirituality, knowledge about mental illness and acceptance of the illness, mutual aid, and significant others were the most prevalent factors that individuals with mental illness identified as ingredients to recovery, according to a study conducted by Sullivan (1994). As people reflect upon ingredients that helped them internalize recovery, they often reference the presence of people who believed in them and gave them hope that recovery was possible (Leete, 1988). Practitioners must demonstrate their belief in the recovery process and help people believe in their inherent capacity to grow, develop a personal vision of a better future, and identify practical strategies to achieve that vision (Trochim & Cook, 1993; Curtis, 1993). Lefley (1994) affirms the importance of the recovery vision, but reminds practitioners that imbuing a person with hope does not mean promoting an unrealistic vision and advises practitioners to "give adequate support to those who have a good potential for speedy recovery, and avoid pressuring those whose progress takes longer."

Empowerment is a critical ingredient of recovery. Gaining control, mastery, and power over one's life are associated with empowerment. Empowerment is promoted in environments that maximize the availability of choices, provide people the skills and knowledge necessary to make informed decisions, and give people the responsibility to make choices among true alternatives. It is important to respect the choices people make and to advocate for self-determination. The process of empowerment also means allowing people to take risks, holding them responsible for the consequences of their decisions and providing a supportive environment to learn from mistakes (Williams, 1994; Hughes). Empowerment is imbued in the philosophy of psychosocial rehabilitation.

It has become synonymous with the mission of mutual support organizations. Daniel Fisher, a psychiatrist and a person in recovery, emphasizes the essential role that peer support groups and networks play in providing safe environments that are characterized by unconditional social acceptance, empathic understanding, feedback and modeling. People can disclose their personal stories, which is vital for continued recovery (Fisher, 1993).

Competency 6

Build on successes and minimize failures.

Dincin (1975) observes that individuals with mental illness have experienced failures in one or more important functions in their lives and that generating successful experiences is one of the most creative and important uses of psychosocial rehabilitation. Practitioners help restore a person's self confidence as they point out and celebrate success no matter how small, teach individuals how to acknowledge each of their successes, review and reframe failures as learning experiences, and support risk-taking behaviors as people seek ways to learn new behaviors (Trochim & Cook, 1993; Friday & McPheeters; 1985).

Hodges (1990) suggests practitioners place an emphasis on day-to-day successes by developing an ability to expect good things to happen, finding something positive to reinforce during each contact; and defining goals in small and reasonable steps. Not only should the practitioner use verbal praises but also recognize the value of nonverbal cues, such as positive facial expressions, smiles, direct eye contact with an affirmative nod, leaning forward during a dialogue, reducing interpersonal distance, etc. (Gambrill, 1983).

Practitioners need to realize that the vision of achieving a long-term rehabilitation goal may not be an adequate incentive to remain motivated on a daily basis; they also need to develop methods to frequently recognize incremental goal directed behaviors (Anthony, Pierce, Cohen, & Cannon, 1980). Anthony, Pierce, Cohen, and Cannon, (1980) advise practitioners that the "particular behavior that is selected as the reinforcer must come from the individual's frame of reference" rather than be a reinforcer that works for the practitioner. Positive changes can be charted or recorded in a diary that can be reviewed as a visible reminder of progress. While reinforcers of successful behaviors are important, PSR practitioners should teach each person to self-acknowledge successes and devise personal reinforcers to reward himself.

People also learn from their failures and practitioners should remember the expression "nothing ventured nothing gained" applies to all people. Interfering or rescuing someone from a risky or potentially poor decision can ultimately impede confidence building, decision making, and learning the unpleasant consequences of flawed choices (Williams, 1994; Hughes).

Competency 7

Demonstrate connecting skills.

Practitioners must have the ability to develop close bonds with the individuals they serve (Anthony, Cohen & Farkas, 1990). Connecting is premised on accepting the person where they are and being interested in their interpretations of events and needs. It exists in a caring relationship but not in a controlling one (Trochim & Cook, 1993). Developing a close bond and providing the ongoing personal support needed are activities that practitioners need to pursue throughout the rehabilitation diagnostic, planning and intervention process (Anthony, Cohen & Farkas, 1990.)

Mosher and Burti (1989) describe the *joiner* technique as one of the methods that facilitates rapport and is premised on non-judgmental behavior, respect, and total attentiveness upon the part of the practitioner. It is reinforced when the worker is informal during interactions and can be viewed as a person who shares information. Informality diminishes attributions of power. Sharing something about the world that is common (e.g., elaborating upon a com-

mon interest in old movies) facilitates connectiveness and is particularly useful when initiating a new relationship. Using the person's descriptive language, exact phraseology, or metaphors to garner clarification or additional information is another joiner or connecting technique.

Competency 8

Normalize interactions and program practices.

Normalizing services and service settings is one of the guiding principles in the philosophy of the community support system (Stroul, 1986). It is embraced in the practice of psychosocial rehabilitation and is demonstrated by practitioners when they design and structure approaches that are similar or comparable to normal lifestyles in the community and utilize learning environments that encourage social acceptability, minimize individual shortcomings, and provide opportunities to explore and practice new skills (Pernell-Arnold & Finley, 1992).

Programmatic expectations must be consistent with those of the broader community and practitioners need to develop the ability to generalize program experiences to interactions with members of the community at large (Trochim & Cook, 1993). The objective of normalizing interactions and program practices is to promote integration and community inclusion. However, Condeluci (1994) observes "You can't get inclusion through exclusion," and advises practitioners to eliminate agency practices that are barriers to community participation. PSR practitioners need to examine the rationale behind modalities that separate people with disabilities from their nondisabled peers. Providing services in the least restrictive environment, helping people establish and maintain natural supports, and utilizing generic community resources are ways to enhance normative interactions and integration (Curtis, Tanzman & McCabe, 1992).

Inclusion does not mean that a person has to deny their disability, but rather true inclusion acknowledges one's differences while also respecting and celebrating diversity (Candeluci, 1994). To facilitate inclusion, practitioners and rehabilitation programs need to establish limits or basic rules that replicate those of the community at large. These include responding to illegal activities (petty crime such as stealing, bizarre or disruptive behaviors, dangerous behaviors, etc.), to provide program participants with the reasons these limits have been set, as well as an opportunity to develop program guidelines and rules to handle transgressions (Trochim & Cook, 1993; Pernell-Arnold, 1992).

Competency 9

Relate to others effectively.

A person who relates well to others is someone who "genuinely likes people" and demonstrates a capacity to establish authentic and honest relationships with a wide variety of people (Curtis, Tanzman, & McCabe, 1992; Friday & McPheeters, 1985). The practitioner must have the ability to relate to individuals with mental illness, peers, family members, and others in the broader mental health system and community at large. Demonstrating involvement in a caring way promotes a joining with the participants in the support system, while sharing feelings facilitates an open commu-

nication system and interactions that can be seen as coming from equals (Hoetlzel & Finley, 1992).

Gambrill (1983) emphasizes that being genuine parallels congruence in relationships whereby the practitioner does not hide behind his or her "professional role" in order to protect oneself, but instead interacts in a nondefensive manner when confronted about negative information about oneself and yet can still be confrontive, be spontaneous, and self-disclose. Compton and Galaway (1984) describe genuineness as being demonstrated by practitioners when they can "enter a relationship without anything of themselves to prove or protect, so they are unafraid of the emotions of others." Relating well to others means being a person who is honest and humble, talks with people and not at them, and demonstrates a willingness to acknowledge one's own fallibility while simultaneously exhibiting a determination to do one's best.

Competency 10

Generate energy and enthusiasm.

PSR practitioners need to exhibit a "can do" attitude, and show a sense of spirit and optimism (Curtis, Tanzman, & McCabe, 1992). Generating energy and enthusiasm is demonstrated in people who are willing to roll up their sleeves when work needs to be done and employ their own initiative to start and finish tasks. Hodge (1990) notes that it is the worker's role to help a person feel better, which can be facilitated when the worker is seen as a source of energy and motivation. Practitioners need to remember that some individuals with mental illness sometimes feel that they have very little reason for getting up or do not have a support system in place that reinforces their productivity. The energy of the practitioner can serve as a mobilization force to encourage people to actively participate in their rehabilitation process.

Competency 11

Demonstrate an ability to nurture.

A capacity for nurturance fosters development and growth. Nurturance is demonstrated by showing warmth, interest, respect, and approval, as well as conveying positive regard through a non-evaluative and nonpossessive caring relationship (Finley, 1990; Gambrill, 1983; Friday, 1986; Friday & McPheeters, 1985). Nurturance is an adjunct to other supportive behaviors that practitioners employ when people are venturing into new and frightening territories, discarding dysfunctional behaviors, or attempting constructive changes (Hoetlzel & Finley, 1992).

According to the Well-Being Project, a survey conducted by The California Network of Mental Health Clients, prejudgements of a person that are based on stereotypic misconceptions reduce the possibility for warmth and getting close to others (Campbell et al., 1989). Unfortunately, when a person experiences rejection, he or she may socially withdraw from other opportunities to develop a nurturing relationship. Offering assistance and suggestions for change in a non-judgmental environment that emphasizes attentive listening and positive feedback are methods that demonstrate warmth and promote participation in a rehabilitation process (Gambrill, 1983).

Competency 12

Demonstrate an ability to empathize.

Empathic understanding and empathic acceptance are characteristics of a helping relationship (Finley, 1990; Gambrill, 1983). Empathy requires practitioners to be sensitive to the subjective world of the individual and is demonstrated by an accurate communication of another person's feelings, thoughts, and experiences in a genuine manner (Friday, 1986; Friday & McPheeters; 1985). Anthony, Pierce, Cohen and Cannon (1980) note that the interpersonal interviewing skills of attending, observing, listening, and responding are often summarized under the term *empathy*.

Gambrill (1983) emphasizes the need for practitioners to offer "empirically grounded assessment and intervention methods" as key components of an empathic relationship and identifies the following common stumbling blocks when a practitioner fails to be seen as empathic: saying nothing when a comment should be offered, distorting the message, misinterpreting a person's feeling, prematurely offering a solution, belaboring an exploration of an issue when it is time to move on, or failing to understand their own feelings or distracting behaviors which interfere in their ability to be viewed as empathic.

Competency 13

Demonstrate an ability to interact and provide support in a nonjudgmental fashion.

Being non-judgmental is a critical aspect of connecting with an individual with a mental illness (Mosher & Burti, 1994). It is demonstrated by communicating positive regard to others in ways that do not belittle, demean, or patronize them; using language and behavior that shows respect, perpetuates the dignity of an individual, and maintains privacy; and providing feedback about an individual's behavior without making pejorative global assumptions about the person (Trochim & Cook, 1993; Friday & McPheeters, 1985; Curtis, 1993). According to Gambrill (1983), "There is no more important task you have than to be non-judgmental."

However, practitioners may be unaware of personal biases and how they communicate them, making this a more difficult task than perhaps initially thought. While practitioners should avoid imposing their values on others, this does not mean that they must agree to help individuals with mental illness pursue outcomes that conflict with the practitioner's personal value system (Gambrill, 1983). It is critical that practitioners consult with supervisors when personal conflicts arise and impede one's ability to be objective and non-judgmental.

Competency 14

Work effectively with colleagues who have psychiatric disabilities.

Psychosocial rehabilitation has promoted the employment of practitioners who have personal experience with mental illness. Some practitioners openly disclose information about their psychiatric disability and involvement with the mental health system, while other workers do not choose to self-identify. Consumer colleagues bring experience with mental illness and practice coping with a psychiatric disability to the psychosocial rehabilitation process.

PSR practitioners must avoid using pejorative stereotypes and derogatory terms that stigmatize those individuals with mental illness. Workers should act in a straightforward and honest manner among colleagues who self-identify that is comparable to interactions with any other worker and should show sensitivity to a colleague who is encountering difficulties in their dual role as practitioner and consumer (Trochim & Cook, 1993; Fridays & McPheeters, 1985).

Deegan (1992) raises issues that are relevant to resolve for collaboration among practitioner co-workers:

- Are there incongruencies between the stated ideal of consumer participation and its actual practice?

- What is the impact of tokenism?

- What is the effect of a lack of representativeness when only "reasonable" individuals with mental illness are hired and expected to speak for a very diverse population?

- How do colleagues help staff with mental illness deal with role strain that occurs when a practitioner with a mental illness employs roles and functions that are effective outside of the workplace setting, but are considered inappropriate with workplace performance?

- Does the use of mental health jargon exclude staff members with mental illness who have not been taught or familiarized with these communication styles?

- Are there economic or other factors that are barriers for real integration such as lower wages, dependency upon public transportation, or inability to attend educational or professional trainings or social gatherings outside of work etc.?

Friday and McPheeters (1985) observe that employee support programs and staff retreats are ways that organizations can improve worker satisfaction, motivation, and productivity, and renew worker commitment to the overarching goals of an agency while assuring workers that their basic needs are recognized. In these settings, staff members with mental illness and their colleagues are provided excellent opportunities to develop staff cohesiveness; to learn from each other; and to examine values, attitudes, and interpersonal reactions.

Competency 15

Follow code of ethics.

Professional Role Competencies for Direct Service Staff

Ethical Conduct of a Psychosocial Practitioner Encompasses the Following:

It is essential that practitioners comport their behavior within the recognized standards of ethical conduct. Sometimes practitioners fail to realize the extent of their influence over others. An inadvertent failure to do so may harm individuals with mental illness, practitioners, the profession or the community. The following ethical areas are based on the Code of Ethics for Psychiatric Rehabilitation Practitioners (IAPSRS, 1996):

- *Propriety*—The psychosocial rehabilitation practitioner maintains high standards of personal conduct. He or she does not engage in personal conduct that compromises the fulfillment of professional responsibilities. One must be knowledgeable and obey all laws and statutes applicable to one's work. A practitioner distinguishes between statements and actions that are made as a private person versus those as a practitioner; and refrains from any activity in which personal problems are likely to impair performance.

- *Competence and Professional Development*—The practitioner strives to become and remain proficient in the performance of functions and in the practice of the field.

- *Integrity*—The psychosocial rehabilitation practitioner acts in accordance with the highest standards of practitioner integrity and impartiality which includes being alert to and resisting influences that interfere with the exercising of practitioner discretion and impartial judgment. The practitioner does not exploit relationships for personal gain, but is continually cognizant of personal needs, values and one's potential influence with individuals being served. The practitioner avoids any exploitation of trust and dependency of the persons served and never accepts or gives anything of value for receiving or making a referral.

The Psychosocial Rehabilitation Practitioner's Ethical Responsibility to Persons Receiving Services Encompasses the Following:

- *Primacy of the interests of individuals with mental illness*—The practitioner serves individuals with mental illness with the maximum application of professional skill, competence, and advocacy. He or she does not exploit relationships for personal advantage. A provider does not practice, condone, facilitate or collaborate with any form of discrimination. He or she avoids relationships or commitments that conflict with the interests of the individuals being served and under no circumstances engages in sexual activities with individuals being served.

The practitioner provides individuals being served with complete and accurate information regarding the extent and nature of services available, their legal and fiscal limitations, criteria for discharge, and information about the practitioner's qualifications to provide services. He or she apprises rehabilitation participants of their risks, rights, opportunities and obligations.

The provider coordinates services with other providers in a cooperative manner while respecting the wishes of the individuals being served. He or she recognizes that families can be an important factor in rehabilitation process and, with the consent of the individual being served, strives to enlist family understanding and involvement. The practitioner seeks advice and counsel of colleagues and supervisors whenever it is in the best interest of the person being served. He or she also discontinues the practitioner relationship when it is in the best interest of the rehabilitation recipient and services are no longer required.

The practitioner anticipates the interruption of services and promptly notifies persons receiving services. He or she does not allow personal or fiscal considerations to influence rehabilitation objectives. The practitioner engages in discharge planning with all individuals being served and making transfers to other practitioners when appropriate.

- *Rights and prerogatives of individuals being served*—The practitioner makes every effort to support self determination. When acting on behalf of individuals with mental illness adjudged legally incapacitated, the practitioner should safeguard their interests, rights and previously expressed choices. And when dealing with another individual that has been legally authorized to act on behalf of a individual with mental illness, the practitioner should always take into consideration previously expressed desires of the individual.

- *Confidentiality and privacy*—The practitioner respects the privacy of person being served, holds in confidence information obtained in the course of rehabilitation and releases such information only at the request of the person receiving services and as prescribed by law. Individuals are given timely access to any official records concerning them. The practitioner obtains written permission before taping, recording or permitting third party observation of activities and thoroughly briefs all persons who must have access to the records of the standards of confidentiality to be observed. He or she safeguards the maintenance, storage, and disposal of records to prevent unauthorized persons accessing them.

- **Fees**—Fees are fair, reasonable, considerate, and commensurate with the services performed when they are set, and with due regard for the person's ability to pay.

The Psychosocial Rehabilitation Practitioner's Ethical Responsibility to Colleagues Encompasses the Following:
- **Respect, fairness, and courtesy**—A provider creates and maintains conditions of practice that facilitate ethical and competent professional performance by colleagues. He or she respects confidences shared by colleagues in the course of their professional relationships and transactions. He or she treats others with respect and accurately and fairly represents their work.

- **Working with individuals who are served by a colleague**—A provider relates to individuals served by a colleague with full professional consideration.

- **Collaborative working relationships**—He or she collaborates fully with other practitioners providing services to the same individual to assure the most effective services.

- **Upholding ethical conduct**—The psychosocial rehabilitation practitioner supports ethical conduct, such as a code of ethics, in dealing with colleagues.

The Psychosocial Rehabilitation Practitioner's Ethical Responsibility to the Profession Encompasses the Following:
- **Maintaining the integrity of the profession**—A practitioner upholds and advances the values, ethics, knowledge and mission of the profession.

- **Professional service**—He or she assists the profession through the promotion of the field of psychosocial rehabilitation, and participates in professional activities which develop the competence of the profession.

- **Development of knowledge**—The psychosocial rehabilitation practitioner takes responsibility for identifying, developing, and fully utilizing knowledge for professional practice. Practice is based upon recognized knowledge relevant to psychosocial rehabilitation, and a practitioner critically examines and keeps current with emerging knowledge relevant to the field. He or she contributes to the knowledge of the field and shares research, knowledge, and practice wisdom with colleagues.

The Psychosocial Rehabilitation Practitioner's Ethical Responsibility to Society includes Promoting the General Welfare of Society:
- **General welfare**—The psychosocial rehabilitation practitioner promotes social justice and the general welfare of society which includes promoting the acceptance of persons who experience mental illness. The practitioner advocates for changes in policy and legislation to improve social conditions, to promote social justice, and to encourage informed participation by the public in shaping social policies and institutions.

- **Empowerment**—The practitioner acts to expand choice and opportunity for all persons, with special regard to groups of persons who are disadvantaged or disabled. He or she strives to eliminate attitudinal barriers, including stereotyping and discrimination toward people with disabilities. Practitioners work to enhance their own sensitivity and awareness toward people with disabilities.

- *Cultural competence*—The psychosocial rehabilitation worker promotes conditions that encourage respect for the diversity of cultures that constitute our society.

Competency 16

Demonstrate a mastery of negotiation and mediation skills.

The ability to negotiate effectively with people receiving your services, supervisors, peers, and other significant stakeholders is dependent upon effective communication skills (Trochim & Cook, 1993). The rehabilitation process requires practitioners to maintain reciprocal relationships with representatives of each component of the community support system and any other individual that is involved in a person's support system. Negotiation and mediation for the purpose of goal attainment relies on practitioners seeking constructive feedback from all of the significant stakeholders and helping them recognize that "each win is for the good of the whole team" (Hemenway, 1994). Fisher and Ury (1981) in their book, *Getting to Yes,* draw on their backgrounds in law and anthropology and recommend the following negotiation strategies that have application to the work of rehabilitation practitioners to pursue and teach win-win strategies:

- Separate the people from the problem that needs to be addressed;

- Focus on the interests of the stakeholders and not their positions;

- Establish precise goals at the outset of negotiations;

- Work together with the parties involved to create options that satisfy everyone; and

- Develop methods to respond to stakeholders who refuse to play by the rules, resort to "dirty tricks," or are more powerful.

When a negotiation process breaks down, a practitioner may want to invite non stakeholders such as a supervisor, peers, or other consumers to participate. Weiland (1994) recommends the incorporation of nonstakeholders as a strategy to generate solutions. This helps the practitioner see the presenting problem from a different view or from multiple perspectives, become aware of personal blindspots, or avoid polarization which can occur when stakeholders have different positions.

Competency 17

Work in cooperative and collaborative manner.

Rehabilitation practitioners collaborate with the persons receiving services, with family members and significant others, and with colleagues throughout the service system. Rehabilitation practitioners must be adept at the coordination of all services in a person's support system, as well as those that they are responsible for delivering. Collaboration is dependent upon the candid exchange of accurate information among all partners, a willingness to be flexible and open to alternative strategies reflecting the of insights all of the significant players, and the practitioner's trust that information received from other network individual with mental illness is accurate, and that any information shared will not used inappropriately (Hoeltzel & Finley, 1992).

Recognizing one's own personality traits and working style facilitates team work; for example, some people like routine work and a high degree of structure and organization, while other people prefer constant challenges and are always exploring new approaches. Hemenway (1994) recommends the following strategies to optimize communication among team members:

- understand differences and do not blame or make assumptions about one another;

- resolve past conflicts and focus on present issues,

- encourage one another,

- be flexible,

- applaud strengths and view the so-called weaknesses of others as opportunities for growth,

- believe that each "win" is for the benefit of the individual with mental illness or the whole team,

- establish and maintain clear boundaries,

- and always be respectful of others.

Curtis, Tanzman and McCabe (1992) observe that team-oriented people share their knowledge and skills, help the people they serve and their colleagues develop solutions to real issues, and make requests for consultations and insights to solve problems.

Assist in building positive relationships.

The rehabilitation process is dependent on the practitioner building positive relationships with each person receiving rehabilitation services, family members and the community support system. Hodges (1990) observes that "positive relationships usually result when there is optimism and when there is an emphasis on the individual's strengths and assets." Maintaining a positive relationship requires the practitioner to be available and responsive when needed. It also means persevering when the going gets tough (Friday, 1986).

There are varying experiences and levels of knowledge that direct service practitioners in the same agency bring to their work (Bunker & Wijnberg, 1988). Although all workers at an agency may be competent, practitioners are at different stages in their career. Some colleagues have acquired expertise from their experiences as service recipients or specialized training that predispose the worker to particular strengths and innovations that would benefit others. Each worker also has areas of weakness, or will experience an ambiguous situation that will benefit from consultation and feedback from a broader reference group. Soliciting, accepting, and providing consultation and feedback; negotiating differences; and accepting criticism from collaborators in the rehabilitation process are mechanisms that improve worker morale and build enduring positive relationships.

Competency 19

Be willing to have fun with others.

People are more inclined to be receptive to learning when their environment is joyful rather than burdened with a tone of seriousness. Humor is a way that practitioners expose the real person within them and show that they are fun to be with (Curtis, Tanzman, & McCabe, 1992). Mosher (1994) notes that "good staff don't generally take themselves too seriously." Humor and having fun on the job is a way to broaden one's vision, feel a sense of freedom, and become reinvigorated after experiencing darker moments and tap into a "new energy source to find solutions to our vexing problems" (Hughes, 1988). Practitioners not only need to bring levity into their work, but they also need to respond to jokes, humor, and a sense of playfulness that individuals in the rehabilitation process bring.

Some people with a mental illness have found that their sense of humor on "heavy" topics, including psychiatric treatment modalities, has helped them survive (Campbell et al., 1989). The ability to jump in and have fun during an activity shows the worker is a team player and can comfortably work in consort with other practitioners, individuals with mental illness, or others in the community. Anhedonia, one of the negative symptoms of schizophrenia, is a diminished ability to experience pleasure and is associated with a loss of interest or sense of emptiness (American Psychiatric Association, DSM-IV, 1994). It is important for practitioners to serve as role models to individuals who may be depressed, unable or unaware of their diminished capacity to initiate playfulness, and where, when and how to use play-

fulness, silliness, or humor to develop and enhance relationships.

Competency 20

Demonstrate tenacity in work activities.

An important component of good rehabilitation practice is being there over the long haul for persons receiving rehabilitation. Tenacity includes perseverance in the task of finding effective and acceptable interventions for each individual person, a capacity to endure repetitious or mundane tasks that need to be performed throughout the duration of the rehabilitation relationship to provide necessary supports and resources, teach a skill, or maintain one, and a willingness to stick with difficult tasks (Curtis, Tanzman, & McCabe, 1992). Tenacity on the job is dependent upon the worker having the ability to set goals for oneself, effectively managing and organizing personal time to accomplish those goals, and not giving up or stopping until all of the tasks that are necessary to do the job well are completed.

Competency 21

Demonstrate the ability to set limits.

Setting limits helps practitioners to identify skills, resources, and expectations as they determine desirable choices that are simultaneously achievable (Trochim & Cook, 1993). Williams (et al,1994) notes that setting appropriate limits and learning when it is necessary to say no is not used to disregard individual choices, but can provide a needed structure in some relationships, particularly when working with people who are overly dependent or demanding. Used appropriately, limits can be perceived as recognition that the practitioner cared enough about the person to be firm, and yet risk a hostile response (Compton & Galaway, 1984). Finley (1990) observes that setting limits is an assertive message that allows the practitioner to both acknowledge the individual's point of view while also making explicit conditions under which the practitioner can be helpful. Furthermore, it allows individuals to learn appropriate behavioral boundaries, when to establish internal controls and self monitor selected behaviors. Finley (1990) recommends that practitioners' clearly and firmly state limits, repeat them if necessary, work out alternate guidelines when possible, maintain a nonjudgmental manner, and acknowledge and praise the resultant positive behaviors.

Competency 22

Have the ability to let go.

As practitioners provide long-term services, one of the dangers is to become too protective or to not recognize when an individual is ready to take new risks and be more independent. The ability of practitioners to let go and to facilitate moving on is an essential component of recovery in rehabilitation.

Valuing self determination implies that each person is provided opportunities to choose among alternative choices. When practitioners present options in their role as active partners in the rehabilitation process, they often present the pros and cons of the various options. The concept of self determination requires practitioners to give each person the freedom to adopt or reject any of the strategies that have been discussed, which can be difficult when it is

feared that a person's choice may have negative consequences (Compton & Galaway, 1984). "Letting go" is difficult but necessary in these situations. (When the choice of action that is selected poses imminent danger to the individual with mental illness or other persons, the practitioner is obligated to intervene.)

Competency 23

Demonstrate the ability to use self as a role model.

Direct service workers need to consistently act as role models and mutually share experiences and ideas to achieve goals through a partnership in the helping relationship (Trochim & Cook, 1993). When people are viewed as models, they have the capacity to inhibit or disinhibit behavior (Gambrill, 1983). Without explicitly drawing attention to what workers are doing, they are almost always demonstrating effective communication, social, and problem solving skills, such as how to use public transportation, ask for directions, and seek information and support from community resources. As a constant model, the personal behaviors of the practitioner on the job must comport with those behaviors that are being asked of others, in particular, being honest, prompt, and appropriate in language, interactions, and dress (Friday & McPheeters, 1985). In other words, direct service workers must practice what they preach. Not only must the practitioner consistently demonstrate good social skills and interact comfortably with all kinds of people in the community, but he or she must also not embarrass easily when teaching a wide range of normative behaviors to others (Curtis, Tanzman, & McCabe, 1992).

Practitioners can enhance the individual's acquisition of the behaviors that they are modeling by the following: being receptive to questions, criticism and praise; identifying critical components of the behavior being modeled; practicing the behavior as needed for its retention (Gambrill, 1983). Just as important as modeling how to achieve success is modeling how to deal with adversity, or simply put, coping with mistakes. In these instances, modeling how to reframe outcomes that you did not expect or want as a learning opportunity and determining how to reapproach the situation in a new or alternative way is another valuable role modeling experience.

"Negative expectations and stereotypes are among the greatest obstacles to recovery and keep many mentally ill persons immobilized by defeat and despair." (Lovejoy, 1982). Gambrill (1983) refers to a study that found that human service professionals were more likely than lay persons to focus on the negative characteristics of persons with mental illness. More experienced professionals placed even greater emphasis on a person's negative traits.

Stereotyping people impedes accurate observations and Gambrill(1983) recommends that practitioners employ "anticipatory empathy" as a technique to be more receptive to the situation of others who may have engaged in dysfunctional behaviors, and focus on a method to understand and feel what it is like to be in their position. Anticipatory empathy makes a distinction between the form of a behavior and its function in order to elicit the individual's views of an event without the practitioner displaying messages of disapproval. Practitioners can facilitate rapport by considering what they or an acquaintance would have done in the same circumstances, asking what are the concerns that the individual has about the practitioner and the agency setting, and determining whether there are any cultural, ethnic, sexual, age, or class issues that are relevant factors to understand. Just as the role of positive expectations by practitioners can promote success, negative practitioner perceptions, biases and attitudes can become self-fulfilling prophecies that heavily influence the outcome of a relationship in a pejorative fashion. When practitioners have positive regard and expectations for people with mental illness, they are more likely to be motivated to engage and participate in the rehabilitation process that promotes positive changes.

One of the most important ways that direct service practitioners can develop themselves is seeking appropriate help with problems (Trochim & Cook, 1993). Bunker and Wijnberg (1988) recommend the following methods to promote practitioner development:

- using agency supervisors to hone old skills and acquire new ones,
- developing self awareness about one's impact on others that impedes or promotes efficacy,
- participating in peer support groups,
- and developing skills to solve complex and persistent problems.

Practitioners need to be willing to question their beliefs during discussions with colleagues, rather than be wedded to dogma. When challenged, competent practitioners should seek out the most up-to-date knowledge (Gambrill, 1983).

A belief in lifelong learning is important if practitioners want to remain on the cutting edge of psychosocial rehabilitation. This can be accomplished by reading current periodicals, such as the *Psychiatric Rehabilitation Journal* and numerous other publications that focus on mental health and related issues; consulting with experts on issues related to mental illness and rehabilitation; attending local, state, and national conferences; taking continuing education classes in work related topics; and joining organizations that focus on issues relevant to people with disabilities.

Practitioners also need to pursue activities and hobbies that develop their personal growth and be willing to share and role model the rewards that are experienced through lifelong endeavors like sports, dance, art, music, film, cooking, surfing the internet, etc. to motivate and inspire individuals with mental illness to similarly fill their lives with recreational and educational pursuits that have restorative qualities for personal well-being.

Two community support programs in Kansas City, Missouri worked with an anthropologist, social worker, and two musicians to establish an African drum ensemble based on traditional music from the Dagbami people of Ghana (Longhofer & Floersch, 1993). Mime and theater ensembles that creatively merge the arts and healing have been established at rehabilitation programs throughout the country, taking advantage of practitioners with knowledge and interest in the performing arts, as practitioners at other agencies with fine arts skills promote art by individuals with mental illness that can be exhibited and marketed. At Thresholds in Chicago, a practitioner with a degree in dance therapy is helping individuals with mental illness use dance to become more aware of their actions and reactions while they improve their communication skills and simultaneously swing to the sounds of jazz (Thresholds, 1995).

Competency 26

Maintain self-awareness.

Intrapersonal Competencies for Direct Service Staff

A person's actions, whether they are intentional or not, are imbued with social meaning and influence the perceptions and reactions of others (Gambrill, 1983). The presentation of self reveals information about one's role, status, social identities etc., and helps those around us know what to expect and how to react (Compton & Galaway, 1984). Hemenway (1994) recommends practitioners take advantage of standardized instruments, such as the Myer-Briggs Type Indicator, to further self-awareness about their unique set of personality traits that influences how a person acquires information and makes decisions. "You cannot *not* influence others" observes Gambrill (1983). What people believe they can accomplish, can in fact influence the outcome. Thus "in defining ourselves to others we also define ourselves to ourselves" (Gambrill, 1983). Self-awareness or self-understanding entails the practitioner's comprehending one's personal impact in the work environment and developing the capacity to consciously rethink a situation and modify one's approach (Bunker & Wijnberg, 1988).

Practitioners need to recognize and select behaviors that are useful in their working relationships, such as slowing down the conversational pace, being nonjudgmental, paraphrasing, reflecting and summarizing a conversation and refraining from these behaviors when they are detrimental in work or in social relationships,etc. (Fleck-Henderson, 1989). In order for practitioners to demonstrate good social judgment, according to Friday and McPheeters (1985) they must know and use basic social skills, be aware of their personal social habits, recognize their effect on others, articulate and respond appropriately to social situations, and understand the trade-offs or cost and benefits of personal actions in diverse situations.

Competency 27

Demonstrate personal stability.

Experts in the practice of psychosocial rehabilitation looking at direct practitioner competencies considered consistent and congruent responses to social and environmental demands representative of personal stability in a worker (Trochim & Cook, 1993). Mosher (1994) warns agencies to be wary of practitioners who brag about their virtues or charisma because of their potential to create mischief, and instead he recommends agencies select workers who demonstrate humility, humor, and do not take themselves too seriously. He also warns agencies to avoid hiring those who hold a "rescue fantasy" and see themselves as vitally important or indispensable to an individual's recovery. Practitioners must develop the ability to anticipate and be sensitive to the social implications of diverse situations, articulate and execute appropriate re-

sponses relevant to the circumstances—in other words, exercise good judgment. (Friday & McPheeters, 1985).

Competency 28

Demonstrate the ability to handle personal stress.

A practitioner must separate personal needs and behaviors from those of the job to prevent issues in one's personal life affecting job performance (Trochim & Cook, 1993). Without realizing it, a practitioner may send indirect messages related to personal problems, such as work absences, tardiness, diminished quality of work, increasing the burden of work on other practitioners, or becoming emotional, sensitive, remote, labile etc. (Shulman, 1994). Effective social behavior that is displayed by the practitioner has a positive influence on the behavior and feelings of co-workers and individuals with mental illness (Gambrill, 1983).

It is natural that people may be influenced by a troubling personal problem, which in turn may negatively impact relationships with colleagues and client outcomes with individuals with mental illness. Shulman (1994) notes that a good supervisor should recognize signs of worker stress, explore their origin, assess their implications for workplace performance, and collaborate with the practitioner on ways to diminish stress. When stressors are non-work related, direct service workers need to seek assistance from appropriate sources outside of the workplace in order to maintain the focus of the work environment on those persons participating in rehabilitation.

The work of rehabilitation is dynamic. Consistent effectiveness is dependent on the practitioner's ability to be flexible in his or her use of multiple rehabilitation strategies in order to implement those that best fit the unique behaviors, interests, and circumstances of each individual at a given point in time (Gambrill, 1983). Mosher (1994) considers "response flexibility" a necessary trait of psychosocial rehabilitation practice. Workers must always remain alert and have the capacity to quickly respond to situational changes that affect a person's emotional, physical, social, and economic well-being by using interventions that are relevant rather than relying on interventions from only one theoretical model. Not only must workers be willing to modify old approaches and try out new ones, they must also be comfortable with a lack of structure and ambiguity in order to respond effectively to diverse circumstances (Curtis, Tanzman, & McCabe, 1992).

Practitioners need to believe that an ever-changing world is one that promotes growth, and they need to have the capacity to seize opportune moments that will bring forth positive changes. Gambrill (1983) recommends workers have the skill to perform "on the spot cost-benefit analyses" that consider short-term as well as long-term consequences. Flexibility is demonstrated by workers who have the ability to adapt quickly to situations that do not comport with preconceived expectations or previous experiences and who set aside the prepared strategy for a new one that has the potential to help a person succeed (Trochim & Cook, 1993).

Being supportive to a person with mental illness includes "letting be." A practitioner is supportive without being over intrusive, over talkative, over demanding or projecting unrealistic expectations in unreasonable time frames (Mosher, 1994). Having patience means that practitioners must learn to appreciate small or incremental positive changes and calmly wait until the overall objective is achieved (Trochim & Cook, 1993; Friday & McPheeters, 1985).

Humor is a powerful connecting tool that can be shared at many levels, among close friends, casual acquaintances, and at the workplace. Victor Borge, an internationally acclaimed entertainer, has been quoted as saying "laughter is the shortest distance between two people" (Rowes, 1980). The appropriate use of humor has a therapeutic value (Hoeltzel & Finley, 1992) In spite of difficulties that individuals with a serious mental illness experience, like everyone else in the world, they need to share and experience joyful moments. Sokol (1995) writes in *The Altered State,* a publication by individuals with mental illness, "Joking around feels good inside. When we laugh we begin to heal. Smiling and laughter makes our hearts warm. Many of us are ever so familiar with the cold (anxiety, fear, anger). Humor is part of the healing process."

Demonstrating humor on the job is a way for practitioners to model how people let go of what cannot be changed or controlled. It is a way to reduce tension and can be a legitimate response to some of life's uncertainties. Bringing levity to a situation that has become overly serious may introduce a more hopeful perspective, or provide an opportunity to turn a negative exchange into a positive one (Gambrill, 1983). Hoeltzel and Finley (1992) recommend that humor should never be used to be hurtful and that its appropriate timing is crucial. Not every practitioner needs to have a comedic gift of telling jokes, but all people can learn how to recognize humor and respond to humorous situations by laughing at what is funny, laughing at oneself, and laughing with others (Pernell-Arnold & Finley, 1992; Trochim & Cook, 1993).

Competency 32

Recognize the limits of the practitioner's ability to help.

Practitioners will not always be able to assist everyone that comes to them or they may have exhausted their capacity to work with an individual. Gambrill (1983) notes that in some situations, no one will be able to help the person find an amenable solution to a particular problem. The inability to achieve desired outcomes may be a result of uncontrollable external factors, or relate to the worker reaching a personal emotional limit and level of tolerance. Practitioners must recognize their limits and know when it is necessary to stop and ask for help or additional assistance (Trochim & Cook, 1993). Friday (1986) correlates liking oneself and knowing oneself with understanding one's limits and being realistic about what the direct service worker, the individual with mental illness and the agency can do. Establishing appropriate work limitations can help pre-

vent burnout (Finch & Krantz, 1991). In a study examining worker burnout, Finch and Krantz (1991) found that while workers had diverse places where they drew the line to extra hours, employment tasks and demands, learning when to say no was an adaptive limit setting skill to effectively cope with the emotional and physical demands that are associated with psychosocial rehabilitation.

Self Management Competencies for Direct Service Staff

Competency 33

Have the ability to be pragmatic and do hands-on work.

At its heart, psychosocial rehabilitation is an active process that requires practitioners to be involved in all the day to day activities of the people participating in the rehabilitation program. Often productive working relationships are developed through the process of doing tasks together, such as fixing lunch, taking the bus, and cleaning the program site. Practitioners do what needs to be done, even though it often is not part of the job description.

Competency 34

Demonstrate the ability to handle multiple tasks, prioritize and manage time, and partialize tasks.

Throughout the rehabilitation process, the practitioner helps people to establish priorities and develop a plan to achieve identified goals. Developing and sequencing primary and secondary steps, developing timelines and reinforcements, helping individuals apply old skills and resources or acquire new ones, and monitoring the retention of skills to ensure goals are achieved are programming skills that the practitioner must master to respond to diverse and complex situations (Anthony, Pierce, Cohen, & Cohen, 1980).

Practitioners must similarly apply these skills in the overall management of the panoply of tasks associated with their jobs to be effective and not experience burnout. Feeling angry and frustrated about a job, procrastinating about the performance of tasks or blaming others for their incompletion are some of the signs that a worker is not dealing effectively with multiple job task (Trochim & Cook, 1993). Psychosocial rehabilitation experts participating in the Trochim and Cook (1993) workforce competency concept mapping exercise emphasized the need for practitioners to develop the following time management and task prioritization abilities:

- recognize the total number of tasks inherent in job responsibilities;

- apply an organization's agreed upon prioritization standard to identify critical tasks;

- gauge the level of effort and time necessary to complete discrete tasks;

- involve individuals with mental illness in the completion of organizational tasks and teach them time management techniques;

- recognize signs of job stress and employ stress management techniques.

Direct service workers should also be prepared to bring ideas to their supervisors and agency management regarding suggestions that would improve practitioner and overall organizational productivity. Friday and McPheeters (1985) observe that clarifications and revisions in program philosophies and goals, organizational structure and procedures, agency technologies, utilization of human resources and agency facilities, etc. can improve individual- and system-wide productivity and morale. Simple things like the standard times for staff trainings, required meetings, meal breaks etc. may be impediments that are easily remedied when brought to the attention of supervisors and management. In order to optimize growth and shape productive behaviors, practitioners must cope with uncertainties and tolerate unpredictable circumstances, even those that appear chaotic or uncontrollable (Friday & McPheeters, 1985). Peterson (1994) observes that "disequilibrium as opposed to the status quo, is necessary for systems growth and for self-organizing systems." People must be open to change to prevent entropy, or systems decay. Practitioners must not lose sight of the uncertainty inherent in mental illness, and the unpredictability of outcomes (Gambrill, 1983).

Competency 35

Tolerate ambiguity.

Participants in the Trochim and Cook (1993) concept mapping exercise generated three primary abilities that a practitioner needs in order to tolerate ambiguity. The first ability is related to problem solving in ambiguous situations. The problem solving steps include seeking involvement of others to help in problem identification, the generation of potential solutions, critical evaluation of posed solutions and feedback to determine viability, selection, implementation, and evaluation of solutions. These problem solving skills are necessary for the practitioner to manage ambiguity, as well as for those persons participating in rehabilitation.

The second ability relates to the recognition and acceptance of unresolvable ambiguities. The employment of techniques that facilitate letting go, acceptance, and humor can be very helpful. Providing ongoing support when you are unable to change a painful situation is just as important as facilitating change. Being there through the difficult times and the good times is part of the recovery process.

The third ability is learning how to distinguish between truly ambiguous situations and those that arise from lack of information, training, and feedback. These require the worker to know how to seek all of the information that is necessary to problem solve. Acquiring decision making skills, such as identifying and operationalizing relevant values for a specific decision, and brainstorming, researching, and choosing among potential alternatives for the optimal one are pragmatic approaches that the practitioner can employ in a systematic decision-making process (Anthony, Pierce, Cohen & Cannon, 1980).

Ambiguity regarding the staff role can also become an issue as the person's role changes from recipient of treatment and rehabilitation to independent citizen (Curtis, Tanzman, & McCabe, 1992). In public venues, Curtis, Tanzman, and McCabe (1992) recommend that workers maximize integrative and normative interactions that minimize their "professional" role and the individual's "patient" role. Interactions in the public domain will also occur outside of planned workday tasks, such as at movie theaters, places of worship, educational programs, and medical offices. The blurring of personal and professional roles can create an ambiguous situation and should be addressed by acting naturally, being polite and respectful, and maintaining the confidential nature of your work relationship. However, practitioners can not deviate from ethical conduct in any circumstances, despite their ambiguous nature (Curtis, 1995).

Recognition of relationship boundaries are even more important in the informal environment that is often characteristic of rehabilitation services. Guidelines of ethical conduct have been established to safeguard the rights of the persons receiving services and must be internal guideposts for practitioners at all times (IAPSRS; NASW). Under no circumstances may a practitioner exploit the rehabilitation relationship for personal gain.

Competency 36
Enjoy diversity.

The attitudes, values, beliefs, and behaviors of all people are influenced by ethnic, racial, cultural, class, sexual, age, and disability factors. Without this understanding of multiculturalism, practitioners and the agencies that employ them would be unable to "nourish and empower" individuals with mental illness, families and the communities that they endeavor to effectively serve (Daniel, 1994). Agencies that value diversity will find that hiring a heterogeneous workforce with varied educational backgrounds and who also share demographic, cultural, and linguistic characteristics of the community are ways to facilitate effective rehabilitation (Williams et al., 1994).

Furthermore, practitioners need to develop an understanding of specific subcultures that influence lifestyle decisions, needs, and intervention strategies (Friday, 1986). Persons who choose to be involved in activities of the gay/lesbian community, individuals who are deaf and prefer association with others who uniquely share their concerns, interests and mode of optimal communication are some of the subcultures that practitioners need to understand. Even among these subcultures, there are enormous differences from person to person.

A creative and effective use of practitioners was developed in Miami, Florida, when it was realized that homeless persons with severe mental illness who were from Latino and Hispanic communities were underutilizing community support program services. Ethnic teams of practitioners were initiated to do extensive outreach and increase the services accessibility of these homeless subpopulations (NRCHMI, 1994). When working with persons who are homeless, practitioners must realize that cultural differences will influence how a person seeks help, defines a problem and responds to a treatment strategy (Milstrey, 1994). Practitioners who value diversity must have the capacity to identify the opportunities presented by diversity and employ positive ways to incorporate diversity into the rehabilitation process, such as realizing when alternative explanations and solutions that consider a person's unique background need to be explored (Trochim & Cook, 1993).

Competency 37

Be willing to take risks.

Creative practitioners are willing to challenge boundaries, such as using old resources in a nontraditional way, assigning an alternative interpretation to an event that opens the door for a more effective intervention, or perhaps introducing a new approach to solve a prob-

lem that has not previously been used by other practitioners at the agency (Curtis, Tanzman, & McCabe, 1992; Trochim & Cook, 1993). When practitioners are in an environment that has a "shared sense of purpose, they are more likely to respond creatively to change without being bound by regimen or supervision" (Peterson, 1994). The field of psychosocial rehabilitation was premised on innovative community-based practices and it must continue to encourage and support all levels of workers who exhibit the motivation, energy, and excitement that come from taking risks to continually explore and try new and more effective approaches (Zipple et al., 1993).

However, practitioners must not wait for organizational encouragement to bring about innovations. Practitioners need to assume personal responsibility to initiate productive changes (Spaniol, Zipple, & Cohen, 1991). Furthermore, practitioners need to support and assist those receiving rehabilitation services in their own risk-taking behaviors to move closer toward independence, recovery, mastery and control over their lives. While no one wants to see a person fail, it is not possible for a person to achieve great heights without the freedom to fly or tackle difficult tasks.

Competency 38

Positively reframe potential stressors.

A study by Finch and Krantz (1994) found that practitioners who have successfully adapted to this work are more likely to employ positive statements about job characteristics that reinforce their personal accomplishments. They demonstrate successful coping strategies with workplace stressors that other people might interpret differently. For example, workers who have a good fit with psychosocial rehabilitation will be more likely to make statements about enjoying a fast work pace, never wanting to be bored, and liking autonomy, creativity, and flexibility. Positive reframing or providing an alternative interpretation of stressors as possible assets is a cognitive strategy that rehabilitation workers often use with persons receiving services (Gambrill, 1983). Practitioners will similarly find this strategy applicable in the management of workplace stressors in order to avoid worker burnout and emotional exhaustion from the constant pace, demands and challenges of their work (Finch & Krantz, 1991).

Competency 39

Demonstrate the ability to read and write effectively.

Proficiency in the use of terminology that is specific to psychosocial rehabilitation and the treatment of serious and persistent mental illnesses, the capacity to learn about topics relevant to rehabilitation, and an ability to write with clarity when communicating with others are required. Reading and writing skills must be at a level to develop and record detailed rehabilitation programs that describe in behavioral language the objectives and goals of individuals with mental illness and to document their progress (Anthony, Pierce, Cohen & Cohen, 1980). Accurate documentation is used to evaluate the effectiveness of practitioner intervention strategies and overall agency performance and the completion of various forms may be required to determine the rate of reimbursements for agency/practitioner services. (Trochim & Cook, 1993).

References

Anthony, W.A. (1993). Recovery from mental illness: The guiding vision of the mental health service system in the 1990s. *Psychosocial Rehabilitation Journal, 16* (4): 11-23.

_____ (1980). *The principles of psychosocial rehabilitation.* Baltimore, MD: University Park Press.

Anthony, W. A., Cohen, M., & Farkas, M. (1990). *Psychosocial rehabilitation.* Boston, MA: Center for Psychosocial rehabilitation, Boston University.

Anthony, W.A., Pierce, R.M., Cohen, M.R., & Cannon, J.R. (1980). *The skills of diagnostic planning: Psychosocial rehabilitation practice series book 1.* Baltimore MD: University Park Press.

_____ (1980). *The skills of rehabilitation programming: Psychosocial rehabilitation practice series book 2.* Baltimore MD: University Park Press.

Blankertz, L.E., Hughes, R., Rutman, I.D., Robinson, S.E., & Baron, R.C. *A national survey of the psychosocial rehabilitation workforce* (Draft). Philadelphia, PA: Matrix Research Institute: A project of Matrix Research Institute and the International Association of Psychosocial Rehabilitation Services.

Bunker, D.R. & Wijnberg, M.H. (1988). *Supervision and performance: managing professional work in human service organizations.* San Francisco: Jossey-Bass Publications.

Campbell, J., Schraiber, R., Temkin, T., & ten Tusscher, T. (1989). *The well-being project: Mental health clients speak for themselves.* Sacramento, CA: The California Network of Mental Health Clients.

Carkhuff, R.R. (1972). The art of helping. Amherst, MA: Human Resource Development Press.

_____ (1977) *The art of helping trainer's guide.* Amherst, MA: Human Resource Development Press.

_____ (1973). *The art of problem solving*. Amherst, MA: Human Resource Development Press.

Carkhuff, R.R. & Behenson, D.H. (1977). *Beyond counseling and therapy.* New York: Hold, Rinehart & Winston.

_____ (1976). *Teaching as treatment: An introduction to counseling and psychotherapy*. Amherst, MA: Human Resource Development Press.

Carkhuff, R.R., Behenson, D.H & Pierce, R.M. *The skills of teaching: Interpersonal skills.* Amherst, MA: Human Resource Development Press. Corey & Corey. Self assessment of group leadership skills. In J.

Hoelzel, & L. Finley(1992) *Developing groups and group skills.* Philadelphia, PA: Division of Mental Health Education at Medical College of Pennsylvania, Eastern Pennsylvania at Psychiatric Institute.

Condeluci, A. (1994). Inclusion: Do we understand it, are we ready? (1994*). Field Report, Special Double Issue Positive Behavioral Supports, 4*(4): 5. University of Northern Colorado: Center for Technical Assistance.

Compton, B.R. & Galway, B. (1984). *Social work processes* (3rd ed.). Chicago: Dorsey Press.

Curtis, L, Tanzman, B.H. & McCabe, S.S. (1992*). Orientation manual for local level supported housing staff.* Burlington, VT: The Center for Community Change through Housing and Support.

Curtis, L. (1993). *Workforce competencies for direct service staff to support adults with psychiatric disabilities in community mental health services.* Burlington, VT: The Center for Community Change through Housing and Support.

_____ (1995). *Yes, no, maybe: A discussion about relationship boundaries in community support services.* Paper presented at the International Association of Psychosocial Rehabilitation Services' national conference in Boston, MA, June 9, 1995. Burlington VT: The Center for Community Change through Housing and Support.

Daniel, R. (1994). Cultural competency. *Western New York Mental Health World, 2*(4): 5.

Danley, K.S. & Mellen; V. (1987). Training and personnel issues for supported employment programs which serve persons who are severely mentally ill. *Psychosocial Rehabilitation Journal, 11* (2): 87-102.

Deegan, P.E. (1992). The independent living movement and people with psychiatric disabilities: Taking back control over our own lives. *Psychosocial Rehabilitation Journal, 15*(3): 3-19.

Dincin. J. (1975). Psychosocial rehabilitation. *Schizophrenia Bulletin, 13* (Summer): 131-47.

Finch, E.S. & Krantz, S.R. (1991). Low burnout in a high-stress setting: A study of staff adaption at Fountain House. *Psychosocial Rehabilitation Journal, 14*(3): 15-26.

Finley, L.Y. (1990). *People skills in the art of healing: Lecture notes and workbook; revised 1992.* Philadelphia, PA: Division of Mental Health Education at Medical College of Pennsylvania, Eastern Pennsylvania at Psychiatric Institute.

Fisher, R. & Ury, W. (1981). *Getting to yes.* New York: Penguin Books, or Houghton Mifflin Company.

Fleck-Henderson, A. (1989). Personality theory and clinical social work practice. *Clinical Social Work Journal, 17* (2): 128-37.

Friday, J.C. (1986). *Case managers for the chronically mentally ill: Assessing and improving their performance.* Atlanta, GA: Southern Regional Education Board.

Friday, J.C. & McPheeters, H.L. (1985). *Assessing and improving the performance of psychosocial rehabilitation staff*. Atlanta, GA: Southern Regional Education Board.

Gambrill, E.D. (1983). *Casework: A competency-based approach*. Englewood Cliffs, NJ: Prentice-Hall Inc.

Hatfield, A.B. & Lefley, H.P. (1993). *Surviving mental illness: Stress, coping, and adaptation*. New York: Guilford Press.

Hemenway, C. (1994). Myers-Briggs Indicator helps us know ourselves and each other better. *Resources: Workforce Issues in Mental Health Systems, 6*(5): 15.

Hoeltzel, J. & Finley, L. (1992). *Developing groups and group skills*. Philadelphia, PA: Division of Mental Health Education at Medical College of Pennsylvania, Eastern Pennsylvania at Psychiatric Institute.

Hodge, M. (1990). The helping relationship: Appendix module 1. In Finley, L. (Ed) *People skills in the art of healing: Lecture notes and workbook*. Philadelphia, PA: Division of Mental Health Education at Medical College of Pennsylvania, Eastern Pennsylvania at Psychiatric Institute.

Hughes, R.A. *Process of empowerment*. Columbia, MD: International Association of Psychosocial Rehabilitation.

Hughes, S.R. (1988). Introduction. *Accent On Humor: A Look At The Lighter Side Of Philanthropy*. Silver Spring, MD: Philanthropic Service for Institutions.

Human Services Research Institute (HSRI). (1995). *Skills standards document* (Draft). Boston MA: The Community Support Skills Standard Project, Human Services Research Institute.

International Association of Psychosocial Rehabilitation Services(1996). *Code of ethics for psychiatric rehabilitation practitioners*. Columbia, MD: International Association of Psychosocial Rehabilitation Services.

Jonikas, J.A. (1993). *Staff competencies for service-delivery staff in psychosocial rehabilitation programs.*Chicago, IL: Thresholds National Research and Training Center on Rehabilitation and Mental Illness.

Kuehnel, T.G., Howard, E., Backer, T.E., & Liberman, R.P. (1994). *Psychosocial rehabilitation competencies for mental health workers* (Draft). Los Angeles, CA: Center for Improving Mental Health Systems, Human Interaction Research Institute.

Koehler, M. (1994). Values and love in recovery: Is there life after coping? *Innovations and Research, 3*(2): 31-32.

Leete, E. (1988). A consumer perspective on psychosocial treatment. *Psychosocial Rehabilitation Journal, 12* (2): 45-52.

_____. (1993). The interpersonal environment: A consumer's personal recollection, Chapter 10 in A.B. Hatfield H.P. & Lefley, H.P. (Eds.) *Surving mental illness: Stress, coping, and adaptation*. New York: Guilford Press.

Lefley, H.P. (1994). Thinking about recovery: Paradigms and pitfalls. *Innovation and Research, 3*(4):9-23.

Link, D. (1993). Life on the ledge: My recovery from a major mental illness— A consumer's personal recollection. Chapter 14 in A.B. Hatfield H.P. & Lefley, H.P. (Eds.) *Surviving mental illness: Stress, coping, and adaptation.* New York: Guilford Press.

Longhofer, J & Floersch, J. (1993). African drumming and psychosocial rehabilitation. *Psychosocial Rehabilitation Journal, 16*(4): 3-10.

Lovejoy, M. (1982). Expectations and the recovery process. *Schizophrenia Bulletin, 8*(4).

Milstrey, S.E. (1994). Response to homelessness requires culture competence. *Access, 6* (1): 1. Delmar, NY: National Resource Center on Homelessness and Mental Illness, Policy Research Associates.

Mosher, L.R & Burti, L. (1994). *Community mental health: A practical guide.* New York: W.W. Norton and Company.

National Association of Social Workers (NASW). The NASW Code of Ethics. In B.R. Compton & B. Galaway (Eds.) *Social Work Processes.* (3rd ed.). Chicago: Dorsey Press.

National Resource Center on Homelessness and Mental Illness (NRCHMI). (1994). Miami mental health center reaches out to homeless minorities. *Access, 6* (1): 1. Delmar, NY: National Resource Center on Homelessness and Mental Illness, Policy Research Associates.

Pernell-Arnold, A.& Finley, L. (1990). *Psychosocial rehabilitation services in action: Principles and strategies that result in rehabilitation.* South Carolina Department of Mental Health.

Peterson, P. (1994). Learning to live creatively with chaos. *Resources: Workforce Issues in Mental Health Systems, 6*(5): 9.

Rogers, C.R (1959). A theory of therapy, personality, and interpersonal relationships, as developed in the client-centered framework. In S. Koch (Ed.) *Psychology: A Study Of Science, 3*: 184-256. New York: McGraw-Hill.

Rowes, B. (1980). *The book of quotes.* New York: Ballantine Books.

Shulman, L. (1994). Practitioner as manager: The parallel process. *Resources: Workforce Issues in Mental Health Systems, 6*(5): 3-7.

Sokol, M. (1995). *The Altered State, 3* (3): 10. Lauderdale by the Sea, FL: Altered States.

Spaniol, L. & Koehler, M. (1994). The foundations of coping for people with psychiatric disability. *Psychosocial Rehabilitation Journal, 3*(2): 1-2.

Spaniol, L., Zipple, A., & Fitzgerald, S. (1984). How professionals can share power with families: Practical ap-proaches to working with families of the mentally ill. *Psychosocial Rehabilitation Journal, 8*(2): 76-84.

Spaulding, W., Harig, R., & Schwab, L.O. (1987). Preferred clinical skills for transitional living specialists. *Psychosocial Rehabilitation Journal, 11*(1): 5-21.

Stroul, B.A. (1986). *Models of community support services: Approaches to helping persons with long-term mental illness.* Rockville, MD: National Institute of Mental Health, Community Support Program.

_____. (1993). *Psychiatric crisis response systems: A descriptive study.* Rockville, MD: National Institute of Mental Health, Community Support Program.

Sullivan, W.P. (1994) A long and winding road: The process of recovery from severe mental illness. *Innovations and Research 3*(3): 19-27.

Swayze, F.V. (1994). Jumping in: A lesson well learned. *Resources: Workforce Issues in Mental Health Systems, 6*(5): 13-14.

Thresholds. (1995). Dance therapy takes center stage. *Thresholds Open Door,* 7.

Trochim, W.M. & Cook, J. (1993). *Workforce competencies for psychosocial rehabilitation workers: A concept mapping project.* Final report for project conducted for the International Association of Psychosocial Rehabilitation Services: Columbia, MD.

Weiland, P. (1994). The reflecting team, a model for supervision. *Resources: Workforce Issues in Mental Health Systems, 6*(5): 17.

Weingarten, R. (1994). Despair, learned helplessness and recovery. *Innovations and Research, 3*(2): 31-32.

Williams, M.L., Forster, P., McCarthy, G.D., & Hargreaves, W.A. (1994). Managing case management: What makes it work? *Psychosocial Rehabilitation Journal, 18*(1): 49-59.

Williams, X. (1994). Consumer empowerment vs. bundling of services: Why bundling of services is counterproductive. *Consumer Connection, 3*(2). Salem NH: New Hampshire Mental Health Consumer Council.

Yalom, I.D. (1985). *The theory and practice of group psychotherapy* (3rd ed.). New York: Basic Books, Inc.

Zipple, A.M., Selden, D., Spaniol, L., & Bycoff, S. (1993). Leading for the future: Essential characteristics of successful psychosocial rehabilitation program managers. *Psychosocial Rehabilitation Journal, 16*(4): 85-94.

Assessment in Psychosocial Rehabilitation

Barbara Caldwell

Introduction

This chapter will present a comprehensive review of assessment in psychosocial rehabilitation. Rehabilitation planning and assessment is integral to providing quality services in an accountable process. Assessment and planning are based in an ongoing partnership with the persons receiving services and should be driven by the their goals, desires, and needs. Assessment and planning are not just a paper work exercise but a set of interventions to make the rehabilitation process more powerful and useful. A review of the literature is presented with the tools and techniques to effectively conduct comprehensive assessments.

Direct Practitioner competencies for assessments conducted in psychosocial rehabilitation programs include the ability to:

- Complete a functional assessment.
- Complete a symptom assessment.
- Complete a resource assessment
- Assess and access appropriate housing.
- Assess active addiction and co-dependency.
- Assess the need for crisis interventions.
- Assess the role of family support.

These competencies are an integral component of clinical practice in the psychosocial rehabilitation arena. Competencies evolve over time through working in the field and through formal and informal education and readings in the literature.

Overall Assessment Process in Psychosocial Rehabilitation

Psychosocial rehabilitation assessment differs from the traditional medical/psychiatric/diagnostic approach. Psychiatric diagnosis is imbedded in the use of the *Diagnostic Statistical Manual*. This manual has categorized symptoms and relates them to a diagnostic label. The diagnostic classification does assist in the clustering and labeling of symptoms and associated treatment strategies but does not address a holistic approach which assesses the rehabilitation potential of individuals with mental illness. The overall function of psychosocial rehabilitation is to return or integrate the psychiatrically disabled individual into a home, work, or community setting (Anthony, 1977). Psychosocial rehabilitation is accomplished by providing the disabled person with the physical, intellectual and emotional skills to live, learn, and work in the community with the least amount of supports or resources. Psychosocial rehabilitation practice integrates not only the aspects of the definition of psychiatric rehabilitation but also the philosophical component composed of the guiding principles and values.

The delivery of services to individuals with serious mental illness is a complex, comprehensive, and ongoing process. In order to ensure quality service delivery, a systematic methodology has been identified for rehabilitation practitioners. The psychosocial rehabilitation process (Anthony, Cohen & Cohen ,1983) provides a framework for professional practitioners to ensure that all aspects of service delivery are considered, analyzed, planned for, implemented, and continuously evaluated. The psychosocial rehabilitation process includes **four phases**: assessment phase, planning phase, intervention phase, and the continuous evaluation phase. **Rehabilitation assessment** is the first phase that consists of specific practitioner activities. These practitioner activities (Anthony, Cohen & Farkas, 1990) include setting the overall rehabilitation goals and conducting a functional and resource assessment. The practitioner collaborates with the individual with mental illness to evaluate their skill and supports strengths and weaknesses. With this information, the practitioner and individual with mental illness can formulate a rehabilitation plan which is the second phase of the rehabilitation process.

The second phase is the **development of the rehabilitation plan**. The associated practitioner activities include: priority selecting short- and long-term goals stated in measurable terms and accompanied by time frames, outlining specific skills and behaviors to be acquired, organizing responsibilities, and projecting time frames for accomplishment of the objectives. This second phase leads to the development of the individualized service rehabilitation plan. The plan is a collaborative effort between the individual requesting services and the practitioner. The ability to engage the individual in this plan will create the working relationship that is fostered during the course of rehabilitation.

The third phase is **rehabilitation intervention**. The overall practitioner activities focus on the psychological, social, residential, vocational, educational, recreational skill and resource development. Further emphasis is on enhancing community supports, such as family or residential psychoeducation, relapse prevention education, medication education, personal health care education, and anger management. Strategic interventions include direct skill teaching, resource coordination, and/or modification. Providing **continuous evaluation** of the psychosocial rehabilitation interventions is integral. Ongoing assessment and reassessment of the person is mandated in light of the ever changing status and environmental stressors on the person. The ultimate outcome of psychosocial rehabilitation is the prevention of further deterioration of individuals with mental illness and/or the prevention of a reoccurrence of psychiatric disability (Anthony, 1977) with the evolving improvement in the quality of life for the individual.

In summary, the overall philosophy guiding principles and core values of psychosocial rehabilitation provides the framework for clinical practice. Psychosocial rehabilitation practice contains a vast array of assessment techniques and strategic interventions which can include development of the person's skills and the development of environmental supports that enable them to fulfill a chosen role in their preferred living, learning, social and work settings (Farkas, O'Brien, Cohen & Anthony, 1990).

Psychosocial Rehabilitation Assessment

The psychosocial rehabilitation assessment is the first phase of the psychiatric rehabilitation process. It is considered critical in that it provides the practitioner and individual with mental illness with a comprehensive and holistic understanding of the person. The assessment phase is designed to collect and analyze objective and subjective data in collaboration with individual persons to identify the skills and resources that the persons currently have or do not have in relation to being successful in the chosen environment they have selected. The psychosocial rehabilitation assessment is carried out in a series of individual with mental illness interviews. Anthony, Cohen & Nemec (1990) utilize two guiding principles in the interview to foster the individual ownership (i.e., maximizing the involvement of the individual with mental illness in the interview process; and sharing with the individual with mental illness the information collected facilitating the individual's understanding of the results).

The assessment interview requires critical practitioner skills (Cohen, Farkas & Cohen 1986) used to involve the individual with mental illness: (1) orienting, (2) requesting information, and (3) demonstrating understanding. These communication skills involve explaining to individuals with mental illness their role in the rehabilitation process and what will be expected from them. The language used needs to be appropriate for the individual with mental illness understanding. The use of open-ended ques-

tions about a person's thoughts, actions, and feelings assists with increasing participation. Additional communication skills that facilitate the person's involvement in the assessment process are clarifying, paraphrasing, giving feedback, and checking perceptions of the person concerning the process. The person's involvement is also dependent on the development of trust and an atmosphere of concern and support.

The core values provide the practitioner with a philosophy to develop the necessary therapeutic relationship. Specific qualities are necessary in order to develop a support relationship where change and growth can occur. These qualities include respect for the individual with mental illness, acceptance, sensitivity, hope, empathy, availability, and vision. The psychosocial rehabilitation practitioner's actual implementation of these qualities will be evident in their capacity to creatively provide strategic interventions and connect with persons who are seriously impaired and disabled.

Psychosocial Rehabilitation Assessment Areas

Psychosocial rehabilitation assessment can be divided into three areas: (1) Functional/Situational assessments, (2) Individual Assessment inventories, and (3) Program assessment inventories that can be utilized by PSR agencies.

Competency I

Complete a functional assessment.

Functional/Resource Assessment:
Functional assessment is a process that provides data on the current or required capabilities of individuals needed to sustain themselves in their chosen environment. The functional assessment assists

individuals with mental illness to better understand what skills they need to achieve their rehabilitation goals (Cohen and Anthony, 1984). It can be utilized as a means for communication during admission, continuation of services and discharge as an objective basis of functional level. The psychosocial rehabilitation practitioner gathers data from a multidimensional perspective in order to complete the functional assessment.

Vaccaro, Pitts & Wallace (1986) indicate that the process of functional assessment integrates not only the identification of goals that are congruent with the person's life roles but also measures to be taken to enhance coping skills, competencies, and to add resources or supports for impairment areas. The practitioner guides the individual with mental illness toward realistic and reachable roles in their personal, social, occupational, and psychosexual domains. The goal for functional assessment is to integrate the data into a meaningful and mutually developed treatment plan with the individual with mental illness. The areas included in a functional assessment are:

- Social, community, occupational, and family roles presently engaged in and roles that the individual chooses to strive toward;

- Coping skills which include: basic living skills, communication skills, assertiveness skills, management and leisure time skills, problem solving skills, financial skills, household skills, anger/self-destructive behavior management skills;

- Cognitive or psychiatric impairments that will require alteration in environmental supports;

- Environmental barriers or impediments requiring additional resources or changes to promote the individual's transition into the new role;

- Educational knowledge/utilization needed to expand their understanding of their impairment and function more effectively: medication use and compliance, relapse prevention, and symptom management.

The functional assessment analysis also requires that the practitioner focus on the individual's strengths; have knowledge of what resources, skills, and behaviors are needed to function successfully in the individual's chosen environment; and have the ability to sustain the individual's commitment in the treatment plan and interventions over time.

Several functional assessment tools are currently in the literature that can assist the practitioner. The first is the Multi-Function Needs Assessment (MFNA). The MFNA was originally developed by Angelini (1982) and identified seven key factors that need to be assessed in order to plan for service needs. The MFNA was revised by Weiner (1993) and consists of 118 items divided into 13 subscales or areas of functioning:

- physical self-maintenance
- physical health
- substance use
- motor behavior
- psychiatric symptoms
- attitude and motivation
- attention and memory
- verbal communication
- family interaction
- social interaction
- independent living skills
- public behavior
- work/school/leisure.

A mean score is calculated and represents a current level of individual- with-mental-illness functioning. The results can be utilized for treatment planning, assignments, program planning, and evaluation.

Another tool is the Boston University (BU) Functional Assessment Approach. It is a comprehensive interviewing format to assess needed skills in specific environments. In this assessment chart are identified strengths and deficits, critical skills, skill use descriptions, and skill evaluations. Cohen, Farkas & Cohen (1986) have developed a format for this assessment into a series of training modules.

The Functional Assessment Scale (FAS [Krowinski, & Fitt, 1978]) is composed of five subscales: task orientation scale, social functioning scale, emotional scale, independent living-personal self-care scale, and a global level of functioning scale. It can also be used to evaluate the quality of the interventions but also serve as a model for evaluating service programs.

Barker, Barron, McRanlandy and Bigelow (1994) describe a 17 item instrument that measures the level of functioning or severity of disability of persons with serious mental illness. The Multhomah Community Ability Scale is designed to be completed by case managers. Accordingly, it is effective in measuring individual with mental illness progress, assignment of individuals with mental illness to different levels of service and assisting in the determination of reimbursement. Wyles and Sturt (1986) describe the MRC Social Behavior Schedule that covers 21 individual with mental illness behaviors areas such as hygiene, initiating conversation, self-harming behaviors, concentration, etc. It is a standardized tool that can be uti-

lized both in hospital and community settings.

The Self-Care Assessment Schedule presented by Barnes and Benjamin (1987) provides a self-administered tool to measure overt behaviors and essential elements of self-care. It is a ten-item questionnaire that can generate a level of disability that will facilitate program development and interventions.

Gorden and Gorden (1991) report an equation that employs measures of aggravating stress, biomedical impairment, coping skills, directive power and environmental supports to predict level of functioning. Practitioners, facilities, program evaluators, and third party payers would benefit from data that demonstrates whether a program is providing individuals with mental illness with effective interventions to improve their level of functioning or just symptom relief.

Weissman, Sholomskas & John (1981) provide a review of 12 tools for assessment of social adjustment that can be utilized in an assortment of settings for individual assessment and intervention evaluation. Yankowitz and Musante (1994) present examples of a cognitive functional assessment instrument which consist of six areas: short term attention, sustained attention (concentration), memory, flexibility, initiative, and organization that is integrated into a vocational rehabilitation program. There is also an individual with mental illness awareness version of the cognitive function assessment for increasing understanding of the impact of the illness through psychoeducational programs.

In summary, functional assessment provides crucial information for both the individual and practitioner to better plan and develop interventions for enhancing the skills, knowledge, and capabilities in the individual's selected living environment. Tools are currently available in the

Functional/Situational Assessment Tools

TOOL	AUTHOR	AREAS OF ASSESSMENT
MultiFunction Needs Assessment	Angelini (1982) Weiner & Michael (1987)(Revised Tool)	Household skills; personal appearance; self-care; Family intervention; psychological functioning; Community living skills. Revised tool also included substance abuse; attitude and motivation; attention and memory; verbal communication; family and social interaction; public behavior; work/school & leisure.
Functional Assessment Scale (FAS)	Krowinski & Fitt (1978)	5 Subscales: Task orientation; social functioning scale; emotional scale; independent living-personal self-care scale; global level of functioning.
MRC Social Performance Schedule tive	Wykes & Sturt (1986)	21 behaviors are included such as: communication, conversation, social contacts, suicidal and self-harming behaviors; restlessness; acting out behaviors; destruc- behavior; personal appearence; concentration; leisure activities, etc.
Self Care Assessment Schedule (SCAS)	Barnes & Benjamin (1987)	Self-care activities such as: dressing, appearence; personal hygiene; mobility; domestic activities; and occupational activities.
Role Functioning Scale (RFS)	Goodman, Swell, Cooley & Leavitt (1993)	4 domains: Personal self-care; cognitive-affective functioning; social-familial relationships; and vocational-educational functioning.
Social Adjustment Scale-II (SAS II)	Schooler, Hogerty & Weissman(1979)	52 questions, semistructured interview covering: work role, extended family relationships, social-leisure activities personal well-being, relationship with household individual with mental illness; sexual adjustment.
Denver Community Mental Health Questionnaire (DCMHQ)	Ciarlo & Davis (1977)	79 item, semi-structured interview covering: personal and social functioning, social behavior, psychological distress, interpersonal isolation, home and work, alcohol and drug use, interpersonal aggression, legal difficulties.
St. Louis Inventory of Community Living Skills	Everson & Boyd (1993)	15 items each rated on 7 point scale including: personal hygiene, self-care, communication, safety, handling time & money, leisure activity, meal preparation, use of resources, problem solving, health practices.

Functional/Situational Assessment Tools

TOOL	AUTHOR	AREAS OF ASSESSMENT
Specific Level of Functioning Scale (SLOF)	Schneider & Struenig (1983)	43 item rating scale which uses a 5 point Likert-type scale to assess the adequacy of 6 functioning areas: (1) Physical functioning; (2) Personal care skills; (3) Interpersonal relationships; (4) Social Acceptability; (5) Activities; (6) Work Skills.
Thresholds Monthly Work Evaluation Form (TMWEF)	(Cook, Bond, Hoffschmidt, Jonas, Razzano & Weakland, 1991)	22 item rating scale comprised of 4 dimensions: work readiness(e.g. attendance, grooming,control of inappropriate behavior), work attitudes (e.g. initiative, acceptance of responsibility), interpersonal relations (cooperation with supervisor and peers) and work quality (e. g. accuracy and productivity).
Work Personality Profile (WPP)	(Cook, Bond, Hoffschmidt, Jonas, Razzano & Weakland, 1991)	58 item behaviorally work oriented assessment rating scale completed by the practitioner. Sample items include:"Learns new assignments easily" and "Shows pride in group effort."

literature for use in various settings. Practitioners should also consider the unique needs of individuals with mental illness and adapt tools or design their own to suit their special populations and service needs. Practitioners should enlist the assistance of individuals with mental illness in the development, implementation, and ongoing evaluation of functional assessment tools and their use in agencies and programs.

Competency 2

Complete a symptom assessment.

Individual Assessment Inventories
Psychosocial rehabilitation practitioners need to appreciate that each individual with mental illness in their program will demonstrate changing behaviors depending on the setting, situations, medication, use of self-medication, or stress level. Behaviors that indicate that the individual with mental illness is struggling with their illness require continual assessment and attention by psychosocial rehabilitation practitioners. The purpose of symptom assessment is to:
- understand the complex behaviors that the individual with mental illness presents;
- differentiate deteriorating symptoms from situational stress symptoms;
- identify symptoms related to adverse reactions or side effects of medication;

- identify self-medication or drug and alcohol effects

- assist the individual in their understanding of what these symptoms mean in the person's life;

- develop appropriate interventions in order to reduce symptoms that interfere with daily functioning.

The goal of symptom assessment is to continually evaluate the individual's behavior with the ultimate practitioner role of providing ongoing interventions for development of coping strategies and skill development. Furthermore, the medication schedule of the individual with mental illness will require assessment so that the practitioner understands the actions of the medication on a person's behavior and what side effects or adverse reactions can develop. Antipsychotic drugs ameliorate various symptoms of schizophrenia and other psychotic behaviors. Positive symptoms respond to antipsychotic medication in comparison to negative symptoms. The table below categorizes negative and positive symptoms of schizophrenia. A rank order of symptoms from greatest to least responsive to antipsychotic medication would include: combativeness and hostility, tension and hyperactivity, hallucinations, sleep disturbances, delusions, poor social skills, realistic planning, judgment and insight (DeVane, 1990).

Rehabilitation practitioners need to be familiar with the most common side effects and adverse reactions of common antipsychotic drugs. The table on the next page provides a review of potential side effects and adverse reactions of antipsychotic medication. Individuals with mental illness on lithium also need to be observed for side effects and possible adverse reactions. Another table has a listing of the changes possible based throughout the body. Psychosocial rehabilitation practitioners are responsible for having an understanding of the side effects of antipsychotic drug therapy not only for monitoring but also to assist with the education of the rehabilitation participants to be knowledgeable about drugs. Side effects and adverse reactions will require referral to medical personnel for follow-up.

The recognition and documentation of individual with mental illness symptoms over time dictates that psychosocial rehabilitation practitioners utilize objective, measurable, and verifiable criteria for classification of behavioral manifestations. Psychosocial rehabilitation service programs have the opportunity to refine assessment by utilizing assessment tools that provide interpractitioner agreement on specific measures of symptom assessment. The severity of certain symptoms can be correlated with

Positive and Negative Symptoms Response to Antipsychotic Therapy

POSITIVE SYMPTOMS	NEGATIVE SYMPTOMS
Delusions	Poor social skills
Hallucinations	Impaired judgment
Inappropriate behaviors	Inability to prioritize tasks
Grandiosity	Social withdrawal
Paranoid ideation	Loss of punctuality

Side Effects/Adverse Reactions
Antipsychotic Medication (Excluding Clozapine)

System Affected	Side Effects Seen
Central Nervous System	Daytime sleepiness; muscle spasms, tremors; inner sense of restlessness and agitation; Tardive dyskinesia: Repetitive movements of wrist and hand; random movements of lips, tongue or jaw; difficulty swallowing, eating; seizures. Anticholinergic Effects: Dry mouth; nasal stuffiness; blurred vision; constipation; urinary retention. Neuroleptic Malignant Syndrome: Fever, muscle rigidness, altered mental status including delirium.
Cardiovascular System	Low blood pressure causing lightheadedness, weakness, and fainting.
Gastrointestinal System	Weight gain
Skin and Eye System	Rashes, eye swelling, hives; phototoxic reaction to the sun.

Side Effects and Adverse Reactions to Lithium (Arama & Hyman, 1991)

System Affected	Side Effects and Adverse Reactions
Gastrointestinal System	Nausea, vomiting, lack of appetite, diarrhea or abdominal pain.
Renal System	Urinary frequency during the day and night time; increase thirst.
Neurological System	Lethargy, fatigue, weakness and tremors, headache, blurred vision, irritability, twitching, stumbling, poor coordination, difficulty concentrating, confusion, visual disturbance, hallucinations, and delirium.
Cognitive and Psychological System	Individuals with mental illness complain of dulling affect, sense of depersonalization, loss of creativity, memory disturbances.
Dermatological System	Acne, psoriasis, rashes.

specific interventions to ensure quality of service and utilization of appropriate strategies.

The Brief Psychiatric Rating Scale originally designed by Overall and Gorham(1962) and expanded to 24 items by Lukoff, Liberman & Nuechterlein (1986) assesses many nonpsychotic symptoms present that occur prior to relapse. The Brief Psychiatric Rating Scale is composed of 18 items scored on an eight point scale. This is an interviewer assessment tool which will provide continuity over time and give an overall score for rating symptoms. These tools can be utilized as one method to evaluate effectiveness of interventions and improvement in individual with mental illness functioning over time. It has been widely utilized in clinical practice areas and has a manual available from the UCLA Clinical Research Center for Schizophrenia and Psychosocial Rehabilitation (Box 6022, Camarillo, CA 93011).

The Schedule for Assessment of Negative Symptoms (SANS [Anderson, 1982]) and Negative Symptom Assessment (NSA [Raskin, Pelchat, Sood, Alphs & Levine, 1993]) were developed to provide methods for assessment of the negative symptoms of schizophrenia. These symptoms have been linked as predictors of rehabilitation outcomes. The recognition of symptoms not only by the practitioner but also collaboratively working with the individual and family members to identify that the person's idiosyncratic signs will be the first step in symptom assessment and ultimately relapse prevention. Williams (1994), in his exploratory study of the recovery process, identified that 63% of the respondents described their ability to control or successfully monitor their illness. Success, the study indicated, lies in the ability to recognize symptoms and to take action to counteract them.

Other tools such as rating scales for depression and anxiety can be incorporated into ongoing assessments and evaluations. The Beck Depression Inventory (Beck, Ward, Mendelson, Mock, and Erbaugh, 1961) or the Hamilton Rating Scale (Hamilton, 1960) are tools available to evaluate the degree of depression. Zung (1965) and Zung (1974) have developed depression and anxiety assessment tools. The Symptom Checklist (SCL-90) (Derogatis, Lipman & Covi, 1973) is a self-report inventory of symptoms commonly found in the psychiatric population. The SCL-90 tool is a highly structured instrument covering five domains:

- somatization
- obsessive-compulsive
- interpersonal sensitivity
- depression
- anxiety

Global Assessment

The Global Assessment Scale (GAS [Endicott, Spitzer, Fleiss & Cohen, 1976]) is a rating scale for evaluating the overall functioning of an individual during a specified time period on a continuum from psychological or psychiatric illness to indicators of more positive behaviors of mental health functioning. The scale is divided into ten equal interval ranges beginning with 1–10, 11–20, and ending with 91–100. GAS covers an entire range of severity, providing the practitioner with an overall assessment tool for risk of readmission or relapse. Scores lower than 40 have been found to substantially increase the probability of rehospitalization. This tool can be utilized at the time of entrance to a program and administered routinely at specific intervals throughout the course of individual with mental illness participation. The modified version of the GAS is included in the DSM-IV as the Global Assessment of Functioning (GAF) Scale.

Skill Assessment

Skill assessment provides vital information concerning individual with mental illness strengths and weaknesses and assists in the identification of targeting resources for treatment planning and service programming. Assessment of skills for individuals can be accomplished through diverse settings and experiences. The first objective method of gathering data on individual skill level is through the functional assessment. The summary of findings taken together with the needs and requests of the individual will provide information to plan for skills development program. The second method is through observation of the person's performance in role play or simulated interactions can be utilized to gather pertinent information on individual with mental illness skill ability (Corrigan, Schade & Liberman, 1992). The skill functioning assessment survey consists of personal care skills, interpersonal skills, social acceptability skills, work and living skills. The Skill Assessment Scale (SAS) developed by Lowell, MacLean & Carroll (1985) can identify groups of individuals with mental illness with similar behavioral profiles. This can facilitate effective development of strategies for skills development programs in a cost-effective manner. Another tool, the Independent Living Skills Survey (Wallace, 1986) is also available. One important aspect of skill assessment is to collaborate with the individual with mental illness to determine what reinforcements or incentives can be used to enhance their participation in the treatment and rehabilitation strategies (Vaccaro, Liberman, Wallace & Blackwell, 1992). These reinforcements can be money, articles of clothing, food, or books.

Skills assessment and training is an essential aspect of the rehabilitation process. Individuals with mental illness experience not only deficits from the illness but also suffer from the lack of abilities in communication and interpersonal relationships. Basic living skills and self-maintenance behaviors are integral to independent living. Social skills are defined as the ability to give and obtain information and to express and exchange attitudes, opinions, and feelings (Liberman, 1982). Deficits can occur as a result of inadequate social learning environments appropriate to the individual, such as supportive family settings; loss of previously learned social skills due to institutionalization; excessive anxiety and affective states; and impairments in cognitive, informational processing skills, and stimulus overload. While psychotropic medication assists in reducing the positive symptoms—hallucinations, delusions, and florid thought symptoms—little relief is found in reducing the negative symptoms of the illness—poverty of speech, psychomotor retardation, and flat affect. The negative symptoms represent deficits in interpersonal behavior relative to social expectations (Pogue-Geile & Harrow, 1984). Skills have been defined as behaviors that must be performed at a required level to succeed in a particular environment (Cohen, Danley & Nemec, 1985). Two methods to provide interventions with skill acquisition is skills training (Liberman et al, 1986) and direct skills teaching (Cohen, Danley & Nemec, 1985). This area will be explored in more detail in the chapter on interventions.

Disability Rating Scales

The Disability Rating Scale (DRS [Hoyle, Nietzel, Guthrie, Baker-Prewitt & Heine, 1992]) provides a global rating on the basis of practitioners' synthesis of the behavioral patterns in five domains: activities of daily living, social functioning, concentration and task performance, adaptation for change, and impulse control. These domains correspond to the Social Securities Act disability criterion. A training manual is available to standardize the administration of the DRS. It has the capability of providing a brief and straightforward approach to assessment and detection of changes produced by treatment interventions.

Another measure available to assess general function and extent of disability for individuals diagnosed with schizophrenia is the Life Skills Profile (LSP [Rossen, Hadzi-Pavlovic & Parker, 1989]). Rehabilitation strategies that address not only relieving acute symptoms but also the associated dysfunction and disability provides a more in-depth approach. The LSP can be utilized both as an assessment tool in addition to evaluation of clinical service delivery.

Cognitive Assessment

Cognitive deficits suffered by individuals with mental illness include impaired attention and concentration; language processing difficulties due to memory deficits or associational inferences and difficulty in holding information; maintaining a given topic of conversation or engaging in prolonged discussion; and the inability to modify the interpretation of events or situations with appropriate social feedback (Ahmed & Goldman, 1994). Reed, Sullivan, Penn, Stuve, and Spaulding (1992) have identified cognitive deficits that need to be considered in all areas of rehabilitation: inability to maintain vigilance and continuous performance, distractibility, disorientation, difficulty with concept formation and processing, attributional problems such as delusions, and difficulty with mediating complex social functioning. These cognitive deficits require careful assessment especially in relationship to skills training. Cognitive processes can vary depending on medication compliance and extent of psychiatric disability, may be significant obstacles to personal functioning, and may impede efforts at psychosocial rehabilitation.

The psychiatric mental status examination (MSE) is a component of the comprehensive psychiatric evaluation that includes observing the individual's behavior and describing it in an objective, non-judgmental manner. MSE is gathered during the course of the initial interview and evaluated on an ongoing basis throughout the individual's participation in the program. The component parts to be included in a MSE are: appearance, attitude, mood, affect, speech and language, thought content, thought process and perceptions, cognition, insight, and judgment. The purpose of the MSE is to detect cognitive impairment both gradual and sudden onset. It provides vital information on changes in cognitive functioning as a result of decompensation, medication compliance, substance use/abuse, or an undiagnosed co-occurring physical illness.

The Mini-Mental State Exam (Folstein, Folstein, & McHugh, 1975) is a brief widely-used screening test that superficially assesses several dimensions of language and cognitive functioning: orientation, registration, immediate recall, concentration, naming, articulation, construction, sentence writing, and three-stage command comprehension. Detection of cognitive impairment is of vital importance and contributes to the individual's recovery and rehabilitation.

The Neurobehavioral Cognitive Status Examination (NCSE [Mitrushina, Abara & Blumenfelf, 1994]) provides the practitioner with a sensitive tool for the detection of cognitive impairment due to organic brain disorders. It can assist in providing information about the possible contribution of organic factors to the individual's present symptoms to enhance accuracy of treatment and rehabilitation strategies. The NCSE can be used to determine the need of a referral for further diagnostic work-up. It assesses the following cognitive domains: orientation, attention, comprehension, repetition, naming, construction, memory, calculation, similarities and judgment.

The Executive Interview (Royall, Mahurin & Gray, 1992) is a new neuro-psychological test that evaluates frontal lobe executive control functions. These are considered cognitive processes that orchestrate relatively simple ideas, movements, and actions into complex goal-directed behaviors. They assist in maintaining goal-directed behavior with internal and external distraction. Examples of executive control function include sequencing, self-monitoring, and inhibition of inappropriate behavior. According to Royall, without executive controls, complex behaviors such as cooking, cleaning, and self-care cannot be carried out. The Executive Interview is a structured clinical interview with 25 items that takes 15 minutes to administer by lay personnel. This instrument can be valuable in identification of levels of functioning and problem behaviors that interfere with rehabilitation training.

Competency 3

Complete a resource assessment.

Resource assessment evaluates the presence or absence of supports critical to the individual achieving success in the goals that the individual with mental illness wishes to attain. The rehabilitation practitioner involves the individual with mental illness in listing those persons, places, and things that are necessary for the individual with mental illness to be successful in their selected living arena (Anthony, Cohen, & Farkas, 1987). The focus of the practitioner is to reduce the barriers in the environment to achieve the goals. The resource assessment is completed in the process of the overall comprehensive rehabilitation assessment. The rehabilitation practitioner identifies the necessary supports that are required to accomplish each goal established. Resource supports, modification, and coordination are the interventions that correlate with resource assessment. The practitioner's actions are directed toward increasing, improving, or adding resources in the individual's environments. There is no immediate expectation of change in the individual's behavior as a result of resource interventions.

The community support system (CSS [Stroul, 1989]) is a concept that identifies an entire array of services, supports, and opportunities needed by people in order to function successfully in a community setting. It can be utilized as methodology to assist in resource assessment. The following outline is a list of critical questions practitioners can utilize as an assessment guide for the individual with mental illness. Components of resource assessment within the framework of CSS are (Stroul, 1989):

Identification and Outreach:

1. Are individuals with mental illness connected to the appropriate systems of services necessary for community tenure?
2. Is there a need for transportation assistance or access to other van/ community transportation networks?

3. What component of the population served are homeless and how are services provided to these individuals?

4. What are their unique needs and issues in order to ensure that services are targeted and pertinent?

Mental Health Treatment
1. What resources are needed to ensure appropriate follow-up and medication compliance?

2. What family education needs to be provided for understanding the needs of the mentally ill?

3. What residential staff also need education in creating a supportive, low demand environment, a medication monitoring program, and a behavioral approach to problem-solving (Ranz, Horen, McFarland, & Zito, 1991)?

Medication and medication compliance have been isolated by individuals with mental illness as being the single most important factors associated with success in individual with mental illness recovery (Sullivan, 1994). Ensuring that the individual with mental illness has accessibility to medication supervision and transportation along with satisfaction with the clinician are responsibilities of the rehabilitation practitioner.

Crisis Response Services:
1. Do individuals with mental illness have accessibility to crisis assistance resources in their community? Are there 24 hour hotlines available?

2. Are respite beds available?

3. Will outreach workers stay with individual with mental illness during crisis to prevent further hospitalization?

4. Are residential crisis services available and are they accessible by individuals with mental illness?

Housing Supports:
1. Are there transitional housing opportunities available?

2. If not, can programs take active roles in the initiation and development of housing?

3. Are programs available for developing and implementing supported housing or transitional housing opportunities?

4. Is there training and consultation to residential care providers/ development of collaborative relationships with practitioners to support individual with mental illness goals(Heritage, Sudol & Connery, 1987)?

5. Is there a continuum of supervision and structure in housing opportunities to meet the needs and offer choices to individuals with mental illness.

Income Supports and Entitlements:
1. What are individual additional entitlements (Social Security Income, Medicaid)?

2. What resources are necessary so that individuals with mental illness can participate in obtaining eligibility?

Social Recreation/ Peer Support:

1. What resources are necessary to ensure involvement in self-help services?

2. What recreational activities are accessible to individuals with mental illness and what accommodations need to be in place so that they can be tailored to the individual's needs?

3. Pyke & Atcheson (1993) suggest increasing access by:
- advocating for lower fees;
- providing for transportation;
- meeting with social recreation services to discuss activities and supports that would increase utilization;
- providing consultation and support to mainstream services to make them more user friendly;
- identifying people who can assist in linkages, escorting and supporting individual with mental illness in use of social recreation service;
- identifying and reducing actual or potential barriers (e.g. hours of attendance, attendance expectations)

Protection and Advocacy:

1. Are individual rights to receiving treatment in the least restrictive environments being upheld?

2. Are there systems in place to protect the legal rights of individuals with mental illness? Is there access and are there efforts to provide these supports?

3. Are there procedures to ensure individuals with mental illness and families are aware of their rights?

Case Management Services:

1. Are individuals with mental illness connected to ongoing services through case management?

2. What agency is taking responsibility for the coordination and continuity of care and services provided?

3. Are special populations such as the homeless population being provided with adequate services and entitlements?

Health Care and Dental Services:

1. Given the high incidence of medical illness among individuals with serious and persistent mental illness, are there coordinated services for health care maintenance and acute and chronic illnesses?

2. Are these services accessible and is transportation available?

Tools available for use in resource assessment can be utilized to effectively assess the diverse and complex needs of the individual with mental illness. The first tool is the Level of Community Support Systems Scale (LOCSS), developed by Kazarian and Joseph (1994), which is a screening tool to measure the needs of psychiatric individuals with mental illness for community support services. Ratings are based on individual characteristics (Stein, Ronald & Factor, 1990) and the person's need for core services provided by the Community Support System (Stroul, 1989). The second tool is the Uniform Individual with Mental Illness Data Instrument (UCDI), developed by the National Institute of Mental

Health, utilized to assess the Community Support Program (Tessler & Goldman, 1982; Mulkern & Manderscheid, 1989). Two measures from this instrument, the Community Living Skills and the Social Activities Index, provide a level of response categories to elicit levels of resources required for survival in community settings(Wadlak, McKee, Greenberg & Greenley, 1992). A third tool, the Multnomah Community Ability Scale (Barker, Barron, McFarland & Bigelow, 1994) is utilized to serve as a program evaluation tool, measure individual with mental illness change over time, help in resource allocation, and assist with individual with mental illness assessment.

The concept of access, representing the degree of fit between individual with mental illness needs and the system response is explored in the dimensions of access (Penchansky & Thomas, 1981). They are:

- accessibility: the location of the service in relation to the individual with mental illness;

- accommodation: the manner in which the services are provided in relation to the individual's ability to accommodate to those factors (e.g. hours);

- affordability: the cost of the service in relationship to the individual's ability to pay;

- acceptability: the characteristics of service providers in relation to the individual with mental illness preferred characteristics of service providers, and vice versa;

- availability: the volume and type of service available in relationship to individual with mental illness need for such service.

In summary, assessment of resources for each person requires extensive data collection and the integration of tools in order to formulate a comprehensive plan with the individual with mental illness. The process of assessment serves as a learning experience for the individual with mental illness to identify necessary resources and begin to plan and problem solve in improving the access and availability of services in the community setting. The practitioner is dependent on his or her knowledge and skills in resource assessment and service coordination to effectively implement strategic interventions.

Vocational Assessment

Practitioners in the psychosocial rehabilitation field realize the importance of work to individual with mental illness self-esteem and quality of life. The development of vocational approaches are being utilized as an integral part of rehabilitation and ongoing service delivery. There are currently five programs identified with vocational approaches in psychosocial rehabilitation: Boston University Model, Job Clubs, Assertive Community Treatment Model, PSR/Transitional Employment Model, and the Job Bank (Bond, 1992). Each model has specific strengths and weaknesses associated with their implementation. The primary goal of vocational rehabilitation for people with psychiatric disabilities is to reduce the functional limitations of the disability and to empower individuals to be gainfully employed.

In order to implement vocational service delivery, a comprehensive vocational assessment process is necessary to evaluate the individual with mental illness, develop an individualized action plan and evaluate the plan for its strengths and weaknesses and make appropriate vocationally related changes. Further, vocational assessment is utilized as a process to educate the individual, family, and the multidisciplinary team to gauge the person's work success over time. The data is collected not only from the individual with mental illness but from family, former employers, supervisors, and observation and evaluation on current job tasks. Each assessment area incorporates an array of tools to formalize the assessment process. These vocational assessment tools include: (1) situational, (2) batteries, (3) clinical interviewing, and (4) interest scales.

The vocational assessment process includes data collection in the following areas:

Previous work history

Data should be collected on the type of jobs, length of time, duties, hours, and reason for leaving. The individual's perceived strengths and weaknesses, along with the extent of interruption of work by symptoms/illness, further factors that interfered with success on the job, and side effects/adverse reaction of medication should be included. Also, interpersonal/social/emotional factors that the individual with mental illness identifies as possible supports necessary for success may include: (1) personal assistance, (2) work supports, and /or (3) special accommodations. Vocational assessment tools utilized in this area are classified as vocational assessment batteries. These vocational assessment batteries (Botterbush, 1982) are designed to provide reliable assessment of an individual's abilities and skills, job readiness, and job attitudes.

Academic history

This information will include grade completion, courses, or special educa-tion that was achieved. The individual's level of satisfaction with past academic history should be explored. In addition, a discussion of the individual's perceived strengths and weaknesses related to academic performance should also be included.

Current/projected individual with mental illness preferences/interests/expectations concerning job choice

Danley and Anthony (1987) identified the Choose-Get-Keep Model where individual with mental illness choice and involvement drives the vocational rehabilitation process, particularly supported employment. Five assessment areas outlined in this model are: (1) identifying individual interests, (2) identifying personal work capabilities, (3) matching personal traits to job requirements, (4) evaluating alternatives based on personal values, and (5) listing employment options. Since engagement and empowerment are inherent in all practitioner practice strategies, these assessment areas are important in eliciting individual with mental illness involvement.

Situational work assessment of a individual with mental illness performing in any real work setting

An example of a situational assessment tool is the Job Performance Evaluation Form (JPEF [Bond & Freidmeyer, 1987]). This form has four (4) subscales: Work Readiness (e.g. attendance, controls inappropriate behavior), Work Attitude (e.g., accepts responsibility, persistence with task), Interpersonal Relations (e.g. cooperation and rapport with co-workers) and Work Quality and Performance (e.g. follows direction and accuracy). Another example of a situational assessment tool is the Work Personality Profile (Bolton & Roessler, 1986) which identifies

5 performance areas: task orientation, social skills, work motivation, work conformance, and personal presentation. The Job Club Model uses behavioral assessment to identify a person's deficits in terms of skills needed for the job acquisition (Jacobs, 1984).

Physical and motor capabilities

Each person will need to be evaluated for his or her strength and endurance for different work roles. Assessment of gross and fine motor skills will need to be considered in light of medication side effects. Special accommodations can be made to ensure the appropriate fit between the requirements of the position and the capabilities of the individual under the Americans with Disabilities Act.

Social, psychological and emotional patterns

Consideration of overall psychological functioning and the demands of work role will be necessary. Skill building and training for the individual and education for the employer and other workers will provide the resources for successful work roles.

Skills for preparing, seeking and maintaining a work role

A thorough assessment of working skills and role change over time will provide the psychosocial rehabilitation practitioner with information to plan and intervene accordingly with particular attention on transition periods. Cook , Bond, Hoffschmidt, Jonas, Razzano & Weakland (1991) have developed a comprehensive manual designed to provide the situational assessment guides, vocational assessment batteries, clinical interviewing forms, vocational interest scales, vocational service log, and individual with mental illness choice in employ-

ment evaluations along with other scales and measures for implementing and evaluating vocational rehabilitation services. The manual can be utilized as a reference guide in addition to providing research on vocational outcomes of a service agency. Two scales have been utilized as good situational assessment tools: the Thresholds Monthly Work Evaluation Form (TMWEF) and the Work Personality Profile (WPP). These scales are further described in the first table in this chapter and are available from the authors for purchase.

Competency 4

Assess and access appropriate housing.

The ongoing shift of inpatient services to community settings requires that psychosocial rehabilitation practitioners evaluate the ability of the residential setting to meet the needs of the individual with mental illness. Ideally, the concept of supported housing (NIMH, 1987) focuses on community integration of individuals with psychiatric disabilities with an emphasis on individual with mental illness goals and preferences, and on normal housing (Blanch, et al., 1988; Carling et al., 1987). Guiding principles (Hogan & Carling, 1992) are suggested to assist in the selection of "normal" housing:

- Housing must be chosen by the individual with full involvement in the selection process.

- Neighborhoods should be chosen based on the capacity to assimilate and support the person. Specific emphasis on range of necessary commercial facilities (e.g. post office, library, grocery store, drug store, recreational facilities).

- The number of residents with mental illness in relation to total residents in overall housing unit is critical and should be limited and consistent with community norms. This principle assumes that each community has a limited capacity for assimilation of disabled individuals.

- The appearance of the housing should be consistent with the neighborhood norms.

- Housing should be easily manageable to facilitate individual with mental illness adjustment and stable quality of life.

- Housing should promote individual with mental illness stability and not be transitional.

- Housing should provide opportunities for the individual with mental illness to exert control over their environment and utilize their practical living skills.

Massey & Wu (1993) identify a list of items developed in collaboration with individuals with mental illness and family members that are important characteristics in community settings. These items are: (1) independence and personal choice; (2) social opportunity; (3) safety and comfort; (4) privacy; (5) convenient location; (6) proximity to mental health services; and (7) proximity to family. Each category has a subheading that can be incorporated into a thorough assessment. This same study also indicates that case managers and individuals with mental illness had rated characteristics differently with recommendations that individuals with mental illness and case managers work more closely together in creating alternative community housing.

Part of residential setting assessment is the role of social supports in residential environments. Social support network is operationally defined as the intimate psychosocial network which is a subset of the larger personal social network (Pattison & Pattison, 1998). These social networks have been refined as including emotional support, information, personal feedback, material aid, guidance, physical assistance, social participation, family, and friendship relationships. The Arizona Social Support Interview Schedule (ASSIS [Barrera, 1981]) inquires about several of the functional areas noted. Bogart and Solarz (1990) reported a positive correlation between the number of friends and satisfaction with support. Peer support becomes an important variable linked to potential success in residential arenas. Baker, Jodrey & Intagliata (1992) findings support that satisfaction with life areas may be more affected by the availability of social support with the additional dimension of engaging in social activities. Goering, Durkin, Foster, Boyles, Babiak & Lancee (1992) indicate that monitoring social network composition and function is important especially since the social environments are artificial and can have potential negative consequences. The Community Oriented Programs Evaluation Scale (COPES) developed by Moos(1971) and associates is designed specifically to measure the social environments of community care facilities. The dimensions included are staff involvement, support, spontaneity, autonomy, practical orientation, personal problem orientation, anger and aggression, order and organization, program clarity and staff control. It has been widely utilized in community facilities and established norms. It can be utilized not only for assessment but also to improve the communication and collaboration between home managers and mental health practitioners.

The Uniform Consumer Data Instrument (UCDI) developed by the National Institute of Mental Health (NIMH) was utilized to evaluate Community Support Programs (CSP). It was designed to collect individual with mental illness level data using case managers. Two component measures from the UCDI are the Community Living Skills (CLS) and Social Activities Scale that can be utilized to evaluate residential living. Correspondence between case managers and individuals with mental illness on these two scales was examined in the study completed by Widlak, McKee, Greenberg and Greenley (1992). The St. Louis Inventory of Community Living Skills developed by Everson and Boyd (1993) was designed to be useful in measuring the level of specific skills needed for community or group home tenure and also as an important part of the level of functioning. The positive aspects of the scale are the two categories of basic skills such as personal hygiene, appropriate behavior, and exercise to advanced skills (e.g., handling time, meal preparation, appropriate sexuality, and literacy). Psychiatric rehabilitation interventions can be identified easier with tools that can differentiate skills required for community living.

The housing environment has been demonstrated to impact community adjustment. Baker and Douglas (1990) identify residential assessment to include not only the type of housing situation and setting but also the physical condition of the housing, the neighborhood, the exterior/ interior of the residence, the individual's property, physical layout for sleeping, maintaining personal hygiene, eating, preparing food, solitary relaxation and socializing with others. The results of the study indicate that resident adequacy had a significant impact on Global Assessment Scale score and perceived quality of life. The study supports that when people live in housing that is physically unappealing and is inappropriate, then their degree of maladaptive behavior also increases. The Behavior Setting Assessment (BSA) (Perkins & Baker, 1991) follows the concept of person-environment fit to determine the effectiveness of residential and program placements.

Competency 5

Assess active addiction and co-dependency.

Individuals with dual diagnosis of serious mental illness and substance disorder are particularly challenging to psychosocial rehabilitation practitioners. The assessment to establish the diagnosis for substance use and abuse is critical. Kofoed (1991) indicates that missing the diagnosis has serious implications, since unrecognized substance abuse will compromise the psychiatric diagnosis and further assessment and treatment planning.

Employing substance assessment tools can overcome the denial that accompanies these disorders. Denial can be understood as the inability of the individual with mental illness to admit the extent of their drug or alcohol use and its connection to their current dysfunctions.

Assessment parameters depend on stage of individual with mental illness in the system and current individual with mental illness functioning. If the assessment is part of an initial intake, then specific screening tools have been developed to facilitate the assessment process. Questionnaires such as the CAGE

Questions for Review of Substance Abuse History

Questions to Consider	Areas to Review with Individual
History of substance use	• History of past experimentation or self-medication. • Drugs that are or were used. • Last use. • Method to support drug use. • History of needle use.
Effects of drug use	• Mental Effects: depression, suicidal thoughts, impaired or improved thinking, hallucinations, shaking. • Physical Effects: nausea, abdominal pain, chills, runny nose and eyes, violence toward others. • Impact on family or significant other. • Sexual behavior: unsafe sex, rape or impotence.
Treatment history	• Efforts at self-stopping. • Treatment programs and outcomes. • Periods of success.
Family History	• Two generation review of all relatives.
Consequences of use	• Losses of job, home, social support, incarceration, health. • Legal involvement

(Mayfield, McCleod, & Hall, 1974) and CAGEAID (Brown, 1992) is a four item validated tool that provides a rapid and accurate profile for assessment and treatment planning. The Michigan Alcoholism Screening Test (MAST [Selzer, 1971]) has also been utilized in identification of substance use and abuse. Drake et al (1990) found that the MAST was 84.2% sensitive for current and 86.8% sensitive for lifetime alcoholism in schizophrenic individuals with mental illness.

The Addiction Severity Index (ASI [MCLellan, Luborsky, Woody & O'Brien, 1980]) is an instrument that guides the interviewer through a series of questions about drug use and its consequences as does the American Psychiatric Association's Structured Clinical Interview for the DSM-IV (SCID). Collateral informants (i.e., relatives and close friends) are often helpful in determining the presence of substance use and abuse patterns.

A comprehensive substance abuse history should include the following areas noted above. Other biological assessments are: alcohol on breath, positive drug tests, injuries, traumas or accidents, withdrawal symptoms or impaired cognitive capabilities, physical symptoms (yellow sclera, hand shaking, histories of tuberculosis & hepatitis), and medication compliance. Psychological assessment includes intoxicated behaviors, denial and manipulation, and history of alcohol or substance use. Social assessment includes social supports, family history, legality, housing and employment histories, and nutritional deficits. All assessments incorporate five major areas: (1) readiness to address what events or situations resulted in the need for treatment, (2) relationships both past and present, (3) rational view of attitudes and beliefs about the problem, (4) resources both internal strengths and external supports, and (5) motivation for change and recovery .

Competency 6

Assess the need for crisis intervention.

Crisis situations are common occurrences when working with individuals with mental illness susceptible to chronic stress from their disability, stigma, hopelessness, and powerlessness. Further, changes in medication compliance along with use of non-prescriptive drugs and alcohol and frequent changes in mood place individuals with serious and persistent mental illness in high risk for harming self and others. The assessment of these areas requires the psychosocial rehabilitation practitioner to be an astute observer and listener to ensure that proactive strategies are established in the event of a crisis situation. The individual's own belief of what constitutes a crisis needs to be elicited. The individual may believe that a change in housing arrangements is extremely upsetting and that the person cannot cope with such a change. In this situation the practitioner needs to provide necessary supports and resources to ensure an easier transition. The potential of relapse as a result of a pending crisis always requires consideration and intervention.

Therefore, the first step in a crisis assessment is to have an outline of past crisis situations in the individual's life,

how they coped, and what was the outcome. Baseline data on past crisis events will provide the practitioner with a clear understanding of the coping abilities of the individual, their strengths and weaknesses under stressful conditions, and residual effects of the outcomes. This data will provide a guide to the practitioner to be proactive in planning for potential crisis and meeting the individual's needs when a crisis does develop.

The first area for assessment is suicidality. The practitioner should follow six steps as part of the clinical interview to ensure a comprehensive assessment:

1. **Document and review all suicidal behaviors, thoughts, and attempts.** For this current crisis situation, it is important to document the frequency, intensity, and duration (Chiles & Stroosahl, 1995). Frequency refers to how often specific episodes of suicidal behavior, ideation, or verbalization occur. Intensity is a measure of how concentrated the behavior is at any given point in time. Duration refers to how long an episode of suicidal behavior lasts. Chiles & Strosahl (1995) look at increases in frequency, intensity, and duration as an indicator of severity. Acknowledgment and monitoring of the individual with mental illness and family helps reduce shame and distress associated with suicidal ideation.

2. **Identify high risk individuals.** Initiate a screening process for possible hospitalization or 24 hour supervision.

3. **Provide an ongoing assessment of what the individual with mental illness is experiencing and the practitioner's interventions for prevention of harmful acts.** Review of

the plan-availability-lethality triad is important with questions that include: Do you have a plan? Do you have a method? How lethal is plan?

4. **Ensure an assertive position in the assessment and as discussed in the next chapter, the intervention process.** The problems such as depression, anxiety, and mental pain are at the heart of such behaviors, and it is the practitioner's responsibility to acknowledge and provide a safe and trusting place to explore alternative coping strategies. Efforts to identify positive forces that would deter the person from attempting or completing the suicide are critical interventions. Truly understanding the negative impact suicide has on solving a person's problem and the others that are part of the individual's life becomes an important assessment and problem-solving intervention area.

5. **Utilize self-report inventories and assessment scales.** Several self-reported inventories are available for use by practitioners to gather additional information and understanding of the individual's feelings. The Beck Hopelessness Scale (Beck & Steer, 1988) and the Reasons for Living Inventory Items (Chiles & Strosahl, 1995) and the Suicidal Thinking and Behavior Questionnaire(Chiles & Strosahl, 1995) can be provided depending on the individual and the rationale for its use in the assessment process. The Suicide Probability Scale (SPS [Cull & Gill, 1988]) is a 36 item inventory measuring an individual's self-reported attributes and behaviors which have a bearing on their suicidal risk (p.3).

6. **Ensure that proper supervision is provided from a senior practitioner, supervisor, or team to the practitioner in the review of all possible assessment efforts and intervention strategies.** Harm to others will be further discussed under the violence assessment and a similar assessment process should be followed.

Multicultural Assessment

Intrapersonal awareness is the first step toward cultural awareness. This is accomplished by an examination of one's own beliefs, attitudes, and values through introspection and reflective self-evaluation (Sodowsky, Taffe, Gutkin & Wise, 1994). Espin (1987) notes that if counselors were aware of the influences of their race or ethnicity on their own personality and interpersonal style, they could better recognize the ways in which ethnicity influences individual with mental illness behaviors, interactions, values, and life goals. An understanding of the individual's worldview along with self-examination of cultural competencies will allow for improved assessment and appropriate intervention strategies and techniques. Further, the ongoing process of learning other ethno-cultural perspectives and the process of understanding the dynamics of the difference are key activities for practitioners.

Multcultural assessment assumes more importance as we are learning more about the possibility of misdiagnosis and therefore mistreatment of people based on incomplete or insensitive understanding of cultural and ethnic considerations influencing individual behaviors and attitudes. In an unpublished manuscript, Finley has developed a cross-cultural assessment framework which suggests an inverse pyramid of layered domains proceeding from the social system variables through the ethno-graphic variable and demographic variables to acculturation and adaptational styles, ethnic identify development, and finally, the intra-personal variables. This process places the emphasis on the practitioner's consideration of a variety of ethno-cultural factors before evaluating the intra-personal or intra-psychic dynamics.

Arnold (1990) has developed an Initial Strength Assessment Inventory which includes a section entitled Multi-Cultural Psychosocial Assessment Tool. This five-page practitioner interview tool allows for the assessment of 15 areas with the ability to rate the relative importance of each in these areas of need assessment. Garrison & Podell (1981) discuss the practical problems of economically assessing an individual's support system in the context of a psychiatric emergency service. Using an open-ended interview format, this instrument focuses on the naturally occurring supports with particular sensitivity to the cultural understanding of these supports, including the areas of ethnicity/cultural background, household composition, extended family/kin, religious involvement, and illness beliefs. Pederson (1987b) indicates that counselors are culturally competent when they can look at their own culture from an outsider's perspective.

Quality of Life Assessment

Quality of life has gained significant importance as a mental health service outcome that includes both an objective and a subjective component (Baker & Intagliatia, 1982; Bigelow, Brodsky, Stewart & Olson, 1982; Bigelow, McFarland & Olson, 1991; Lehman, 1982). Several instruments are available for practitioners to utilize in their overall comprehensive assessments with individuals with mental illness. Further, ongoing successful rehabilitation interventions should be evaluated with quality of life questionnaires on an ongoing basis for all individuals with mental illness in the community setting.

The Quality of Life Interview's (QOLI [Lehman, 1982,1988]) overall purpose is to assess the life circumstances of persons with serious mental illness both in terms of what they actually do and their experience and feelings about these experiences. It incorporates both the objective and subjective perspective of individuals with mental illness. The QOLI is a structured self-report interview that consists of 143 items and requires 45 minutes to administer. Quality of Life Scale (QLS) was developed to assess the deficit syndrome in individuals with mental illness with schizophrenia. It is a semi-structured interview and has 21 items rated on fixed interval scales based on the interviewer's judgment of the individual with mental illness' functioning. The 21 items are reduced to four scales: intrapsychic foundation, interpersonal relations, instrumental role, and total score.

Oregon Quality of Life Questionnaire (OQLQ [Bigelow & McFarland, 1991]) has been updated since its original form, which was published in 1981. The authors' definition of quality of life consists of fulfilling needs, meeting social expectations, and accessing opportunities by using abilities. Mental health services are intended to moderate social demand, increase opportunities, and improve abilities. The OQLQ tool yields 14 scale scores: psychological distress and well-being, tolerance of stress, total basic need satisfaction, independence, interpersonal interactions, spousal role, social support, work at home, employability, work on the job, meaningful use of time, and negative consequences of drug and alcohol use. The OQLQ was developed to assess the impact of mental health services on the individual with mental illness' quality of life.

The Community Adjustment Form (CAF [Stein & Test, 1980]) is a semi-structured self-report interview which was developed to assess life satisfaction and other quality of life indicators. It consists of 140 items and requires 45 minutes to administer. Areas assessed are: quality of life situation, employment status and history, income sources and amounts, meal patterns, social and family contacts, legal patterns, life satisfaction, self esteem, medical care, and agency utilization.

Quality of Life (QLC [Malm, 1981]) was developed to provide information about which aspects of quality of life are important to individuals with mental illness and practitioners to assist in therapeutic planning. The areas assessed are leisure activities, work, vocational rehabilitation, economic dependency, social relationships, knowledge and education, psychological dependency, inner experience, housing, medical care, and religion. It is a 93-item rating scale completed by a trained interviewee in one semi-structured interview.

Satisfaction with Life Domain Scale (SDLE [Baker & Intagliata, 1982]) is an instrument developed to evaluate the impact of the Community Support Program on the quality of life of individuals with serious mental illness. It is a self-report scale, consisting of 15 items and requires ten minutes to administer. Items covered are: satisfaction with housing neighborhood, sustenance, clothing, health, services and facilities, economic situation, and relationship to state hospital.

Medication Compliance Assessment

Effective treatment and rehabilitation interventions rely on compliance on neuroleptic medication maintenance. Understanding individual with mental illness perceptions of medical self-administration will provide the entire multi-disciplinary team with information to plan and evaluate strategic interventions on an ongoing basis. It is the individual with mental illness subjective interpretation of an altered physical experience with medication that will determine their degree of medication compliance.

Two tools currently in the literature are the Drug Attitude Inventory (Award, 1993) and the Rating of Medication Influences (Weiden, Rapkin, Mott, Zygmunt, Goldman, Horvitz-Lennon & Frances, 1994). Perceived daily benefit, relationships with prescribing clinician, family beliefs, distress from side effects, and financial obstacles are among several of the areas identified on the scales. These tools can be utilized to monitor medication compliance over time.

Satisfaction Assessment

The identification of service elements that persons with mental illness find to support their recovery is a key in successful rehabilitation planning and intervention delivery. Corrigan (1990) has identified four superordinate factors that underlie individual with mental illness satisfaction decision making. They are: concerns about qualities of the staff (e.g., sensitive, interested, involved, active accessible, nondominant); physical environment (e.g., clean and quiet, private and safe); treatment services (e.g., interesting, dignifying, and making a difference); and activities that foster individual with mental illness autonomy (e.g., ward management and aftercare opportunities). Recommendations indicate that programming should conform to individual with mental illness perspectives and increased collaboration between individual with mental illness and practitioners support individual with mental illness satisfaction.

Competency 7

Assess the role of family support.

Families have been recognized as a vital resource in the care of relatives with severe psychiatric disabilities. The multidiscplinary mental health team needs to adequately prepare families with the knowledge, skills, and attitudes to cope with and manage their individual with mental illness. Practitioners need to fully develop family as a resource. Families, like individuals with mental illness, are all unique and will require different interventions based on their particular needs and perspectives. Program location, population, cultural and ethnic considerations are all impact variables to the assessment, planning, and intervention programs for families. Anderson, Reiss & Hogerty (1986) have developed programs of psychoeducation for families that can be used as a foundational material. Johnson (1990) provides an outline of what families want from professionals: (1) Information: causes of mental illness, prevention of relapse, role of medication and side effects, medication compliance, dealing with inappropriate behaviors, violence, entitlements, and work opportunities; (2) Access to resources: referral to a full spectrum of available services such as crisis management to employment; (3) Continuity of care: information concerning case management and support during community

living; (4) Respect and understanding: acknow-ledgement of the family's efforts and humanness in managing the everyday struggle of providing care. Family satisfaction tools (Hanson & Rapp, 1992) provide a good assessment as to what is and what is not being provided in the mental health care delivery system.

Family satisfaction with the level of interventions directed in effectively dealing with their relatives provides a view of their perceptions concerning the type of services they believe are necessary and supportive of their role. In their survey of individuals with mental illness of the National Alliance for the Mentally Ill (NAMI), Kasper, Steinwachs & Skinner (1992) found that individual with mental illness families identified six areas of functioning that needed assistance, including illness management, community living skills, managing relationships, and engaging in productive activities. According to the data analysis, the last two areas of managing relationships and engaging in productive activities remain largely unmet. Solomon & Marcenko (1992) identify a comprehensive set of items in 2 domains: (1) family satisfaction with meeting the relative's needs in 15 areas; and (2) family satisfaction in meeting the family's need for information, skill building, resources, and supports.

Sexual Abuse Assessment

Sexual abuse and the subsequent residual trauma requires all practitioners to increase their vigilance around assessment and identification of these individuals. Survivors of sexual abuse will require specific interventions and ongoing evaluation to ensure positive trauma resolution. Hutchings and Dutton (1993) utilized a questionnaire to screen for sexual assault and abuse. The following three areas were included:

1. "Have you had sexual intercourse or sexual acts (anal or oral intercourse or penetration by objects other than a penis) when you did not want to (because someone used a position of authority, threatened you, or used physical force to make you)?" [Rape]

2. "Has anyone ever attempted sexual intercourse or attempted sexual acts (oral or anal intercourse or penetration by objects other than a penis) when you did not want to (by using a position of authority, by threatening you, or by using physical force to make you)?" [Attempted Rape]

3. "Have you had sexual activity (fondling, kissing or touching, but not intercourse) when you did not want to (because someone used a position of authority, threatened you, or used physical force to make you)?" [Molestation] (p.60)

Further, adult survivors experience negative trauma resolution with the following symptoms: nightmares, recurrent and intrusive thoughts and memories of the event, hyperarousal (difficulty falling asleep, irritability, difficulty concentrating, and exaggerated startle reflex), emotional numbing, depression, anger, guilt, and shame. Ongoing mental status examination over time will enable the psychosocial rehabilitation practitioner to differentiate symptoms and provide linkages to appropriate resources.

Violence Assessment

Specific factors have been isolated as strong predictors of violence in the population with psychiatric disabilities. These predictors can be utilized not only for practitioners but also for the families of individuals with mental illness and com-munity residential providers. Straznickas et al (1993) reported that among individuals with mental illness who have been admitted to psychiatric hospitals as a result of physically attacking someone within the previous two weeks, families of individuals with mental illness had been the object of the assault 56% of the time. Specific predictors have been isolated that should be part of individual with mental illness' ongoing harm assessment. They are history of violent behavior, concurrent alcohol or drug use non-compliant with medication, psychotic symptoms, presence of delusions, hallucinations, and neurological impairment such as a previous head injury. These items can be utilized as a checklist and monitored over course of rehabilitation. Further, specific interventions can be targets to high risk individuals to reduce the potential for assault and violence.

Physical Health Assessment

The stress from everyday life is certainly apparent in individuals struggling with psychiatric illness. The Vulnerability-Stress-Coping Model (Nuechterlein & Dawson, 1984) provides evidence that exposure to stressful situations has potential to trigger relapse of symptoms. Persons with serious mental illness are vulnerable to stress due to their problem solving capabilities and deficits in social skills. The Hassles Scale (Kenner, Coyne, Schaefer & Lazarus, 1981) has been shortened and studied with the psychiatric population (Segal & Vander-Voort, 1993) with results that indicate that daily stress plays an important role in psychological and physical health status. It can be utilized to assess stress levels and provide appropriate interventions.

Another important area is the extent of physical illness in the psychiatric population. There is strong evidence that persons with serious mental illness have a high prevalence of co-occurring medical problems (Marcile, Hoffman, Bloom, Faulkner & Keepers, 1987; Lima and Pai, 1987; Hoffman and Koran, 1984; Koranyi, 1972) that are undiagnosed or not evaluated due to lack of primary medical care. Psychosocial rehabilitation practitioners who have extensive knowledge of and contact with this population need to be aware and to provide a limited ongoing assessment of the medical problems and appropriate referrals.

A simple checklist that incorporates the last medical examination and follow-up care for specific medical problems can be a useful tool or section of already existing assessment tool. Nevertheless, this area requires monitoring to ensure that the individual with mental illness is receiving the medical services necessary for recovery.

Persons with severe psychiatric disabilities are identified as being at risk for HIV infection. Seven to twenty percent of admissions to private and public mental health facilities are reported to test positive for HIV antibodies (Sacks, Dermatis, Looser-Ott, Burton & Perry, 1992); National Institute of Mental Health, 1990). Further, a recent survey of the literature indicates that a significant proportion of this group are sexually active (Carman & Brady, 1990) and are engaging in high risk sexual practice and drug use behaviors (Cournos, McKennin, Meyer-Bahlburg, Guido, & Meyer, 1993; Sacks, Perry, Graver, Schindledecker & Hall, 1990; Sacks, Silberstein, Weiler, & Perry, 1990). Approaches can be developed to educate and provide necessary resources in order to effectively prevent the spread of the virus and other sexually transmitted diseases. In addition, the psychosocial rehabilitation practitioner can have an important role in prevention through education and early detection and referral.

A high risk assessment screening tool described by Carman and Brady (1990) can be utilized to identify potential individuals with mental illness and provide strategic interventions. Assessment areas included items relevant to intravenous drugs, recreational drugs, alcohol abuse, sexual history, history of sexually transmitted diseases (STDs), and frequent use of condoms. Also included were items covering the testing for HIV and knowledge of transmission and prevention of HIV. Other areas for consideration are behavior patterns when individuals with mental illness are experiencing crises (Sacks, Dermatitis, Button, Hull & Perky, 1994).

Program Assessment : Level of Need-Care Assessment

The Level of Need-Care Assessment method (LONCA [Uehara, Smukler & Newman, 1994]) was developed by a team of service system planners to match resources to individual with mental illness level of need. It first measures the incidence and intensity of need in specific functioning domains. The LONCA Method emphasizes three key functional status areas: physical functioning, social functioning, and psychological functioning. With the preliminary data on the type and intensity of services, planning occurs to address specific individual with mental illness needs, calculated service costs, and the identification of clusters of individuals with mental illness with similar need-cost profiles. The LONCA may assist in the allocation of scarce resources across diverse individual with mental illness and service options. The table on the next page has a summary of other program assessment tools and their specific characteristics such as empowerment, program values, program outcomes, individual service plan and individual with mental illness goals, and advocacy efforts.

In summary, the assessment process in psychosocial rehabilitation requires a combination of knowledge, skills, and attitudes to provide a comprehensive review of individual with mental illness needs and goals. The assessment process utilizes both interviewing and counseling techniques along with standardized tools to validate the individual with mental illness' level of functioning in psychological, social, vocational, residential, and educational areas. Additionally, related variables pertinent to the rehabilitation and recovery process such as multicultural needs, physical health care status, family involvement, harm assessment and past traumas should also be evaluated and considered in the overall development and implementation of interventions with individuals with mental illness. The process of assessment is not only a requirement of good psychosocial rehabilitation practice but also allows the practitioner an opportunity to understand the complete and personal life of the individual with mental illness. The individual with mental illness, in turn, is provided with the experience of taking a responsible approach to what has happened in the past and what he or she is currently experiencing and how to be a partner who actively participates in the personal rehabilitation and recovery process. The individual with mental illness' role is to support what he or she believes can be realistically accomplished given the summary data on both long- and short-term goals. The PSR practitioner's role is to actively engage individuals with mental illness, develop rehabilitation plans based on comprehensive assessment techniques and implement interventions that are individually based, utilizing the best practices available in the PSR literature and research.

Program Assessment Tools

Program Assessment Tool	Characteristics
Level of Community Support Systems Scale (LOCSS) (Kazarian & Joseph, 1994)	Screening tool to measure needs of individuals for community support services based on core components of CSS.
Multnomah Community Ability Scale (Barker, Barron, McFarlans & Bigelow, 1994)	Instrument provides a measure of the individual with mental illness' severity of disability that in turn may be used to: a. Describe the agency case mix. b. Measure individual with mental illness progress. c. Assign individuals with mental illness to different levels of service. d. Assist payors in determination of reinbursement.
Community-Oriented Programs Environment Scale (COPES)(Moos, 1974)	Instrument has a 100 point scale with ten questions in each subscale. Contains the following dimensions and subscales concerning the individual with mental illness in relationship to the service program: (1) Staff involvement; support; autonomy; practical orientation, anger and aggression order and organization, program clarity and staff control; (2) Personal Growth; (3) Systems Maintenance.
Jerrell and Hargreaves' Community Program Philosophy Scale (CPPS) (Hargreaves, 1991)	80 item instrument that measures program-wide values and emphases as perceived by the practitioner providing services.
Uniform Individual with Mental Illness Data Instrument(UCDI) developed by the National Institute of Mental Health (Tessler & Goldman, 1982)	Composed of several subscales that measure individual with mental illness functioning with data collected by case managers in the Community Support Program.
Colorado Individual with mental illness Assessment Record (CCAR) (Ellis, Wilson & Foster, 1984)	Composed of 9 different dimensions of functioning to evaluate program outcomes on statewide level.
Goal Individualization Measure (Arns & Linney, 1995)	Instrument to measure the level of service individualization in psychosocial rehabilitation and community support programs through the goals established in the individual with mental illness' treatment plans.
Personal Empowerment Scale, Organizational Empowerment Scale and the Extra-Organizational Scale (Segal, Silverman & Temkin, 1995)	Instruments that measure empowerment as a program principle and individual with mental illness outcome.
Advocacy Needs Assessment Instrument (Moxley & Freddolino, 1990)	Open-ended designed instrument allowing maximum opportunity for individual with mental illness to identify self-perceived needs as part of the Individual with mental illness Support and Representational Model of advocacy services.
CSP Implementation Analysis (Brekke & Test, 1992)	8 dimensions are identified with corresponding assessment tools.
Behavior Setting Assessment (BSA) (Perkins & Barker, 1991)	A two-page instrument to evaluate the concept of person and environment fit to determine the effectiveness of residential placements.

Individual Assessment Areas

Area of Assessment	Assessment Tools
1. Symptom Assessment	a. Brief Psychiatric Rating Scale (Overall and Gorham, 1962). b. Schedule for Assessment of Negative Symptoms (Andreson, 1982). c. Negative Symptom Assessment (Raskin, Pelchat, Alphs & Levine, 1993). d. Beck Depression Inventory (Beck, Ward, Mendelson, Mock & Erbaugh, 1961). e. Hamilton Rating Scale (Hamilton, 1960). f. Symptom Checklist (SCL-90) (Derogatis, Lipman & Covi, 1973).
2. Global Assessment	a. Global Assessment Scale (Endicott, Spitzer, Fleiss & Cohen, 1976).
3. Skill Assessment	a. Skill Assessment Scale (Lowell, MacLean & Carroll, 1985). b. Independent Living Skills Survey (Wallace, 1986).
4. Disability Rating Assessment	a. Disabilty Rating Scale (Hoyle, Nietxel, Guthrie, Baker-Prewitt & Heine, 1992). b. Life Skills Profile (Rosen, Hadzi-Paavlovic & Parker, 1989).
5. Cognitive Assessment	a. Psychiatric Mental Status Examination b. Mini-Mental State Exam (Folstein, Folstein & McHugh, 1975). b. Neurobehavioral Cognitive Status Exam (Mitrushina, Abara, & Blumenfelf, 1994). c. Executive Interview (Royall, Mahurin & Gray, 1992).
6. Resource Assessment	a. Community Living Skills & Social Activities Index (Wadlak, McKee, Greenberg & Greenley, 1992). b. Also See Program Assessment Tools.
7. Vocational Assessment	a. Job Performance Evaluation Form (Bond and Freidmeyer, 1987). b. Work Personality Profile (Bolton & Roessler, 1986). c. Also see tools under functional assessment.
8. Residential Assessment	a. Arizona Social Support Interview Schedule (Barrera, 1981). b. Community Oriented Program Evaluation Scale (Moos, 1971). c. Uniform Individual with Mental Illness Data Instrument/Community Living Skills & Social Activities Scale (NIMH). d. St. Louis Inventory of Community Living Skills (Everson & Boyd, 1993). e. Behavior Setting Assessment (Perkins & Barker, 1991). f. Social Network & Support Interview Tool (Moxley, 1988). g. Network Analysis Profile (Sokolovsky & Cohen, 1981).
9. Substance Use/Abuse Assessment	a. CAGE (Mayfield, McCleod & Hall, 1974). b. CAGEAID (Brown, 1992) c. MAST (Selzer, 1971). d. Addiction Severity Index (McLellan, Luborsky, Woody and O'Brien, 1980).

Individual Assessment Areas

Area of Assessment	Assessment Tools
10. Crisis Assessment	a. Beck Hopelessness Scale (Beck & Steer, 1988).
	b. Reasons for Living Inventory and Suicidal Thinking Behavior Questionnaire (Chiles & Strosahl, 1995).
	c. Suicide Probability Scale (Cull & Gill, 1988).
11. Multicultural Assessment	a. Finley (citation unknown).
	b. Initial Strength Assessment Inventory, Arnold (1990).
12. Quality of Life Assessment	a. Quality of Life Interview (Lehman, 1992;1988).
	b. Quality of Life Scale (Heinrick, Hanlon &Carpenter, 1984).
	c. Oregon Quality of Life Questionnaire (Bigelow and McFarland, 1991).
	d. Community Adjustment Form (Stein & Test, 1980).
	e. Quality of Life (Malm, 1981).
	f. Satisfaction with Life Domain Scale (Baker &Intaglia, 1982).
13. Medication Compliance Assessment	a. Drug Attitude Inventory (Award, 1993).
	b. Rating of Medication Influences (Weiden, Rapkin, Mott, Zygmunt, Goldman, Horvitz-Lennon & Frances, 1994).

References

Accordino, M. P. & Guerney, B. G. (1993). Effects of the relationship enhancement program on community residential rehabilitation staff and clients. *Psychosocial Rehabilitation Journal, 17*(2), 131-144.

Ahmed, M. & Goldman, J. (1994).Clinical care update: Cognitive rehabilitation of adults with severe and persistent illness: A group model. *Community Mental Health Journal, 30*(4), 385-394.

Anderson, C.M., Reiss, D.J. & Hogarty, G.E. (1986). *Schizophrenia and the family.* New York: Guilford Press.

Andreason, N.C. (1982). Negative symptoms in schizophrenia: Definition and reliability. *Archives of General Psychiatry, 39*, 784-788.

Angelini, D. (1982). Functional needs of the chronically mentally ill: Implications for service delivery. *Psychosocial Rehabilitation Journal, 5*(1), 29-33.

Anthony, W. A. (1994).The vocational rehabilitation of people with serious mental illness: Issues and Myths. *Innovations and Research. 3*(2),17-23.

_____.(1977). Psychological rehabilitation: A concept in need of a method. *American Psychologist, 32*(8), 658-662.

Anthony, W. , Cohen, M. R. & Farkas, M. (1990). *Psychosocial rehabilitation.* Boston: Boston University, Center for Psychosocial rehabilitation.

Anthony, W. A., Cohen, M.R. & Farkas, M.D. (1987).Training and technical assistance in psychosocial rehabilitation. In A. Myerson & T. Fine (Eds.) *Psychiatric disability: Clinical, legal and administrative dimensions.* Washington, D.C.: American Psychiatric Press.

Anthony, W. Cohen, M.R., & Cohen, B. F. (1983). Philosophy, treatment process, and principles of psychosocial rehabilitation approach.In L.L. Bachrach (Ed.)

Deinstitutionalization (New Directions for Mental Health Services), 17, 67- 69. San Francisco: Jossey-Bass.

Anthony, W. Cohen, M. & Nemec, P. *Assessment in psychosocial rehabilitation.*

Arana, G. & Hyman, S. (1991). *Handbook of psychiatric drug therapy.* Boston: Little, Brown and Company.

Arana, J., Hastings, B., Heron, E. (1991). Continuous care teams in intensive outpatient treatment of chronic mentally ill patients. *Hospital and Community Psychiatry, 42*(5), 503-507.

Arns, P. G. & Linney, J.A. (1995). The relationship of service individualization to client functioning in programs for severely mentally ill persons. *Community Mental Health Journal, 31*(2), 127-137.

Barker, S., Barron, N., McRarlandy, B., and Bigelow, D. (1994). A community ability scale for chronically mentally ill consumers: Part I. reliability and validity. *Community Mental Health Journal, 30*(4), 363-383.

Baker F., Jodrey, D. & Intagliata, J. (1992). Social support and quality of life of community support clients. *Community Mental Health Journal, 28*(5), 397-411.

Baker, F. & Douglas, C. (1990). Housing environments and community adjustment of severely mentally ill persons. *Community Mental Health Journal, 26*(6), 497-505.

Baker, F. & Intagliata, J. (1982). Quality of life in the evaluation of community support systems. *Evaluation and Program Planning, 5,* 69-79.

Barker, S., Barron, N., McFarland, B., & Bigelow, D.A.(1994). A community ability scale for chronically mentally ill consumers: Part I. reliability and validity. *Community Mental Health Journal, 30*(4), 363-383.

Barnes, D. & Benjamin, S. (1987). The Self Care Assessment Schedule(SCAS)-The purpose and construction of a new assessment of self care behaviors. *Psychosomatic Research, 31*(2), 191-202.

Barrera, M. Jr. (1981). Social support in the adjustment of pregnant adolescents. In B.H. Gottlieb (Ed.) *Social Networks and Social Support* (pp. 69-96). Beverly Hills: Sage Publication.

Bartels, S. & Thomas, W. (1991). Lesson from a pilot residential treatment program for people with dual diagnosis of severe mental illness and substance use disorder. *Psychosocial Rehabilitation Journal, 15*(2), 19-30.

Beck, A.T., Ward, C.H., Mendelson, M., Mock, J. & Erbaugh, J. (1961). An inventory for measuring depression. *Archives of General Psychiatry, 4,* 561-571.

Beck, A. T. & Steer, R. A. (1988). *Manual for the Beck Hopelessness Scale.* San Antonio, TX: Psychological Corporation.

Becker, D. & Drake, R. (1994). Individual placement and support: A community mental health center approach to vocational rehabilitation. *Community Mental Health Journal, 30*(2), 193-205.

Benoit, B. (1992). Promoting the rehabilitative potential of community residential facilities. *Psychosocial Rehabilitation Journal, 16*(1), 109–113.

Berman, C. & Rozensky, R. (1984). Sex education for the chronic psychiatric patient: The effects of a sexual-issues group on knowledge and attitudes. *Psychosocial Rehabilitation Journal, 1,* 29-33.

Bigelow, D.A., McFarland, B.H., & Olson, M.M. (1991). Quality of life of community mental health program clients: Validating a measure. *Community Mental Health Journal, 27*(1) 43-55.

Blanch, A.K., Carling, P.J. & Ridgway, P. (1988). Normal housing with specialized support: A psychosocial rehabilitation approach to living in the community. *Rehabilitation Psychology, 4*(32), 47-55.

Bolton, B,.& Roessler, R. (1986). *Manual for the work personality profile.* Fayetteville, Arkansas Research and Training Center in Vocational Research.

Bond, G. R. & Freidmeyer, M.H. (1987). Predictive validity of situational assessment at a psychosocial rehabilitation center. *Rehabilitation Psychology, 32*, 99-112.

Botterbusch, K.F. (1982). *A comparison of commercial vocational evaluation systems* (2nd. ed.). Menonomie, WI: Materials Development Center, University of Wisconsin-Stout, Stout Vocational Institute, School of Education and Human Resources.

Brekke, J. S. & Test, M.A. (1992). A model for measuring the implementation of community support programs: Results of three sites. *Community Mental Health Journal, 28*(3), 227-247.

Campanelli, P., Sacks, J., Heckart, K., Ades, Y., Frecknall, P., & Yee, P. (1992). Integrating psychosocial rehabilitation within a community residence framework. *Psychosocial Rehabilitation Journal, 16*(1),135-153.

Carling, P.J. & Ridway, P. (1987). Overview of psychosocial rehabilitation approach to housing. In W. Anthony & M. Farkas, Psychosocial rehabilitation: Turning theory into practice, (pp. 28-80). Baltimore: John Hopkins University Press.

Cates, J. & Graham, L. (1993). HIV and Serious mental illness: Reducing the risk. *Community Mental Health Journal, 29*(1), 35-47.

Chiles, J.A. & Strosahl, K. (1995). *The suicidal patient: Principles of assessment, treatment and case management.* Washington, D.C.: American Psychiatric Press.

Ciarlo, J.A., Reihman, J. (1977). The Denver Community Mental Health Questionnaire: Development of a multi-dimensional program evaluation instrument. In R. Coursey, G. Spector, S. Murrell et al (Eds.) *Program Evaluation For Mental Health: Methods, Strategies, And Participants.* New York: Grune & Stratton, Inc. pp. 131-167.

Cnaan, R., Blankertz, L., Messinger, K. & Gardner, J. (1990). Experts' assessment of psychosocial rehabilitation principles. *Psychosocial Rehabilitation Journal, 13*(3), 59-73.

Cohen, B. & Anthony, W. (1984). Functional assessment in psychosocial rehabilitation. In A.S. Halpern & M.J. Fuhrer (Eds.). *Functional Assessment in Rehabilitation.* (pp. 79-100). Baltimore: Paul Brookes.

Cohen, M.R., Farkas, M.D. & Cohen, B. (1986). *Functional assessment: Trainer package.* Boston: Center for Psychosocial rehabilitation.

Cook, J. A., Bond, G. R., Hoffschmidt, S. J., Jones, E.A., Razzano, L., & Weakland, R.(1991). *Assessing vocational performance among persons with severe mental illness.* Chicago: Illinois: Thresholds National Research and Training Center on Rehabilitation and Mental Illness.

Corrigan, P.W., Schade, M., & Liberman, R.P. (1992). Social skills training. In R.P. Liberman (Ed.) *Handbook of psychosocial rehabilitation.* New York: Macmillan Publishing Company.

Corrigan, P. & Storzbach, D. (1993). Behavioral interventions for alleviating psychotic symptoms. *Hospital and Community Psychiatry, 44*(4), 341-347.

Cull, J. G. & Gill, W. S. (1988). *Suicide probability scale (SPS) manual.* Los Angeles: Western Psychological Services.

Danley, K. & Anthony, W. (1987). The choose-get-keep model serving severely psychiatrically disable people. *American Rehabilitation, 13*(4),6-9.

Derogatis, L.R., Lipman, R.S. & Covi, L. (1973). The SCL-90: An outpatient psychiatric rating scale. *Psychopharmacology Bulletin, 9,* 13-28.

DeVane, C. (1990). *Fundamentals Of Monitoring Psychoactive Drug Therapy.* Baltimore: Williams & Wilkins.

Donat, D.C., McKeegan, G.F. & Neal, B. (1991). Training inpatient psychiatric staff in the use of behavioral methods. Psychosocial Rehabilitation Journal, 15(1), 60-74. Downs, M. & Fox, J. (1993). Social environments of adult homes. *Community Mental Health Journal, 29*(1), 15-23.

Drake, R.E., Osher, F.C., Noordsy, D.L., Hurlbut, S.C. Teague, G.B. & Beaudett, M.S. (1990). Diagnosis of alcohol use disorders in schizophrenia. *Schizophrenic Bulletin, 16,* 57-67.

Espin, O. M. (1987). Psychotherapy with Hispanic women: Some considerations. In P. Pederson (Ed.). *Handbook Of Cross-Cultural Counseling And Psychotherapy* (pp. 165-171). New York: Praeger.

Evans, B., Souma, A., Maier, G. (1989). A vocational assessment and training program for individuals in an inpatient forensic mental health center. *Psychosocial Rehabilitation Journal, 13*(2), 61-69.

Folstein, M.F., Folstein, S.E. & McHugh, P.R. (1975). Mini-mental state: A practical method for grading the cognitive state of patients for the clinician. *Journal of Psychiatric Research, 12,* 189-198.

Endicott, J., Spitzer, R., Fleiss, J. & Cohen, J. (1976). The global assessment scale. *Archives of General Psychiatry, 33,* 766-771.

Evenson, R. & Boyd, M. (1993). The St. Louis Inventory of Community Living Skills. *Psychosocial Rehabilitation Journal, 17*(2), 93-99.

Farkas, M.D., Anthony, W. A. & Cohen, M.R. (1989). Psychosocial rehabilitation: The approach and its programs. In M.R. Farkas, & W. A. Anthony (Eds.), *Psychosocial Rehabilitation: Putting Theory Into Practice* (pp. 1-27). Baltimore: The John Hopkins University Press.

Freddolino, P. & Moxley, D. (1992). Clinical care update: Refining an advocacy model for homeless people coping with psychiatric disabilities. *Community Mental Health Journal, 28*(4), 337-352.

Gillies, L.A., Wasylenki, D.A., Lancee, W.J., James, S., Clark, C.C., Lewis, J., & Goering, P. (1993). Differential outcomes in social network therapy. *Psychosocial Rehabilitation Journal, 16*(3), 141-145.

Goering, P., Durbin, J., Foster, R.. Boyles, S., Babiak, T., & Lancee, B. (1992). Social networks of residents in supportive housing. *Community Mental Health Journal, 28*(3), 199-214.

Goodman, S., Swell, D., Cooley, E. & Leavitt, N. (1993). Assessing levels of adaptive functioning: The role functioning scale. *Community Mental Health Journal, 29*(2), 119-131.

Gorden, R. & Gordon, K. (1991). Assessing the elements of biopsychosocial functioning. *Hospital and Community Psychiatry, 42*(5), 508-512.

Heritage, S., Sudol, R., & Connery, L.(1987). Training and consultation to residential care providers serving adults with serious mental illness. *Psychosocial Rehabilitation Journal, 10*(3), 11-19.

Hill, D. & Balk, D. (1987). The effect of an education program for families of the chronically mentally ill on stress and anxiety. *Psychosocial Rehabilitation Journal, 10*(4), 25-40.

Hogan M. & Carling, P. (1992). Normal housing: A key element of a supported housing approach for people with psychiatric disabilities. *Psychosocial Rehabilitation Journal, 28*(3), 215-226.

Hoyle, R., Nietzel, M., Guthrie, P., Baker-Prewitt, J. & Heine, R. (1993). The disability rating form: A brief schedule for rating disability associate with severe mental illness. *Psychosocial Rehabilitation Journal, 16*(1), 77-94.

Hyde, A. & Goldman, C. (1992). Use of multi-modal multiple family group in the comprehensive treatment and rehabilitation of people with schizophrenia. *Psychosocial Rehabilitation Journal, 15*(4), 77-86.

Jacobs, H. E., Collier, R. & Wissusik, D. (1992). The job-finding module: Training skills for seeking competitive community employment. In *New Directions for Mental Health Services, 53*, 105-115.

Jerrel, J.M. & Hargreaves, W.A. (1991). *The operating philosophy of community programs.* Berkeley: Institute for Mental Health Services Research Working Paper #18.

Kanner, A.P., Coyne, J.C., Schaefer, C., & Lazarus, R.S. (1981) Comparison of two modes of stress measurement: Daily hassles and uplifts versus major life events. *Journal of Behavioral Medicine, 4,* 1-39.

Kazarian, S.K. & Joseph, L. (1994). A brief scale to help identify outpatients' level of need for community support services. *Hospital and Community Psychiatry, 45*(9), 935-938.

Kazarian, S. & Vanderheyden, D. (1992). Family education of relatives of people with psychiatric disability: A review. *Psychosocial Rehabilitation Journal, 15*(3), 67-83.

Kofoed, L. (1991). Assessment of comorbid psychiatric illness and substance disorders. In *New Directions for Mental Health Services, 50,* 43-55.

Krowinski, W.J. & Fitt, D. X. (1978). A model for evaluating mental health programs: The functional baseline system. *Administration in Mental Health, 6,* 22-41.

Lam, D. (1991). Psychosocial family interventions in schizophrenia: A review of empirical studies. *Psychological Medicine, 21,* 423-441.

Liberman, R. P. (1982). Assessment of social skills. *Schizophrenic Bulletin, 8*(1), 62-83.

Lehman, A.F. , Ward, N.C. & Linn, L. S. (1982). Chronic mental patients: The quality of life issue. *American Journal of Psychiatry, 10,* 1271-1276.

_____. (1988). A quality of life interview for the chronically mentally ill. *Evaluation and Program Planning, 11,* 51-62.

Lukoff, D., Liberman, R. P.& Nuechterlein, K. H. (1986). Symptom monitoring in the rehabilitation of schizophrenic patients. *Schizophrenia Bulletin, 12,* 578-602.

Mannion, E., Mueser, K. & Soloman, P. (1994) Designing psychoeducational services for spouses of persons with serious mental illness. *Community Mental Health Journal, 30*(2), 177-189.

Marsh, D. (1992). Working with families of people with serious mental illness. In L. VandeeCreek, S. Knapp & T. L. Jackson (Eds.). *Innovations in Clinical Practice: A Source Book.* Sarasota, FL: Professional Resource Press.

Mayfield, D., McCleod, G., & Hall, P. (1974). The CAGE Questionnaire: Validation of a New Alcoholism screening instrument. *American Journal of Psychiatry, 131,* 1121-1123.

McCue, M., Pramuka, M., Chase, S. & Fabry, P. (1994). Functional assessment procedures for individuals with severe cognitive disabilities. *American Rehabilitation, 20*(3), 17-27.

Mills, P. & Hansen, J. (1991). Short-term group interventions for mentally ill young adults living in a community residence and their families. *Hospital and Community Psychiatry, 42*(11), 1144-1149.

Nikkel, R. & Coiner, R. (1991). Critical interventions and tasks in delivering dual-diagnosis services. *Psychosocial Rehabilitation Journal, 15*(2), 57-66.

Noordsy, D. & Fox, L. (1991). Group intervention techniques for people with dual disorders. *Psychosocial Rehabilitation Journal, 15*(2), 67-78.

Overall, J. E. & Gorham, D. R. (1962). The brief psychiatric rating scale. *Psychological Reports, 10,* 799-812.

Massey, O. & Wu, L. (1993). Important characteristics of independent housing for people with mental illness: Perspectives of case managers and consumers. *Psychosocial Rehabilitation Journal, 17*(2),81-92.

Malm, U, May, P.R. A. & Dencker, S.J. (1981). Evaluation of the quality of life of the schizophrenic outpatient: A checklist. *Schizophrenia Bulletin, 7,* 477-487.

Mayfield, D., McCleod, G. & Hall, P. (1974). The CAGE questionnaire: Validation of a new alcoholism screening instrument. *American Journal of Psychiatry, 131,* 1121-1123.

McKeegan, G.F., Geczy, B., & Donat, D.S. (1993). Applying behavioral methods in the inpatient setting: Patients with mixed borderline and dependent traits. *Psychosocial Rehabilitation Journal, 16*(3), 55-64.

McLellan, A. T. , Luborsky, L., Woody, G.E. & O'Brien, C.P. (1980). An improved diagnostic evaluation instrument for substance abuse patients: The addiction severity index. *Journal of Mental and Nervous Disease, 168,* 26-33.

Mills, P. & Hansen, J. (1991). Short-term group interventions for mentally ill young adults living in a community residence and their families. *Hospital and Community Psychiatry, 42*(11), 1144-1149.

Mitrushina, M., Abara, J., Blumenfeld, A. (1994). The neuorbehavioral cognitive status examination as a screening tool for organicity in psychiatric patients. *Hospital and Community Psychiatry, 45*(3), 252-256.

Moos, R. (1974). *Community oriented programs environment scale manual.* Palo Alto, California: Consulting Psychologists Press.

Mowbray, C., Wellwood, R. & Chamberlain, P. (1988). Project stay: A consumer-run support service. *Psychosocial Rehabilitation Journal, 12*(1),33-42.

Moxley, D. P. & Freddolino, P. P. (1990). A model of advocacy for promoting client self-determination in psychosocial rehabilitation. *Psychosocial Rehabilitation Journal, 14*(2), 69-82.

Mulkern, V.M. & Manderscheid, R.W. (1989). Characteristics of community support program clients in 1980 and 1984. *Hospital and Community Psychiatry, 40*(2), 165-172.

Overall, J. E. & Gorham, D.R. (1962). Brief psychiatric rating scale. *Psychological Reports, 10,* 799-812.

Pattison, E. M. & Pattison, , M.L. (1981). Analysis of a schizophrenic psychosocial network. *Schizophrenia Bulletin, 7*(1), 135-142.

Pelham, T. W., Campagna, P. D., Ritvo, P.G., & Birnie, W.(1993). The effects of exercise therapy on clients in a psychosocial rehabilitation program. *Psychosocial Rehabilitation Journal, 16*(4), 75-83.

Perkins, D. & Baker, F. (1991). A behavior setting assessment for community programs and residences. *Community Mental Health Journal, 27*(5), 313-325.

Pyke, J. & Atcheson, V. (1993). Social recreation services: Issues from a case management perspective. *Psychosocial Rehabilitation Journal, 17*(2), 121-130.

Ranz, J., Horan, B., McFarland, W. & Zito, J. (1991) Creating a supportive environment using staff psychoeducation in a supervised residence. *Hospital and Community Psychiatry, 42*(11), 1154-1159.

Raskin, A., Pelchat, R., Sood, R., Alphs, D. & Levine, J. (1993). Negative symptom assessment of chronic schizophrenia patients. *Schizophrenia Bulletin, 19*(3), 627-635.

Reed, D., Sullivan, M., Penn, D., Stuve, P., & Spaulding, W.(1992). Assessment and treatment of cognitive impairments. *New Directions in Mental Health Services, 53,* 7-19.

Rosen, A., Hadzi-Pavlovic, D. & Parker, g. (1989). The life skills profile: A measure assessing function and disability in schizophrenia. *Schizophrenia Bulletin, 15*(2),325-337.

Royall, D. , Mahurin, R., & Gray, K. (1992). Bedside assessment of executive cognitive impairment: *The Executive Interview* (EXIT). JAGS, 40, 1221-1226.

Ryglewicz, H. (1991). Psychoeducation for clients and families: A way in, out and through in working with people with dual diagnosis. *Psychosocial Rehabilitation Journal, 15*(2), 79-89.

Schneider, L.C. & Struenig, E. L. (1983). SLOF: A behavioral rating scale for assessing the mentally ill. *Social Work Research and Abstracts, 19,* 9-21.

Schoenfeld, R., Dott, J.H., Hemley-van der Velden, E., & Ruhf, L. (1986). Long-term outcome of network therapy. *Hospital and Community Psychiatry, 37,* 373-376.

Selzer, M.L. (1971). The Michigan Alcoholism Screening Test: The quest for a new diagnostic instrument. *American Journal of Psychiatry, 127,* 89-94.

Segal, S. P. & VanderVoort, D. (1993). Daily hassles and health among person with severe mental disabilities. *Psychosocial Rehabilitation Journal, 16*(3), 27-37.

Segal, S. P., Silverman, C., & Temkin, T. (1995). Measuring empowerment in client-run self-help agencies. *Community Mental Health Journal, 31*(3), 215-227.

Shilony, E., Lacey, D., O'Hagan, P., & Curto, M. (1993). All in one neighborhood: A community-based rehabilitation treatment program for homeless adults with mental illness and alcohol/ substance abuse disorders. *Psychosocial Rehabilitation Journal, 16*(4), 103-116.

Soloman , P. & Marcenko, M. (1992). Families of adult with severe mental illness: Their satisfaction with inpatient and outpatient treatment. *Psychosocial Rehabilitation Journal, 16*(1), 121-131.

Solomon, P. (1988). Services to severely mentally disabled homeless persons and to emergency food and shelter providers. *Psychosocial Rehabilitation Journal, 12*(2), 3-13.

Stein, L.I. & Test, M.A. (1980). Alternatives to mental hospital treatment: Conceptual model, treatment program and clinical evaluation. *Archives of General Psychiatry, 37,* 392-397.

Stroul, B. (1989). Community support systems for persons with long term mental illness: A conceptual framework. *Psychosocial Rehabilitation Journal, 12*(3), 9-26.

Sodowsky, G.R., Taffe, R., Gutkin, T. & Wise, S. (1994). Development of the multicultural counseling inventory: A self-report measure of muticultural competencies. *Journal of Counseling Psychology, 41*(2), 137-148.

Solarz, A. & Bogart, G.A. (1990). When social support fails: the homeless. *Journal of Community Psychology, 18,* 79-96.

Stein, L. I., Ronald, J., & Factor, R.M. (1990). A system approach to the care of persons with schizophrenia. In M.I. Herz, S.J. Keith, J.P. Docherty. New York: Elsevier.

Sullivan, W. P. (1994). A long and winding road: The process of recovery from severe mental illness. *Innovations And Research. 3*(3), 19-27.

Susser, E., Goldfinger, S., & White, A. (1990). Some clinical approaches to the homeless mentally ill. *Community Mental Health Journal, 26*(5), 463-479.

Tessler, R.C. & Goldman, H.H. (1982). The chronically mentally ill: Assessing community support programs. Cambridge, Massachusetts: Ballinger.

Trzepacz, P. & Baker, R. (1993). *The Psychiatric Mental Status Examination.* New York: Oxford University Press.

Tuffy, L., Belanger, J., & Gregory, B. (1993). An evaluation of redirection through education: A psychosocial rehabilitation program for young adults with psychiatric disability. *Psychosocial Rehabilitation Journal, 16*(3),7-25.

Unger, K.V., Skrinar, G.S., Hutchinson, D., & Yelmokas, A. (1992). Fitness: A viable adjunct to treatment for young adults with psychiatric disabilities. *Psychosocial Rehabilitation Journal, 15*(3), 21-27.

Unger, K. V., Danley, K. S. , Kohn, L. & Hutchinson, D. (1988). Rehabilitation through education: A university-based continuing education program for young adults with psychiatric disability on a university campus. *Psychosocial Rehabilitation Journal, 10*(3), 35-49.

Vaccaro, J., Pitts, D. & Wallace, C.(1992). Functional assessment. In R. P. Liberman, (Ed.) *Handbook Of Psychosocial Rehabilitation.* New York: Macmillan Publishing Company.

Wells, D. (1992). Management of early postdischarge adjustment reactions following psychiatric hospitalization. *Hospital and Community Psychiatry, 43*(10), 1000-10004.

Weiner, H. (1993). Multi-functional needs assessment: The development of a functional assessment instrument. *Psychosocial Rehabilitation Journal, 16*(4), 51-61.

Weissman, M., Skolomskas, D. & John, K. (1981). The assessment of social adjustment. *Archives of General Psychiatry, 38*,1250-1258.

Widlak, P.A., McKee, D., Greenberg, J.R. & Greenley, J.R. (1992) An assessment of client functioning scales in the Uniform Client Data Instrument (UCDI). *Psychosocial Rehabilitation Journal, 15*(4), 19-3.

Wintersteen, R. & Young, L. (1988). Effective professional collaboration with family support groups. *Psychosocial Rehabilitation Journal, 12*(1), 19-31.

Wykes, T. & Sturt, E. (1986). The measurement of social behavior in psychiatric patients: An assessment of the reliability and validity of the SBS Schedule. *British Journal of Psychiatry, 148*, 1-11.

Yankowitz, R. & Musante, S. (1994). The use of cognitive functional assessment in a psychiatric vocational rehabilitation program. *American Rehabilitation, 20*(3), 32-36.

Zung, W. W. K. (1971). A self- rating anxiety scale. *Archives of General Psychiatry, 26*, 112-118.

Zung, W.W. K. (1965). A self-rating depression scale. *Archives of General Psychiatry, 12*, 63-70.

7

Interventions in Psychosocial Rehabilitation

Barbara Caldwell and John Woods

Introduction

The focus of the intervention phase of the psychosocial rehabilitation process consists of several related steps: setting priorities, setting short- and long-term goals, and the planning and implementation of interventions. The goals upon which the interventions are based need to be individualized, realistic, achievable, measurable, customer-centered, and time limited. Several assumptions concerning the process of interventions are considered.

The process of psychosocial rehabilitation intervention requires that the practitioner operationalize these assumptions as part of their intervention strategies:

- Individuals with mental illness and practitioners are functioning in adult partnership roles;

- Interventions are concrete and functional, have a direct impact on the quality of life, and are designed and implemented to help people in their educational, recreational, social, vocational, residential and psychological life areas;

- Community supports and resources will facilitate the progression toward the resumption of normalized roles and responsibility in family and community life.

- Programmatic elements necessary to facilitate the implementation of the interventions exist; and

- Interventions must include an assessment phase followed by a measurable outcome phase.

These assumptions are part of the overall perspective that the practitioner brings to the interpersonal process of providing services. Further, specific skills are required for practitioners to possess in order to accomplish psychosocial rehabilitation interventions. One of the key skills that overrides all other interventions is the capacity to work with individuals with mental illness in non-stigmatizing ways. This skill involves placing the person first and believing that the people served can and must have an equal role in developing personal goals, the services to achieve these goals, and the supports to maintain their goals.

Systems Framework for Psychosocial Rehabilitation Interventions

Interventions are the third phase to the psychosocial rehabilitation process. This phase implements the mutually determined objectives and goals established by the individual with mental illness and the direct practitioner. The actual practice of carrying out psychosocial rehabilitation is derived from the mix of information from six sources:

- the communicated strengths, vulnerabilities, beliefs and attitudes of the person served;
- the skills and knowledge the practitioner utilizes in carrying out specific objectives or goals;
- the clinical judgment of the practitioner;
- the past professional experiences (successes and failures) of the practitioner;
- the prevailing scientific research and literature base; and
- the practitioner's own personal views and beliefs on human capacity.

Interventions need to be viewed in a systems framework. A systems approach to the practice of psychosocial rehabilitation ensures that no aspect of the individual with mental illness' life is left out or denied necessary assessments and interventions. Individuals with serious mental illness are part of many different systems that need to be coordinated and developed. Each part of the system can be the focus of an intervention, but in order to achieve the most success, the practitioner will consider the system the individual is a part of and how each aspect of the system functions to support and empower the individual. Therefore, interventions can be individually fo-

cused, group focused, family focused, or systems focused. The systems framework allows practitioners to appreciate the resources of the multidisciplinary team approach valued in working with complex issues that cut across disciplines.

Competency I

Demonstrate crisis intervention strategies.

Crisis Intervention Strategies

A crisis refers to an individual's ability to solve a problem using traditional coping abilities that were successful in the part. The person experiencing a crisis feels helpless and experiences emotional turmoil. The goals of crisis intervention are:

- To stabilize emergency situations.

- To decrease the stressor(s) that precipitated the crisis.

- To mobilize the resources and supports to resolve the circumstances and prevent hospitalization if possible.

- To improve the individual's overall functioning at or above the pre-crisis level.

Crisis intervention is utilized in all aspects of psychosocial rehabilitation and can arise when there are unplanned or perceived changes in personal, social, psychological, residential, or family circumstances. Each individual perceives stress and change according to their own perspective. Situational or maturational crisis will be present for most individuals with serious mental illness. These can include episodes with increased psychotic or delusional symptoms, suicidal behaviors or thinking, episodes of violence, loss of significant persons in the individual's life, an abrupt change, or unexpected stressful event.

Anticipatory guidance (Caplan, 1989) is the first line of intervention for practitioners and can be fully developed and implemented during treatment planning. Areas such as prevention interventions, relapse prevention, and signs of symptoms clusters that indicate deteriorating functioning are integrated into the treatment plan with members of the multidisciplinary team including the family and social network as prime players in the intervention process.

The practitioner is responsible for a clear understanding of the individual's base line symptomatology, past history of crisis situations and their precipitating factors, and any past suicidal behaviors. Interventions for crisis situations are diverse and dependent on the following set of variables: active listening, communicating a sense of acceptance and safe environment, evaluation and referral for suicidal behaviors, positive proactive control over the situation, emphasis on problem solving with a focus on reducing mood changes and anger, enhancing a sense of self-control and self-esteem, short-term suicidal contracts, evaluation of current medication, increasing contact with the individual in crisis, reducing stressors, identifying family and social support network members (family and friends, 12-step group, peer support groups), referral to specialized services depending on setting, respite beds, hospitalization evaluation, increased clinical services, and pharmacology services. Practitioners should also be prepared to assist in the linkage or coordination of special crisis intervention services such as mobile outreach programs, crisis case managers, and use of police emergency services.

The risk of completion of a suicide is a major consideration to practitioners in the management of individuals with serious mental illness. Caldwell and Gottesman (1990) report a 10% incidence of suicide in the first 10 years of schizophrenic illness; and Cohen, Test and Brown (1990) report a 15% lifetime incidence. According to Fremouw, de Perczell & Ellis (1990), intervention strategies to reduce suicidal risk fall under the heading of "therapeutic activities": delaying impulses, restoring hope, environmental interventions and hospitalization. One of the advantages of most PSR environments is the ability to include a broad array of environmental supports at times of crisis. For instance, peers and friends who are also involved in the PSR program, family members, fellow-members of 12 step programs, as well as other PSR staff can be called upon (with the consent of the individual experiencing the crisis) to assist him or her in making it through the night or until suicidal impulses decrease.

Therapeutic activities focus on increasing the level of contact with the individual, becoming more actively involved and directive, and organizing the support of the multidisciplinary team (in settings where they exist). Overwhelming problems should be broken into smaller ones that are more manageable and solvable. Contingency plans will need planning and initiation, such as calling a telephone hotline or visiting a hospital emergency room in the event that the primary plan fails. Preparing a "crisis card" with the phone numbers of various sources can be helpful (Fremouw, de, Percsel & Ellis, 1990). Intervention strategies that delay suicidal impulses are crucial. These strategies can include impressing alternative options, recalling and reviewing the use of self-control strategies during previous painful times, completing verbal and written anti-suicidal contracts and other alternative options. Practitioners provide an instillation of hope to the individual by communicating that they will do what it takes to see that the person is safe and comes through the crisis.

Environmental interventions (Fremouw, de Perczel & Ellis, 1990) for the practitioner include: (1) removing the means for suicide, (2) involving family and support networks, such as persons who can provide 24 hour supervision, (3) referring the individual to 24 hour hotlines, mobile outreach teams, transitional crisis programs and agencies that perform hospitalization screening, (4) evaluating the potential for medication overdose by collaborating with the prescribing physician, (5) assisting the individual and other support systems with problem solving and conflict resolution, and (6) increasing service contact.

Mobile Psychiatric Crisis Intervention Teams

Reading and Raphelson (1995) utilized a mobile psychiatric crisis intervention team with the goal of achieving hospital diversion, minimal stigmatization, access to the most ill individuals with mental illness and adequate treatment in the least restrictive environments. Interventions focused on alleviating the symptoms of the acute psychotic episode, organization of the individual's support system by integrating family and friends in the education and treatment strategy, and rapid pharmacological interventions. This was followed by home visits several times per day, 24 hour telephone access and periodic "check-up" by telephone.

Suicide is a leading cause of premature death in the long-term mentally ill population. Pyke and Steers (1992) in their study reported that practitioners and in particular case managers need to direct particular attention to the post discharge period especially with individuals who tend to be socially isolated, unmarried, unemployed, and who have unstable housing, problems with substance abuse and problems establishing a working alliance.

In summary, crisis intervention is an ongoing aspect of the psychosocial rehabilitation process. Practitioners can anticipate crisis periods and collaborate with the individual and members of their family and broader support system to develop intervention strategies that reflect the optimal and least restrictive environments available for crisis stabilization and recovery. The use of hospitalization should always be considered when impulse control is lacking and neither support network members nor service resources can provide the necessary structure to keep the individual safe.

Postdischarge Interventions

Individuals with mental illness frequently experience serious symptoms during the postdischarge period. Well (1992) describes a team approach to management of the early postdischarge reaction with specific interventions. The individual with mental illness is educated about the problems creating the crisis, their potential for reoccurrence, and coping skills that can be developed. The team also integrates social skills training and family counseling. In addition, plans for future post discharge home visits can be developed that explore crisis management in situations that constitute an emergency situation and interventions for suicidal behaviors.

Relapse Prevention Intervention Strategies

Marlatt (1985) states that the goal of relapse prevention is to teach individuals who are trying to change their behavior how to anticipate and cope with the problem of recurrent symptoms. **Relapse** is defined as a break or setback in a person's attempt to change or modify a target behavior. For individuals experiencing serious and persistent mental illness, interventions to reverse, reduce or slow down the process of relapse will improve the quality of life and the problem solving capacity for these individuals. Symptoms serve not only as diagnostic indicators of a person's condition, but also as early warning signs of an impending relapse and the foundation for preventing future relapse. Specific educational programs have been developed for relapse prevention.

Docherty and associates (1978) formulated stages leading to relapse based on symptoms patterns. Predominant symptoms in the early stages were anxiety based and depressive in nature. Symptoms in the later stages were identified by impulsive thoughts and behaviors followed by perceptual and cognitive symptoms. Birchwood, Smith, & Mac Millan (1989) developed an early symptom rating scale completed by the individual and family members every 2 weeks for a period of 9 months or until relapse. Herz and Melville (1980) found that 70% of the sample reported changes in thoughts, feelings and behaviors that led them to believe that they were becoming sick and may need hospitalization.

One intervention that will assist in relapse prevention is to conduct an inventory with the person reviewing the events, thoughts, and feelings that were presented prior to a previous relapse. This inventory will identity key personal symptom clusters that are unique to the individual. These early warning signals will require close attention by practitioners involved with the individual and other significant family and support network members. For example, disturbed sleep patterns, changes in medication compliance, social withdrawal, development of loss of concentration and other more individualized symptom clusters can be identified. From these key symptom clusters, intervention strategies are pre-established in a mutual process and specific actions are formulated at pre-agreed points at early symptom development and the first signs of decompensation.The practitioner will then intervene in order to prevent further symptom escalation. For instance, a reduction in vocational activities, increase in practitioner contact along with medication adjustment and peer support to take medications may be accomplished to initiate the reversal of symptoms.

If symptom reversal is not successful, the practitioner will need to determine whether a crisis intervention framework or other intervention strategy is indicated. Specific behaviors and attitudes will be present in the individual that are indicators that the individual is beyond the rationality of the established advanced directives. It is at this point in an individual's illness that the practitioner will move from relapse prevention to crisis intervention management. Specific indicators are an increasing intensity, frequency and duration of harmful thoughts, feelings or behaviors toward self or others that require direct intervention.

Relapse Prevention Programs

There are numerous relapse prevention programs that have already been developed by experts in the field which can be reviewed by practitioners and agencies. Two outstanding examples include:

1. A Wellness Approach to the Management of Chronic Neurobiological Disorders developed by Moller and Miller which focuses on three aspects of patient and family education: relapse, recovery and rehabilitation (Moller and Miller, 1991).

2. Relapse prevention skills training modules that have been developed by the UCLA Clinical Research Center for Schizophrenia and Psychosocial Rehabilitation. These modules consist of a trainer's guide, workbook for participants, demonstration video and user's guide (Liberman, Wallace, Blackwell, Echman, Vaccaro and Kuehnel, 1993).

Competency 3

Demonstrate individual supportive counseling intervention strategies.

Individual Supportive Counseling

The rehabilitation relationship (Dincin, 1974) includes a strong element of reaching out to the individual with mental illness, attempting to overcome his reluctance to participate and taking an active role in increasing his level of motivation. The practitioner strives to influence and create an environment that is rich in hopefulness and courage to preserve in the face of extreme obstacles, resistance, and persistent symptoms. The rehabilitation relationship requires intensive contact where the primary goals are to change behavior, increase personal power to control and improve one's quality of life. The counseling relationship is an ongoing process from which the practitioner can move from the "persuasion" mode to an empathetic confrontation (Minkoff, 1993). Empathetic confrontation within a counseling relationship enables the practitioner to help individuals deal with the obstacles and barriers preventing them from achieving their personal goals. Individuals with mental illness who are dually diagnosed may require such interpersonal strategies to reduce self-destructive behaviors.

The individual counseling relationship in the PSR field is always developed in a context characterized by a reliance on rehabilitation activity. The context is the prevailing program philosophy that drives the attributes of the counseling relationship. One needs to distinguish generic counseling skills required in any setting of PSR from the more focused skills development counseling used in some forms of PSR. Generic individual counseling skills are practiced in many milieus of PSR such as the Clubhouse, the Fairweather Lodge, or Compeer programs. The function and form of individual counseling in these settings is influenced by the particular philosophy of the program. Nevertheless, there are generic interventions for individual supportive counseling in PSR that include:

1. **Engagement:** Key interventions include active listening, creating a sense of trust, positive regard, and acceptance. In addition, attention to the cultural patterns presented by the individual allows for understand-

ing the personal story brought to the counseling relationship. The engagement process (Shea, 1988) refers to the ongoing development of a sense of safety and respect from which the individual feels increasingly free to share their problems and strengths. It is in the rehabilitation relationship that the trusting alliance is developed and the individual experiences are being heard, understood, and challenged to change. At the same time, unknown and unrecognized strengths and inner resources are located through active listening. The type and quality of past relationships impacts the engagement process, which will influence the quality of the current therapeutic alliance.

2. **Empowerment**: Key interventions include partnership building and plan development that is individual with mental illness-driven. Empowerment (Segal, Silverman & Temkin, 1995) reflects a process by which individuals with lesser power gain control over their lives and influence the organizational and societal structures within which they live. The role of the practitioner in PSR is to facilitate the individual with mental illness' efforts towards personal change and improved quality of life.

Partnership building interventions begin with the practitioner communicating their acceptance of the person first in spite of any challenging conditions. PSR programs often communicate this by encouraging staff and members to share mutual responsibilities, using the same facilities as individuals with mental illness without "staff only" or "client only"

designations, sharing major programmatic decisions with the constituent community, involving individuals with mental illness in the staff selection and hiring process, and encouraging them to show initiative and creativity in achieving their goals.

Intervention plans that are developed and driven by the persons receiving services focus on listening to the individual's vision of their own future, creating a communication environment where the individual with mental illness can begin to imagine a future which may presently seem unattainable, shaping and extrapolating immediate objectives from more general goals. When the intervention planning process is centered on the individuals receiving services, services are organized around their goal attainment as opposed to the elevation of practitioner or agency goals.

3. **Encouragement**: Key interventions involve the use of supportive feedback, reflection of feelings, paraphrasing, and self-disclosure. The effective use of problem solving in the counseling relationship helps people learn new ways of viewing their world. Change can be further facilitated by providing the logical consequences of actions, providing information and direction, and engaging the individual in a review of alternative options. Appropriate sharing of practitioner's own struggles in attaining similar goals helps reduce the distance felt by many because of mental illness stigma.

Environments That Facilitate Engagement and are Testimonies to Empowerment

Physical environments in PSR services are almost as important as interpersonal factors in creating a sense of welcome and acceptance. Typically PSR environments are characterized by multicultural wall hangings, photos of program participants at work, and a homelike atmosphere jointly created by staff and program members.

For example, the MICA Club program in New Jersey has created an environment pre-vocational unit whose job it is to continually evaluate the "look" of the program, to make suggestions for improvements and to carry out these improvements. Recently, concern was raised by members about the lack of physical reminders of the program's commitment to multiculturalism. The Environmental Unit rallied group consensus on the issue, and helped to motivate members to bring meaningful and culturally oriented wall hangings and other decorations to the program. The result was a place that much more clearly invokes the program's commitment to multiculturalism, a place that members proudly show when giving tours, and increased sense of empowerment for members involved in this activity.

4. **Evaluation**: Key interventions involve an ongoing process of working with the individual to monitor the progress, successes, and setbacks, as established in the mutual goals that were developed. Practitioner sensitivity to the changing level of functioning, changing life goals, and developmental changes are part of the intervention process. The onset of a serious and persistent mental illness is usually in late adolescence or early adult years. Not only are individuals faced with the struggle of overcoming their illness, but also progressing through the normal developmental stages that all members of society face. Adler, Pajer, Ellison, Dorwart, Siris, Goldman, Lehman & Berlant (1995) provide a range of interventions based not only on illness and recovery but also normal life cycle roles and tasks of individuals.

In summary, individual counseling in PSR is context-based around real rehabilitative activities. Good counseling includes building an adult partnership with individuals with mental illness which provides opportunities for them to grow in self esteem, respect, and power.

The Relationship Enhancement Program

The Relationship Enhancement Program (REP) (Accordino & Guerney, 1993) integrates the principles and methods from individual with mental illness-centered, social learning theories to train staff to establish, maintain, and deepen intimate interpersonal relationships. It involves training in the following skill areas: empathic, expressive discussion and negotiation skills; problem-conflict resolution; and self-change skills. The results of the training enhanced the staff's capacity for interaction with their individuals with mental illness and the individual with mental illness' capacity for interacting with the staff, sharing feeling and thoughts, and being more motivated to accomplish goals.

Components of Rogers Therapeutic Relationship

EMPATHY—The capacity of the practitioner to experience the other person's feelings and perceptions and respond to them in a sensitive and clear manner. The practitioner can maintain respect for what the other is experiencing so that the person seeking help feels understood and accepted.

RESPECT—The practitioner believes that the person deserves and has a right to be regarded as a human being with dignity.

GENIALITY—The practitioner is sincere, honest, and authentic in his or her relationship with the person. The establishment of role modeling behavior can be the result of such an authentic relationship.

SELF DISCLOSURE—Appropriate exposing of one's attitude, feelings, and beliefs provides an opportunity for the person to experience another who can be a role model.

CONCRETENESS AND SPECIFICITY—The ability to locate and identify feelings and attitudes by skillful listening of the person's needs and desires.

CONFRONTATION—Discussion of discrepancies in a person's behavior with the purpose of assisting the person in assuming more appropriate and socially acceptable behaviors can be accomplished (when a strong trust relationship has been established).

IMMEDIACY OF THE RELATIONSHIP—Sharing appropriate, spontaneous feelings with the person strengthens the therapeutic relationship and fosters a realistic picture of interpersonal relationships.

SELF EXPLORATION—The practitioner needs to explore the overall competencies and strengths that the person has, along with understanding how the person operates in different situations. Through the journal of introspection, the person can learn to develop improved coping and problem solving capabilities.

Rogers, 1961

Competency 4

Demonstrate group intervention strategies.

Group intervention strategies

The use of group counseling as an intervention has been widely utilized in the psychosocial rehabilitation field. The group process can be adapted for many of the interventions needed by individuals with serious mental illness from medication groups to family psychoeducational groups. Group counseling has not only preventive and educational purposes but can also provide orientation, socialization, rehabilitation, and treatment.

Group modalities are crucial to PSR in that they function to provide the individual with mental illness with the following critical elements:

- Role modeling interactions(staff/ individuals with mental illness;
- Foundation of individual with mental illness' community supports and socialization development;
- Opportunities to experience leadership roles;
- Peer feedback;
- Problem solving, reality testing and improved coping strategies;
- Learning opportunities;
- Building self-esteem: reflection on strengths and progress; and
- Involvement of the family or individual of the individual with mental illness' social network.

Psychosocial rehabilitation practitioners will be presented with diverse opportunities to take roles, either as a leader or facilitator, in planning, development, and implementation of group processes. The types of groups that will be utilized in a particular setting depends on the needs of the individuals being provided services. Types of groups may include: psychoeducational groups, skill building groups, support groups, active treatment groups, supporting self-help groups, prevocational groups, job clubs, recreational groups, residential living groups, and medication groups.

Yalom (1985) has identified twelve therapeutic factors operating in the group dynamic: altruism, universalization, instillation of hope, imparting information, imitative behavior, catharsis, identification, family re-enactment, self-understanding, guidance, interpersonal learning both about self and others, and group cohesiveness. These therapeutic or curative factors operate to facilitate the main goal of the group experience: changing patterns of behavior, thinking and feelings about the self and others. Psychosocial rehabilitation practitioners need to be familiar with the factors identified by Yalom (1985) to ensure that they are meeting similar goals.

Within the group process certain skills must be mastered in order to take on the various roles that the group process rests. The type of skills (Corey & Corey, 1992) required of the PSR practitioner include:

- **Active listening**: Being aware of both the verbal and non-verbal communication along with acknowledgement of what the person is stating and the congruence/incongruence with behaviors.

- **Reflecting**: Responding to an individual in a way that the person feels heard and understood. Part of reflecting involves recognizing destructive patterns in behavior and works that need to be confronted in a direct and persuasive approach.

- **Clarifying**: Asking for clear and concise picture of information so that individual can sort out and understand what is really occurring.

- **Summarizing**: Taking time to reflect on past issues and place events in perspective.

- **Facilitating**: Providing the opportunity for individual with mental illness to openly express their feelings within a climate of trust and safety. In addition, the practitioner encourages and supports conflict and new ideas and eases the way for more direct communication.

- **Empathizing**: Expressing the sensitivity to each individual with mental illness of the group and the group as a whole concerning their fears, anxieties, shame, guilt and pain.

- **Interpreting**: Providing explanations of possible reasons for behavior or symptoms. It is normally presented as a working hypothesis and can change given additional information.

- **Supporting**: Being able to provide acknowledgement for behavior that is constructive and also during times of crisis where the individual is at a loss for what to do and where to turn.

- **Evaluating**: The practitioner must continually evaluate the dynamics of the group to ensure all individual with mental illness are moving forward and are receiving the support and encouragement needed.

The interventions that are part of the PSR practitioner role in group counseling are:

- **Forming a group**. This involves the development of guidelines for the group, recruiting individual with mental illness, screening and selection, assisting individuals to join the group. Specific considerations are decisions of group size, frequency and duration, open versus closed groups and place to hold group meetings. The establishment of the rules for the group are formulated.

- **Initiating the group**. This role includes building on group's initiatives to encourage individual with mental illness active participation, development of a safe and trusting atmosphere, delegating tasks such as agenda development or coffee set-up, and link up/matching of individual with mental illness needs and wants with current group goals and objectives. Other important interventions include: outreach to individual with mental illness who miss meetings; facilitating peer advocacy; utilizing opportunities for teaching and discovery. Norms and procedures that facilitate group progress and goals also develops in the early stages.

- **Working Stage of the Group**. The PSR practitioner role includes dealing with the fears, anxieties, issues of control and conflict, challenges to goal accomplishment and participation, hostility, etc. Interventions for this stage of group development are: teaching individual with mental illness through role modeling, facilitating leadership roles of individual with mental illness, encouraging individual with mental illness to ex-

press a range of feelings, provide acknowledgement, support and feedback, demonstrating a commitment for change and the use of humor. Group "work" toward established group goals and the development of cohesion is important during this phase.

- **Termination**. The PSR practitioner role will need to summarize the learning that occurred during the group process, effectively acknowledging and dealing with feelings of separation and loss of the social group. A discussion of unfinished work began in group and opportunities to continue to hold on to these goals or change is important. A final intervention is to assure that continuity is provided and additional resources are available for support.

Examples of Types of Groups:

1. **Psychoeducational Groups**: Primarily designed to educate families about mental illness on their individual with mental illness. The primary goals and objectives are: support, understanding and coping strategies for families; information on mental illness using a biopsychosocial approach for effective treatment and rehabilitation; understanding medication and compliance; relapse prevention strategies; crisis intervention and services available for support; increase in social network; working toward recovery. Marsh (1992) presents an excellent review for practitioners who want to design and implement educational programs/groups for families of individuals with serious mental illness. Hyde and Goldman(1992) utilize a multimodal multiple family group inter-

vention strategy which incorporates a biopsychosocial approach, use of medical model for psychopharmacology, patient and family education, focus on strengths, good health habits, gradual, step-wise progression and dealing with personality versus schizophrenic behaviors.

2. **Skill Building Groups**: A group treatment approach that include cognitive rehabilitation and the development of effective communication and social skills training was developed by Ahmed and Goldman (1994). The format included 4 areas: (1) use of relaxation techniques; (2) paper and pencil exercises to challenge associative, sequential, and logical thinking; (3) exercises and their relation to core psychiatric symptoms; and (4) a discussion of personal and current issues in a person's life. The enhancement of task attention and concentration as well as opportunities for supportive group environments and the experience of success and accomplishments are outcomes of the intervention program.

3. **Support Groups**: Mills and Hansen (1991) provided group interventions for mentally ill young adults living in a community residence and their families where the results demonstrated that group individual with mental illness become more cohesive, manage conflict more effectively, express support, and allow for a more realistic expectation of the illness as chronic condition.

4. **Active Treatment Groups**: Noordsy & Fox (1991) describe group intervention techniques for people with dual disorders. According to the authors, active treatment groups pro-

vide more focused, behavioral, abstinence-oriented interventions with an emphasis on social skills training, anxiety management, assertiveness and avoidance of drug and alcohol. Specific group leadership techniques and integration are presented. Sciacca (1991) describes an integrated treatment approach for severely mentally ill individuals with substance disorders. The group treatment program is presented in detail with a step by step methodology.

5. **Supporting Self-Help Groups**: Martin & Bratter(1993) describe an innovative program from community residing older adults with serious mental illness where a range of services is provided. What is unique about this project is that professional intervention is used only as needed and is present to provide a sense of support and community empowerment by fostering multiple supports and making new roles available to individuals with mental illness. Peer counseling has been developed with a program manual for seniors, use of volunteerism for a variety of roles and group health education. The support of the group through self-help is an excellent role for PSR practitioners to consider in all areas of service delivery.

6. **Recreational Groups**: The use of exercise therapy (Pelham, Cam-pagna, Ritvo & Birnie, 1993) on individuals with mental illness has been demonstrated to effect higher levels of aerobic fitness and lower levels of self-reported depression. The authors suggest that exercise may be a safe and cost-effective treatment for many individuals with mental illness in community settings. Fitness pro-

grams as adjunct to treatment have also demonstrated benefits for individuals with serious mental illness (Unger, Skrinar, Hutchinson & Yelmokas, 1992).

7. **Health Education Groups**: Groups such as "Stress Reduction," "Smoking Cessation,"and "AIDS and Sex." Pepper (1988) describes a group for individuals to become more comfortable with their sexuality and level of knowledge and awareness. Topics are provided and content for the 13 sessions. Educational intervention techniques are developed and critiqued for reducing the risk of HIV in persons with serious mental illness (Cates & Graham, 1993). The interventions include the use of videos, didactic presentations including topic on modes of transmission, risk behaviors, symptoms, and testing for HIV infection. Gender sensitive groups were conducted to deal with specific issues.

Competency 5

Demonstrate skills training intervention strategies.

Skills training intervention strategies

PSR can be enhanced with a structured educational process that aims at assisting individuals with mental illness in acquiring the knowledge and skills to function in the community. Social skills training significantly improves individuals with mental illness' social behavior and self-perception and reduces social anxiety (Benton and Schroeder, 1990; Echman, Wirshing, Marder, Liberman,

Johnston-Cronk, Zimmerman and Mintz, 1992). Skills training can be accomplished by the practitioner either with an individual or as part of a group. The PSR practitioner will need to assume the role as teacher and educator and will need to possess the requisite skills to function effectively.

The skills and corresponding interventions that are an integral part of the teacher/trainer role are:

Understand and utilize educational principles of teaching and learning as it relates to rehabilitation and treatment.
Carkhuff and Berenson (1976) combine two strategies of social learning theory and educational methods into a "teaching as treatment approach." This method has been utilized by the Center for Rehabilitation Research and Training at Boston University, and a series of programs are available for purchase for training with individuals with serious mental illness. A series of modules for training social and independent living skills has been developed by the Clinical Research Center for Schizophrenia and Psychosocial rehabilitation at UCLA. The models consist of a trainer's manual, individual with mental illness' workbook, demonstration video and user's guide (Liberman, Wallace, Blackwell, Echman, Vaccaro and Kuehnel, 1993). An understanding of cognitive deficits is taken into consideration with interventions such as focused instructions, prompting, and coaching with positive feedback (Echman, Wirshing, Marder et al, 1992).

Integrate teaching/learning principles into effective teaching plan.
The practitioner needs to be knowledgeable of the content presented or obtain consultation on the content required. For instance, training in medication man-

agement may require guidance from psychiatrists or nurses who have advanced skills and expertise in pharmacology. It is also important to be knowledgeable of the audience's prior learning skills and motivation and readiness to engage with the teacher/trainer around the particular skill development. Assessment of skills deficits is an important first step in the skills training process (Liberman, 1982). Lastly, the practitioner needs to develop content for each teaching session with objectives and appropriate teaching strategies such as take home activities and, in particular, the ability to break up larger goals into smaller achievable objectives on a time line basis.

Demonstrate effective teaching strategies for skills.

Teaching strategies are selected that are best suited for content presented: use of diverse teaching tools such as multimedia, participatory, narrative, computer generated learning tools, role modeling, videotaping skill progression, and critique. The practitioner needs to create an environment of enthusiasm and cheerleading. Learning styles require consideration to improve teaching. Price, Dunn and Dunn (1982b) suggest teaching strategies that should include:

- The use of precise oral directions and explanations when giving assignments, setting tasks, reviewing progress, or for any performance requiring comprehension or understanding.

- The use of auditory system for primary presentation and reinforcement through the visual, kinesthetic, and tactile modalities.

- The encouragement of peer meetings and joint meetings; facilitate learners to assist each other in pairs and groups; seek group learning experiences; use team learning and small group techniques.

- The use of brief uncomplicated tasks; provide frequent supervision.

- Experiment with motivators and reinforcers.

- Scheduling periodic breaks and short assignments.

- The maintenance of basic routines, patterns and schedules; avoid frequent changes.

Sex, Games and Video Tape

Valencia & Torres (1994) present an HIV-prevention intervention program, "Sex, Games, and Videotape" to reduce high-risk behaviors among homeless mentally ill men. It has a fully developed curriculum that can be adapted to other settings and provides engaging and social activities to sustain motivation and learning. Cook, Razzano, Jayaraj, Myers, Nathanson, Scott & Stein (1994) describe an assessment and program for preparing individuals with mental illness in avoiding HIV infections and in dealing with it when it has been diagnosed. Included in the article are topics suggested by individuals with mental illness of an HIV support group for men with mental illness. Knox, Davis & Friedrich (1994) have developed an excellent review on how to manage HIV in the mental health system. A spectrum of individual with mental illness issues related to the type of mental health service required with an emphasis on the educational needs and skills for the individuals with mental illness in the system.

Illness Self Management

Eckman, Wirshing, Marder, Liberman, Johnston-Cronk, Zimmerman & Mintz (1992) incorporate the use of structured learning and cognitive therapy to design modules to teach illness self-management skills. Two modules, one on symptom management, were developed to teach the skills of identification of early signs of relapse, managing the warning signs, coping with persistent symptoms, and avoiding alcohol and street drugs. The second module focuses on medication management to include information on antipsychotic medication, knowing correct self-administration and evaluation, and knowing side effects and negotiating medication issues with health care providers.

Involvement of the learner in the teaching process.

The practitioner creates opportunities for the learner to participate in the teaching session in which they can demonstrate an expert role related to specific content.

Effective application by the individual to transfer of skills to natural environments.

It is important that each person have opportunities to try out the new set of skills and practice them in a supportive environment where feedback is available and reinforcing.

Continued evaluation to reassess the level of individual's progression.

The psychosocial rehabilitation practitioner supports each person's efforts to motivate and encourage themselves to look at new areas for skill development.

Competency 6

Demonstrate family intervention strategies.

Family intervention strategies

The experience of mental illness for an individual is not self-contained but reaches the heart of all family members. Deinstitutionalization has forced a different view of the role of family in the lives of its family member with mental illness. Practitioners need to gain an understanding of the family's role and an appreciation for the family's expertise in dealing with the person who has a serious mental illness. As a result of this natural role of the family, the practitioner needs to fully involve families based on a competency model (Marsh, 1992) in the overall treatment, rehabilitation, and recovery process of PSR individuals with mental illness.

The overall objectives of family interventions are:

- Increase competence through knowledge and skills of families to deal effectively with their loved one experiencing mental illness,

- Facilitate a balance between the family's role in overall treatment, rehabilitation and recovery, and their capacity to meet their own individual needs and life roles,

- Empower the family to act as advocate and leader for their family member and with other families experiencing similar life circumstances,

- Appreciate the family as a core emotional, psychological, and social structure for individuals with mental illness that contains the strengths and potential for healing and recovery, and

- Sustain an ongoing, open and trusting relationship between family, individual with mental illness and multidisciplinary team.

The primary interventions for PSR practitioners with families are to:

Engage family members as part of the multidisciplinary team in the support of the person with mental illness. Terkelsen (1990) indicates that there is a need for families and clinicians to evolve a culture of collaboration, a habit of including each other in their thoughts and their actions on behalf of the patient. Consideration of the stages that families progress will determine the role family members will play in the care and rehabilitation process (Tessler, Killian, and Gubman 1987). Further, each family possesses different capacity and endurance for involvement in the daily direct support and management. Consideration of the cultural and ethnic background of the family will greatly influence the support.

Understand and appreciate the family's emotional struggles and experiences. The family can be the only support that an individual has as one progresses through the illness and on to recovery. Family members, whether they are the mother, father, sister, brother, or aunt experience a full spectrum of emotions related to the experience of dealing with the everyday events in the life of the individual who is mentally ill. Severe guilt, despair, shame, embarrassment and self-blame along with anger, depression and rage will be felt but also will need to be acknowledged. The PSR practitioner's intimate involvement with the individual with mental illness provides the conduit for understanding what the needs are not only of the individual with mental illness, but the person imbedded in the family

system. Noh and Turner (1987) have been helpful in demonstrating how families are disrupted and a psychological burden is incurred as a result of living with families of individuals with mental illness experiencing psychiatric disability. Hyde and Goldman (1993) provide an excellent and comprehensive review of interventions to deal with issues confronting families:

- "Sell" families on a treatment and rehabilitation program; encourage new families to observe an already constituted group.

- Confront and acknowledge poor past experiences in the mental health system, poor management of the family member's pharmacology, communication problems with mental health staff and expenses, and time devoted to treatment issues.

- Confront issues related to the fear of stress and capabilities of the individual with mental illness with emphasis on an evolving increase in being involved in living and working roles; emphasis on stress management education for families and individuals with mental illness to effectively deal with the every day stress is provided; a review of do's and don'ts is provided by authors.

- Threats, intimidation, and violence— either real or perceived— must be discussed openly and action plans, contracts, and sanctions developed to deal with real problem behaviors.

- Families need education and support with drugs and alcohol using individuals with mental illness and encouragement to utilize AA or NA and Al-Anon; persuasive group pressure to stop use.

- Reduction in family polarization and isolation by persuading all individuals with mental illness to back one another and support the treatment and rehabilitation process.

- Use of anti-negative symptom techniques: (1) aerobic exercise; (2) volunteer or paid work; (3) development and sustaining close friendships; and (4) steady, comfortable, useful activity throughout the day.

- Guidance in handling immature behavior and guidelines for providing increasing responsibility as recovery occurs.

Spaniol, Zipple & Fitzgerald (1984) provide guidelines to support families in their roles. The authors highlight the need for practitioners to learn to respond to the intense emotions of families and acknowledge their own biases and limitations in working with families.

Social Network Therapy

The social network of individuals with mental illness has been isolated as increasingly important to the person's stability and recovery. Social networks are considered an important aspect of the individual with mental illness' social support. Social Network Therapy's main goal is to reduce dysfunctional patterns of interaction within the family and promote healthy communication styles (Schoenfeld, Dott, Hemley-van der Velden & Ruhf, 1986). The use of this intervention has been demonstrated to improve growth of reciprocal relationships which may in turn contribute to increase in the number of relatives in the network. The reduction of psychiatric symptoms has been linked to increased social networks (Gillies, Wasylenki, Lancee, Clark , Lewis & Goering, 1993).

Demonstrate community resource and environmental support intervention strategies.

Community Resource and Environmental Support Intervention Strategies

The acquisition of competence in psychosocial rehabilitation interventions specific to the development of environmental resources in the community are dependent upon the practitioner being knowledgeable in several critical areas:

Community Resource Development and Utilization

A critical aspect of PSR practice is the ability of the practitioner to link the often poor and/or undermotivated persons with mental illness to critical resources in the community. For many persons with mental illness, social isolation and economic poverty go hand in hand. In order for larger rehabilitation goals to be identified and achieved individuals first need to be connected to basic service and entitlements. Maslow's hierarchy of needs established basic needs primary to functioning. Recognizing that until basic safety existence needs are met, individuals find it difficult, if not impossible, to achieve self-esteem and community integration needs.

Interventions specific to environment resources include: linking individuals with mental illness with needed entitlements including Social Security SSI and SSD, Medicare and Medicaid, county food stamps, aid to family with dependent children, Municipal Welfare, food banks and second hand clothing stores and thrift shops, hospital resources for people with limited or no benefits, alcohol or drug treatment resources for individuals with few or no benefits. Knowledge of these resources includes not only knowing where they are and what fundamental services they provide but also how they work. For instance, if it's Tuesday and a participant in your program needs to go to the Social Security office, it's important to know that Social Security worker Betty is on the front desk as opposed to Social Security worker Frank, because Betty is much more effective and helpful in getting individuals with mental illness in to see a counselor.

Outreach

One of the key negative symptoms of schizophrenia and other serious mental illnesses consists of struggles with motivation, impoverished feelings, and general underachieving. For PSR practitioners to work successfully with these individuals, they must develop interventions within the context of persistent outreach. Outreach services in PSR takes many forms, from as simple as telephone outreach to calling a perspective individual a day before they are due for an intake interview to physical outreach to a person in a day program who does not come in as expected. The practitioner needs to develop the skill of demonstrating his or her sincerity about their concern for the person as opposed to being perceived as meddling in the individual's private affairs. Other outreach interventions include: mailing birthday cards and/or holiday cards to those who have been absent, sending program newsletters to individuals who have been rehospitalized, inviting inactive persons to holiday parties at the PSR agency, and including everyone in satisfaction surveys and other research surveys within the agency, etc.

Advocacy

In addition to some of the negative symptoms experienced by individuals with mental illness, the significant stigma about these mental illnesses within our society as a whole also exists. Often, people will not get the services they are entitled to because of this stigma. Therefore, practitioners need to develop an array of interventions involving advocacy. For instance, Peter is experiencing headache pain on the weekend and takes himself to the emergency room of the local hospital. Peter's communication skills are hampered by the fact that he has a severe headache. When the psychiatric resident at the emergency room pulls his chart from the hospital records department, he discovers that Peter has a history of psychiatric problems and interprets Peter's reporting his headache symptoms to be psychiatric in nature and refers him to the local screening center for psychiatric hospital admission. These kinds of "miscommunications" happen in much greater numbers to individuals with mental illness because of the ignorance and stigma attached to most people's knowledge of these illnesses.

Advocacy interventions include: practitioners accompanying individuals to entitlements offices to assist in negotiating their claim for benefits, accompanying persons in their visits with psychiatrists and other clinical personnel to assist in making sure that the medical practitioner has the full story before making clinical decisions, and assisting local groups to join voter registration drives.

Development of vocational resources

Perhaps there is no area of greater importance than the development by practitioners of successful vocational interventions for individuals with mental illness. Indeed the success that practitioners and participants in rehabilitation have in this area will often be the most significant determinant of recovery as an outcome in psychosocial rehabilitation. As noted in the chapter on assessment, there is a growing body of knowledge about how to successfully assess vocational strengths, deficits, desires and motivations. Interventions in this area include:

- The ability to take seriously the individual with mental illness' own desire for vocational rehabilitation.

- Access to real opportunities for pre-vocational and employment work.

- The ability to support individuals with mental illness over time in their vocational growth.

- The ability to engage other individuals with mental illness as role models and supporters of newer individuals with mental illness taking on employment activities.

- A number of tools have been developed in psychosocial rehabilitation to assist in providing vocational interventions.

Pre-vocational areas

Pre-vocational areas as an intervention provide a place usually located within a PSR agency or affiliate where individuals can "try out" real work tasks in the safety and support of the rehabilitation community. In clubhouses members and staff (1) work side by side to actually run the program activities such as: housekeeping, clerical, research, food service, transportation, outreach and many others consisting of one or more staff and numerous individuals with mental ill-

ness; (2) this approach allows the practitioner to establish a trusting relationship with the individual with mental illness to evaluate his or her strengths and weaknesses in the pre-vocational area; (3) it allows for the individual with mental illness to receive ongoing feedback from both other individuals with mental illness and staff on their ability to take on and complete certain activities; and (4) it provides a basis for recommending with the individual with mental illness when it is time to move on to a more normalized working environment. In summary, vocational interventions span a wide range of activities including: assessment, marketing, development of support networks for individual with mental illness employees, development of real employment opportunities, and individual counseling skills which are focused on individuals with mental illness ability to work and achieve in real employment settings.

Transitional employment

Transitional employment is a tool employed by many PSR programs which empowers individuals to work in real work settings for real wages for a period of time to test out their ability to work. Typically the agency approaches local businesses and asks the business to give the agency a job for which it will hold itself responsible. An agency staff person will then learn the job and often break that job into two part-time jobs. Individuals will then complete the personnel process with the industry and work on that job for a 4 to 6 month period of time. Typically the agency guarantees the employer that the job will be done on a year round basis. Transitional employment allows the person to test out their generic work skills including: ability to get to work on time and stay the designated course, ability to get along with co-workers, ability to interact successfully with supervisors, ability to handle the pressures of work productivity standards, in a setting where a link remains with the PSR agency through the staff worker who is responsible for this account. Typically a person can work one or many placements until he is ready to move on to his own full or part time job or career oriented job training.

- This intervention has the effect for many individuals with mental illness of convincing them that they can either once again or for the first time do a real job in the community.

- Adds to a growing sense of self-esteem and mutual self reliance.

- Often has the effect of reducing or eliminating stigma in the minds of other workers and supervisors in the industry.

Supported employment

Supported Employment is a term used for a variety of individual with mental illness-oriented and career-oriented job acquisition, placement, and support activities. Typically Supported Employment models can be described as either the Job Coach Model or the Enclave Model. The focus of Supported Employment assessment is on the person's strengths, motivation and desires for vocational achievement. Significant time and energy is spent in Supported Employment efforts in testing individual's interests and motivations, shaping a vocational plan that meets the interest of that person, and developing real work opportunities that are in line with the person's area of desired employment. Supported Employment interventions

therefore need to be extremely flexible, requiring a high degree of practitioner creativity, a high degree of negotiation skills to match the person's interest and desires with existing opportunities in the labor market, stronger reliance on existing and creation of new employment training opportunities and the skill to provide ongoing support, advocacy and problem solving with individuals with mental illness over time. The desired outcome for many people in Supported Employment is being placed in supported, career-oriented jobs and receiving the necessary support, training, and mobility counseling which will allow that person to continue to grow toward a particular career.

Placements in Supported Employment are usually not seen as time limited but, rather, ongoing. Other interventions include: support groups concerning employment issues, marketing training skills for practitioners, designing and implementing educational programs for and with local industry.

Affirmative businesses

A relatively new vocational intervention involves the development of affirmative businesses. These businesses are either for-profit or not-for-profit companies which employ people with psychiatric disabilities, people with other disabilities, and employees without any clearly identifiable disabilities. These companies may be seeded with funds from public and/or private sources with the intention of becoming fully self-supported and able to either invest profits in the business or to reward share holders in private for profit ventures. In these businesses practitioners need to learn how to operate a successful business with maximal respect for the "bottom line."

Innovative Vocational Programs

One vocational intervention that is noted for its innovative design is the Job-Finding Module (Jacobs, Collier & Wissusik, 1992) designed to assist persons capable of competitive employment find work. The module consists of four parts: (1) technical manual on the design and operation of job finding clubs, (2) a job-seeking skills training curriculum, 3) an individual with mental illness workbook, and (4) a video training tape that demonstrates actual job-seeking skills. It presents a clear and direct methodology for program implementation. Another approach to enhance vocational rehabilitation interventions is the individual placement and support (IPS [Becker & Drake, 1994]), which draws from other models. The overriding principles from this New Hampshire mental health system indicate that vocational rehabilitation is integrated into mental health treatment, that the goal of IPS is competitive employment in integrated work settings, that individuals can obtain jobs rapidly without pre-vocational programs, that vocational assessment is continuous, that follow-up supports are necessary to sustain employment, that services are based on individual with mental illness' preferences and choices, and that the team approach fosters integration of employment with rehabilitation services. Employment specialists are a critical component of the IPS model.

Another innovative program is the Redirection Through Education (RTE [Tuffy, Belanger & Gregory, 1993]). RTE is a program designed to address both the employment and interpersonal needs of young psychiatrically disabled adults. The educational component is a crucial element that allows for completion of high school and job training experience. The RTE Program is structured and demands that students regularly attend class, interact with other students, and concentrate on school work. It acts as a bridge to other programs and opportunities.

Supported education

The formulation of an overall picture concerning wants or needs related to the desire to return to school for further education or training is part of the role of PSR practitioners. The process includes the ability to link needs and wants with a realistic vision of themselves in the future and to be clear as to what will be expected as students and what support is available at the academic program. Psychological testing, such as aptitude, motivation to return to formal education in addition to evaluation of the person's best formal educational experience and the person's worst formal experience. Understanding whether the person's life stresses played a role in their symptoms and/or educational performance will be important for planning. Attitudinally, it will then be important to assess how things have changed and evaluate the person's willingness to explore, pursue, and participate in formal academic programs. A useful intervention is to have DVR have career aptitude testing and interest testing. A full review of local academic programs and how they are able and willing to accommodate the needs of the individual will be needed. Other interventions include the establishment of groups such as GED, support groups in local colleges who are doing course work, and liaison with academic counselors to ensure coordinated services.

References

Accordino, M.P. & Guerney, B.G. (1993). Effects of the relationship enhancement program on community residential rehabilitation staff and clients. *Psychosocial Rehabilitation Journal, 17* (2), 131-144.

Adler, D.A., Pajer, J., Ellison, J.M., Dorwart, R., Siris, S., Goldman, H., Lehman, A. and Berlant, J. (1995). Schizophrenia and the life cycle. *Community Mental Health Journal, 31*(3), 249-262.

Ahmed, M. and Goldman, J.A. (1994). Cognitive rehabilitation of adults with severe and persistent mental illness: a group model. *Community Mental Health Journal, 30*(4), 385-394.

Anthony, W.A., Cohen, M.R., Farkas, M.D. and Cohen, B.F. (1988). Clinical care update: Case management - more than a response to dysfunctional system. *Community Mental Health Journal, 24,* 219-228.

Arana, J., Hastings, B., and Herron, E. (1991). Continuous care teams in intensive outpatient treatment of chronic mentally ill patients. *Hospital and Community Psychiatry 42*(5), 503-507.

Bataille, G.G. (1990). Psychotherapy and community support: community mental health systems in transition. *Using Psychodynamic Principles in Public Mental Health (New Directions for Mental Health Services, 46,* 9-17. San Francisco: Jossey-Bass.

Becker, D.R. & Drake, R.E., (1994). Individual placement and support: A community mental health center approach to vocational rehabilitation. *Community Mental Health Journal 30* (2), 193-205.

Berman, C., & Rozensky, R. (1984). Sex education for the chronic psychiatric patient: The effects of a sexual-issues group on knowledge and attitudes. *Psychosocial Rehabilitation Journal, 1,* 29-33.

Birchwood, M., Smith, J. and MacMilian, F. (1989). Predicting relapse in schizophrenia: The development & implementation of an early sign monitoring system using patient and families as observers: a preliminary investigation. *Psychological Medicine, 19,* 64-656.

Bond, G.R. (1991). Variations in an assertive outreach model. Psychiatric Outreach to the Mentally Ill. (New Directions for Mental Health Services, 52, 65-80). San Francisco: Jossey-Bass.

Brekke, J.S. and Test, M.A. (1987). An empirical analysis of services delivered in a model community support program. *Psychosocial Rehabilitation Journal, X* (4), 51-61.

Burns, B. J. and Santos, A.B. (1995). Assertive community treatment: an update of randomized trials. *Psychiatric Services, 46*(7), 669-675.

Caldwell, B. and Gottesman, I.I. (1990) Schizophrenics kill themselves too: A review of risk factors for suicide. *Schizophrenia Bulletin, 16* (4) 571-589.

Carkuff, R.R. and Berensen, B.G. (1976). *Teaching as treatment. An introduction to counseling and psychotherapy* Amherst, M.A. Human Resources Development Press.

Cates, J.A. and Graham, L.L. (1993). HIV and serious mental illness: reducing the risk. *Community Mental Health Journal, 29*(1), 35-47.

Chiles, J. & Strosohl, K. (1995). *The suicidal patient.* Washington, D.C.: American Psychiatric Press.

Cohen, B.F., Ridley, D.E., and Cohen, M.R. (1983). Teaching skills to psychiatrically disabled persons. In. H.A. Marlowe (Ed.) *Developing Competence.* Tampa: University of Florida Press.

Cohen, L. J., Test, M.A. and Brown, R.L. (1990). Suicide and Schizophrenia: Data from a prospective community treatment study. *American Journal of Psychiatry, 147* (5) 602-606.

Cohen, N.L. and Tsemberis, S. (1991). Emergency psychiatric intervention on the street. Psychiatric Outreach to the Mentally Ill (New Directions for Mental Health Services, 52, 3-14). San Francisco: Jossey-Bass, Inc.

Cook, J.A., Razzano, L., Jayaraj, A., Myers, Mr., Nathanson, F. Stott, M.A. and Stein, M. (1994). HIV-risk assessment for psychosocial rehabilitation clientele: Implications for community-based services. *Psychosocial Rehabilitation Journal, 17*(4), 105-115.

Corrigan, P.W. and Kayton-Weinberg, D. (1993). "Aggressive" and "problem-focused" models of case management for the severely mentally ill. *Community Mental Health Journal 29*(5), 449-457.

Corrigan, P.W. & Storzbach, D.M. (1993). Behavioral interventions for alleviating psychotic symptoms. *Hospital and Community Psychiatry, 44* (4), 341-347.

Corey, M.S. & Corey, G. (1992). *Group process and practice.* California: Brooks/Cole Publishing Company.

Daley, D.C., Salloum, I., and Jones-Barlock, A. (1990). Integrating a dual-disorders program in an acute-care psychiatric hospital. *Psychosocial Rehabilitation Journal, 13*(4) 45-56.

Deci, P.A., Santos, A.B., Hiott, D.W., Schoenwald, S. and Dias, J. (1995). Dissemination of assertive community treatment program. *Psychiatric Services, 46*(7), 676-678.

Detrick, A. and Stiepock, V. ( ) Treating persons with mental illness, substance abuse and legal problems: the Rhode Island experience. *Innovative Community Mental Health Programs* (New Directions for Mental Health Services, 65-77). San Francisco: Jossey-Bass.

Dixon, L.B., Krauss, N., Kernan, E., Lehman, A.F. and DeForge, B.R. (1995). Modifying the PACT model to serve homeless persons with severe mental illness. *Psychiatric Services, 46* (7), 684-688.

Dobson, D.J.G., McDougall, G., Busheikin, J. and Aldous, J. (1995). Effects of social skills training and social milieu treatment on symptoms of schizophrenia. *Psychiatric Services, 46*(4), 376-380.

Docherty, J., Van Kammen, D. , Siris, S. and Marder, S. (1978). Stages of onset of schizophrenic psychosis. *American Journal of Psychiatry, 135,* 420-426.

Drake, R.E. and Burns, B.J. (1995). Special section on assertive community treatment: an introduction. *Psychiatric Services 46*(7) 667-668.

Eckman, T.A., Wirshing, W.C., Marder, S.R., Lieberman, R.P., Johnston-Cronk, K., Zimmermann, K. and Mintz, J. (1992). Technique for training schizophrenic patients in illness self-management: A controlled trial. *American Journal of Psychiatry, 149*(11), 1549-1555.

Essock, S.M. and Kontos, N. (1995) Implementing assertive community treatment teams. *Psychiatric Services, 46*(7) 679-683.

Fremouw, W.J. de Perczel, M. and Ellis T. (1990) *Suicide risk: assessment and response guidelines.* New York: Pergamon Press.

Gillies, L.A., Wasylenki, D.A., Lancee, W.J., James, S., Clark C.C., Lewis, J. & Goering, P. (1993). Differential outcomes in social network therapy. *Psychosocial Rehabilitation Journal, 16*(3) 141-145.

Greenfield, S.F., Weiss, R.D. & Tohen M. (1995). Substance abuse and the chronically mentally ill: A description of dual diagnosis treatment services in a psychiatric hospital. *Community Mental Health Journal, 31*(3) 265-277.

Hanson, J.G. and Rapp, C.A. (1992). Families' perceptions of community mental health programs for their relatives with a severe mental illness. *Community Mental Health Journal, 28*(3), 181-197.

Heritage, S., Sudol, R. and Connery, L. (1987). Training and consultation to residential care providers serving adults with severe mental illness. *Psychosocial Rehabilitation Journal, X*(3), 11-19.

Herz, M.I. and Melville, C. (1980). Relapse in schizophrenia. *American Journal of Psychiatry, 137,* 801-805.

Hill, D. & Balk, D. (1987). The effect of an education program for families of the chronically mentally ill on stress and anxiety. *Psychosocial Rehabilitation Journal, 10*(4), 25-40.

Honeycutt, N. and Belcher, J.R. (1991). Schizophrenia and social skills: An "identify and train' approach. *Community Mental Health Journal, 27*(1) 57-68.

Hromco, J.G., Lyons, J.S. and Nikkel, R.E. (1995). Mental health case management: Characteristics, job function and occupational stress. *Community Mental Health Journal 31*(2), 111-114.

Hyde, A.P. & Goldman, C.R. (1993). Common family issues that interfere with the treatment and rehabilitation of people with schizophrenia. *Psychosocial Rehabilitation Journal, 16*(4) 63-73.

Hyde, A.P. & Goldman, C.R. (1993). Use of multi-modal multiple family group in the comprehensive treatment and rehabilitation of people with schizophrenia. *Psychosocial Rehabilitation Journal, 15*(4), 77-86.

Isaacs, A.D. & Bebbington, P.E. (1991). Strategies for the management of sever psychiatric illness in the community. *International Review of Psychiatry, 3*(1), 71-82.

Kasper, J.D., Steinwachs, D.M., and Skinner, E.A. (1992). Family perspectives on the service needs of people with serious and persistent mental illness: Part II: Needs for assistance and needs that go unmet. *Innovations and Research, 1*(4), 21-33.

Kazarian, S. and Vanderheyden, D. (1992). Family education of relatives of people with psychiatric disability: A review. *Psychosocial Rehabilitation Journal, 15*(3), 67-83.

Keith-Spiegel, D. and Koocher, G. (1985). *Ethics in psychology.* New York: McGraw Hill, Inc.

Knight, B.G. (1991). Outreach to older adults: matching programs to specific needs. Psychiatric Outreach to the Mentally Ill. *New Directions for Mental Health Services, 51,* 93-111. San Francisco: Jossey-Bass.

Knox, M.D., Davis, M. and Friedrich, M.A., (1994). The HIV mental health spectrum. *Community Mental Health Journal, 30*(1) 75-89.

Lam, D.H. (1991). Psychosocial family intervention in schizophrenia: a review of empirical studies. *Psychological Medicine, 21,* 423-441.

Liberman, R.P. (1982). Assessment of social skills. *Schizophrenic Bulletin, 8* (1), 62-83.

Mannion, E.., Mueser, K., and Solomon P. (1994). Designing psychoeducational services for spouses of persons with serious mental illness. *Community Mental Health Journal, 30*(2), 177-189.

Marcenko, M.O., Herman, S.E. and Hazel K.L. (1992). A comparison of how families and their service providers rate family generated quality of service factors. *Community Mental Health Journal, 28*(5), 441-449.

Marsh, D. (1992). Working with families of people with serious mental illness. In L. VandeeCreek, S. Knapp & T.L. Jackson (Eds.). *Innovations in clinical practice: A source book.* Sarasota FL: Professional Resource Press.

McFarlane, W.R., Stastny, P. and Deakins, R., (1992). Family-aided assertive community treatment: A comprehensive rehabilitation and intensive case management approach for persons with schizophrenic disorders. Effective Psychosocial rehabilitation. *New Directions for Mental Health Services, 53,* 43-53. San Francisco: Jossey-Bass, Inc.

McGrew, J.H., Bond, G.R., Dietzen, L., McKasson, M. and Miller, L.D. (1995). A multisite study of client outcomes in assertive community treatment. *Psychiatric Services, 46*(7), 696-701.

McQuistion, H.L., D'Ercole, A. and Kopelson E. (1991). Urban street outreach: using clinical principles to steer the system. Psychiatric Outreach to the Mentally Ill. *New Directions for Mental Health Services, 52,* 17-27. San Francisco: Jossey-Bass.

Mills, P.D. and Hansen, J.C. (1991). Short-term group interventions for mentally ill young adults living in a community residence and their families. *Hospital and Community Psychiatry, 42*(11), 1144-1149.

Minkoff, K. (1993). Intervention strategies for people with dual diagnosis. *Innovations and Research*, 2(4), 11-17.

Minkoff, K. (1991). Program components of a comprehensive integrated care system for serious mentally ill patients with substance disorders. Dual Diagnosis of Major Mental Illness and Substance Disorder. *New Directions for Mental Health Services, 50,* 13-25. San Francisco: Jossey-Bass, Inc.

Moller, M.D. and Murphy, M. (1991). *The three "R" program, relapse, recovery and rehabilitation.* Center for Patient and Family Mental Health Education. Nine Miles Falls, WA.

Moxley, D.P. and Freddolino, P.P., (199). A model of advocacy for promoting client self-determination in psychosocial rehabilitation. *Psychosocial Rehabilitation Journal, 14*(2), 70-82.

Nemec, P.B., McNamara, S. & Walsh, D. (1992). Direct skills training. *Psychosocial Rehabilitation Journal, 16*(1), 15-25.

Nikkel, R.E. (1994). Areas of skill training for persons with mental illness and substance use disorders: building skills for successful community living. *Community Mental Health Journal, 30* (1), 61-72.

Nikkel, R. and Coiner, R., (1991). Critical interventions and tasks in delivering dual-diagnosis services. *Psychosocial Rehabilitation Journal, 15*(2), 58-66.

Noh, S. and Turner, R.J. (1987). Living with psychiatric patients: Implications for the mental health of family members. *Med., 25*(3) 263-272.

Noordsy, D.L. and Fox, L. (1991). Group intervention techniques for people with dual disorders. *Psychosocial Rehabilitation Journal, 15*(2) 68-78.

Pelham, T.W., Campagna, P.D., Ritvo, P. G. & Birnie, W. (1993). The effects of exercise therapy on clients in psychosocial rehabilitation program. *Psychosocial Rehabilitation Journal, 16*(4) 75-83.

Pepper, E. (1988). Sexual awareness groups in a psychiatric day treatment program. *Psychosocial Rehabilitation Journal, 11*(3), 45-53.

Pyke, J. and Steers, M.J. (1992). Suicide in a community based case management service. *Community Mental Health Journal, 28*(6) 483-489.

Ranz, J.M., Horen, B.T., McFarlane, W.R., and Zito, J.M. (1991). Creating a supportive environment using staff psychoeducation in a supervised residence. *Hospital and Community Psychiatry, 42*(11), 1154-1159.

Rapp, C.A. and Wintersteen, R. (1989). The strengths model of case management: results from twelve demonstrations. *Psychosocial Rehabilitation Journal, 13*(1), 23-31.

Reed, D., Sullivan, M.E., Penn, D.L., Stuve, P. and Spaulding, W.D. (1992). Assessment and treatment of cognitive impairments. Effective Psychosocial rehabilitation. *New Directions for Mental Health Services, 53,* 7-19. San Francisco: Jossey-Bass.

Reding, G.R. & Raphelson, M. (1995). Around-the-clock mobile psychiatric crisis intervention: Another effective alternative to psychiatric hospitalization. *Community Mental Health Journal, 31*(2), 179-187.

Ridgely, M.S. (1991). Creating integrated programs for severely mentally ill persons with substance disorders. Dual Diagnosis of Major Mental Illness and Substance Disorder. *New Directions for Mental Health Services, 50,* 29-41. San Francisco: Jossey-Bass, Inc.

Rogers, C. (1961). *On becoming a person.* Boston: Houghton Mefflin.

Ryglewicz, H. (1991). Psychoeducation for clients and families: A way in, out and through in working with people with dual diagnosis. *Psychosocial Rehabilitation Journal, 15*(2), 79-89.

Schoenfeld, R., Dott, J.H., Hemley-van der Velden, E. & Ruhf, L. (1986). Long-term outcome of network therapy. *Hospital and Community Psychiatry, 37,* 373-376.

Sciacca, K., (1991). An integrated treatment approach for severely mentally ill individuals with substance disorders. Dual Diagnosis of Major Mental Illness and Substance Disorder. *New Directions for Mental Health Services, 50,* 69-84.

Segal, S.P. and Holschuh, J. (1991). Effects of sheltered care environments and resident characteristics on the development of social networks. *Hospital and Community Psychiatry, 42*(11), 1125-1131.

Segal, S. P., Silverman, C. & Temkin, T. (1995). Measuring empowerment in client-run self-help agencies. *Community Mental Health Journal, 31*(3), 215-227.

Shea, S.C. (1988). *Psychiatric interviewing: The art of understanding.* Philadelphia: W.S. Saunders Company.

Shelton, R. and Rissmeyer, D. (1989). Involving consumers in the discharge process. *Psychosocial Rehabilitation Journal, 12*(4), 19-28.

Solomon, P. (1988). Services to severely mentally disabled homeless persons and to emergency food and shelter providers. *Psychosocial Rehabilitation Journal, 12*(2) 3-13.

_____ (1993. The efficacy of case management services for severely mentally disabled clients. *Community Mental Health Journal, 28*(3), 163-179.

Srebnik, D., Livingston, Gordon, L. and King, D. (1995). Housing choice and community success for individuals with serious and persistent mental illness. *Community Mental Health Journal, 31*(2), 139-151.

Stein, L.I. & Test, M.A. (1980). Alternatives to mental hospital treatment. *Archives of General Psychiatry, 37,* 392-398.

Stroul, B. (1989). Community support systems for persons with long term mental illness: A conceptual framework. *Psychosocial Rehabilitation Journal, 12*(3) 9-26.

Susser, E., Goldfinger, S.M. and White, A. (1990). Some clinical approaches to the homeless mentally ill. *Community Mental Health Journal, 26*(5), 463-479.

Teague, G.B., Drake, R.E. and Ackerson, T.H. (1995). Evaluating use of continuous treatment teams for persons with mental illness and substance abuse. *Psychiatric Services, 46*(7), 689-695.

Telles, L. ( ) The clustered apartment project: a conceptually coherent supported housing model. Innovative Community Mental Health Programs. *New Directions For Mental Health Services*, 53-64. San Francisco: Jossey-Bass.

Terkelsen, K. (1990). A historical perspective on family-provider relationship. In. H. Lefley and D. Johnson (Eds.). *Families As Allies In the Treatment of the Mentally Ill*. Washington, D.C. American Psychiatric Press.

Tessler, R.C., Killian, L.M., and Gubman, G.D. (1987). Stages in family response to mental illness: An ideal type. *Psychosocial Rehabilitation Journal, X*(4), 3-15.

Unger, K. V., Skrinar, G.S., Hutchinson, D. & Yelmokas, A. (1992) Fitness: A viable adjunct to treatment for young adults with psychiatric disabilities. *Psychosocial Rehabilitation Journal, 15*(3), 21-27.

Vaccaro, J.V., Liberman, R.P., Wallace, C.J. and Blackwell, G. (1992). Combing social skills training and assertive case management: The social and independent living skills program of the Brentwood veterans affairs medical center. Effective Psychosocial rehabilitation. *New Directions for Mental Health Services, 53*, 33-41. San Francisco: Jossey-Bass, Inc.

Well, D. (1992). Management of early post-discharge adjustment reactions following psychiatric hospitalization. *Hospital and Community Psychiatry, 43*(10), 1000-1004.

Wenocur, S. and Belcher, J.R. (1990). Strategies for overcoming barriers to community-based housing for the chronically mentally ill. *Community Mental Health Journal, 26*(4) 319-333.

Wintersteen R. & Young, L. (1988). Effective professional collaboration with family support groups. *Psychosocial Rehabilitation Journal, 12*(1), 19-31.

Yalom, I.D. (1985). *The theory and practice of group psychotherapy.* New York: Basic Books, Inc.

Zipple, A.M., Langle, S., Spaniol, L. and Fisher, H. (1990). Client confidentiality and the family's need to know: Strategies for resolving the conflict. *Community Mental Health Journal, 26* (6), 533-545.

8

Integrating Multicultural Competence in Psychosocial Rehabilitation

Anita Pernell-Arnold and Laurene Finley

Introduction

The authors use the assumption "everyone has an ethnicity" as the basic tenet of inclusion. This reduces intergroup conflict and promotes acceptance and understanding in an area that is riddled with accusations and antagonisms. It also leads to the study of any and all cultures to which PSR can relate. The authors define culture by many variables: race, religion, disability, gender, sexual orientation, and class.

The incorporation of cultural competence into the core of PSR principles and values is a critical process that will increase the applicability of PSR services across racial, ethnical, cultural, and national boundaries. This chapter is designed to identify assumptions that promote universal approaches that preclude analysis from cultural perspectives. PSR has long accepted the necessity of exploring individual functioning biologically, psychologically, and socially. *Social* has generally come to mean interpersonal, hence the requirement for adding culture. The individual and family must both be understood within their cultural context.

Administrators, supervisors, and practitioners will be able to use this chapter to begin the process of introducing cultural competency into their programs. Information is included that forms the basis for staff competencies and their evaluations, training programs, program development, and evaluation. The principles and values that must inform culturally competent organizations are enumerated and operationalized.

The authors propose that PSR is a natural home for culturally competent services in mental health. Many of the approaches and strategies are user-friendly and promote the integration of culturally competent methods. The differences in the building blocks that are required to ensure PSR programs' responsiveness and accomodation are described. Models are identified that can equip professionals to create programs that fit the cultural, environmental, and economical demands of their various locales. A PSR professional must mediate between mainstream mental health programs (culture-broker) and/or modify existing programs to increase their compatibility and effectiveness with various racial, ethnic, and cultural groups. These are the skills and competencies that professionals must have to carry out these complex tasks.

It is imperative that PSR increase its commitment to incorporate multi-cultural philosophies, principles, and values in the daily details of the relationship between the professional and the consumer and in the major machinations of the overall agency.

Historical Context

The roots of the multicultural movement in the United States can be found among social psychiatry pioneers such as Karen Horney (1937). She recognized that human problems were incomprehensible apart from their cultural context. Erickson, a human development theorists provided a framework for understanding how the individual might be linked to the ethnic group and the society. In his description, the final stage of human development involves coming to terms with one's own cultural identity as the basis for psychosocial equilibrium (Erickson, 1950). Lewin (1948), in the development his field theory, formulated questions and assumptions about the role and importance of group membership in the formation of one's identity. He maintained that an early, clear, and positive feeling of belonging to one's group was an essential foundation perceived necessary to the individual's security, direction, and eventual development of identity. Following his theory, several studies demonstrated a positive relationship between a solid, clear, ethnic group identification and self-esteem, sense of well-being, and positive self-concept (Weiss, 1957; Radke-Yarrow, 1958; Janov, 1960; Proshansky & Newton, 1968; Rutchik, 1968; Mobley, 1974; Klein, 1980; Hehm, 1990; Parham, 1992).

The social climate of the 1960s and 1970s exploded! A surge of ethnic group consciousness emerged resulting in increased protest and demands for human services to perform more effectively and equitably. A concept of *new pluralism*

was reasserted as a framework for increasing the acceptance and sensitivity to group differences. Human services would be delivered by public institutions according to cultural needs and lifestyles (Friedman, 1971; Levine & Herman, 1971; Novak, 1971; Feinstein, 1974).

A wide array of social programs came into existence during this same period. The community mental health movement was one system of services enacted to make mental health services more accessible to persons within their communities and to involve the individual with mental illness in institutional decision-making. Giordano (1976) suggests that the movement had a limited national impact on effective service delivery for several reasons, one of which was an insensitivity to diversity within American communities based on ethnic, racial, religious, and regional differences and a lack of recognition of the natural strength within these communities. Messages that mental health services were out-of-tune with the life style and culture of people emerged from this tumultuous period.

The historical review of the mental health literature from the organizational perspective has paid relatively little attention to either agency organizational structure or program development, supportive of healthy cross-cultural relationships and services. There are, however, several notable exceptions. An exploratory investigation of a group developed at Hill House was designed for African Americans with mental illness to impact on their length of stay in the program (Stillman, 1974). Black professional leadership, group membership, and specific use of culture seemed to increase identification with the agency and involvement in the program (Stillman, 1974). Research at Thresholds, another PSR program, demonstrated that intensity of participation and length of stay were positively correlated with goal achievement (Dincin & Kaberon, 1979). Finley (1978) and Primm (1990) have also described culturally oriented group models and their effectiveness at reaching ethnic subgroups.

Lefley and Bestmen (1974) developed a nontraditional, multicultural mental health agency targeting diverse communities of Cubans, Puerto Ricans, Haitians, Bahamians, and Southern African Americans. Major features of this program included: culture-specific mobile treatment teams which provided outreach to each ethnic community; neighborhood surveys; and integration of a prevention program model aimed at environmental stress reduction through specific interventions such as child care, better housing, employment, medical services with psychiatric treatment models. Three concepts frequently experienced by ethnic group members were considered in the development of this agency:

- acculturation stress experienced by refugees who were often forced to migrate by choice or fear and forced to adapt to a new culture;

- environmental stress, (i.e. the lack of equal access to resources such as education, employment, housing and medical care); and

- use of folk healers and alternative healing practices because of the presence of culture-bound syndromes such as spirit possession, "ataque," rootwork.

Lefley and Bestman hypothesized that a model which integrated the above features would result in more effective treatment outcomes, greater use of therapeutic resources, higher levels-of-functioning and improved social relationships. A random sample of 150 individuals with mental illness, when compared to rates from more traditional programs, reported the effectiveness of outreach approaches, a decrease in no-show rates and drop-out rates. About half of the individuals with mental illness reported a higher degree of satisfaction with services offered (1974).

Martin (1988) reported on an NIMH conference during which reviews of mental health programs designed to meet the needs of the culturally different were identified. Several recommendations were generated that could guide the development of culturally competent programming for Hispanics, Asian and Pacific Island Communities (Naranjo, 1988; Fujiwara & Christian; Townsend, 1988; Cook, 1988). Suggested recommendations were:

- the term "minority" and "minority relevant" must be defined in specific detail,

- culturally appropriate assessment tools must be developed,

- model programs and clinical treatment standards that are culturally and ethnically appropriate must be developed,

- quality assurance indicators must be developed to measure the quality of services provided to minorities,

- a needs assessment mechanism must be developed to ensure that programming is responsive to the culturally different, and

- various models of community care should be reviewed so as to learn the most effective programs which enable people to stay in their respective communities.

Multicultural organizational development (MCOD) has been most fully described by consultants in response to companies needing to adapt to newly changing markets. The focus has been on: 1) how organizations and systems can be more culturally adaptive; and 2) the role of culture on leadership styles, organizational styles, and changing societal demands (Kilman, 1985; Peters, 1987; Smith and Peterson, 1988).

The overall goal of MCOD is the involvement of the entire membership or staff of an organization in the creation of a multicultural environment. MCOD is a total organizational approach that must be initiated by the leadership and must include all levels and functions of the organization. A major assumption of this method is that racism, sexism, ageism, discrimination, and oppression have all had a major impact on the cultural styles of the organization. Frequently, an internal team, representative of the major stakeholders, spearheads the change process. A review of goals, objectives, policies and procedures to determine their compatibility with the organization's mission is required in order to achieve a more multicultural environment. Often outside consultants are used to facilitate this review process and may suggest needed staff training and problem identification. It is essential that organizational members or staff receive training on the implementation of the revised mission, policies and procedures (Jackson & Hardiman, 1994). A consensus model is utilized to actually guide the dynamics of the change process. This model, as opposed to a more competitive, encounter, conflict model, promotes finding and strengthening commonalties, mutual interests, and collaborations as strategies to overcome resistances that are often generated in cross cultural exchanges (Hardiman & Jackson, 1994; Chesler, 1994).

Many mental health organizations, including some psychosocial rehabilitation programs, have been structured according to principles that relate to power, authority, status, roles, and behavior. Furthermore, each program function (e.g., day treatment, residential) often has a separate, semi-autonomous structure. Frequently referred to as a medical model, this type of program structure has been soundly rejected by the psychosocial rehabilitation movement (Rutman, 1994). Most psychosocial rehabilitation programs have adopted structures that are more closely aligned with democratic and humanitarian principles such as egalitarianism, reduced hierarchy, and empowerment of both those participating in the program and staff (Dincin & Kaberon, 1979).

The concept of universality, interwoven with other values and principles, has also been infused into the structure of PSR programs. Universality implies that models and practices formed on the basis of experience with one group can be applied to persons of any culture and race. The phrase "people are all the same" is one way that this concept is expressed by professionals. Though it is true that human needs are similar, how these needs may be expressed are culturally determined (Randall, 1989; McGoldrick, Pearce and Giordano, 1982). Values and belief systems derive from diverse cultural contexts and cannot be analyzed from a universal perspective. The effect of a universality concept is a reluctance of PSR programs similar to medical model programs that it sought to reject, to accept, to study, and to integrate how race, gender, culture, sexual orientation, and disability might impact rehabilitation services and outcomes.

Overview: Mental Health and Multiculturalism

There is a compelling need for mental health professionals to intervene more effectively with diverse ethnic populations. It is estimated that people of diverse ethnic groups account for one quarter or more of those persons currently using the public mental health system (Cheung, 1991) and the estimated growth of peoples of color and service demands are likely to increase (U.S. Department of Commerce, 1989). The reassertion of American ethnicity through the multicultural movement, therefore, is much more than a passing fad and much deeper than romanticizing the past. It denotes social characteristics as well as the biological origins of a people which have been the carriers of culture through the emotional language of families over generations. Ethnicity is critical for the determination of values, attitudes, perceptions, needs, expressive modes, behavior, and identity formation (Tumin, 1964; Feinstein, 1974; McGoldrick, Pearce & Giordano, 1982). It forms the basis for the search for a sense of belonging and self-esteem (Giordano, 1973).

Twenty-five years later, mental health services continue to be out-of-tune with the cultural movement. Many of the mental health approaches utilized to treat persons of diversity remain inherently insensitive and incompatible with their cultures (Sue, 1992; Sue & Sue, 1990; Smith, 1973; Karno, 1966; President's Commission on Mental Health, 1978; Chavey, 1986). Socio-cultural variables are not acknowledged by service planners and providers, leaving many individuals with mental illness disenchanted with current service practices.

Mental Health System Barriers

Epidemiological surveys report major barriers to the delivery of mental health services to persons from different ethnic backgrounds. Rates for non-whites hospitalized in psychiatric institutions have consistently been reported to be higher than for those of whites (Cannon & Locke, 1977; Myers & King, 1980; Snowden & Cheung, 1990). Racial discrepancies between non-whites and whites for involuntary commitments are pronounced. Non-white rates are 3.5 times greater than whites for involuntary criminal commitments and nearly 2.5 times higher for involuntary noncriminal commitments (Rosenstein, Millazzo-Sayre, MacAskill & Manderscheid, 1987). Danger to self or others, the major criterion for involuntary commitment, may depend on clinical judgements which are readily influenced by stereotypes and prejudices. These decisions leave considerable room for the intrusion of racial bias (Snowden & Cheung, 1990).

Significant disparities between the diagnostic assessment of nonwhites and whites continue to be discriminatory and unfairly stigmatizing to some individuals with mental illness. African-Americans, for example, have typically been assigned more severe diagnoses such as paranoid schizophrenia, while whites are more likely to be diagnosed with the less severe depressive disorders (Cannon & Locke, 1976; Jones & Gray, 1986; Snowden & Cheung, 1990). Depressive disorders for blacks have been under represented (Jones & Gray, 1986). Furthermore, depressive symptoms among African Americans, for example, have been found to have a different quality of mood than for whites. Blacks have been shown to manifest more worry, muscular tension, general anxiety, and bodily symptoms (Cannon & Locke, 1977). Some of the more classic signs of fatigue, loss of appetite and sleep, crying and dejected mood may be masked by a more agitated, active and self-destructive expression of depression (Block, 1981). Psychosocial assessments have most times not reflected the differential cultural expression and pattern of psychiatric symptomatology and behaviors for ethnic group individuals with mental illness.

What is multiculturalism?

Multiculturalism, the cultural movement of today, poses unique challenges to mental health and specifically to PSR. Multiculturalism is the study of one's own culture and ethnicity as the basis for understanding and identifying with those of others. It recognizes and values diversity. It views our nation as a mosaic in which each culture makes valuable contributions to the entire society. Belonging to one's group implies that there are values about what it means to belong and that these values form the basis for the conscious or unconscious decisions made regarding the role and importance of culture in one's life. Persons may choose to reject his/her personal culture, selectively incorporate aspects of the mainstream culture, or become bicultural.

Given these assumptions, all behavior occurs within a cultural context. The behaviors and lifestyles of all persons with mental illness are viewed through "a cultural lens" so that the development of multiple perspectives and integration of broad and conflicting bodies of information may occur. Initial assumptions about behavior are suspended in favor of active query regarding the individual's and family's worldview and the personal meaning of behavior within the cultural context in order to arrive at sound judgments. Individuals with mental illness are

actively discouraged from inappropriately personalizing problems that may reside within the system at-large.

Theory, rehabilitation, and treatment interventions are often viewed as "culture-bound" (Sue, 1992). Through cultural flexibility, treatment is both modified and tailored to maximize compatibility with the individual's ethnic background, worldview, values, beliefs, and expectations of what is acceptable. Providers and programs continuously struggle to eliminate biases, stereotypes, and prejudices which often result in culturally destructive or ineffective practices and structures.

Lack of mainstream familiarity with the burgeoning field of multiculturalism, as a whole, may generate tremendous fear regarding major adjustments anticipated in current PSR theories, values, principles and practices thereby increasing the reluctance to embrace this orientation and to integrate it within our ranks. What then are the major points of departure between psychosocial rehabilitation and multiculturalism? Conversely, at what points do they converge?

Comparison of PSR and Multiculturalism

A comparison between the psychosocial rehabilitation and multicultural models can further highlight these "points of contact" using the following parameters as a guide:
- goals and objectives,
- context for treatment and rehabilitation,
- theoretical framework,
- professional roles, and
- approaches and methods.

Goals and objectives
Psychosocial rehabilitation's primary goals are to maximize each person's

strengths and skills in the environments of living, learning, working and playing (Anthony, 1977; 1979; 1982; Anthony & Liberman, 1994). The multicultural model also emphasizes strengths but further acknowledges that these strengths are "rooted" in each person's culture (Lewin, 1948; Erickson, 1950). These embedded strengths contribute to a sense of self while also providing psychic energy for coping, which enriches the lives of each individual with mental illness (Levine, 1976). Solutions to problems are also found within the culture. For example, broadening the concept of family to include persons not just living within a person's household but across geographic lines or the inclusion of "non-blood" kin (i.e., good friends, neighbors, godparents) may expand the resources available in the social network. In another example, a Vietnamese person who rejects social skill training and participation in verbal social groups might be better served by immediate placement in a business or community organization in the Vietnamese community where he can work extended hours and be more useful to his family.

The integration of PSR with multi-culturalism utilizes cultural strengths to address individual goals. Furthermore, individual goals and the processes used to meet these goals are compatible with the individual's worldview in order to maximize attainment. Sue (1981 & 1990) outlines three major conditions which may occur when goals and processes are incongruent:

- goals are appropriate to the culture but the strategies needed to help individuals with mental illness meet their goals are incompatible with the individual's experiences;

- goals are questionable but methods or approaches are compatible;

- both the selected goals and methods are inappropriately matched to the individual with mental illness' ethnic background.

Consider, for example, a young African-American male with mental illness from the inner-city, who consistently gets into fights with others. Using behavioral, structural approaches to eliminate "fighting" behaviors may be a culturally compatible strategy, yet, stopping the "fighting behaviors" may be incompatible with defensive, survival, coping behaviors needed for self protection.

Emancipation from one's family with placement in a residential program, for example, is frequently a PSR goal. This goal reflects American values of individualism and independence. Potential conflict may emerge when the "multicultural lens" is used with individuals with mental illness from different ethnic groups to the point that this goal may not be appropriate. Family expectations of loyalty, often found in Italian, Asian and Polish American families, may mitigate against familiar provider and institutional values (McGoldrick, et al 1982).

Biculturality, the ability to adaptively function in both mainstream and ethnic communities is a goal which must also be integrated with PSR. Individuals with mental illness will need to be adequately prepared to differentiate norms, rules, and expectations in more than one cultural environment. Specific instruction in skills may be required to assist individuals with mental illness as they transition to different cultural milieus so that intercultural movement will be enhanced (Gross, 1989).

Service context
Psychosocial rehabilitation practices need not be limited to particular settings or modalities. In fact, helping individuals

with mental illness practice their skills in settings where they will be used such as job sites, Y's, churches, and other community settings may maximize generalization (Anthony, 1977; 1979; 1982; Anthony & Liberman,1994). The individual's cultural context can provide a rich, creative array of informal settings in which rehabilitation methods may be applied. The use of testimonials and prayer in African American churches; mutual aide associations across different ethnic communities; participation in neighborhood, community block meetings, and community cultural celebrations are just a few of the many settings where rehabilitation can occur (Griffith, English, and Mayfield, 1980; Finley, 1986).

Theoretical framework

Psychosocial rehabilitation sometimes refers to particular types of programs or interventions, sometimes to a philosophy of care, and sometimes to a professional movement (Rutman, 1994). There is a general lack of precision regarding its theoretical underpinnings (Rutman, 1994). Dincin (1975) and Cnaan, Blankertz, Messinger, and Gardner (1989) have described PSR as an integration of different theories. Psychodynamic theory, for example, could be utilized as a means of understanding basic personality dynamics. From behaviorism and social learning theory we "borrow" educational and skills training approaches (Cohen, Ridley, and Cohen, 1983; Wallace and Liberman, 1985); and from humanism, we "borrow" an emphasis on genuiness and respect for individuals with mental illness (Rogers, 1942; 1957; Carkhuff, 1972; Holden, Carkhuff, & Berenson, 1967). The medical field provides a source of understanding about the biological basis of mental illness responsible for both the etiology and maintenance of the disorder as well as the resulting impair-

ments (Anthony, 1994). The importance of psychotropic medication in mediating symptoms has also been a major contribution of the medical field. From rehabilitation we have derived an emphasis on the restoration of residual functional capacities, remediating disabilities and compensating for handicaps (Wood, 1980; Frey, 1984).

At this stage of its development, multiculturalism has been described as both a philosophy and a movement. Like PSR it is conceptually and theoretically imprecise. According to Pederson (1990) it is a "fourth force" in the mental health field following other historical "forces" such as psychodynamic theory, humanism, and behaviorism. The "fourth force" implies that there are multicultural dimensions to every treatment relationship in which differences are treated as a normative part of our interactions with others (i.e. age differences, ethnicity, nationality, religion, gender, sexual orientation, and region of the country). It does have its roots, as does PSR, in other theoretical formulations such as developmental theory (Erickson, 1950), social psychiatry (Horney, 1937), and field theory (Lewin, 1948).

Traditional theories are so often culture-bound, emphasizing only one dimension of the human condition such as the "thinking self," the "feeling self," the "behavior self," or the "social self" (Sue, 1992). Conversely, multiculturalism endorses the totality of the human experience, including both the cultural, spiritual, and political self. It can be inclusive of other theories providing that a cultural lens or filter is used as they are applied to individuals of different ethnic groups. For example, it would be almost impossible to work with persons of some ethnic groups (i.e., Latinos, African Americans, or Asian Americans) if the provider was unfamiliar with their religious and spiritual beliefs. These beliefs often provide cultural explanations of the etiology of misfortune or disease and the culturally acceptable help-seeking strategies to be used to ameliorate the illness. Providers are to be reminded that consumers bring these values and perceptions into the program, causing cultural gaps in the building of relationships.

Practitioners' roles
The practitioner's role in both the PSR and multicultural models is similar in that both emphasize building upon individual strengths. The person's choice, while highly valued in PSR, may conflict directly with the worldview of different ethnic groups for whom individual choice either does not exist or, if at all, comes second to what is best for the family group. Providers would do well to work within the cultural framework of the individual's family.

Often informal provider roles in PSR emphasize less hierarchical and more egalitarian relationships with individuals with mental illness (Hoeltzel, 1988; Dincin, 1975). Some less acculturated individuals of different ethnic subgroups might be expected to be more responsive to formal and more hierarchical relationships where communication flows from the top down. Persons from such cultures may not feel as comfortable with the more democratic ideals upon which many of our institutions are based. They have come to expect "inequality" in role functions and may be more comfortable in mental health care settings when an expert role is maintained.

Active engagement of individuals with mental illness through gentle persuasion, encouragement, and influence is another important PSR provider role (Dincin, 1975). Identifying and developing provider engagement strategies for individuals with mental illness from different ethnic communities can be quite challenging because the historical relationship between some ethnic groups has frequently been a conflict, evoking distrust and communication barriers. Native Americans, for example, might find active engagement approaches intrusive or perceive them as "interference" (Sue, 1990). Culturally syntonic engagement strategies are required. Asking each person how they might feel relating to a service provider from a different culture may be helpful in diffusing potential barriers.

Practitioner roles in PSR frequently emphasize empowerment and advocacy. While equally compatible with a multicultural frame of reference, it must be kept in mind that people from different ethnic backgrounds have experienced the multiplicative effects of discrimination via their membership in several subcultures such as mental illness, substance abuse, and/or ethnic, gender and different sexually-oriented subgroups. The effects from these various subgroup memberships have produced individuals who have been caught in the "victim system" (Pinderhughes, 1982). Institutional oppression has produced differential access to goods and resources in the mainstream for both the individual with mental illness and his/her family. Sue (1981) recommends that practitioners intervene not only in the individual system, but also within the broader service systems that perpetuates inequities. Practitioners actively confront discriminatory service practices as well as the negative, internalized stereotypes which affect a person's self-image and ability to visualize different goals.

A role function which needs to be incorporated in PSR is the instruction of individuals with mental illness who must enter and effectively manage different, multiple, cultural milieus where they are least familiar with the norms and values. Transitioning to different milieus can be highly stressful and requires skill development and a desensitization to potential environmental stressors and discrimination. The development of different strategies for the purpose of building up resistances against potentially noxious, stigmatizing, and discriminatory experiences is called "inoculation" (Miechenbaum, 1974; Finley & Pernell-Arnold, 1993). Staff enhance personal resources, coping, and problem solving strategies in order to reduce anxiety and to assist consumers in managing the multiplicative effects of race, gender, sexual orientation and/or mental illness in addition to their mental illness and/or substance abuse. These approaches, patterned after Meichenbaum's (1975; 1985) social learning technique of stress inoculation, utilize a variety of self-management procedures such as: role play activities, rehearsal, problem solving strategies, cognitively self-reinforcing statements, self-dialogue during actual simulations with confrontations with a discriminatory stressor. Four phases are emphasized:

- First, the person builds a reservoir of positive thoughts and feelings that include strengths and skills, favorite pictures, songs, poems and stories, which can be used a s buffers against negative experiences.

- Second, each person is given a didactic session on the nature of discrimination and its effects. This phase is called the "nibble theory" of discrimination (Jamison, 1984). Suggestions of possible coping responses are generated.

- Third, these ideas are rehearsed.

- Finally, the individual's ability to apply techniques is tested.

Approaches & methods

Rehabilitation is never to be used as an agent of social, political, or economic control of those who may deviate in thought and behavior from the "accepted" norms of Western society (Pernell-Arnold, 1989). Instead it is acknowledged and understood that the treatment of ethnic individuals with mental illness within their familial, historical, sociopolitical context is indispensable to the interpretation of issues related to: 1) self esteem, 2) identity formation, 3) acculturation and assimilation, and 4) role assumption.

A multicultural lens can be applied to those multiple approaches utilized in the PSR field to promote engagement and progress (e.g., skills teaching, functional assessments, family participation, use of natural community supports, and curative factors in the agency milieu). Assertiveness training to improve social skills, for example, would need to be redefined when working with women from cultures where the family systems are more patriarchal. The physical environment, for example, must reflect aspects of the surface culture of those individuals with mental illness who are attending the program. Pictures, magazines, music, colors, foods, and languages spoken are to be culturally representative.

PSR functional and symptom assessments in the multicultural model are more inclusive, for example, in assessing a person's abilities to access goods and resources in *both* mainstream *and* ethnic communities, acculturation and adaptational styles to mainstream communities, and differentiation of culturalogical symptoms or survival behaviors from those of the disease process. Assessment tools and diagnostic procedures should be properly normed and not inappropriately used to exclude persons from either educational or vocational placements and/or psychiatric or rehabilitative treatment.

Service offerings would include, as currently exists in PSR, individual counseling as needed, psychoeducational groups and inclusion of ethnic families. Experimentation with ethnically homogeneous psychoeducational groups has been found to be particularly useful for engaging individuals with mental illness to the PSR organization and for creating the much needed feelings of commonality and safety for persons who might otherwise view the agency as alien (Finley, 1978; Primm, 1990; Stillman, 1973). Natural systems such as the family, community, church, and folk healers are viewed in multiculturalism as primary to the rehabilitation process rather than ancillary or adjunctive. Ethnic family members are engaged with strategies compatible with their culture. Providing concrete, individualized, direct assistance in the homes of ethnic family members with severe and persistent mental illness, for example, has been one psychoeducational family approach that has been reported to be successful in increasing the connection with ethnic families (Falloon, 1985; 1988). Psychoeducational family group approaches would be facilitated by the availability of whole or extended family meetings with child care services available, provision of transportation, motivational, ethnic/cultural speakers, and opportunities for recognition awards, testimonials and leadership.

Multicultural Staff Competencies

Staff require requisite awareness, knowledge and skills in order to facilitate the integration of culture into PSR. There has been an impetus over the past 15-20 years for the psychiatric, counseling, and psychological professional fields to in-

corporate issues of cultural diversity in response to the compelling need for mental health professionals to intervene more effectively with diverse ethnic populations (Allison, Crawford, Echemendia, Robinson, & Knepp, 1994). Training practitioners who are capable of demonstrating effectiveness with individuals with mental illness from a wide range of ethnic, cultural, and socioeconomic backgrounds and who may have a severe and persistent mental illness present another specific challenge to those of us in psychosocial rehabilitation (PSR). These challenges are complicated by the fact that many practitioners have not addressed issues related to their own ethnicity (Giordano & Giordano, 1977).

Recent attempts have been made by PSR to both identify and clarify needed attributes and skills of practitioners who are to practice in the field (Trochim & Cook, 1993; Jonikas, 1993; Curtis, 1993). PSR, as it continues to seriously address the challenges of rehabilitation for individuals with mental illness from diverse backgrounds, might find it beneficial to look more closely at the process and struggles of other professional groups also grappling with the development of more specific, comprehensive competencies and standards for persons working across cultures. Multicultural counseling and counseling psychology are two such groups defining and evaluating multi-cultural competencies that will guide future training strategies designed to go well beyond knowing that cultural differences matter to knowing how to apply sensitivity to practice.

Cultural competence has been defined as more than:
- being sensitive to ethnic differences
- not being a bigot
- treating everyone in a similar way (Isaacs, 1991).

It is a "set of congruent behaviors, attitudes, and policies that come together in a system, agency, or among professionals which enable the system, the agency, or professionals to work more effectively in cross cultural situations" (Cross, Bazron, Dennis, and Issacs, 1989, p. iv). Competence implies having the capacity to function effectively by achieving a level of mastery and skill development (Isaacs, 1991). It is a continual, active process. Implicit is a recognition of the complexity of diversity and the acknowledgment of one's own personal limitations. The practice of a monocultural worldview in a pluralistic society could be seen as a form of maladjustment, engaging in cultural oppression using unethical and harmful practices (Szapocznik, Santisteban, Durtines, Perez-Vidal, & Herves, 1983; Kornian, 1974).

The Division of Counseling Psychology in a position paper entitled: "Position Paper: Cross-cultural Counseling Competencies (Sue, Bernier, Durran, Feinberg, Pedelsen, Smith, Vasquez-Nuttal, 1982) and the "Guidelines for Providers of Psychological Services to Ethnic and Culturally Diverse Populations" (APA, 1993) has provided the conceptual framework for defining multicultural competencies. These competencies and standards have been widely endorsed and currently represent the best that various groups and organizations have to offer.

The conceptual framework typically classifies multicultural competencies into three categories:

- personal attitudes, values and beliefs;

- knowledge about others' history and worldviews;

- skills, e.g., the appropriate application of goals and interventions (Sue et al, 1982 and 1990).

The first category incorporates a self-recognition that one's own personal worldviews may be a product of cultural conditioning which may potentially contribute to negative emotional reactions towards other racial and ethnic groups. Understanding one's own worldview forms the basis for a more accurate understanding and knowledge of the worldviews of others in the second category. Practitioners acquire knowledge that includes but is not limited to the history, migration, and acculturation patterns; family styles; communication styles; beliefs about health and illness; coping; and psychological adjustment styles of persons from different ethnic groups. The third category requires that the practitioners translate personal and intuitive understanding of self and others into skills that can apply culturally compatible interventions and strategies.

Sue, Arredondo, and McDavis (1992) have suggested that each of the three categories may, in fact, have a subset of concomitant attitudes, knowledge, and skill dimensions so that a 3 x 3 matrix is created in which nine potentially different competency areas can be identified. So, for example, acquiring knowledge and information about the history and worldviews of others has requisite beliefs and attitudes, knowledge, and skills. (See the table on the next page.)

A summary of multicultural competencies recommended for mental health practitioners follows. These competencies were formulated using the framework proposed by Sue (1990) and tailored to mental health providers. They were first developed for a multicultural mental health training program for the

Understanding The Culture and Worldview of Others (Sue, Arredondo, & McDavis, 1992)

Beliefs and Attitudes—Practitioners who are culturally competent:
Are aware of personal biases and stereotypes which they may hold against individuals with mental illness of other ethnic groups. They are able to identify and list them.

Knowledge—Practitioners who are culturally competent:
Understand how race, culture, and ethnicity may affect the formation of the individual's personality, vocational choices, symptom display, help-seeking behaviors, etc. They demonstrate specific knowledge of the history, life experiences and the cultural heritage of persons with whom they work.

Skills—Practitioners who are culturally competent:
Seek out relevant research regarding the mental health and mental disorders of various ethnic and racial groups. They become actively involved with persons from different ethnic subgroups outside of the agency setting in social and political functions, community events, celebrations, and friendships so that the multicultural perspective is more than just an academic exercise.

Capital District Psychiatric Center, Albany, New York (Finley & Pernell-Arnold, 1991). Currently they have been further refined and adapted for the Advanced Certificate Program in Multiculturalism, sponsored by the Multicultural Research and Training Institute, Temple University School of Social Administration (Pernell-Arnold & Finley, 1993).

Professional Standards of Multicultural Clinical Competence

Staff are expected to develop competencies in three areas:
- Awareness
- Knowledge
- Skills

Awareness of own assumptions, values, and beliefs

Staff should possess personal characteristics of genuineness, empathy, warmth, and a nonjudgmental stance. They should also have accurate and appropriate attitudes, opinions, and assumptions about others who may be different. A willingness to modify and to correct biases and stereotypes and understand how they influence relationships with consumers is essential. A psychosocial rehabilitation practitioner will:

Competencies 1–2

Move from being culturally unaware to aware.

Value and celebrate differences of others.

Knowledge

Competencies 3–6

Acquire knowledge regarding the socio-political systems operation and its treatment of ethnic group members.

Have a clear and explicit knowledge of traditional theories and principles concerning human behavior, development, psychopathology, therapy, rehabilitation and community functions. the psychosocial rehabilitation practitioner can describe theoretical delimitations as they relate to cultural group members.

Describe current theories, processes and practice models in the literature that have specific applicability and relevance to the treatment needs of ethnic/cultural group members.

Have knowledge of institutional, class, culture and language barriers that prevent ethnic group members from using PSR mental health services.

Skills

Staff demonstrate behaviors for enhancing the interactions with persons from other cultures. Staff are able to identify appropriate behaviors that will facilitate acceptance by persons from the culture. They have the ability to determine what information is needed about the client's problem and are able to access different traditional or alternative resources compatible with the client's culture. Appropriate goals are selected and appropri-

ate processes are utilized to assist the client in reaching these goals. Specifically, a staff member will:

Competencies 7–14

Generate a wide variety of verbal, non-verbal responses, interventions, and strategies.

Demonstrate behaviors for enhancing engagement with the culturally different person.

Conduct a multicultural assessment.

Assess cultural strengths, their impact on level of functioning, and integrate them into the ongoing treatment plan.

Conduct an accurate diagnostic assessment in which culturally derived symptoms are differentiated from psychiatric symptoms.

Select appropriate assessment tools and diagnostic procedures that are properly normed and not used as methods of exclusion from service opportunities.

Spell out strategies in the rehabilitation plan to specifically engage individuals from different ethnic communities.

Select appropriate goals for each person served. Select appropriate methods for goal attainment which are compatible with the person's cultural background. Try to match services to the needs of the persons served.

Document attempts to integrate the person's natural support system, (i.e., folk healers, family, friends, minister, church members, community organizations, and/or neighbors) into the rehabilitation program.

Design creative and motivational programming as structured methods to develop opportunities that will assist each person in growth and goal attainment.

Devise rehabilitation plans and refers to community resources when necessary.

Demonstrate advocacy and negotiating skills when coordinating agency and community services. Challenge service systems when appropriate and takes actions to correct identified issues.

Consult with supervisors, colleagues, same-cultural group representatives for feedback and monitoring of performance.

Recognize direct and indirect communication styles.

Demonstrate a sensitivity to nonverbal cues.

Recognize differences between cultural institutions and traditional institutions. Assist either the person served or institutions in making necessary adjustments in order to maximize the person's engagement in the agency setting.

Use language of each person's culture appropriately.

Identify features of his/her professional style. Recognize limitations and strengths.

In spite of the recent attention in the counseling profession to multi-culturalism, there is not a clear consensus as to how these competencies are to be empirically assessed (Sabnani, Ponterotto, and Borodovsky, 1991; Sue & Sue, 1990) using psychometrically sound and conceptually anchored instrumentation. Multicultural instrumentation is in its infancy.

Ponterotto, Reixer, Barrett, and Sparks (1994) have critiqued four current instruments designed to measure the cultural competence of professional counselors. Each have utilized the Sue (1882; 1990) conceptual framework for instrument design. Several recommendations are outlined:

- Continued investigation and modification with systematic and longitudinal validation data are needed. Concurrent validity and test-retest reliability studies are also required.

- Large-scale factor-analytic studies that incorporate two or more of the instruments simultaneously so as to more clearly identify the nature of the competency construct.

- Utilization of multiple methodologies, e.g. qualitative research (case studies; life histories of expert multicultural professionals; interview formats of individuals with mental illness in order to assess the qualities culturally different individuals look for in a professional) in order to further define the competency construct.

- Outcome studies are required to examine whether or not individuals with mental illness who work with practitioners rated highly in multicultural competence evaluate them more positively (Ponterotto & Furlong, 1985).

Recognizing Multiculturalism Within the Organizational Context

The integration of multiculturalism into PSR programs is best achieved by the development of culturally competent staff within an organizational structure supportive of diversity, an organization which strives to be multiculturally competent. A multicultural organization demonstrates the value of diversity by involving persons who are racially, ethnically, and culturally different including disabilities, gender differences and sexual orientation, at all levels and functions of the organization. The organization is committed to the identification of even unanticipated barriers (Cross, Katz, Miller & Seashore, 1994).

Multicultural organizations have accountability processes that recognize the insidious nature of prejudice, discrimination, and oppression. Open discussion of interpersonal problems, separation of prejudice and bias from personal style issues and confrontation of discriminatory behaviors at all levels of the organization is encouraged and reinforced. The organization promotes advocacy activities both inside and outside of the organization. These types of organizations take primary responsibility for providing training for individuals with

mental illness and employees to acquire the skills needed to work and live in diverse environments (Cross, Bazron, Dennis, Issacs, 1989; Cross, Katz, Miller, Seashore, 1994; Jamison, 1984).

Multicultural organizations promote internal culture that include multiple world views and perspectives, values, culturally determined styles and behaviors. The foundation of a multicultural organization is respect for any type of human difference.

A multicultural organization values and encourages diversity because this expands the number and/or types of options, ideas, solutions and methods that are generated thereby expanding the number and type of environments and people to which it can respond (MRTI, 1993; Randall, 1989). The complexity of society, the information explosion, and the rapidity with which environments change requires flexible creative organizations that utilize organized chaos and the presence of multiple, often competing perspectives (Peters, 1987).

Multicultural organizations emphasize the adaptive stage of organizational development rather than homeostasis or stabilization. Adapting to rapidly changing technologies, markets and people is the key characteristic of a multicultural organization (Gallegos, 1982; Peters, 1987). The appreciation and acceptance of differences permeates the vision, mission, goals, policies, procedures, and products or outcomes of multicultural organizations (Cross et al, 1994). In mental health organizations, this respect becomes the willingness to enter various cultural perspectives in order to understand the interaction between the person's mental illness and his or her race, culture, or ethnicity (Asante, Gudykunst, 1989).

Mental health, psychosocial rehabilitation organizations ultimately become multiculturally competent by requiring the study of culture, and exploring the relationship of personal cultural heritage to current behavior and skills. The number and types of diverse groups which the program is able to serve are expanded as it develops linkages and connections with racial, cultural and ethnic organizations represented in the community (Cross et al, 1989).

Defining Multicultural Organizational Competencies

A culturally competent organization must continually answer the following questions:
- Do the mission, policies, procedures, and organizational culture create a multicultural environment in which cultural responsiveness regularly occurs? Is the organizational atmosphere welcoming and supportive of diversity? What is the process utilized for multicultural organizational development?

- What steps has the organization taken to ensure that all levels are representative of the cultural, racial and ethnic groups in their service areas? What steps have been taken to develop linkages with cultural, racial, ethnic groups in the community? How are families involved in the program?

- What steps have been taken to ferret out covert and overt practices of prejudice, ethnic slurs, jokes, destructive assumptions and stereotypes towards staff and individuals with mental illness? Do these steps lead to problem resolution?

- How do services, programs and activities encourage the expression of cultural, racial, and ethnic differences through world view, the arts, communication and learning styles? Are services designed to meet the different needs of various cultural, racial, and ethnic groups? Are services culturally accommodating?

- How does the organization ensure that the staff and administration have the skills and competencies needed to implement culturally competent services?

- Is the quality assurance program consistent with multicultural values (Jamison, 1984); Marin & Marin, 1991; Mason, 1995; Peters, 1987; Cross, et al, 1994; Cross, et al, 1989; Dana, 1992)?

Developmental Stages of Cultural Competence

A developmental stage model has been used to assist organizations in the description and assessment of cultural competencies. At one end of the continuum organizations may be culturally destructive (CD) and at the other end, cultural proficiency (CP) (Cross et al, 1984). A brief description of each anchor point along the continuum is presented with an accompanying example provided:
- **Cultural destructiveness**
  Cultural destructiveness represents a set of attitudes, practices, and/or policies that is designed to promote the superiority of the dominant culture and that purposefully attempts to eradicate the "lesser" or "inferior" culture because it is viewed as "different" or "distasteful." A Korean

family, for example, requests that the individual with mental illness receive a job placement that is located in the family's business. The staff's response is that the business has not been evaluated as part of the agency's employment program so the person cannot be placed there. This is culturally destructive because it forces the person to make a mutually exclusive choice between the family business and the rehabilitation program.

- **Cultural incapacity**

  Cultural incapacity refers to a set of attitudes, practices, and/or policies that, while not explicitly promoting the superiority of the dominant culture, adheres either explicitly or implicitly to the traditional idea of "separate but equal" treatment. These programs tend to segregate or discriminate against difference which may become institutionalized. A Middle Eastern family, for example, blocks the residential placement of a daughter. The worker embarks on a long discourse of the rights of women in the United States. When this fails to gain the family's permission for placement the agency decides that it cannot work with Middle Eastern families or that it will hire Middle Eastern professionals who will only work with them. This is a cultural incapacity.

- **Cultural blindness**

  Cultural Blindness refers to a set of attitudes, practices, and/or policies that adhere to the traditional philosophy of being unbiased and universal in both theory and method. Under this paradigm, culture and people are basically all alike, and what works with one culture should,

therefore work as well with another (Cross et al, 1989). Uniform services, therefore, are designed to meet the needs of all individuals with mental illness regardless of their race, ethnicity, sexual orientation, etc.

- **Culturally open**

  The culturally open (CO) organization adheres to attitudes, practices, and/or policies that promote receptivity to and learning about new ideas and solutions to improve services rendered to one's particular target group. CO organizations may hire one or two bilingual, bicultural staff, but usually have only "token" representatives. Commitment to a fully diverse service population and staff population is often superficial. Training may be provided but is limited to "one shot" programs that are unable to provide the knowledge and skills required to achieve staff competency. This type of program may expect the "token" staff member or the person with mental illness to inform them about their group. They may have a Black History Month, a Cinco De Mayo event or an annual multicultural festival. The culturally different person is treated as a representative of his/her group and then perceived as an exception to group stereotypes. The culturally different person often feels uncomfortable may drop out or resign.

- **Culturally competent**

  Culturally competent agencies are characterized by a set of attitudes, practices, and/or policies that respects, rather than merely shows receptivity to different cultures. In the process of enhancing the quality of services, such agencies actively seek advice and consultation from ethnic/racial communities and actively incorporates such practices into the organization with a sense of commitment.

- **Culturally proficient**
  Cultural proficiency is characterized by a set of attitudes, practices, and/or policies that holds cultural differences and diversity in the highest esteem. Culturally proficient organizations hold a "proactive" posture regarding cultural difference. Their aim is to improve the existing quality of services through active research into cultural issues in preventive and therapeutic approaches that affect the service outcome. They not only engage in the dissemination of such research findings, but also promote improved cultural relations among diverse groups in society through public education and awareness campaigns. During the intake and assessment period, a Haitian individual with mental illness declares that his problems are caused by his parent's spirits who died after he left Haiti with his wife and children. The intake staff member arranges a meeting with a Haitian minister and requests help in determining how much of the man's problem is a cultural explanation of the feelings of guilt, the result of immigration and difficulties of coping in a new culture, spiritual possession, or depression over his inability to return due to political reasons. This is a culturally competent assessment. The next step could be the study of how Haitians tend to respond to immigrant or refugee status or the study of research conducted on treatment outcomes when professional helpers collaborate with natural helpers. This step would promote cultural proficiency.

Guiding Principles for the Development of Culturally Competent Programs

Development of a psychosocial rehabilitation, multicultural program cannot rely upon specific strategies and techniques that are designed in advance for each cultural, ethnic, racial group that may be encountered. Several basic principles, however, can be used to guide processes in the development of culturally competent programs: 1) cultural accommodation; 2) linkage to the community; 3) problem-resolution; 4) training and education; and 5) evaluation.

Cultural Accommodation

The organization must encourage the presence of multiple human behavioral styles. Each culture has a system of values and behaviors that it incorporates to facilitate group unity. An early step to organizational cultural competence is the creation of an environment where various cultural styles can be expressed and accepted (Cross et al, 1994).

Culturally competent programs typically address each of the issues:

- Communication styles: the expressive, stoic, verbal, and non-verbal language of choice;

- Ethnic identity development: the level of acculturation and the attitudes and values each member holds about his or her cultural group membership;

- Learning styles: the mode in which the person is most comfortable learning new information, e.g. observing, reading, listening, talking, thinking; working alone or with others;

- Leadership styles: the extent to which individuals with mental illness respond more positively to expert authority, non-directive support, and or peer support;

- Inclusion of surface culture: the visible presence of music, art, literature, or food representative of different cultures throughout the program (Orlandi, et al, 1992; Smith & Peterson, 1988; Lefley, 1990);

- Family involvement: utilization of different strategies consistent with the person's culture which best engages family members from different ethnic groups, e.g. home visits, extended family therapy, network therapy, and self-help.

- Help-seeking behavior: builds upon the awareness of ethnic group member's perceptions of the professional role, natural helpers, styles of interacting; interventions utilized; compatibility with typical treatment norms such as self disclosure

Organizations seek to further accommodate to the cultural needs of staff and individuals with mental illness by increasing the degree of "cultural fit" between rehabilitative, social, residential and educational services provided and the culture of the individual with mental illness. Psychoeducational groups and educational methods use program media, music, dance, storytelling, arts and crafts for example, to help people resolve personal, emotional, social and societal problems. These groups, therefore, incorporate aspects of the individual's surface culture providing individuals with mental illness with a cultural bridge that communicates both uniqueness and commonality with others. The sharing of artistic experiences can be used to help people with mental illness explore the

connections between emotions, attitudes, and behaviors within familiar and unfamiliar cultural contexts (Wilson & Ryland, 1949; Vinter, 1985).

Psychoeducational activities serve additional needs. When related to the cultural, ethnic and racial groups' history they can promote self-acceptance, positive self image and self-esteem. Individuals with mental illness who are new arrivals to the U.S. also need information and education on expected values, attitudes and behaviors.

Reading poetry, listening to music, reading ethnic literature, attending festivals, ethnic, racial and cultural movies (surface culture) can begin a process through which staff and participants in the program can explore their identities. They provide structure while increasing the understanding of one another's values and beliefs (deep culture). These activities can also help demonstrate that racial, cultural and ethnic differences need not be threatening. We can begin to understand how to balance differences and commonalties in relationships rather than reject one or the other (Middleman, 1983; Guzie, 1957).

Psychoeducational activities and groups that are based on, at least in part, expressive arts of specific groups can promote the exploration of feelings, attitudes and values first towards self, others and one's illness in culturally syntonic modes. Second, these experiences can be used to increase options and the solution of people's problems and third, understand the context from which others' feelings, attitudes, and values may emerge (Dodson, Pernell-Arnold, and Finley, 1993).

Organizations striving to be more accommodating to diversity acknowledge the current and historical context of discrimination toward specific groups so that stereotypes are not inadvertently reinforced. For example, a service may be "misfit" when providing work opportunities for a young woman from a newly arrived Hmong family outside of her home; placing an African-American woman in a "stereotypical" housekeeping work crew; expecting to "emancipate" an unmarried, Italian man with severe and persistent mental illness by placing him in an independent, residential program away from the watchful eye of his family.

Discrimination can operate so subtly that there must be a continual review of programs and activities to determine whether anyone perceives discrimination, e.g. are there women on the maintenance work group? Are there Latinos working on the newsletter? Are there Asians on the reception and/or telephone detail? In addition, some activities may be designed to help individuals with mental illness from specific groups learn to cope with and solve problem related to cultural expectations, discrimination, racial identity, or cultural affiliation. If a gay woman experiences isolation as a result of rejection by her family, then she needs informal and structured groups designed to reaffirm her positive self-image. She needs to learn how others have created new families in which mates or potential mates will be accepted. The program needs to provide information and education on gay lifestyles to promote understanding (Pernell-Arnold, 1993).

Linkage to the Community

The organization must be aware of the cultural, ethnic, and racial groups that are residents of the community they serve. The organization's boundaries must be permeable and accepting of open interaction with cultural, ethnic, and racial community leaders and representatives.

Cultures generate varying institutional styles (Smith & Petersen, 1988; Asante & Gundykunst, 1989). Some have complex hierarchies; others emphasize peer relationships; some emphasize informality. Other organizations exist to meet the need for recognition and respect. People from different cultures have different expectations for organizations that may result in misunderstandings and feelings of rejection (Austin & Hershey, 1982). The hierarchy/organizational structure may interfere with effective community interaction and involvement. The organization must be representative of the community it serves at all levels. Recruitment processes must be reasonably open, have procedures that can be published and discussed with community representatives. The organization must also participate in the community's cultural life, activities and provide opportunities for the inclusion of the various group's cultural and artistic expressions in the program.

Problem-Resolution

The organization must have established mechanisms that identify, examine, and resolve misunderstandings and disputes based on personal and cultural differences.

Opportunities for open discussion and redress of actual or perceived discrimination and prejudice must be regularly available in order to prevent blatant or subtle forms of sexism, racism, ageism, etc. from becoming a part of the milieu or organizational culture. The organization needs to develop internal growth mechanisms that use differences as a basis for expanding strategies that are to be used for solving problems and providing rehabilitation experiences (Jamison, 1984).

Training and Education

The organization must provide training and educational opportunities to maximize the cultural competency of board members, administrators, supervisors and staff.

There are at least five types of training activities which may occur in any agency setting in order to increase staff and organizational competence: 1) generic; 2) culture specific; 3) skill development; 4) program development and 5) organizational development.

Generic training activities target the enhancement of staff self-awareness regarding issues of diversity. Staff are exposed to the psychological dynamics of difference and learn information that is applicable across ethnic groups, e.g. learning styles, communication styles, ethnic identity development. Racism, oppression and discrimination are explored experientially and cognitively in order to:

- understand the similarities and differences between the various expressions of prejudice, e.g. racism, sexism, and ageism;

- recognize the behaviors and responses of oppressors and victims;

- identify survival and coping skills that people may use and/or need to transcend these experiences (Ponterotto, 1991; Pedersen, 1988; Essed, 1991).

Culture specific, in-depth training activities enhance knowledge about the history, values, norms, and perceptions of illness and help seeking behaviors of several racial, ethnic, and cultural groups. The selection of specific ethnic groups, however, encompass more than just people of color. Training is targeted to a variety of groups present within the community e.g. Italians, Slovakian, deaf and hearing impaired, gender, and sexual orientation differences. Trainers utilized are representative members of each group and are bilingual, bicultural professionals.

Training for skill development may occur in areas such as: development of engagement strategies; conducting a multicultural assessment and diagnosis; resource development; interviewing and counseling skills; family therapy as well as bridging cultural gaps in communication. Modifications needed in mental health and psychosocial rehabilitation modalities are emphasized in order to maximize the match or fit of ethnic populations to current service options. Staff, at the conclusion of such training activities, can be expected to demonstrate specific skill attainment in designated areas.

Staff will require assistance in integrating and applying values, self-awareness and skills to areas where additional services which are culturally appropriate and relevant are needed. Training may include the development of psycho-educational groups, self-help programs; family support groups, and/or an orientation program specifically targeted to increase the person's comfort with the organization as well as other specialized activities required to assist in retention.

Organizations interested in renovating their entire program so as to be more competent may select training and consultation in areas such as: multicultural team building; designing a quality assurance program; supervision of culturally different staff; review and revision of the mission, policies and procedures in order to insure compatibility with principles of a multicultural organization.

Training activities may be provided within several arenas:

- Training may occur within the organizational setting, conducted either by senior staff or invited outside speakers. There is an organizational commitment to incorporate all training activities, whether or not directly related to cultural diversity, with content applicable to staff working with persons from different ethnic groups. In this way, the organization avoids a major pitfall of providing "one shot" training devoted to cultural diversity.

- Staff may be sent to courses, conferences, workshops which provide opportunities to increase cultural competencies. The organization provides follow up of such activities by incorporating new ideas and approaches into programs. Opportunities are also provided for staff to both inform and train others.

- Connections may be developed to college and university based programs in which staff can obtain academic credentials with agency support through released compensatory time and/or financial contributions. Entry level staff, particularly those from different racial and ethnic groups, may be able to benefit from this training strategy in that their opportunities for advancement within the organization may be increased.

The number and type of cultural, ethnic, and racial differences is so great that the process of learning to be culturally competent is a never ending quest. The degree to which the organization accepts responsibility for assisting staff in this quest will directly affect its program outcomes with individuals and families from various cultural groups.

Evaluation

The organization must develop multidimensional, qualitative and quantitative information that is designed to document the benefits and outcomes experienced by the cultural, racial and ethnic group individuals with mental illness participating in its programs.

There are several evaluation issues which must be addressed in order for programs to become more culturally competent. First, there is a need to collect statistical data on the presence of different ethnic groups both within the agency and within the community at large. Maintaining statistical data according to federal, standard racial group designations such as African-American, Hispanic, White, Asian/Pacific Islander and Native American cannot facilitate an analysis of the operation and effectiveness of a multicultural program (Lefley & Best-man, 1994; Rogler, et al, 1987). The assumption is promulgated that each of these designations is monolithic and homogeneous. The African-American group, for example, could be expected to include persons from various sections of the U.S., people from the Caribbean, as well as those from the continent of Africa. The designated "white" group includes Swedes, English, Germans, Hungarians, Ukrainians, Italians, Irish, and numerous other ethnic groups.

Tremendous within-group variability may impact assessment outcomes, perception of illness, help-seeking behaviors as well as required program modifications. African-Americans from the rural South, for example, are more likely to believe in "roots," spirits or a lack of faith in God as the cause of mental illness than second or third generation urban African

Americans (Snow, 1983). Though Italians and Irish may primarily be Catholic, there are, however, vast differences in their belief systems (McGoldrick et al, 1982). Statistical documentation might be more beneficial if it were kept on the basis of self report. Responses to two questions (e.g., "from where did your ancestors come?" and "with which group do you identify?") may provide the most useful information (Pernell-Arnold and Finley, 1993).

Second, the presence of each ethnic group within the service area and level of need for rehabilitative services requires documentation. Data on who is currently being served and those requiring services are compared as well as comparisons made with numbers of individual with mental illness served in relation to the dominant European groups (Jackson et al, 1991).

Third, program modifications introduced to accommodate specific cultural differences must be reviewed in order to determine effects on program participation; units of services utilized; length of stay, ongoing progress and goal attainment. Does, for example, an ethno-therapy group increase the participation of African American young men in a program and improve their service outcomes? Does program intake through home visits or the use of an agency orientation film increase the participation of Latinos in programs (Rogler et al, 1987)?

Fourth, methods of determining individual with mental illness satisfaction are required. A regular, structured feedback process through focus groups or questionnaires can be developed to determine individual with mental illness perceptions of the content and quality of the program (Ennis & Hodge, 1993; Peters, 1987; Orlandi et al, 1982). Community groups need to receive informa-

tion on whether this information has been incorporated into the program. A formal structure is required for incorporating the information received.

Summary

Much work continues to be needed as the field of multiculturalism develops. PSR could benefit from the rigorous efforts of other groups to more fully incorporate multicultural competencies which are consistent with its "best practices." Psychosocial rehabilitation practitioners could join forces with others in taking a strong stand in adopting a cultural competence model so that a proactive means of correcting many of the inadequacies and inequities that historically have plagued ethnic group members in mental health.

References

Adebimpe, V.R. (1994). Race, Racism, and Epidemiological Surveys. *Hospital and Community Psychiatry, 45(1),* 27 - 31.

Allison, Crawford, Echemendia, Robinson, & Knepp (1994). Human Diversity and Professional Competence Training in Clinical and Counseling Psychology Revisited. *American Psychologist,* 792-811.

Anthony, W.A. (1982). Explaining 'Psychosocial Rehabilitation' by an Analogy to 'Physical, Rehabilitation.' *Psychosocial Rehabilitation Journal, 5,* 61-65.

_____ (1979). *Principles of Psychosocial Rehabilitation.* Baltimore, MD: University Park Press.

_____ (1977). Psychological Rehabilitation: A Concept in Need of a Method. *American Psychologist, 32,* 659-662.

Anthony, W.A. & R. P. Liberman (1994). The Practice of Psychosocial Rehabilitation: Historical, Conceptual, and Research Base. Publications Committee of IAPSRS (Eds.). *An introduction to psychosocial rehabilitation* (pp. 18-41). International Association of Psychosocial Rehabilitation Services.

Asante, M.K. & W.B. Gudykunst (1989). *Handbook of international and cultural communication.* Newburg Park: Sage.

Bell, C.C. (1994) "Race as a Variable in Research: Being Specific and Fair." *Hospital and Community Psychiatry, 45*(1).

Bernal, G. and V. Flores-Ortiz (1988). *Latino families: Sociohistorical perspective and cultural issues.* Washington, D.C.: Nueva Epoca.

Block. C. (1981). Black americans and the cross-ultural counseling and psychotherapy experiences. A. Marsella and P. Pedersen (Eds.), *Cross-cultural counseling and psychotherapy* (pp 177-194). New York.: Pergamon Press.

Boyd-Franklin, N. *(1989). Black families in therapy—A multi-systems approach.* New York: Guilford Press.

Brislin, R. & T. Yoshida (1994). *Intercultural communications training: An introduction.* Newburg Park, CA.: Sage Publications.

Bromley, M.A. (1997). New beginnings for cambodian refuges—or further disruptions? *Journal of the National Association of Social Workers.*

Campinha-Bacote, J. (1993). *Readings in transcultural health care* (4th Ed.) Cincinnati Ohio: Transcultural C.A.R.E.

Cannon, M. & B. Locke (1977). Being Black is Detrimental to One's Mental Health: Myth or Reality? *Phylon.* 38: 409-429.

Carkhuff, R.R. (1972). *The art of helping.* Amherst, Mass.: Human Resource Development Press.

Carleton-LaNey, L. (1992). Elderly Black Farm Women: A Population at Risk. *Journal of the National Association of Social Workers. 37*(6): 517-523.

Carney, C.G. and K.B Karn. (1994). Budding competencies for effective cross-cultural counseling: A developmental view. *The Counseling Psychologist. 22:* 111-119.

Carter, R.T. (1984). *The relationship between black students' value orientations and their racial attitudes.* Unpublished manuscript. University of Maryland, College Park, MD.

Chavez, N. *(1995). Mental health service delivery to minority populations. hispanics—a perspective.* Paper presented at the sponsored workshop, Mental Health Research and Practice in Minority Communities: Development of Culturally Sensitive Training Programs. School of Social Welfare, UCLA.

Chessler, M. (1994) Organizational development is not the same as multi-cultural organizational development. *The Promise of Diversity.* Gross, Kutz, Miller, & Seashore (eds.). New York: Irwin Professional Publishing.

Cheung, F.K. (1991). The Use of Mental Health Services by Ethnic Minorities. Myers, B.F., Wolford, P., Guzman, L.P., & Echemendia, R.L. (Eds.) *Ethnic minority perspectives on clinical training and services in psychology* 23–31. Washington, DC: American Psychological Association.

Cnaan, R., Blankertz, L., Messing, K., & Gardner, L.(1989). Psychosocial rehabilitation: Towards a theoretical base. *Psychosocial Rehabilitation Journal 13*: 12-55.Comas-Diaz, L. and A. Padilla (1992). English-only Movement: Implications for Mental Heath Services. *American Journal of Orthopsychiatry 62*(1): 6.

Coser, L.A. (1956). *The Functions of Social Conflict.* London: Collier-Macmillan Limited.

Costex, G.M. (1994). Providing Services to Hispanic/Latino Populations: Profiles in Diversity. *Social Work 39*(3), 286-296.

Cross, E., Katz, J., Miller, F.A., Seashore, E.W. (1994). *The promise of diversity.* New York: Irwin Professional Publishing.

Cross T., Bazron, B., Dennis, K. and M. Issiacs(1989). *Towards a culturally competent system of care: A monograph on effective services for minority children who are severely emotionally disturbed.* Washington, D.C.: CASSP Technical Assistance Center, Georgetown University Child Development Center.

Curtis, L. (1993). *Workforce Competencies For Direct Service Staff to Support Adults With Psychiatric Disabilities in Community Mental Health Services.* Trinity College of Vermont: The Center for Communicating Change Through Housing and Support.

Dana, R.N. et al (1992). A checklist for the examination of cultural competence in social agencies. *Research an Social Work Practice, 2*(2): 220-223.

Dincin, J. (1975). Psychosocial rehabilitation. *Schizophrenia Bulletin 13.* 1310147, HEW Public Health Services, ADAMHA.

Dincin, L & Kaberon, D.A. (1979). *Attendance as a predictor of success in rehabilitation of former psychiatric patients.* (Final Report to the Chicago Community Trust).

Dodson, L F. *Afrocentrific educational manual: Toward a non-deficit perspective in services to families and children.* Tennessee: University of Tennessee School of Social Work, Office of Continuing Education.

Edwards, A.W. (1982). The Consequences of Error in Selecting Treatment for Blacks. *Social Casework: The Journal of Contemporary Social Work.*

Ennis, J. E. and M. Hodge (1993) Practical Outcome Evaluations: Principles of Evaluation. Research for service *Consumers as Providers* workshop at second national mental health services case management conference, Philadelphia.

Erickson, E.H. (1950). *Childhood and society.* New York., W.W. Norton & Company.

Erickson, F.H. (1968). *Jdentity, youth, and crisis.* New York: W.W. Norton & Company.

Essed, P. (1991). *Understanding everyday racism.* CA: Sage.

Falloon, I.R. (1988). Expressed Emotion: Current Status. *Psychological Medicine, 18*:169-227.

_____ (1985). *Family management of schizophrenia: A study of clinical, social family and economic benefits.* Baltimore, MD: John Hopkins University Press.

Farris, C.E. & Farris, L.S. (1976). Indian children: The struggle for survival. *Journal of the National Association of Social Workers, 2*(5): 386-389.

Feinstein, 0. (1974). Why ethnicity? In D. Hartman (Ed.). *Immigrants and migrants: The detroit ethnic experience.* Detroit Center for Urban Studies and Southeast Michigan Regional Heritage Study Center, Wayne State University.

Finley, L & Pernell-Arnold, A. (1992). *Reducing stigma and promoting job success curriculum.* Philadelphia, PA: Rehabilitation Services Institute, Temple University.

Finley, L (1986). *Psychosocial programming: The neighborhood services curriculum.* Philadelphia, PA: Division of Behavioral Healthcare Education at Allegheny University of the Health Sciences.

_____ (1978). The black experience group: A therapeutic group activity model for the black schizophrenic. In *Innovations In Counseling Services* (pp. 165-171). Falls Church, VA: International Association of Counseling Services.

First, R.J., Roth, D. & Arawa, B.D. (1988). Homelessness: Understanding the dimensions of the problems for minorities. *Social Work, 33(7),* 120-124.

French, W.L., & Bell, C.H. (1973). *Organizational development.* Englewood Cliffs, NJ: Prentice-Hall, Inc.

Frey, J. (1984) A practitioner's guide. Madison, WI: PACT Program.

Friedman, M. (Ed.). (1971). *Overcoming Middle Class Rage.* Philadelphia, Westminster Press.

Fujiwara, T. & Christian, A. (1998). The Asian/Pacific Island community—A diverse cultural and ethnic people. *Community Support Network News, 4(4),* 5.

Gallegos J. (1982). Manning and administering services for minority groups. In M.L. Austin & W.E. Hershery (Eds.). *Handbook on Mental Health Administration.* San Francisco, CA: Jossey-Bass.

Gary, LE. (Ed.). (1978). *Mental health: A challenge to the black community.* Philadelphia and Ardmore, PA: Dorrance & Company.

Garvin, C.D. & Glassor, P.H. (1995). Social group work: The preventive and rehabilitative approach. In R.D. Sundel, P.H. Glassor, R. Surr & R.D. Venter (eds.). *Individual Change Through Groups.* New York: Free Press.

Getzel, G. (1993). Poetry writing groups & the elderly: A reconsideration on of art and social group work. In R. Middleman. *Activities & Action In Group Work.* New York: Haworth Press.

Giordano, J. & Giordano, G.P. (1977). *The ethno-cultural in mental health: A literature- review of bibliography.* New York.- Institute on Pluralism and Group Identity.

Gopaul-McNichol, SA. (1993). *Working with west indian families.* New York- Guilford Press.

Gordon, T.A. & Jones, N.L. (1979). Functions of the social network in the black community. In L.E. Gary (Ed.). *Mental Health: A Challenge To The Black Community.* (pp. 179-195)- Philadelphia & Ardmore, PA: Dorrance & Company.

Gould, K. H. (1939). Asian and pacific islanders: Myth and reality. *Journal of the National Association of Social Workers, 33(2),* 142-147.

Green, R.L. (1987). Ethnicity and MMPI performance: A review. *Journal of Consulting and Clinical Psychology, 55(4),* 497-512.

Griffith, E.E. (1988). A cross-cultural introduction to the therapeutic aspects of a Christian religious retreat. In L. Comas-Diaz & E.E. Griffith (Eds.). (pp. 69 - 89). *Clinical Guidelines in Cross-Cultural Health.* New York, N.Y.: John Wiley & Sons.

Griffith, E.E., English T. & Mayfield, V. (1980). Possession, prayer, and testimony: Therapeutic aspects of the Wednesday night meeting in a black church. *Psychiatry, 439,* 120-128.

Griffith, E.E, Young, J. & Smith, D. (1982). An analysis of the therapeutic elements in a black church service. *Hospital and Community Psychiatry, 35,* 464-469.

Guidelines for providers of psychosocial services to ethnic, linguistic, and culturally diverse populations. (1993). *American Psychologist, 4547.*

Guzie, F. (1957). *Emerging patterns in the use of program in social group work* National Conference on Social Welfare- Group Work Papers. New York: National Association of Social Workers.

Hale, J.E. (1982). *Black children, their roots, culture and learning styles.* Utah: Brigham Young University Press.

Helms, LE. (Ed.). (1990). *Black and white racial identity: theory, research, and practice.* New York: Greenwood Press.

Hoetzel, J. (1989). *Inversional pyramid of psychosocial values.* Philadelphia, PA: Division of Continuing Mental Health Education at Medical College of Pennsylvania/ Hahnemann University.

Holden, T., Carkhuff, R.R. & Berenson, B.G. (1967). Differential effects of the manipulating therapeutic conditions upon high-and-low-functioning clients. *Journal of Counseling Psychology, 14,* 63-66.

Horney, K. (1937). *The neurotic personality of our time.* New York: Norton.

Issacs, M. (Ed.). (1991). *The pennsylvania model: Towards a culturally competent system of care.* PA Department of Public Welfare, Office of Mental Health, Bureau of Children's Services.

Jackson, B.E. & R. Herdiman. (1994) Multicultural Organizational Development. *Promise of Diversity.* Cross, Kutz, Miller, and Seashore, eds. New York: Irwin Professional Publishing.

Jackson, J.S., Hatchett, S.J., Cochran, D.L & Jackson, J.S. (1991). *Life in black america.* Newberry Park, CA.: Sage Publications.

Jacobson, F.M. (1999). Ethnocultural assessment. In L. Comas-Diaz and F.R. Griffith (Eds.). *Clinical Guidelines in Non-Cultural Mental Health.* New York, N.Y.: John Wiley & Sons.

Jamison, K.(1984). *The nibble theory and the kernel of power.* New York: Paulist Press.

Jones, B. and Gray, D. (1986). Problems in diagnosing schizophrenia and affective disorders among blacks. *Hospital and Community Psychiatry, 37,* 61-65.

Jonikas, J. *(1993). Staff competencies direct service delivery staff in psychosocial rehabilitation programs.* Chicago, IL: Thresholds National Research and Training Center on Rehabilitation and Mental Illness.

Kaliski, S.Z. & Zabow, T. (1993). Psychiatry in post-apartheid South Africa. *Hospital and Community Psychiatry, 44(12),* 1191-1193.

Karno, M. (1966). The enigma of ethnicity in a psychiatric clinic. *Archives of General Psychiatry, 14,* 116-125.

Kiev, A. (1964). *Magic, faith and healing.* New York: Free Press of Glencoe.

Kiev, A. (1972). *Transcultural psychiatry.* New York. Free Press of Glencoe.

Kilman, D. (1935). *Learning style inventory.* Boston, MA. McBer & Co.

Kilman, Ralph H. (1984) *Beyond the Quick Fix: Managing Five Tracks to Organizational Success.* San Fransisco: Jossey-Bass.

Korman, M. (1974). National conference on levels and patterns of professional training in psychology: major themes. *American Psychologist, 29,* 301-313.

Lefley, H.P. (1990). Culture and chronic mental illness. *Hospital and Community Psychiatry, 41,* 277-136.

Lefley, H.P. & Bestman, E.W. (1984). Community mental health and minorities: A multi-ethnic approach. In S. Sue and T. Moore, (Eds.). *The Pluralistic Society: A Community Mental Health Perspective* (pp. 116-149). New York: Human Services Press.

Leininger, M. (1984). Transcultural interviewing and heath assessment. In E. Petersen, N. Sanorus, & A.L Marsella (Eds.). *The Cross-Cultural Context* (pp. 109–133). Beverly Hills, CA.: Sage Publication.

Levine, L. (I 976). *Ethnicity and mental health: A social conservation approach.* Paper presented at the White House Conference on Ethnicity and Mental Health. New York: Institute on Pluralism and Group Identity.

————.*(1973). Social policy and multi-ethnicity in the 1970's: Working paper no. 1.* New York: Institute on Pluralism and Group Identity.

Levine, L. & Herman, J. (1971). The new pluralism. In M. Friedman (Ed.). *Overcoming Middle Class Rage.* Philadelphia: Westminster Press.

Lewin, Kurt. (1948) *Resolving social conflicts.* New York: Harper & Bros.

Lewis, R.G. and Ho, M.K (1975). Social work with Native Americans. *Social Work Journal, 20*(5),379-483

Locke, D.C. (1991). *A model of cross cultural understanding.* Raleigh, N.C.: State University of Raleigh.

Marin, G. & Van Oss Marin, M. D. (1991). *Research with Hispanic populations.* Newbury Park, CA: Sage Publications.

Marsella, A.J. (1993). Counseling and psychotherapy with Japanese Americans: Cross-cultural considerations. *American Journal of Orthopsychiatry, 63(2),* 200-208.

Mason, J.L (1995). *Cultural Competence Self Assessment Questionnaire.* Portland, OR: Portland State University, Research and Training Center on Family Support and Children's Mental Health.

Martin, M. (1988). Differences form the basis for inclusion: It is time to consider the needs of ethnic and racial/minority persons. *Community Support Network News, 4(4),* 1-2.

Mayadas N.S. & Lason, D.B. (1983). Minority groups in majority cultures, Techniques of refugee integration into a alien times. In M.N. Goroff (Ed.). *Reaping From the Field Practice to Practice: Proceedings of Social Group Work.*

Meichenbaum, D. (1974). A self-instructional approach to stress management: A proposal for stress inoculation training. In L. Sasrason and C.D. Spielberger (Eds.). *Stress and Anxiety, 2,* 227-263. New York: Wiley.

Middleman, Ruth R. ed. (1983) *Activities and action in group work.* New York: Haworth Press.

Minnich, E.K. (1990). *Transforming knowledge.* Philadelphia: Temple University Press.

Mobley, B. (1974). *Self concept and conceptualization of ethnic identity: The black experience.* Unpublished doctoral dissertation, Purdue University.

Mortland, C.& & Egan, M.G. (1997). Vietnamese youth in American foster care. *Journal of the National Association of Social Workers, 32*(3), 240-245.

Myers, R. & King, L. (1980). Youth of the black underclass: Urban stress and mental health. *Fanon Center Journal, 2,* 22-29.

McGoldrick, M., Pearce, J.K- & Giordano, J. (1982). *Ethnicity and Family Therapy.* New York, NY: Guilford Press.

Naranjo, D. (1998). Mental health services for Hispanics: A personal perspective. *Community Support Network News, 4*(4), 4.

Newhill, C.L. (1990). The role of culture in the development of paranoid symptomatology *American Journal of Orthopsychiatry, 60*(2), 176-185.

Novak, M. (1971). *The Rise of the Unmeltable Ethnics.* New York: Macmillan.

Orlandi, M. A., Weston, R. & Epstein, L. G. (1992). *Cultural competence for evaluators: A guide for alcohol and other drug abuse prevention practitioners working with ethnic/racial communities,* ADAMHA. Rockville, MD.: U.S. Department of Health and Human Services.

Owan T. C. (1985). *Southeast Asian mental health.* Washington, D.C.: U.S. Dept. of Health and Human Services.

Parham, TA. (1982). *The relationship of black students' racial identity to self esteem, affective states, social class, and mental health.* Unpublished doctoral dissertation.

Paster, V.S. 1990. Pinderhughes E. *Journal Orthopsychiatry, 60*(2), 162-163.

Pedersen, P. (1988) *A Handbook For Developing Multicultural Awareness.* Alexandria, VA: American Counseling Association.

_____ (1988). *A Handbook For Development Of Cultural Awareness.* Alexandria, VA.: American Association for Counseling and Development.

Pernell-Arnold, A. (1991) *Coming to america*. Keynote at Second Annual Conference, Mutlicultural Training and Research Institute, Temple University at Philadelphia.

_____ (1993).*Multiculturalism: myth or miracle*. Keynote address IAPSRS Conference, New Orleans, LA.

Pernell-Arnold, A. & Finley, L. (1991). *Multicultural/antistigma training program curriculum*. Albany, NY: Capital Area Psychiatric Center.

Pernell-Arnold A. & Finley, L. (1993). *Multicultural advanced certificate training program curriculum*. Philadelphia, PA: Temple University School of Social Administration, Multicultural Research and Training Institute.

Peters, T. (1987). *Thriving on chaos*. New York, NY: Harper & Row Publishers.

Petzold, J.E. (1991). Southeast Asian refugees and sudden unexplained death syndrome. *Journal of the National Association of Social Workers, 36*(5) 387.

Ponterotto, J.G. and M.J. Furlong. (1985) Evaluating Counselor Effectiveness: A Critical Review of Rating Scale Instruments. *Journal of Counseling Psychology 32*, 597-616.

Ponterotto, J.G., Reiger, Barrett, and Spacks. (1994) Assessing Multicultural Counseling Competences: A Review of Instrumentation. *Journal of Couseling and Development 20*, 64-88.

Ponterotto, J.G. (1991) The nature of prejudice: Implications for counseling intervention. *Journal of Counseling and Development 70*, 216-224.

President's Commission on Mental Health. (1978) *Task panel reports: Black Americans*. In President's Commission on Mental Health, The Report to the President, Vol. 3, 839-844. U.S. Government Printing Office, Washington, D.C.

Primm A. (1990). Group psychotherapy can raise self esteem in mentally ill Black men. *The Psychiatric Times: Medicine and Behavior, 23-25*.

Proctor, E.K- & Davis, L.E. (1994). The challenge of racial difference: Skills for clinical practices. *Social Work, 39*(3), 314-323.

Radin, N. (1995). Socioeducation groups. In R.D. Sundel P.H. Glassor. IL Sarr, & R.D. Vinter. *Individual change through groups*. New York. Free Press.

Radke-Yarrow, M., (1959). Personality development and minority group membership. In J. Sklare (Ed.), *The Jet* (pp. 451-475). Glencoe: Free Press.

Randall, D.E. (1989). *Strategies for working with culturally diverse communities and clients*. Association for the Care of Children's Health through Family Centered Care, Grant # MCH 113793 from the Bureau of Maternal and Child Health and Resource Development, U.S. Dept. of Health and Human Services. Rockville, MD.

Rivera L.R. (1994). *A planetary perspective: Multiculturalism and the Afro/ Latino connection*. Metro Exchange, June.

Rogers, C.R. (1942). *Counseling and psychotherapy*. Boston: Houghton, Mifflin.

Rosenstein, M, Milazzo-Sayre, L, MacAskill IL & Manderscheid, R. (1997). Use of inpatient services by special populations. In R.W. Manderscheid and SA. Barren (Eds.) *Mental Health in the United States*. (DHHS publication Number ADM 87-1518). Washington, DC: U.S. Government Printing Office.

Rutman, I.D. (1994). Introduction. In The Publications Committee of IAPSRS (Ed.). *An Introduction To Psychosocial Rehabilitation* (4-8), International Association of Psychosocial Rehabilitation Services.

Sabnani, Ponterotto, and Borodovsky. (1991). White Racial Identity Development and Cross-cultural Training: A

Stage Model. *The Counseling Psychologist 19*: 76-102.

Sandven, IC and Resnich, M.D. (1990). Informal adoption among black adolescent mothers. *American Journal of Orthopsychiatry, 60*(2),210-224.

Schein, E.H. (1995). *Organizational Culture And Leadership*. San Francisco, CA: Jossey-Bass Publishing.

Shuter, R. (1989). The international marketplace. In M.K. Asante & W.B. Gudykurst, 392- 406, *Handbook of International and Intercultural Communication*. Newbury Park, CA; Sage Publications.

Simons, G.F- (1999). *Working together: how to become more effective in a multicultural organization.* Los Altos, CA: Crisp Publications, Inc.

Smith, E.J. (1973). *Counseling the culturally different black youth.* Ohio: Charles E. Merril.

Smith, P. & Peterson, P. (1989). *Leadership, Organizations, And Cuts.* CA: Sage Publications.

Snow, L.F. (1983). Traditional health beliefs and practices among lower class black Americans. *Western Journal. of Medicine 139*(6), 820-828.

Snowden, L and Cheung, F. (1990). Use of inpatient mental health services by members of ethnic minority group. *American Psychologists, 45*, 347-355.

Stillman, S.M. (1973). *Increasing black client participation in a community social service agency.* Unpublished manuscript.

Sue, D.W. (1981). The challenge of multiculturalism: The road less traveled. *American Counselor, 1*, 6-14.

Sue, Arredondo, and McDavis. (1992) Multicultural counseling and standards: A call to the profession. *Journal of Multicultural Counseling and Development 20,* 64-88.

Sue, Bernier, Durran, Feinberg, Pederson, Smith, and Vasquez-Nuttal. (1982) Position paper: Cross-cultural counseling competencies. *The Counseling Psychologist 10*, 45-52.

Sue, D.W. and D. Sue (1990). *Counseling the culturally different: Theory and practice* (2nd ed.). New York: John Wiley & Sons.

Szapocznik, Santisteban, Durtines, Perez-Vidal, and Hervis. (1983) *Bicultural effectiveness training: A treatment for enhancing intercultural adjustment in cuban american families.* Paper presented at the Ethnicity, Acculturation, and Mental Health Among Hispanics Conference, Albuquerque.

Timberlake, E.M. & Chipungu, S.S. (1992). Grandmotherhood: Contemporary meaning among African American middle class grandmothers. *Journal of the National Association of Social Workers, 37*(3), 216-222.

Townsend, W., Arewa, B., Griffin, G., Waters-Brown, M. & Bennett, C. (1992). *Use of public mental heath services by minorities in Ohio.* A Report by the Minority Concerns Committee to the Ohio Department of Mental Health, Columbus, Ohio.

Trochim, W. and J. Cook. (1993) *Workforce Competencies For Psychosocial Rehabilitation Workers: A Concept Mapping Project.* Project conducted for the International Association of Psychosocial Rehabilitation Services, Albuquerque.

Tumin, M. (1964) Ethnic Groups. Gould and Kolb. (eds.). *A Dictionary of the Social Sciences.* New York: Free Press.

Vinter, R.D. (1985). Program activities: An analysis of their effects on participant behavior. In R.D. Sundel, P.H. Glassor, R. Sarr & R.D. Vinter. *Individual change through groups.* New York- Free Press.

Wade, J.C. (1993). Institutional racism: An analysis of the mental health system.

American Journal of Orthopsychiatry 63, 536-544.

Wallace, C.J. and R.P. Liberman (1985). Social skills training for patients with schizophrenia: A controlled clinical. *Psychiatric Research, 15,* 239-247.

Westermeyer, J. (1997). Clinical considerations in cross-cultural diagnosis. *Hospital and Community Psychiatry, 38*(2),160-139.

White, BOW. (1984). *Color in a white society.* Los Angeles, CA: National Association of Social Workers, Inc.

Wilson, G. & Ryland, G (1994). *Social Group Work Practice.* Cambridge, MA: Houghton Mifflin

Wood, P.H.N. (1980) Appreciating the consequences of disease: The classification of impairments, disability, and handicaps. *The Who Chronicle, 34,* 376-380.

9

Vocational Rehabilitation

Richard Baron

Psychosocial rehabilitation has, at its core, an emphasis on the importance of work, and the best psychosocial rehabilitation programs provide people with psychiatric disabilities with the encouragement, assistance, and ongoing support they need to establish or re-establish themselves as productive members of the broader society. This chapter is designed to provide the reader with an overview of the importance of employment programs for persons with mental illness, the major program models for the delivery of employment services, the roles that various practitioners play in assisting people to work, and the basic competencies that psychosocial rehabilitation workers must develop to play these roles effectively. Underlying the entire chapter, however, is a strong belief that persons with mental illness can and should be working.

The Importance of Work

Numerous studies over the past twenty years that have examined the topic of work and mental illness have demonstrated that employment makes a significant contribution to:

- improved clinical outcomes—such as reduced symptomatology,

increased medication compliance, and the avoidance of hospitalization (PORT, 1994; Bond & Boyer, 1988);

- increased self-esteem and self-efficacy (Anthony, et al., 1988; Neff, 1988; Strauss & Carpenter, 1984; Harding, et al., 1987);

- improved integration into the community (McGurrin, 1994; Rutman, 1993); and

- perceptions of a higher quality of life in the community (Fabian, 1993; Knoedler, 1979).

In addition, there is initial evidence that those individuals who do work make less use of public mental health services, and thus lower the overall costs of their care (Drake, et al., 1993).

Most important, however, persons with mental illness see work as a key priority in their lives (Lehman, 1988; Mulkern & Bradley, 1986; Ball & Havassy, 1984; Rosnow & Tucker, 1985; Roger, Danley & Anthony, 1992). Although most individuals with psychiatric disability can clearly remember both the first time they were told that they "could never work" and the most recent time it was suggested that they "were not ready for a job yet," the great majority would nonetheless like to work (Harp, 1992; Chamberlin, 1987). For many participants in psychosocial rehabilitation agencies, working endures as a critical marker of their current stability and future prospects.

The Rehabilitation Challenge

Widespread unemployment among adults with severe mental illness, however, also endures, with estimates of unemployment ranging from approximately 80% (Anthony, et al., 1978) to 92% (Goldman & Tessler, 1994). There are many contributing reasons for such high rates. In part, unemployment among those with severe mental illness is due to the impact of the illness itself (Rutman, 1993) the resulting cognitive, perceptual, affective and interpersonal deficits (Mueser & Liberman, 1988) and the episodic and/or chronic nature of mental illness make work a particularly difficult challenge. In part, the pervasiveness of unemployment for this group is the result of the perceived disincentives to employment embodied in the Social Security Administration's regulations surrounding SSI and SSDI benefits and their implicit threat to the individual's eligibility for medical benefits. Finally, in part, unemployment is a result of both the relative scarcity of employment-oriented rehabilitation programs, which are unevenly distributed across the country and all but unavailable in some communities, and the limited effectiveness of many of those programs in helping individuals gain employment in the competitive labor market (Bond, 1991).

However, the systems of care that are available to most persons with a psychiatric disability also act to discourage the realization of individual employment aspirations. *Mental health professionals* often downplay or delay the exploration of employment goals: many mental health professionals still tend to focus on the emotional lives of the people they work with and—either because of their academic training or their agency's fiscal priorities—neither explore nor encourage interests in or capabilities for vocational training and a career. *Vocational rehabilitation counselors* have often failed to see the work potential of the individuals with mental illness that are referred to them. The state/federal rehabilitation system reports that of all the disability groups they serve, those with mental illness are least often successful in the rehabilitation process. *Family members* are occasionally an additional barrier. While some parents enthusiastically support the development of career goals, others are both concerned about the emotional consequences of a failure at work and worried about the financial implications of the individual's employment and loss of benefits. *Employers* also offer little support. Reflecting the views of the broader public, they often view those with mental illness as potentially dangerous, deviant, and unproductive. People with mental illness, consequently, are often too readily convinced by others that they are unsuitable candidates for a job and resist the offers of rehabilitation programming or entry-level job opportunities that do come their way. Those with the still more daunting problems of a dual disability—those who have a co-occurring substance abuse or physical disability or who have AIDS or are homeless—are more discouraged. In many communities it is often true that it is only psychosocial rehabilitation programs that continue to offer a coherent and effective challenge to the conventional notion that people with mental illness cannot work.

Program Models

Responding effectively to these challenges in part relies upon a redefinition of what it means to work. Psychosocial programs help others to understand that work can be defined broadly, to include both part-time and full-time work, both ongoing and occasional work, and both fully independent work and work that requires the continuing support of a psychosocial rehabilitation program (Laplan, 1988). Psychosocial programs, further, have traditionally been interested not only in the early stages of the vocational rehabilitation process (e.g., assessment, skill training, placement, and job stabilization) but also in helping the individual to establish a long-term attachment to the labor market. The first job is often seen as the beginning of the individual's career, rather than as the culmination of the vocational rehabilitation process.

Because psychosocial programs are best at responding to the individual needs of participants, employment programs among psychosocial agencies have taken a number of forms (Blankertz, in press; Toms-Barker, 1992; Campbell, 1989). *Clubhouse programs*, often based in a Fountain House comprehensive PSR setting, offer "transitional employment" programs, in which the individual is able to work—part-time, and for no more than six months—in a series of entry-level jobs in local businesses and industries that the clubhouse uses as a way to provide the individual with an introduction to and a mastery of the demands of work in the competitive marketplace (Beard, et al., 1978). *Agency-sponsored entrepreneurial businesses*, which often employ janitorial teams, landscaping crews, restaurant staff, and other small business ventures of nonprofit agencies, offer another in-troduction to the world of work and skill training that will be useful in the real job market (Granger, 1990). *Supported employment programs*, which work to place individuals with mental illness as quickly as possible in real jobs in community settings and then provide needed support (on-site or off-site, in the short-term or months following placement), provide another means to help people attain work (Wehman & Melia, 1991; Wehman, 1981; Anthony & Blanch, 1987). *Fairweather lodges*, which are designed as communal living programs in which the residents either hold jobs in a jointly operated business or pool their resources and supports at individual jobs, see employment as one of the central aspects of successful community living (Fairweather, 1969, 1978). *Consumer-operated businesses*, in which individuals with mental illness themselves own or operate a small business without support (or only minimal support) from professional staff, are a fast growing element in the rehabilitation community, with adults with mental illness starting restaurants and audio-visual production companies, computer service centers, and laundromats.

It is important, however, to recognize two important facts about these varied models. First, they often share some very basic principles: a belief in the individual's ability to work, an emphasis on the rapid placement of the individual into the real world of work rather than a never-ending involvement in pre-vocational and work readiness programs, a commitment to assist each person in the early days and weeks of employment while the individual works toward stabilization, and a recognition that the person who is working is likely to need ongoing support and assistance in order to sustain a long-term attachment to the labor market. Second, many of these models—because of their similar principles and their responsiveness to individual needs—tend to blur into one another, with practitioners in varied settings often engaged in very similar tasks.

Practitioner Competencies

Thus, psychosocial rehabilitation practitioners engaged in employment programming may have very different job titles such as employment specialist, job coach, job development worker, case manager, and counselor and still do very similar tasks day-to-day. They may be in very different settings—private nonprofit independent agencies, partial hospitalization programs within a community mental health center, consumer-run drop-in centers, assertive case management units, and even state hospital or private hospital discharge units—and still be focusing on the same set of fundamental responsibilities: to provide encouragement, assistance, and ongoing support to the person who wants to work.

The competencies needed by psychosocial rehabilitation practitioners are often taught on the job. Although there are still few academic degrees or extended in-service training programs currently available in this important arena, there is a growing body of knowledge of what it takes to help someone enter or re-enter the world of work (Farrell, 1991; Danley & Mellen, 1987).

The following competencies provide an overview of the knowledge base, specialized skills, and general approaches that an effective provider of employment services offers to the individual with severe mental illness (Farrell, 1991; Danley & Mellen, 1987). Few practitioners come to their jobs with many of these competencies fully developed, yet their development over time is a critical responsi-

bility of each worker in the field. To assist the reader, vocational competencies here have been roughly divided into three broad categories: ***encouragement competencies***, in which the psychosocial rehabilitation (PSR) practitioner initiates the rehabilitation process; ***assistance competencies***, in which the PSR practitioner is assisting individuals with mental illness to acquire skills, a real job, and work stability; and ***ongoing support competencies***, in which the PSR practitioner provides the consistent and long-term services the individual may need in order to remain at work.

Encouragement Competencies

It should be highlighted that the person with severe mental illness often comes to the vocational rehabilitation process with mixed feelings, and much of the early work of the employment-focused PSR practitioner is designed to build an alliance with the individual that explicitly values employment.

Competency I

Engagement—Engage the individual with mental illness in the rehabilitation process.

At the heart of any relationship between staff and the person in rehabilitation is a mutual engagement in a therapeutic or rehabilitative process. The PSR practitioner who focuses on employment issues finds effective ways to engage each person in a positive relationship with shared goals. However, as in all the competencies to follow, the specific approaches used will vary with the individual needs of the person in question. It should be noted also that it is not necessary for PSR practitioners to approach the issue of work in an entirely neutral fashion, waiting for people to express interest or motivation. While adults with mental illness are often well aware of the disincentives and barriers to employment that they face, they are often unfamiliar with the world of work and its potential benefits, in part because many people have faced their initial struggles with severe mental illness just when their non-disabled contemporaries are having their first employment experiences. Two approaches to the engagement process address this issue. On the one hand, many people benefit from some form of work exploration, not only talking about different types of jobs and their benefits, but also visiting various work sites and talking with workers (often other people from the agency) about their experiences. On the other hand, effective PSR practitioners are forthright about the value that they attach to work. While it is inappropriate to insist that individuals with mental illness must work or are morally bereft if they are not productively engaged, PSR practitioners need to be clear in the engagement process about the importance they attach to work (Blankertz, 1994; Blankertz & Cnaan, 1993; Cohen, 1989).

practitioners may be the most significant people (and sometimes the only individuals) in an individual's life who are enthusiastic about that person's employment potential. PSR practitioners must honestly believe in that potential and must convey that belief effectively to the people with whom they work. In this regard, it is also important to help everyone understand that can embrace a wide range of employment patterns: full-time or part-time, one job for years or a variety of short-term positions, a career in only one field of endeavor or periodic shifts in roles, and either fully independent employment or jobs in which ongoing support (on- or off-the-job) is provided. Such a redefinition of *work* as a goal can be substantially motivating itself, placing employment within each individual's understanding of personal capacities and interests. (Blank-ertz, 1994; Blankertz & Cnaan, 1993). At the same time, the PSR practitioner must develop and communicate a deep and abiding **belief** in the capacity of adults with psychiatric disabilities, even with the most serious and persistent of mental illnesses, to perform at work, and this belief must then be communicated to the particular individual.

Competency 2

Encouragement —Encourage each person to establish employment as a key goal in the overall rehabilitation process.

Competency 3

Empowerment—Assist the individual with mental illness in establishing the goals, nature, and pace of the rehabilitation process.

Many persons with severe mental illness who wish to seek employment are consistently discouraged by mental health professionals, vocational rehabilitation counselors, and (occasionally) family members, as well as by media portrayals of persons with mental illness. PSR

Notwithstanding the issues of engagement and encouragement noted above, central to an effective vocational rehabilitation process is the degree to which each person feels empowered to have the rehabilitation process address his or her needs. In this regard, individuals with mental illness must be fully engaged in setting both short-term goals (e.g., one person may want to start out tentatively in a very part-time position, while another individual may want to jump quickly into a full-time job) and long-term goals (e.g., one person may want little more than a comfortable entry-level and unskilled post, while another individual may want to develop a career in a particular industry or human services field). Similarly, individuals with mental illness need help in making difficult choices about the nature of the rehabilitation process: pre-vocational programs; transitional and supported employment services; job clubs and mainstream employment agencies; returning to school to obtain a high school diploma, a college degree or advanced academic qualifications; or entering into a technical training program. All are valid ways to pursue employment. Finally, the pace of the rehabilitation process must also be a matter of choice: some will want to proceed cautiously, and others will be more comfortable with risk. The effective PSR practitioner assists each person in making informed choices (Harp, 1992; Blankertz, 1994) in all these areas.

Competency 4

Education—Inform the individual with mental illness about the operations and options of available employment programs.

To help individuals with mental illness make informed choices about the rehabilitation process, PSR practitioners need to know a good deal themselves. It is often helpful to have a sense of the history of employment programming in this field. The PSR practitioner who is unaware of the degree to which pre-vo-

cational programs in the past have been the graveyard of vocational ambition may be inappropriately cautious about a person's ambition to quickly get a 'real' job. The PSR practitioner who is unaware of the degree to which some people have been channeled into unskilled employment despite specific skills or educational accomplishments may be inappropriately enthusiastic about a janitorial opening. At the same time, PSR practitioners need to understand the state/federal vocational rehabilitation program, so that they can help everyone have reasonable expectations of their VR counselors, the VR process and time-frame, and the VR system's funding limitations. Because human services systems are complex, it is often helpful for PSR practitioners to find effective means to provide information that clarifies the various elements of those systems and what people will experience and can expect from each (Blankertz, 1994; Rogers, et al., 1992).

Competency 5

Assessment—Complete both initial and ongoing assessments of a person's employment-related strengths and deficits.

There are a variety of formal and informal mechanisms for assessing the skills and problems that individuals bring to the vocational rehabilitation process. Three broad categories should be noted here. First, assessment instruments—work samples, interest tests, and a variety of batteries to determine specific capabilities—can prove useful in determining both strengths and deficits. Second, most PSR practitioners combine the results of such formal mechanisms with their observations within a more informal interview situation, in which individuals with mental illness have the opportunity to talk about their own work experiences and ambitions. There are a number of formats for such interviews that are especially effective in helping people focus on the issues most important to them. Third, and most important, the psychosocial field has placed its strongest emphasis on situational assessments, in which persons with mental illness are quickly placed in real work settings (either within the operations of the psychosocial agency itself or within a supervised setting in a mainstream business or industry) and their performance in the work context is closely observed. Indeed, many clubhouse program practitioners believe that the single best indicator of readiness for employment is the individual's willingness to try. While this belief does not negate the need to assess a person's strengths or weaknesses, it does have a major impact on the number of real work opportunities made available to participants of the psychosocial program. Finally, the effective PSR practitioner includes the person in all of these assessment processes as a partner (Anthony & Jansen, 1984; Jacobs, 1984; Shepherd, 1990; Blankertz, 1994).

Competency 6

Financial Counseling—Assist the individual with mental illness in understanding the fiscal impact of employment.

There are two broad areas of concern here. The first is that many people do not pursue employment options because they feel that the financial and medical assistance benefits of their status as SSI/SSDI recipients/beneficiaries will change,

leaving them more economically vulnerable than before they started work. PSR practitioners are aware of these concerns and have the information they need to reassure potential workers that working will generally leave them economically ahead, and that there are a variety of ways in which they can retain their medical eligibility, regardless of their work status. People are understandably worried about these issues, but the Work Incentive Provisions of the Social Security Act do indeed make work, for a great many persons, an economically viable alternative to dependency. Second, many people with psychiatric disabilities have never received a paycheck, and both management of those monies and budgeting to insure that they can remain independent may be challenging. Effective PSR practitioners are either able to offer substantial assistance themselves to the worker, or are able to refer the individual to appropriate sources for information and help (Hill, et. al., 1987).

Competency 7

Program Planning—Work together to develop a comprehensive vocational rehabilitation program plan.

The culmination of this first phase of the rehabilitation process is the development of an initial plan that will guide both the practitioner and the individual as they continue to work together. Employment plans, like other rehabilitation plans, need to be: mutually developed between the person receiving services and the practitioner; responsive to individual needs; and adaptable on an ongoing basis to the changing perceptions and preferences of the individual. Effective PSR practitioners are also adept at drawing into the development of a vocational rehabilitation plan all those—the VR counselor, family members, casemanagers, the therapist, etc.—whose contributions to the process are required to make the pursuit of employment successful (Kregel, et al., 1990; Test, 1991; Russert, 1991; Isbister & Donaldson, 1987).

Assistance Competencies

At this point, the PSR practitioner and the person receiving services will continue to work closely together to ensure ongoing progress in the rehabilitation process. While some of the person's involvement in work may be agency-based (in which the agency's operations depend upon a workforce of people with psychiatric disabilities) or agency-supervised (in which the agency's own small business operations employ individuals with mental illness), some of the person's involvement in work may be within mainstream businesses or human service agencies. Whether providing direct supervision on the job or offering less direct counseling services off-site, PSR practitioners need to demonstrate the following competencies (Baron, 1992).

Competency 8

Teaching—Teach the technical and interpersonal skills needed at work.

Once on the job, whether within the agency or out in the community, individuals need to be able to master both the technical/skill areas of employment and the interpersonal dimension of their jobs. The effective PSR practitioner uses a variety of techniques to teach those skills, depending on the circumstances of the individual job and the learning styles of the person. In some instances,

a more academic approach in classroom settings is appropriate, but PSR practitioners often find that a "learn-by-doing" approach is more effective. The PSR practitioner may talk briefly about the skill, demonstrate its application, assist the person in demonstrating the skill, provide correction and encouragement, and ask the individual to demonstrate the skill again. Because many PSR practitioners are often on-the-job themselves, their work behavior also permits them to serve as effective role models. When the PSR practitioner is not on the job, another on-the-job role model (i.e., another employee at the site) may be willing to provide both role modeling and skill teaching on an ongoing basis (Knoedler, 1979; Mueser & Liberman, 1988; Robers, et al., 1992, 1988).

Competency 9

Monitoring—Monitor the individual's acquisition and ability to use both technical and interpersonal skills on the job.

It is critically important for PSR practitioners to regularly monitor an individual's use of technical and interpersonal skills, both to identify those areas where the person may need to review or "brush-up" on skills reviewed in the past and to identify those areas where the person may need to develop new skills to respond to previously unforeseen work demands. When appropriate, PSR practitioners are in touch with employers to review performance records as well. The basic monitoring of work performance, however, combines the practitioners' observations and the employers' comments with the individual's reports and expressed needs. It is important that PSR practitioners become aware that skill development in both technical/skill and interpersonal areas is often a gradual process: skills may develop slowly, and the accumulation of a variety of new skills may take place over time. For this reason, it is vital to be aware that the rehabilitation process is something that is taking place the job rather than the job and makes the PSR practitioners' monitoring and teaching responsibilities critical (Furlong, et al., 1994).

Competency 10

Job Development—Be adept at finding welcoming job opportunities for persons with severe mental illness.

Although there is a strong literature that identifies the fears and concerns of employers with regard to hiring persons with mental illness, there is also a growing recognition that employers are more willing than ever to open work opportunities to those with psychiatric disabilities. Effective PSR practitioners are able to identify employers—whether because of their own altruistic motivations, the imperatives of the Americans with Disabilities Act, or the demands on them with regard to regularly filling higher turnover entry-level positions—who are willing to interview, hire, supervise, and continue to employ persons with severe mental illness. Job developers must be persistent. Employers are most often reached through personal contact (whether through an introduction from someone else or through a "cold contact") and rarely respond to promotional materials in the media. Once contacted and willing, employers rarely open more

than one or two positions at a particular site. Job developers must be able to assess the demands of the positions available, or work with the employer to redefine several dispersed job elements into a single position which a person with mental illness is able to fill. The PSR practitioner must also be able to explain both the financial benefits to the employer (through Targeted Jobs Tax Credits, reduced search and training costs, etc.) as well as the availability of the job developer on a continuing basis to help to handle problems that may emerge (Ebert, et al., 1983; Goodall, 1987; Young, et al., 1986).

Competency 11

Job Finding — Be able to help the individual with mental illness to find a job independently.

Many people with mental illness would like to find a job on their own; the desire may come at the beginning of the rehabilitation process, or it may emerge following a transitional or supported employment training program. This may be the person's way either of establishing independence or of avoiding disclosure of a history of mental illness to a future employer. PSR practitioners can help an individual to review the classified section of the newspaper, develop an effective resume, practice interviewing techniques, and contact their own friends and family members for potential employment leads. This kind of work is often done in *job clubs*, in which a group of individuals work together, with staff leadership, on such assignments (Azrin, 1979).

Because the individual with severe mental illness is often involved with a number of other service providers, effective PSR practitioners take responsibility for insuring that there is regular, open, and cooperative communication with other service elements. This is especially important with regard to collaboration with the local office of vocational rehabilitation (if that office is financially supporting the person's employment programming), and it requires that PSR practitioners have an understanding of the VR counselors' roles, responsibilities, and restraints. But effective PSR practitioners also work to insure that therapists, residential program providers, case-managers, and others are continually aware of employment activities. Changes in medication, clinic appointments during work hours, and residential program restrictions that interfere with shift work are all potential sources of conflict for individuals with mental illness who are working, and PSR practitioners often help them to manage the competing demands of helping agencies (Test, 1991; Russert, 1991; Frey & Godfrey, 1991).

It is often true that people with mental illness need some form of accommodation on the job in order to work effectively. Although interest in job accommodations is in part a response to the demands on employers in the Americans with Disabilities Act to make "reasonable accommodations" that do not pose an "undue hardship" on their enterprise, cooperating employers have long made adjustments to accommodate employees with special needs (Mancuso, 1991; U.S. Congress, 1994). The current literature indicates that most such adjustments are relatively simply made. Changes in schedules, re-assignment of some responsibilities, special training for supervisors and/or co-workers, and flexible leave policies with regard to psychiatric emergencies constitute the majority of accommodations requested and are often made with little or no cost to the employer (U.S. Office of Personnel Management 1989 a,b; Combs & Omuig, 1986). Effective PSR practitioners help the employee and the employer to identify those accommodations that will be helpful and to make them in as simple and unintrusive a fashion as possible (Mancuso, 1990).

In urban, suburban, and rural communities, transportation to and from work on a regular basis is often problematic (Danley et al., 1982). In urban settings, despite the frequent availability of mass transit, some individuals with mental illness may be readily confused or frightened by the systems available to them, and PSR practitioners must be able to help them negotiate public transportation systems. In suburban and rural areas, public transportation is often unavailable, and PSR practitioners must help a person select a job he or she can either reach, call upon friends or family members to play a role in meeting these transportation needs, or develop carpooling arrangements with other workers. For some persons, acquiring a driver's license and an inexpensive car may also provide a motivation for obtaining and maintaining employment.

Competency 15

Stabilization—Help the individual with mental illness to become stabilized in the work environment.

The first few weeks of a new job are often the most stressful for persons with severe mental illness, and effective PSR practitioners are especially attentive and involved in this period, helping the worker to adjust to both the technical and the interpersonal demands of the job. This may involve PSR practitioners in on-the-job coaching or off-the-job counseling, discussions with supervisors and co-workers, and may sometimes require the practitioner to help an overwhelmed person withdraw gracefully from the position (Jacobsen, 1993; Kirszner et al., 1992; McCrory, 1991). In the case of successful placements, PSR practitioners must also develop the capacities to gradually reduce their involvement with the worker so that both on-the-job and off-the-job interventions become less frequent as the worker expresses less need for them. Once an individual has mastered the tasks of the job, supports provided "around the job" are often significantly more useful and important. If job coaches focus too much on "on-the-job" supports, the very real needs for other supports may remain unmet.

Ongoing Support Competencies

With stabilization on the job, the PSR practitioner's responsibilities will shift to those involved in helping the worker to sustain employment. It should be highlighted here that the PSR practitioner is not solely interested in helping the individual with mental illness succeed in that first job, but, rather, works to help the person establish and maintain a satisfying and long-term attachment to the labor market. That is, persons with psychiatric disabilities—like the rest of today's workforce—are likely to hold a number of jobs over their working careers, and part of the PSR practitioner's focus must be on helping individuals to see themselves as individuals who will be working for a living for much of the rest of their lives. However, the individual's work interests are likely to change over time, and it must be anticipated that many of the jobs that people are in today will not be available tomorrow. Ongoing supports offer the individual with a long-term disability a long-term resource for remaining actively engaged in the labor market. To provide those resources requires additional competencies. Some of these supports are offered in one-to-one counseling settings, some in group settings at times convenient to workers, and some within peer support groups, but all seek to meet the person's needs within the context of employment (Blankertz, 1994).

Because the recurrence of symptoms among those with severe mental illness is an all too common occurrence, PSR practitioners must be prepared to respond to these crises in ways that are sensitive to a person's desire to be able to hold onto a job. Sometimes the crisis occurs at work, with symptoms leading to intense workplace conflicts or lowered productivity, and PSR practitioners must be able both to contact treatment resources for the individual and to work with the employer and co-workers to assure them of the short-term nature of the crisis. Sometimes the crisis in question occurs away from the job, and here again the PSR practitioner must work with treatment resources and employers to ensure that a return to work is one of the goals of the crisis response system. Occasionally, even positive events at work—an offered promotion or additional responsibilities—will lead to a crisis, and the PSR practitioner must be prepared to help individuals adjust to these as well.

Some individuals prior to employment will have built a satisfying social life around their involvements in the recreational activities of the psychosocial rehabilitation agency and other individuals will have developed friends and romances around their private interests: these may now conflict with the demands of the work day. PSR practitioners work with individuals to develop new patterns of social interaction, to respond appropriately to social opportunities at work, and to sustain their prior relationships in new ways. While work is an important goal, it must be recognized as only one goal within what is often a complex array of support needs—for therapy, affordable housing, medical attention, and a social life—that must be met if the individual with mental illness is to be able to continue at work (Nisbet & Hagner, 1988; Wehman & Kregel, 1985; Nisbet et al., 1989; Henderson & Argyle, 1985).

Few people in today's society are likely to remain at a single job for their entire career, and effective PSR practitioners recognize that they will often need to assist individuals with mental illness who are working in assessing future career prospects. This will include assessing whether a current job is becoming too stressful or too boring, and with 75% of current TE and SE placements in entry-level and unskilled positions (Kirszner, 1991), this is very possible. Other individuals will indicate when they are ready to move on to more demanding work or back to school, and others may need a period of unemployment before returning to the workforce. Because career planning is stressful, particularly the process of job hunting, persons with severe mental illness can often make use of career counseling while still working (Baumgart, 1987; Ciardiello & Bingham, 1982; Toms-Baker, 1994).

Job loss among those with severe mental illness is a frequent reality, with as many as 50% of those placed in employment without a job a year later (Loeb, 1972). PSR practitioners work to avoid job loss (through the efforts described above) and to respond to job loss in a positive manner. Whatever the reason for job loss—the individual has quit peremptorily, been fired for cause, or been laid off for broader economic reasons—the individual often experiences job loss as a personal failure reconfirming earlier judgements about his or her lack of vocational potential. Effective counseling can be critical at this juncture, helping the individual to realistically assess the reasons for the lost job, to make necessary changes, and to begin as soon as possible to return to work in a new position (Wehman & Kregel, 1985; McLoughlin et al., 1987).

It is important throughout this process of providing ongoing supports for PSR practitioners to be working to help the worker develop more independent styles of functioning. This includes helping the individual to develop the capacity to respond appropriately to crises (at home or on the job), to manage their funds on their own, and to be prepared to seek new employment themselves. Often this involves helping the worker to more independently draw upon other support systems—the natural supports of co-workers and supervisors, the Employee Assistance Plan or Human Resources Coordinator where they work, family members and friends, and mentors and volunteers (MacDonald Wilson, et al., 1989; McLoughlin, et al., 1987)—that can help them address the challenges that they, like everyone else, must address to sustain their careers.

Other Issues

There are, of course, a range of other issues that the PSR practitioner must be concerned with if individuals with mental illness are to be effectively served. It is important to note, for instance, that workplace discrimination can still be a significant problem, and PSR practitioners should be helping workers to respond to both subtle and not-so-subtle assaults on their integrity. Further, work-oriented programs will not long survive if they cannot more definitively demonstrate their effectiveness, and this will require PSR practitioners to respond to system demands for careful record keeping throughout the process. At the same time, it is important to recognize that whatever the statistical or economic success that may be demonstrated by such record keeping, it is even more important for the PSR practitioner to remain sensitive to whether the *individual with mental illness* is satisfied. There must be mechanisms to ensure that the recipients of services are asked both whether they like their jobs and whether they are pleased with the impact that work has had on their lives.

Helping individuals with severe mental illness to gain and maintain employment is a demanding job. The range of competencies required and the challenges of today's labor market, among other stresses associated with this task, make this part of the overall psychosocial rehabilitation agenda particularly difficult. It should be noted, as well, that the PSR practitioner in this arena often feels somewhat unprepared. The additional demand for the PSR practitioner to be out *in the field* working with the individual, the family, or the employer and away from the home agency makes the practitioner's job appear daunting.

Nonetheless, it is a job that thousands of psychosocial practitioners currently do with notable success, success that is absolutely critical. Throughout the psychosocial field, agencies and practitioners have begun to recognize that the people who come to them for help today are quite different from those who turned to psychosocial programs a generation ago. Two decades ago, PSR agencies often served an older age group, addressing the needs of people who had spent years in psychiatric hospitals and who had the relatively modest ambition to live out their days quietly in a supportive community. Today, however, individuals with mental illness are younger, less institutionalized, and fully hopeful that they can find a more independent way to live a more full and a more normal community life. At the center of that hope, quite often, is a vision of themselves at work. Despite discouragement and past failures, despite disincentives and future fears, people with mental illness remain firm in their desire to be productive. At the core of the psychosocial rehabilitation field philosophy, and thus at the center of the complex web of competencies demanded of PSR practitioners, is a commitment to assist individuals with mental illness in attaining their hopes for meaningful and sustaining work.

References

Anthony, W.A., Cohen, M.R., & Danley, K.S. (1988). The psychosocial rehabilitation approach as applied to vocational rehabilitation. In J.A. Ciardiello & M.D. Bell (Eds.), *Vocational Rehabilitation of Persons With Prolonged Psychiatric Disorders*. (pp 59-80). Baltimore: Johns Hopkins University Press.

Anthony, W.A. & Blanch, A. (1987). *Supported employment for persons who are psychiatrically disabled: An historical and conceptual perspective.* Presented at State of the Art Conference on Supported Employment for Chronically Mentally Ill Individuals. Washington, D.C.

Anthony, W.A. & Jansen, M.A. (1984). Predicting the vocational capacity of the chronically mentally ill. *American Psychologist, 39*, 537-544.

Anthony, W.A., Danely, K.S., & Howell, J. (1984). The vocational rehabilitation of the psychiatrically disabled. In M. Mirabi (Ed.), *The Chronically Mentally Ill: Research and Services*. Jamaica, NY: SP Medical and Scientific Books.

Anthony, W.A., Cohen, M.R., & Vitalo, R. (1978). The measurement of rehabilitation outcome, *Schizophrenia Bulletin, 4*, 365-383.

Azrin, N.H. & Phillip, R. A. (1979). The job club method for the job handicapped: A comparative outcome study, *Rehabilitation Counseling Bulletin, 23*, 144-155.

Ball, J. & Havassy, B.E. (1984). A survey of the problems and needs of homeless consumers of acute psychiatric services. *Hospital and Community Psychiatry, 35*(9), 917-921.

Baron, R. C. (Sept. 1992). *Strategies to Secure and Maintain Employment for People with Long-Term Mental Illness: Consensus Statement.* The National Institute on Disability and Rehabilitation Research, 1(3).

Baumgart, D. et al (1987). Career Focus: A curriculum manual for students with moderate or severe handicaps. *Secondary Transition and Employment Project: STEP*, Moscow, ID: Idaho University, Dept. of Special Education.

Blankertz, L. (In press). *An Assessment of Long-Term Employment Support for Persons with Mental Illness Who are Working.* Matrix Research Institute, Philadelphia, PA.

_____ (1994). *The Employment Specialist Manual.* Unpublished Manual. Philadelphia, PA: Matrix Research Institute.

Blankertz, L. & Cnaan, R. (1993). Serving the dually diagnosed homeless: Program development and interventions. *The Journal of Mental Health Administration, 20*(2) 100-112.

Bond, G.R. (1992). Vocational rehabilitation. In R.P. Liberman (Ed.). *The Handbook of Psychosocial Rehabilitation* (pp. 244-275), New York: McMillan.

Bond, G.R. & McDonel, E.C. (1991). Vocational Rehabilitation Outcomes for Persons with Psychiatric Disabilities: An Update. *Journal of Vocational Rehabilitation, 1*(3), 9-20.

Bond, G.R. & Boyer, S.L. (1988). The evaluation of vocational programs for the mentally ill: A review. In J.A. Ciardiello and M.D. Bell (Eds.) *Vocational Rehabilitation of Persons with Prolonged Mental Illness.* Johns Hopkins Press: Baltimore, MD.

Campbell, J.F. (1989). Employment programs for people with a psychiatric disability: An overview. *Community Support Network News, 6*(2), 1-11.

Chamberlin, J. (1987). Speaking for Ourselves. *City issues.* Boston, MA: Episcopal City Mission, 7(1).

Ciardiello, J.A. & Bingham, W.C. (1982). The career maturity of schizophrenic clients. *Rehabilitation Counseling Bulletin,* Sept. pp. 3-9.

Cohen, M.B. (1989). Social work practice with homeless mentally ill people: Engaging the client. *Social Work,* November, 505-508.

Combs, I.H. & Omvig, C.P. (1986). Accommodation of disabled people into employment: Perceptions of employers. *Journal of Rehabilitation, 52*(2) 42-45.

Cook, J.A, Jonikas, J., & Solomon, M. (1992). Models of Vocational Rehabilitation for Youth and Adults with Severe Mental Illness. *American Rehabilitation, 18*, 6-11.

Cook, J.A. & Razzano, L. (1992). Natural Vocational Supports for Persons with Severe Mental Illness: Thresholds Supported Competitive Employment Programs. In L. Stein, (ed.), *Innovations in Mental Health Services* (pp. 23-42). San Francisco: Jossey-Bass.

Cressey, D. E. & Mc Carthy, T.P. (1981). Training VR counselors who work with chronic mental patients. *American Journal of Psychiatry, 138,* 1102-1106.

Curran, J. & van Ryn, M. (1991). *Job search skills: An intervention on coping with job loss.* Michigan Prevention Research Center, Institute for Social Research, University of Michigan, Ann Arbor, MI.

Danley, K.S. & Mellen, V. (1987). Training and personnel issues for supported employment programs which serve persons who are severely mentally ill. *Psychosocial Rehabilitation Journal, 11*(2) 87-102.

Danley, K.S., Ridley, D.E., & Cohen, M.R. (1982). *Review of Skills Teaching Guides,* p. 81.

Drake, R.E. & Mercer-McFadden, C. (1994). Assessment of substance abuse among persons with severe mental disorders. In A.F. Lehman & L. Dixon (Eds.), *Substance Abuse Among Persons with Chronic Mental Illness.* New York: Harwood Academic Publishers.

Drake, R.E., Becker, D.R., Biesanz, J.C., Torrey, W.C., McHugo, G.J., & Wyzik, (1993). Partial hospitalization vs supported employment: I. Vocational Outcomes. *Community Mental Health.*

Ebert, T.A., Bevan, D.J. & Dennis, S.S. (1983). Effective strategies to increase employment placements for persons who are mentally disturbed. *Mental Retardation and Learning Disabilities Bulletin, 11*(2) 50-59.

Fabian, E. (1992). Supported employment and the quality of life: Does a job make a difference? *Rehabilitation Counseling Bulletin.*

Fairweather, G.W. et al (1978). *The Community Lodge Program,* MSU-NIMH Innovation Diffusion Project, Michigan State University.

Fairweather, G. W. et al (1969). *Community Live for the Mentally Ill.* Chicago: Aldine.

Farrell, D. (1991). Case management issues in a supported competitive employment setting for young adults with mental illness. In Cook, J.A. (ed.), *Issues in supported competitive employment for youth with mental illness: Theory, research, and practice.* (pp. 22-40). Chicago, IL: Thresholds, National Research and Training Center.

Frey, J.L. & Godfrey, M. (1991). A comprehensive clinical vocational assessment: The pact approach. *Journal of Applied Rehabilitation Counseling, 22,* 25-28.

Furlong, M., Jonikas, J.A., & Cook, J.A. (1994). *Job coaching and on-going job support for persons with psychiatric dis-abilities.* Chicago, IL: Thresholds National Research and Training Center.

Goodall, P. (ed.) (1987). Benefits to employers who hire workers with disabilities. *Virginia Commonwealth University RRTC Newsletter, 3*(1).

Granger, B. (1990). *Agency-sponsored entrepreneurial business employing individuals with long-term mental illness: Findings from a National Survey.* Unpublished paper. Philadelphia, PA: Matrix Research Institute.

Harding, C. M. et al (1987). The Vermont longitudinal study of persons with severe mental illness, I: Methodology, study sample, and overall current status. *American Journal of Psychiatry, 144,* 718-726.

Harp, H.T. (Sept. 21-23, 1992). *Empowerment of Mental health Consumers in Vocational Rehabilitation.* Consensus Validation Conference Resource Papers. Sponsored by The National Institute on Disability and Rehabilitation Research.

Henderson, M. & Argyle, M. (1985). Social support by four categories of work colleague: Relationships between activities, stress, and satisfaction. *Journal of Occupational Behavior, 6,* 229-239.

Hill, M.L., Wehman, P.H., Kregel, J., Banks, P.D., & Metzler, H.M. (1987). Employment outcomes for people with moderate and severe disabilities: An eight-year longitudinal analysis of supported competitive employment. *JASH 12*(3) 182-189.

Isbister & Donaldson (1987). Supported employment for individuals who are mentally ill: Program Developments. *Psychosocial Rehabilitation Journal, 9*(2) 45-55.

Jacobs, H.E. (Dec. 1984). Skills-oriented model for facilitating employment among psychiatrically disabled persons. *Rehabilitation Counseling Bulletin, 28*(2) 87-96.

Jacobson, S.G. (Nov. 1993). *Use of Work-place Supports to Promote Growth Opportunities for Employees with Mental Illness.* The Baltimore Supported Employment Project, Kennedy Krieger Community Resources. Working Paper 1.

Kaplan, S.R. (1988). The value of work for the mentally ill. In B.J. Black (ed.) *Work and Mental Illness: Transitions to Employment* (pp. 1-19). Baltimore: Paul H. Brookes.

Kirszner, M.L., Baron, R.C., & Rutman, I.D. (1992). *Employer Participation in Supported and Transitional Employment for Persons with Long-Term Mental Illness.* Final Report to The National Institute on Disability and Rehabilitation Research. Philadelphia, PA: Matrix Research Institute.

Knoedler, W. (1979). How training in community living programs helps its patients work. *New Directions in Mental Health Services, 2,* 57-66.

Kregel, J., Schafer, M.S., Wehman, P., & West, M. (1990). Policy and program development in supported employment: Current strategies to promote statewide systems change. In P. Wehman, J. Kregel, and M.S. Schafer, *Emerging trends in the national supported employment initiative: A preliminary analysis of twenty-seven states* (pp. 15-45). Richmond, VA: Rehabilitation Research and Training Center, Virginia Commonwealth University.

Kregel, J., Wehman, P., Revell, W.G., & Hill, M. (1990). Supported employment in Virginia. In F.R. Rusch (Ed.) *Supported employment: Models, methods, and issues* (pp. 15-29). Sycamore, IL: Sycamore Publishing.

Kregel, J., Wehman, P., & Banks, P.D. (1989). The effects of consumer characteristics and type of employment model on individual outcomes in supported employment. *Journal of Applied Behavior Analysis, 22,* 407-415.

Lehman, A. F. (1988). A Quality of Life Interview for the Chronically Mentally Ill. *Evaluation and Program Planning, 11,* 51-62.

MacDonald-Wilson, K.L., Mancuso, L.L., Danley, K.S., & Anthony, W.A. (1989). Supported employment for people with psychiatric disability. *Journal of Applied Rehabilitation Counseling, 20*(3) 50-57.

Mancuso, L. (Dec. 1991a). The americans with disabilities act—implications for people with psychiatric disabilities. *Community Support Network News, 8*(2), 1.

_____ (Dec. 1991b). Questions frequently asked about the ADA by workers with psychiatric disabilities. *Community Support Network News, 8*(2), 4-5,13.

_____ (1990). Reasonable accommodation for workers with psychiatric disabilities. *Psychosocial Rehabilitation Journal, 14*(2), 3-19.

McCrory, D.J. (1991). The Rehabilitation Alliance. *Journal of Vocational Rehabilitation, 1*(3) 58-66.

McGurrin, M.C. (Sept. 21-23, 1992). An Overview of the Effectiveness of Traditional Vocational Rehabilitation Services for the Seriously and Persistently Mentally Ill. *Consensus Validation Conference Resource Papers.* Sponsored by The National Institute on Disability and Rehabilitation Research.

McLoughlin, K., Garner, B., & Callahan, M. (1987). *Getting employed and staying employed.* Baltimore: Paul H. Brookes.

Modrin, M., Rapp, C. A., & Poertner, J. (1988). The evaluation of case management services with the chronically mentally ill. *Journal of Evaluation and Program Planning.*

Mueser, K.T. & Liberman, R.P. (1988). Skills training in vocational rehabilitation. In J.A Ciardiello & M.D. Bell (Eds.), *Vocational rehabilitation of persons with prolonged mental illness* (pp. 81-103). Baltimore, MD: Johns Hopkins Press.

Neff, W.S. (1988). *Work and Human Behavior.* 3rd Edition. New York: Aldine.

Nisbet, J., Rogan, P. & Hagner, D. (1989). Squeezing long-term support out of a short-term program: Independence issues and supported employment. *Journal of Applied Rehabilitation Counseling, 20*(3) 21-25.

Nisbet, J. & Hagner, D. (1988). Natural Supports in the Workplace: A reexamination of supported employment. *Journal of the Association for Persons with Severe Handicaps, 3*(4).

PORT—Patient Outcomes Research Team (1994). *Literature Review Phase 1-A Treatment Approaches for Schizophrenia.* Center for Mental Health Services Research, University of Maryland, Baltimore.

Rogers, S., Danley, K., & Anthony, W.A. (1992). *Survey of client preferences for vocational and educational services.* Unpublished manuscript. Boston, MA: Center for Psychosocial rehabilitation, Boston University.

Rogers, S., Anthony, W.A., & Danely, K.S. (1988). The impact of interagency collaboration on systems and client outcomes. *Rehabilitation Counseling Bulletin, 33*(2) 100-109.

Rosnow, M.J. & Tucker, P. (1985). *Listening to the homeless: A study of homeless mentally ill people in Milwaukee.* Madison, WI: Wisconsin Office of Mental Health.

Russert, M.G. & Frey, J.L. (April, 1991). The PACT vocational model: A step into the future. *Psychosocial Rehabilitation Journal, 14*(4) 7-18.

Rutman, I.D. (1992). Analysis of Vocational Rehabilitation Data for the Mentally Ill, First Report: Characteristics of Persons with Mental Illness Whose Cases were Closed by the *Rehabilitation Services Administration During Fiscal Years 1984-1988.* (Prepared for the Statistical Research Branch, Division of Applied and Services Research, National Institute of Mental Health) Matrix: Philadelphia, PA.

Rutman, I.D. & Armstrong, K. (1985). *A comprehensive national evaluation of transitional employment programs for the psychiatrically disabled.* Unpublished Paper, Matrix Research Institute: Philadelphia, PA.

Shepherd, G. (Jan. 1990). A criterion-oriented approach to skills training. *Psychosocial Rehabilitation Journal, 13*(3) 11-13.

Strauss, J.S. & Carpenter, W.T. (1974). The prediction of outcome in schizophrenia, II: Relationships between predictor and outcome variables. *Archives of General Psychiatry, 31*, 37-42.

Tashjian, M.D., Hayward, B.J., Stoddard, S., & Kraus, L. (1989). *Best Practice Study of Vocational Rehabilitation Services to Severely Mentally Ill Persons.* (Vol. 1: Study Findings). Policy Studies Associates, Inc.: Washington, D.C., 10-14.

Test, M.A. (1991). The training in community living model: Delivering treatment and rehabilitation services through a continuous treatment team. In R.P. Liberman (Ed.), *Handbook of Psychosocial Rehabilitation*, New York: Pergamon Press.

Toms-Barker, L. (1994). *Cultivating a career development orientation in employment programs,* Presented at the 19th Annual IAPSRS Conference, Albuquerque, NM.

_____ (1992). Community Based Models of Employment Services for Persons with Long-Term Mental Illness. NIDRR Consensus Validation

Conference: Strategies to Secure and Maintain Employment for Persons with Long-Term Mental Illness.

U.S. Congress, Office of Technology Assessment (March 1994). Psychiatric Disabilities Employment and the Americans with Disabilities Act, OTA-BP-BBS-124 (Washington, DC: U.S. Government Printing Office).

U.S. Department of Education (Sept. 13-17, 1993). *Severe Mental Illness, Program Administrative Review.* Rehabilitation Services Administration, Region III, Philadelphia, PA, Pennsylvania Office of Vocational Rehabilitation, Harrisburg, PA.

U.S. Office of Personnel Management (1984a). *Handbook of job analysis for reasonable accommodation.* Washington, D.C.

U.S. Office of Personnel Management (1984b). *Handbook of reasonable accommodations.* Washington, D.C.

Wehman, P. & Melia, R. (1991). *A National Analysis of Supported Employment Growth and Implementation.* Rehabilitation Research and Training Center on Supported Employment, Virginia Commonwealth University.

Wehman, P. & Moon, M. (1988). *Vocational Rehabilitation and Supported Employment.* Baltimore: Brookes.

Wehman, P. & Melia, R. (1985). The job coach: Function in transitional and supported employment. *American Rehabilitation, 11,* 4-7.

Wehman, P. (1981). *Competitive employment: New horizons for severely disabled individuals.* Baltimore: Paul Brookes.

Wehman, P. & Hill, J.W. (1987). Competitive Employment for Persons with Mental Retardation: From Research Practice, Vol. II. Virginia Commonwealth University, Rehabilitation Research and Training Center: Richmond, VA.

Young, J., Rosati, R., & Vandergoot, D. (1986). Initiating a marketing strategy by assessing employer needs for rehabilitation services. *Journal of Rehabilitation, 52*(2) 37-41.

Zinman, S. (1982). A patient-run residence. *Psychosocial Rehabilitation Journal, 6*(1), 3-11.

10

Residential Treatment Programs

Betty Dahlquist and Steven Fields

Introduction

Residential treatment programs provide structured and intensive services in a residential setting to individuals who would otherwise be in a 24-hour institutional setting. Residential treatment services, as they are defined for the purposes of this chapter, are not housing resources. Treatment services are offered in a residential setting, and this often creates the impression that the programs are a form of housing. The purpose of residential treatment programs within a system of mental health care is twofold:

- to provide treatment alternatives for those individuals who would otherwise be admitted to, or remain in, acute and long-term hospitals or other institutional settings, including jails, due to the severity and seriousness of their disabilities; and

- to utilize a range of residential settings to transit the mental health system from an institutional dependency to a community-based services capability.

Permanent, affordable housing with necessary support services and vocational opportunities should be the basic building blocks of a community mental health system. For those individuals who require or request more structured settings, a range of residential treatment alternatives to various levels of institutional or custodial care should be conceptualized and developed in order to assure that a system of care utilizes institutional beds only when it is absolutely necessary. No person with a mental illness should have to be treated or held in an hospital psychiatric unit, state hospital, jail cell or skilled nursing facility simply because the individual requires intensive support and there are no available levels of service between supported housing and institutional care.

An appropriate array of residential treatment resources also meets a critical need for community mental health systems which are attempting to move away from institutional dependency and toward community-based systems of care. Crisis residential programs, along with transitional and long-term residential treatment programs are themselves transitional strategies to shift the focus of treatment. Systems that repeatedly attempt to make the leap from state hospitals to permanent housing with a package of support services often find that transitional approaches are required. Over time, the success of such strategies can be measured by the number of individuals who are successfully living in housing of their choice and who rarely require more intensive settings for temporary treatment. Thus as systems attempt to break the cycle of repeated admissions to emergency rooms and hospitals, these alternative 24-hour settings change the patterns of utilization within communities.

Residential treatment programs are often misunderstood and misused resources in community-based systems of care. These settings may be used exclusively for long-term housing, serving individuals who could and should be living independently in the community. Other residential programs are expected to provide an entire range of services, from crisis intervention to long-term treatment, in one facility, creating contradictory demands on staff and program participants. Another common misconception is that a continuum of residential treatment resources represents a mandatory linear progression through which each individual must progress toward more independent living. In fact, the continuum of services described in this chapter represents an array of options, not a mandatory set of required steps. The referring person, the individual with mental illness, family members and the system *gatekeepers* must match the level of service to individual need and moves should be designed to minimize unnecessary transitions from one program to another.

Historical Perspective on the Development of Residential Alternatives to Institutions

Initially, residential treatment programs, known as *halfway houses*, were devel-

oped in the 1960s as post-hospitalization programs. Most recipients of these services were referred to the houses by staff of inpatient units, primarily state hospitals, for follow-up, additional services, and transition to community living. The persons referred were generally stabilized on high levels of medication and came to the houses with a wide range of social, mental health, health, and economic needs.

The task of the staff of residential programs was to determine the social and daily living skills necessary for each person to live more independently in the community and to work with the residents to develop a plan that addressed these needs. It was a common experience that hospitals treated the symptoms and stabilized the crisis (often taking months to achieve these goals) and then discharged individuals to the community programs without addressing the need for social and rehabilitative services.

From the beginning, the staff of residential treatment programs observed that the issues confronting individuals with mental illness were often problems that hospitalization either created or neglected to address. These were the effects of institutionalization—over-medication, dependency on the mental health system, lack of income and other social supports, and stigmatization—which had to be mitigated if the person was to live and fully participate in the community.

In the early 1970s, residential programs began to work with an increasingly acute population. The focus of programs changed from *post*-hospitalization to *diversion from* hospitalization or reduction in hospital lengths-of-stay. The basic principle of these programs was the coincident treatment and rehabilitation approach naturally fostered and supported by the normative settings. Crisis residential treatment settings began diverting people from emergency rooms, or significantly shortening the length-of-stay in hospitals. These programs achieved these results through an intensification of the practices and principles of the traditional *halfway house* service.

As residential programs began working with a more acute population, they also began expanding in another direction. The development of satellite apartments, or cooperative housing, allowed for the expansion of the residential system to provide long-term, supported settings in the community. This evolution of the initial *halfway house* model into acute or crisis settings and development of less intensive, long-term supported housing services represented an attempt to identify a full range of settings which could have a significant impact on the utilization of all levels of institutional mental health care.

The Form and Function of Residential Treatment

One of the ongoing problems in discussions regarding residential treatment is the lack of a clear definition of residential treatment, group homes, and transitional residential programs. These terms are often used interchangeably, but the differences and range of program capability represented by these terms is immense. In one state, an inadequately staffed, large group home may be called a halfway house, or even a residential treatment program. In another state, a well-staffed, rehabilitation oriented residence may be termed a group home. This lack of definitions and generally accepted standards for various levels of residential treatment creates a tendency to generalize from one type of residential service to another.

There are four basic elements to a comprehensive residential treatment systems:

- acute diversion programs (or crisis residential treatment), which provide a community-based residential alternative to acute inpatient care;

- transitional residential treatment programs, which provide a sub-acute level of care as an alternative to psychiatric skilled nursing settings, as well as a rehabilitation-oriented alternative to board and care;

- long-term residential treatment programs as an alternative to state hospital or psychiatric skilled nursing care; and

- supported housing programs, which utilize flexible staff availability to provide varying levels of support for individuals who might otherwise require a more structured program or a 24-hour staffed setting.

Residential treatment programs should be small (a maximum of 15 beds is ideal), well staffed according to the level of disability and acute need of the person served by the program, home-like and normalizing in its environment, and rehabilitation-oriented in programming. The services should be flexible with individually determined lengths-of-stay corresponding to each person's need and the program's role in the overall system of care. Treatment and rehabilitation plans must be individualized and based on the needs of each person.

Residential treatment programs, as therapeutic communities where every interaction is potentially therapeutic, are designed to provide a safe environment to learn and test behaviors which strengthen interpersonal skills and enable the pursuit of individual goals. Residential programs are also settings where individuals can learn basic living skills: cooking, cleaning, money management, etc. While this is an element of residential treatment, the teaching of living skills is only one aspect of most effective programs. Many living skills can best be learned, or strengthened, in more independent living settings.

The programmatic ability to provide intensive support and interventions on a 24-hour basis is particularly effective with persons who represent a risk of self-destructive or violent behavior. The continuous availability of staff members, as well as other persons with mental illnesses, allows residential treatment programs to work with persons who would otherwise require hospitalization. Residential treatment programs are also effective with persons who present active drug or alcohol abuse issues, along with major mental health needs. Dually diagnosed individuals require a high degree of structure and support, particularly in the early intervention stages of treatment. This intervention can often be done more effectively in a residential setting than in a hospital or other institution.

Residential treatment programs are based on a belief that the core of mental health treatment, in the best sense of the term, lies in human interaction and the development of relationships. The following discussion of program practice draws on this critical element.

Program Practice

Residential treatment practice is based on five essential principles which inform the development of all levels of service. The actual implementation of these principles will vary from community to community because of indigenous circumstances and local priorities.

Competency 1

Use the residential, normative setting as a primary treatment tool.

The house itself provides the context within which treatment and rehabilitation takes place. In this intimate, home-like setting, many of the skills which must be developed can be realistically assessed and practiced by observing how people respond to the challenges of operating a household and living communally. The setting is a social-relational environment, within which the opportunity and expectation of interaction between people at unpredictable moments provides critical information for the residents and staff regarding each individual's ability to function within a community of people.

Several authors have noted that hospital-based settings are particularly unsuited to provide this *training in living* function. Stein and Test reported "the failure of in-hospital programs focusing on the teaching of coping skills to have relevance for future community adjustment." (Stein and Test, 1978). Citing Cummings (1963), Stein and Test further note that people often recover from an acutely disorganized state no more able to deal with the requirements of a normal environment than before the acute illness.

The observation that the immediate social environment is as powerful a predictor of behavior as the characteristics of the individual is well established (Polak, 1978, Raush et. al., 1959, Sump et al., (1957). Environments which are based on positive expectations of participation and responsibility promote a sense of safety and ability.

Seeking to create an environment of enthusiasm and pragmatism with strong roots in the community, residential treatment programs employ persons with diverse backgrounds. This mix of skills and experience helps emphasize the peer/fraternal nature of relationships and fosters creative approaches to service planning and provision. An expanded discussion of staff qualities and competencies is found later in the chapter.

Individuals with mental illness—even in the most acute programs—are expected to take part in the cooperative running of the households including: shopping, cooking, cleaning, etc. In fact, it is a basic strategy of residential treatment to involve persons with mental illness in the manipulation of the environment in order to enhance and hasten stabilization from a crisis. Rather than wait until medications take effect, the residential treatment program utilizes incremental expectations of functioning as the primary crisis intervention, supplemented by medications when necessary.

Some believe that such responsibility is a burden on people, particularly those in acute distress. Experience suggests the contrary. As long as responsibility relates to capacity, for most people,

taking responsibility is reassuring. Knowing you can have a positive effect or influence on some aspect of your situation often lessens panic. People learn to recognize increasing anxiety and in addressing problems, the program becomes a symbol for an increased sense of coping.

Each person must also perceive and believe that they have a real opportunity to question and modify elements of the program to meet their needs. Participation in the process of establishing and maintaining program rules and expectations is central to the ability of residential treatment programs to promote self-determination. This participation extends to an explicit partnership in the development of service plans where program staff assist and advise the resident in developing their objectives in using the program.

Residential treatment programs must be adaptable to the changing needs of the people participating in the program. If the programs develop rigid rules and practices, they risk replicating the institutional environments that they are developed to replace. All residential programs must be able to break down structures and adapt to changing circumstances. The ability to respond to specific individual and system needs at a given time dictates that programs be small enough—human scale—and staffed adequately to meet this goal.

Competency 5

Be committed to risk-taking and avoid over-control.

In residential treatment, the primary task is to provide an environment in which a person learns to manage distress, reduce fear and build skills and confidence. This is addressed by focusing on relationships, mutual support and avoiding over-control. The absence of physical controls (e.g., seclusion rooms and restraints) creates an environment that reflects positive expectations, fosters adaptive behavior and supports accepting personal responsibility for actions.

A rehabilitation program's purpose is to foster the joys and conflicts that occur in the course of all human relations and to use those opportunities to enhance interpersonal skills. It is staff's responsibility to be thoughtfully observant as staff and residents mutually face the challenges and obstacles that life presents.

Social and vocational success requires the ability to identify and respond to changing role demands. The myriad tasks entailed in the operation of a residential household provide a wealth of opportunities to experience and practice responding to various situational demands. Programs with very short lengths-of-stay cannot fully address the alienation which results from the experience of being labeled mentally ill. One consequence is the lack of opportunity to hone one's skills of conviviality. Realistically, the development of these skills takes more than 10 days in a crisis program. However, such programs can set the cornerstones and work to eliminate the regression which occurs in institutional settings by providing an environment where adaptation and coping is valued.

Staff Qualities and Competencies

The flexible and shifting nature of the residential treatment environment requires personal qualities that are as important as technical competencies. Staff need to have a level of maturity and self-confidence that enables them to thrive on paradox and ambiguity. The best response to one situation may not be best for a similar event. The ability to be thoughtfully observant and possess a certain psychological mindedness is also important. And most importantly, they must be able to foster a spirit of growth and possibility.

Many persons find a program's most healing aspect is the spirit of hopefulness and belief in their ability to change and grow. The quality in staff which expresses this ability is sometimes referred to as *focused inspirational feedback*.

Historically, programs have hired people from the community who have an ability to get along with others. However, the work environment and increasing demands on programs no longer accommodates people who lack psychological skills. Staff must be able to notice and attach meaning to behaviors and dynamics within the group. However, persons educated and trained as mental health professionals also have a challenge. They may need to unlearn what they've been taught about how they *should* be. Higher education can foster role constriction which is inconsistent with the flattened hierarchy and the non-authoritarian, consensus decision-making processes required in a residential setting. Programs continue to struggle with the paradox of blending education, training and community experience in ways which enhance a program's ability to support self-determination, rehabilitation, and recovery.

Staff must also possess certain technical skills. These competencies have been described in some detail in Section II but they are worth noting here. Staff in residential treatment programs must be able to:

Use the residential environment and peers to enhance the acquisition or refinement of community living and interpersonal skills.

Assess a person's mental health needs, including the potential for injurious behavior to self or others.

Exhibit crisis intervention and stabilization skills including identification of precipitants to crises, focused problem solving, and use of non-pharmacological interventions.

Link, broker, and coordinate services among mental health and other community resources.

Shift in role and power and not experience such behavior as a diminution of status.

Support self-management of symptoms including knowledge of state-of-the-art medications, protocols, and side effects.

Facilitate the development of social skills that promote increased social and vocational performance.

Develop strategies to meet environmental demands including vocational and educational endeavors.

Identify and encourage the use of community resources for social and recreational activities.

Monitor and document progress-related to goals.

Maintain ethical conduct and confidentiality.

Advocate for individual with mental illness and support protection of their civil rights.

Consult and support family members.

Conduct preference and needs assessment to implement discharge plans.

System and Economic Considerations

Despite thirty years of rhetoric to the contrary, NIMH figures showed in 1980 that 70% of the funds spent on mental health were used for hospital-based care (Kiesler, 1982). And while the population of state hospitals has decreased dramatically, the development of local acute inpatient care and the burgeoning growth of skilled nursing facilities for long-term care has continued, if not increased, dependency on institutional settings in some areas of the country.

For almost thirty years research has demonstrated the positive outcomes and cost effectiveness of residential treatment as alternatives to psychiatric hospitalization (Kiesler 1982; Coursey, 1990; Hawthorne, 1994). But decisions to refer to a residential treatment program versus a hospital often have little or nothing to do with the treatment needs of the individual. This is, in part, due to the historic association of treatment for mental disorders with hospitalization and in part to reimbursement structures which prioritize hospital based care and/or treat alternatives as optional services.

However, the tide is changing. Both private and public payers express the need to contain mental health expenditures. This focus on cost containment has created the perfect opportunity for residential treatment programs which have demonstrated their impact on hospitalization rates. A recent Blue Cross study of transitional residential treatment programs reported a reduction in re-hospitalization rates from 79% to 29% (Coursey, 1990). And a study by Hawthorne, et.al. (1994) demonstrates the over-whelming effectiveness of crisis residential treatment programs showing comparable clinical outcomes to hospital-based acute care at one-third to one-fourth the cost.

If our goal is to reduce reliance on expensive and unnecessary institutional care and to provide services which support and promote recovery and successful participation in life, it is essential that a range of non-institutional alternatives be developed. Residential treatment programs are uniquely qualified to be a foundation of a comprehensive, community-based system of care.

References

Bates, T. (1978). Assembly Bill 3052, Community Residential Treatment System Act, California Legislature, Chapter in California Welfare & Institutions Code, Chapter 5, Section 5440, et.seq.

Brook, B.D. (1973). An alternative to psychiatric hospitalization for emergency patients. *Hospital and Community Psychiatry 24.*

Cournos, F. (1987).The impact of environmental factors on outcome in residential programs. *Hospital and Community Psychiatry 38*(8).

Coursey, R., Ward-Alexander L., & Katz B.(1990) Cost-effectiveness of providing insurance benefits for posthospital psychiatric halfway house stays. *American Psychologist, 45*(10).

Cummings, J. (1963). Inadequacy syndrome. *Psychiatric Quarterly, 37.*

Fields, S. (1990).The relationship between residential treatment and supported housing in a community system of services. *Psychosocial Rehabilitation Journal, 13*(4).

————. (1995). The Progress Foundation, San Francisco in *Alternatives to the Hospital for Acute Psychiatric Treatment*, Clinical Practice #32, edited by Richard Warner, MB, DPM. American Psychiatric Press, Inc.

Fields, S. & Weisman, G. K. (Fall 1995). Crisis residential treatment: An alternative to hospitalization. In Michael H. Allen (Ed.), *New directions for mental health services: The growth and specialization of emergency psychiatry.* Jossey-Bass.

Hawthorne, W.B., Cronan-Hillix, T.A., & Woodburn, L.T. (1985). The acute non-hospital: A retrospective study. *Quarterly Journal of Professional School of Psychological Studies 1*(2).

Hawthorne, W.B., Fals-Stewart, W., & Lohr, J. (1994). A treatment outcome study *of community-based residential care. Hospital and Community Psychiatry, 45*(2).

Keisler, C. (1982). Public and professional myths about mental hospitalization: An empirical reassessment of policy-related beliefs. *American Psychiatry 37.*

———. (1982). Mental hospitals and alternative care: Non-institutionalization as potential public policy for mental patients. *American Psychiatry 37*(4).

Lamb, H.R. (1979). Changing concepts in acute twenty-four-hour care, in Lamb, H.R. (Ed) *New Directions for Mental Health Services: Alternatives to Acute Hospitalization.* San Francisco, CA: Jossey-Bass.

Lamb, H.R. & Lamb, D. (1984). A non-hospital alternative to hospitalization. *Hospital and Community Psychiatry 35.*

Minkoff, K. (1987). Beyond deinstitutionalization: A new ideology for the postinstitutional era. *Hospital and Community Psychiatry 38*(9).

Mosher L.R. (1983). Alternatives to psychiatric hospitalization: Why has research failed to be translated into practice? *New England Journal of Medicine,* 309(25).

Mosher, L.R. & Menn, A.Z. (1978). Community residential treatment for schizophrenia:Two-year follow-up. *Hospital and Community Psychiatry 29*(11).

Mosher, L.R., Menn, A.Z., & Matthews, S.M. (1975). Soteria: Evaluation of a home-based treatment for schizophrenia. *American Journal of Orthopsychiatry 45*(3).

Pepper, B. (1987). A public policy for the long-term mentally ill: A positive alternative to reinstitutionalization. *American Journal of Orthopsychiatry 57*(3).

Rausch, H.L. & Rausch, C.L. (1968). *The Halfway House: A Search for Sanity.* New York: Appleton, Century, Crofts.

Rissmeyer, D. (1985). Crisis intervention alternatives to hospitalization: Why so few? *Psychosocial Rehabilitation Journal, 9*(2).

Stein, L.I. & Test, M.A. (Eds.). (1978). *Alternatives to Mental Hospital Treatment.* New York: Plenum Press.

Stein, L.I., Test, M.A., & Marx, A.J. (1975). Alternative to the hospital: A controlled study. *American Journal of Psychiatry 132*(5).

Stroul B. (1986). *Crisis Residential Services: Review of Information.* Prepared for National Institute of Mental Health, Community Support Program.

Weisman, G.K. (1985). Crisis-oriented residential treatment as an alternative to hospitalization. *Hospital Community Psychiatry 36*(12).

Housing

Diane Weinstein

Introduction

Shelter is a fundamental need for all people to achieve a healthy and satisfying life. Psychosocial rehabilitation provides people with a severe mental illness the skills and supports they need to successfully live in the community. Without active rehabilitation, the emotional and behavioral problems associated with a psychiatric disability may interfere with the ability of many people to select and secure an appropriate community living situation (Carling, Randolph, Blanch & Ridgway, 1988).

When deinstitutionalization began, community mental health providers initially believed that community tenure was more likely to be achieved if individuals with mental illness were housed in a series of "progressively less controlled housing environments" until they graduated to normative commercially available housing. However, neither a linear housing continuum, participation in any one residential program model, or singular reliance on supervised housing or a supportive housing paradigm guarantees successful community tenure or satisfaction with housing (Scallet, 1994). There is a need for a broad spectrum of housing options that provide people with

meaningful choices and allow individuals with mental illness access to decent, stable, affordable and safe housing in settings that maximize inclusion and the ability to function independently (IAPSRS, 1992).

Some programs operate or manage one or more residential settings. They may be agency-owned or operated under a special agreement with public authorities or private entitities. Individuals with mental illness may live in supervised housing programs with a therapeutic mission, or congregate living arrangements with minimum agency supervision, no supervision or flexible supports. Housing programs may provide transitional housing, permanent housing, subsidized housing units or assist individuals in the location of commercially available housing that is scattered throughout the community and intentionally separate from the provision of mental health and rehabilitation services (Cook & Hoffschmidt, 1993)

This chapter presents an overview of community housing options and workforce competencies that direct practitioners need to assist people in the selection and retention of housing in the community.

Historical Review of Housing Options

The responsibility for providing services and housing to individuals with a serious mental illness, prior to the deinstitutionalization movement, rested with families and state psychiatric hospitals. As hospitals slowly downsized and some began closing in the 1960–70s, this responsibility gradually shifted to local community mental health authorities and service providers. In the early days of deinstitutionalization, approximately two-thirds of the discharged population returned to their families (Carling, Randolph, Blanch & Ridgway, 1988). Community mental health systems were slow to respond to the housing needs of former hospital patients and often people were discharged from state institutions into nursing homes, for-profit board and care homes, and foster care homes that provided transitional support—residential settings that continued to provide custodial care (Randolph, Ridgway & Carling, 1991; Ridgway & Zipple, 1990). In order to transit people from institutional settings to the communities, a system of transitional housing that included quarter houses on the grounds of psychiatric hospitals, halfway houses in the community, and three quarterway houses was developed in the 1960s. This residential continuum used the congregate living environment as a therapeutic milieu before discharge to permanent housing (Carling, Randolph, Blanch & Ridgway, 1988).

After the National Institute of Mental Health introduced the Community Support System concept in 1974, communities began to develop a wider range of housing options such as agency-supervised group homes and supervised apartments, as well as supportive housing services to individuals with mental illness living in local housing stock. (As discussed in an earlier chapter, residential treatment programs providing acute crisis care services and transitional and long-term treatment to avert utilization of inpatient unit were also developed as part of a comprehensive community support program.) In the 1970s and early 80s, it was believed that discharging patients from a hospital setting to a community residential environment with a high degree of structure and support, and then gradually relocating people to a less structured transitional setting was the optimal approach to increase a person's level of functioning until they were ready to make the final transition to permanent integrated housing. However, by the end of the 1980s, the continuum of residential services was being replaced with more individualized and flexible approaches to housing. Supervised and supportive housing services were increasingly being expanded. Strategies today help people live in housing that offers them the degree of support necessary to remain stable, retain community tenure, and work towards recovery, while receiving encouragement and incentives to assume increasing responsibility and control over their lives (Stroul, 1986).

Descriptions of Prevalent Housing Options

The results of a 1986–87 nationwide survey of residential programs for persons with a severe mental illness identified group homes and supervised apartments as the most prevalent living arrangements, followed by board and care homes and supportive housing arrangements (Randolph, Ridgway, & Carling, 1991). Survey responses from the approximately 1,500 agencies serving about 16,000 individuals in 2,556 programs indicated that more than half of the agencies (64%) offered only one type of residential programming, 17% offered two options, 11% offered three, and less than 9% offered a wider array of housing program options. Fifty percent of the programs had no length of stay restrictions, 20% allowed people to stay more than two years, 11% allowed one to two years, 11% allowed three months to one year, and 8.6% limited the length of stay to less than three months. Scattered site apartment units were available in 24% of the programs.

The following paragraphs describe housing options that are most likely to be available in a community; they are not arranged according to prevalence.

Board and care homes are typically private for-profit residences or facilities that do not have limitations on length of stay and house between three to 25 persons. Facility licensure requirements, occupancy standards, operator and staff credentials, staff training, supervision requirements and the number of hours that each person can remain in the homes during the day vary according to state and local regulations. While some board and care homes provide skills training to improve a person's level of functioning, most are custodial in nature and do not assess or enable the ability of the individual with mental illness to live independently. Proprietary board and care operators are less willing to serve individuals with complex needs or dual diagnoses, preferring people who consistently attend programs during the day or are elderly and have few disruptive symptoms. Mental health systems are reducing their reliance on homes, while increasing their use of other housing options and supports services that enhance functioning and autonomy.

Group homes or community residences have been developed by agencies to assist individuals who need instruction, cueing, or support to carry out essential household tasks. They are designed to replicate family-like settings, and occupancy is usually limited from four to eight persons. These community residences provide transitional or permanent housing, and the intensity of programming and frequency of supervision varies from 24-hour paid live-in staff, daily or weekly visits, and/or flexible supports. Most agency operated group homes are expected to comply with regulations imposed by local mental health authorities and other regulatory bodies which, at a minimum, impose occupancy and supervision standards. Expectations for participation in group home activities or compliance with rules such as attending a program during week day hours, performance of chores etc., vary according to program rules and those agreed upon by the majority of people living in the home.

Some group homes describe themselves as therapeutic communities where persons enter the programs with a volitional desire to improve functioning and acquire individually determined skills (Gardner). The milieu provides each person with the opportunity for social interaction and group activities that are intentionally structured to improve independent living skills and modify dysfunctional behaviors. The therapeutic community is designed to be a democratic social organization that empowers individuals with mental illness to develop and maintain group norms to promote attainment of individual goals (Ellsworth).

The Fairweather Lodge is another group home model that is noted for its emphasis on pursuing employment goals, which are often entrepreneurial ventures developed by the lodge. Peer support, group cohesion, and inclusion in community social and recreational activities, as well as independent living skills are acquired and reinforced in group homes. While some agencies have experienced opposition to group homes, estimated at as many as 50% of the sites initially chosen, the Fair Housing Act Amendments of 1988 have been effective in eliminating restrictive zoning practices, building code obstacles, and other illegal discriminatory actions (Zipple & Anzer, 1994).

Living with family is a common and preferred housing option for many individuals with mental illness. A 1992 survey of members of the National Alliance for the Mentally Ill found that 24% of the respondents had a family member with a serious mental illness living with them, an additional 2% stated a family member was living with another relative (NAMI, 1992). It is estimated that nearly one-third of the adults discharged from psychiatric units return to their family homes (Carling, Randolph, Blanch & Ridgway, 1988). Parents compose the majority of family members providing housing, but spouses, siblings, children, grandparents and other relatives also provide shelter and familial support. As in other residential settings, the expected length of stay with the family may be short- or long-term, and the nature and frequency of services should be negotiated according to individual and family circumstances. Living with the family should not be a forced decision because a direct service worker has not pursued alternative housing options. It is a decision that should represent a free choice for all of the relevant parties (Posey, 1990).

Supervised apartments can be in buildings where all units are leased to individuals with a disability, sections of a building are limited to a disability population, or scattered site apartment units throughout the community. In supervised housing programs, the locus of control and responsibility for a supervision structure rests primarily with an agency or mental health authority. Apartment units or entire buildings may be agency-owned or managed, or the agency may hold the lease for apartment units. The length of stay may be transitional or permanent and the degree of integration among a nondisabled population varies. While one mental health authority or program's supervised apartment program may consist entirely of a building with single room occupancy units only leased to persons with a serious mental illness, another program may have supervised apartment units in integrated buildings with efficiencies, singles, doubles, detached houses, etc. Some programs restrict eligibility to individuals who demonstrate particular independent living skill, although invivo skills training and ongoing supports are central tenets of most supervised apartment programs. Some programs reserve an apartment unit for a live-in residential manager, crisis residential beds, or for use during the day by administrative staff or direct service workers.

Supported housing shifts the locus of control in the delivery of residential support services from the agency worker to the individual with mental illness. The supportive housing paradigm emphasizes the location of permanent housing that has physical as well as social integration, that is safe and affordable for persons with the most severe mental disabilities, and reflects personal lifestyle preferences, values, and interests: "the daily rhythms of a person" (Ridgway and Zipple, 1990; Brown & Wheeler, 1990). A central tenet of supported housing is that individuals with mental illness can access housing that is commercially available through the provision of flexible and individualized support from the mental health system. There is also an emphasis on the utilization of normal social networks to minimize reliance solely on specialized supports from the mental health system (Carling, 1993). As individual needs and functioning change, the direct service worker with the individual continually renegotiate the kinds of interventions and intensity of supports necessary and agreed upon to maintain permanency in one's home. This strategy is different from a system that utilizes a linear residential continuum that relocates the person when level of functioning, behaviors and skill, or symptomatology change (Ridgway & Zipple, 1992).

IAPSRS Position on Housing

The International Association of Psychosocial Rehabilitation Services (1992) has developed a housing position statement that provides guidance to policy planners, psychosocial rehabilitation agencies, and practitioners. IAPSRS believes agencies should be proactive and take a leadership role in securing housing for the individuals that they serve. The following premises combine the central tenets from the Canadian IAPSRS perspective on housing, as well as those from the U.S. membership.

Competencies for Direct Service Staff to Establish and Retain Housing

Competency 1

Collaborate with the individual needing housing to learn personal housing choices and the supports needed.

The right to choose where one lives is an indicator of personal freedom, and one that is highly valued by individuals with mental illness (Bachrach, 1994). Listening to individual choices and preferences are the most important factors that direct practitioners must consider in discussions about housing. In the past, agencies and practitioners discussed housing in terms of "residential placements" and decisions were often based upon the next available slot in an agency operated program or one available in a board and care home (Ridgway & Zipple, 1990; Posey, 1990). Today, there has been a conceptual shift which emphasizes practitioners listening to individuals and collaborating with them to understand their housing preferences and the personal factors that are necessary to turn a housing unit into one's home. Meaningful choices only exist when there are several options to consider (IAPSRS, 1992). Advice from individuals about the importance of choice include the following:

- Practitioners must learn simply to ask people where they want to live and listen to the answers.

- Practitioners must step back from an overprotective and controlling role that attempts to prevent failures.

- Control is an obstacle to treating people as equals and according individuals with mental illness the same dignity and rights that other individuals in the community have.

- Without the risk of failure, a person is not truly empowered and is denied an opportunity for success.

- Without true choices, the mental health system is agency centered rather than a system that is consumer centered (Finkle, Van Tosh, Chamberlin, Posey, Crafts & Howie the Harp, 1990).

Excerpts from the IAPSRS Position Statement on Housing

IAPSRS strongly believes all people with severe and persistent mental illness should be given the option to live in decent, stable, affordable and safe housing in settings that maximize their integration into community activities and their ability to function independently.

Array of Services: Over the last several decades, group homes, apartment programs, and supported living programs have provided the housing resources and support services for many thousands of persons with mental illness. These programs have proven to be not only effective but also desirable to many individuals with mental illness; thus, they are an integral part of the service system. There must be a broad spectrum of options for individuals with mental illness both in the area of their housing as well as the supports associated with that housing. Housing options as well as supported services should be tailored to the needs of the individuals with mental illness and be provided in an individualized manner.

Choice: Individuals with mental illness should be given meaningful choices in terms of where they would like to live. True choice is contingent upon an array of housing options and services. Agencies and practitioners have a responsibility to increase options by advocating for more housing resources, by developing a wide array of housing, and by reviewing preferences with the person in need of housing.

Quality Programming: High quality residential and support services must be the objective of agencies and practitioners. To ensure that these services are of high quality and also effective, it is essential that specific outcomes be identified for these programs. Examples of such outcomes might be: reduced need for hospitalization, obtainment of housing that reflects choice, improved quality of life, and increased levels of self sufficiency—outcomes that are consistent with the values of psychosocial rehabilitation.

Non Discrimination: Individuals with mental illness are denied the opportunity to fully participate in their communities of choice when landlords, property owners and government officials have instituted discriminatory practices. Agencies and practitioners are encouraged to confront them and use laws such as the Fair Housing Act, the Americans with Disabilities Act, (and the Rehabilitation Act) to protect individuals with mental illness from illegal practices. Agencies and practitioners should work with local housing authorities to assure the availability of public housing in accordance with Federal guidelines.

Financing Housing Options: Local, state, provincial and federal authorities have a responsibility to provide sufficient funding for rental subsidies, capital costs, and operating costs of a vastly increased network of housing programs. Without this commitment by governmental funders, adequate housing will never be available. At the same time, the development of housing is part of the "business" of psychosocial rehabilitation agencies. Practitioners and individuals with mental illness can be strong advocates urging public officials to address unmet housing needs. Agencies can participate in a variety of strategies that include forming partnerships with other interested developers or funders.

IAPSRS. (1992). Importance of Housing in the Rehabilitation and Ongoing Support of People with Severe and Persistent Mental Illness. *International Association of Psychosocial Rehabilitation Services:* Columbia, MD.

Learn to assess the personal, social, and cultural factors that impact housing decisions.

Although many individuals with mental illness come into the mental health system as single adults, they are people who have had previous familial roles. As they regain mental health, confidence and control in their lives, they may want to resume parenting roles and intimate relationships or develop these normative and valued adult roles (Nicholson & Blanch, 1994; Jonikas & Zeitz). It is important that direct service workers ascertain personal, social and cultural information that will impact housing decisions and quality of life. Wanting a two bedroom apartment for a child to visit or stay permanently if custody is restored, a private bedroom where one can engage in conjugate relations, a quiet housing complex where there are no children, yard space for gardening, living near a Greek Orthodox church or in the Latino section of town where family members reside, etc., are preferences that turn generic housing into homes and help people establish and retain valued relationships that support housing permanency. A history of homelessness, sexual abuse, substance abuse or other traumatizing experiences are also relevant factors that practitioners need to understand when helping individuals with mental illness determine the style of housing, its location, and the degree of structure and supports that will personally engender safety, control and privacy (Harris, 1994).

While individuals may describe the attributes of a neighborhood that will meet their needs during an assessment process, they are less valid reporters of inadequate housing and neighborhood conditions after they have moved into housing (Newman, 1995). Realistically, no housing unit or neighborhood will be perfect. Accompanying a person on an invivo housing site review before the lease is signed or verbally reviewing the presence of desired characteristics, flagrant violations, or deviations from earlier discussed markers are ways to further assist a person in the clarification of what housing compromises are acceptable and those personal, social, cultural and physical attributes that are not.

Competency 3

Locate affordable and safe housing with public and private providers. Develop linkages with community resources regarding the availability of rental units, fair market values, rental subsidies, home ownership programs, and tenant, landlord, and homeowner responsibilities.

Most individuals with a psychiatric disability relying on income from SSDI or SSI, are unable to afford safe and decent housing without rental assistance. More than 65% of a monthly SSI payment is required to afford an efficiency apartment and more than 80% to rent a one bedroom apartment, according to a nationwide study comparing SSI payments with HUD fair market rents (McCabe et al., 1991). Individuals with monthly SSI benefits less than $500 are facing serious financial hardships to afford any housing. In 1990, only one rental unit, which cost $250 including utilities, existed for every two households needing a unit in that economic range (Kennedy & Manderscheid, 1992).

The Federal government in the past 25 years has drastically cut back its financial commitment to housing. Housings appropriations were 7% of the Federal budget in 1978, and dropped to 0.7% in 1988, diminishing the capacity for local communities to build new low income housing or maintain funds for residential staff, service coordinators and security guards in currently existing public housing stock (Townsend, 1994). The Department of Housing and Urban Development (HUD) identified 5.1 million very low income renters in 1992, who either pay more than half their incomes for housing or live in seriously substandard housing or both. In 1992, the Congress was only asked by the President to consider funding new Section 8 rental subsidy vouchers for approximately 81,000 people. Even if all of those requested new vouchers became available and went to the 500,000 estimated homeless persons (one-third of whom have a serious mental illness), it would take seven years to meet the housing needs of the homeless, leaving unaddressed the 800,000 low income households already on housing subsidy waiting lists. (NLCHP, 1992).

These are daunting obstacles for PSR practitioners assisting individuals with mental illness in the location of affordable and safe housing. However, with the support of their agencies and local mental health authorities, practitioners can develop collaborative relationships with public housing authorities, other government entitities, private housing providers, local industry, foundations, banks, etc., who are willing to redress these barriers. Cooperative agreements that assure the availability of staff to provide supportive services to individuals with psychiatric disabilities in public housing or other government subsidized housing have been developed by agencies and mental health authorities.These agree-

ments can increase the availability of public housing units and rental assistance subsidies that can be used in private housing (CMHS, 1993).

Rental assistance project-based certificates subsidize the cost of living in public housing projects or privately owned projects for the elderly and persons with disabilities. Tenant-based certificates or vouchers that are portable can be used to access privately owned housing at scattered sites throughout a community. Both are available through public housing authorities (McCabe & Tanzman, 1993). Rental assistance certificates allow a person to contribute no more than 30% of their income for rent, with the government entity making payment for the balance due, but not to exceed the *fair market* rental value of the unit. A person with a tenant-based voucher is given a set amount of money that the government entity will contribute towards rental costs. While vouchers allow for more freedom in the location of housing, the percentage of income that the individual pays will depend upon the rent of the unit they select. There are other government and private programs that provide assistance for low income persons who want to purchase cooperative apartments or become homeowners and special programs that provide agencies funds to construct supportive housing for people with disabilities (Section 811 housing). These disability specific projects have attached project-based subsidies available for tenants; however, the supportive services that must be available for individuals with mental illness must come from other funding streams.

Outright discrimination by public and private housing providers towards persons with psychiatric disabilities continues to impede access to affordable and decent housing (Alisky & Iczkowski).

Practitioners need to educate public and private housing providers about the housing needs of people with psychiatric disabilities, reasonable accommodations, and illegal discriminatory practices. Facilitating compliance with tenant obligations (i.e., paying the rent and utilities on time, maintaining a unit's cleanliness inside and outside, and familiarizing the tenants with behaviors and informal norms that are congruent with the other tenants and the neighborhood) have the effect of breaking down previous stereotypes and myths about persons with psychiatric disabilities. As housing providers see individuals with mental illness become good tenants, information about the availability of additional affordable and decent housing units throughout the community often follows.

Competency 4

Coordinate, link, and broker access to supports and services to make housing livable and stable.

Having the capacity to meet regular monthly housing and utility payments is critical. Determining how a person will finance housing, utility deposits, emergency repairs, the costs of appliances such as fans or air conditioning units, furniture that makes the environment livable, and other household items (e.g., curtains) that achieve the appropriate level of privacy and safety are important tasks. While some agencies maintain special housing funds for these kinds of one-time expenses, practitioners may need to investigate other private and public sources. Establishing relationships with other organizations with congruent missions (e.g., local mutual self-help groups, the Alliance for the Mentally Ill, the Mental Health Association, and other mental health and rehabilitation agencies) may generate information about special funds available for loans or direct purchases for needed services or goods. Local social service agencies, charitable organizations, religious organizations, second hand shops, businesses, foundations and individuals with philanthropic missions that assist low income or disability populations are other potential resources. Individuals with mental illness receiving SSI are often eligible for Medicaid, food stamps, meals on wheels, utility assistance and house weather proofing programs which can reduce monthly expenses and increase the ability to meet unexpected housing costs or make discretionary purchases on other items that improve one's quality of life.

Practitioners need to collaborate with tenants to determine the level of support needed to utilize existing resources, services and supports in the community at large. When the individual is not independently going to access these supports and the practitioner is not identified as the appropriate or preferred agent for support, then the practitioner needs to coordinate, link, or assist in brokering the acquisition of supports. Linking a person to natural supports is an important practitioner function to sustain housing (e.g., a group of peers interested in developing reciprocal supportive activities, outreach workers at a neighborhood social center, assistance from compeers or a friendly visitor program, or volunteer services by members of the person's place of worship). While it may initially take more time to link and coordinate the delivery of services and supports rather than the practitioner directly providing them, in the long run diminishing a person's sole reliance on one practitioner or agency will provide that person with the skills to truly become integrated and included in the fabric of their community.

Practitioners in all settings help individuals with mental illness develop strategies to meet environmental demands, instrumental activities of daily living, and age-appropriate normative functions. Instrumental activities of daily living may include maintaining personal hygiene; grooming; budget management; cooking; shopping; laundry; paying bills; personal scheduling; using public transportation, postal and telephone systems, etc. Interventions are always tailored to the individual. For example, while one person needs hands-on assistance to operate a washing machine, another tenant may only need a verbal prompt by telephone that two weeks have elapsed since the last laundering. There is also an emphasis on developing supportive interactive relationships to model, cue, prompt or assist others in the performance of household tasks or recreational activities. While the practitioner may be called upon to provide invivo training or supports in semi-independent or autonomous settings, supervised apartments and supported housing arrangements, there is an increased emphasis on developing alternative supports and, in particular, facilitating a reliance on generic resources in the community. Each person is challenged to develop a greater internal recognition of the skills training

and supports that are necessary to create a satisfactory and personalized home environment, to determine who the preferred source of skills training and supports are, and how to access members of the support system when they are needed. Intervention strategies in any setting should reflect the environment's capacity to allow for the maximum amount of personal lifestyle choices that respect the privacy and rights of other roommates, tenants, or neighbors.

Practitioners responsible for the provision of services in supervised or supportive housing environments not only develop strategies related to the physical maintenance of the housing environment but also help individuals engage in the full spectrum of normative adult tasks that make life meaningful: the pursuit of work, school, social and recreational activities, and attention to spiritual identity. Interventions may include referral, linkage, coordination or the direct provision of skills training and supports that advance these goals. Prompting someone to buy an alarm clock to get to school on time, taking someone to a clothing store to buy a tie for work, reviewing bus routes that go to the prevocational program, making bus tokens available for transportation to a synagogue or church, finding the newspaper section that lists places to go on a date, or meeting someone after a job interview to reduce anxiety and stress are examples of interventions that practitioners could perform in either supervised or supported housing arrangements.

Group homes or therapeutic communities are congregate housing environments that are purposefully designed to improve a person's functioning as individuals interact with peers. Practitioners, whether living on site or being intermittently available, have the role of *change agent* or *social ecologists* in the group residential setting where people have come together because of a common identity or purpose (Jones). In any environment where people come together in groups, the communicating, interacting, group decision making, and social learning that takes place creates dynamics for individual change and growth. It is a skill to participate effectively in group situations. The direct practitioner needs to help individuals in congregate living settings modify those behaviors that are impediments to effective interactions with other persons as they work together on democratic goals and increase their capacity to solve common problems (Pernell-Arnold & Finley, 1992). Groups either have a task structure or a process structure. Practitioners need to know how and when to engage a person in a group activity, to alter the groups to include greater participation, and to respect the individual who does not want to participate in group activities. Group works incorporate knowledge about personality development, the stages of group development and knowledge about group dynamics (Pernell-Arnold & Finley, 1992; Yalom, 1970).

Some residential settings have an established routine when everyone comes together; other homes are more informal. Tenants determine the timing of meetings and their agenda. Typical discussions include the performance of household tasks, the development of social and recreational activities, and any problems and personal interactions. When practitioners feel that individuals are too dependent on them for the performance of basic home activities, they need to examine whether or not they have acted as residential *care takers* rather than facilitators of change (Gardner).

Yalom (1970) suggests eleven curative factors in the ways that groups are instruments of change.

- Group experiences instill hope: seeing other individuals improve inspires people to make positive changes in their lives.

- Understanding that there is a universality in the problems that people experience helps group members feel more in touch with the world and diminishes their feelings of social isolation.

- A skilled group leader can impart helpful information through didactic instruction, such as psychoeducation about mental illness.

- Altruism is a part of the healing process—everyone in the group setting has something of value to give to others.

- Group settings provide an environment to change old patterns that aren't working.

- Group settings are places to develop and practice basic social skills.

- Group settings are places to try out or imitate behaviors of others, keeping those that work, and discarding those that do not.

- Group settings are places where people can learn to recognize their dysfunctional behaviors and develop ways to have gratifying interpersonal relationships.

- Group cohesion facilitates self-disclosure, risk-taking, and the constructive expression of conflicts, all of which are ingredients that promote healthy behavioral changes.

- Group settings are places where people can openly experience and express strong feelings or *catharsis*.

- Group settings allow people to explore and recognize *existential factors*—that life is unfair and unjust at times; one cannot escape from some of life's pain or from death; no matter how close a person gets to others, one still has to face life alone; living one's life more honestly allows one to be less caught up in trivialities; and no matter how much guidance and support a person gets from other people, each person must ultimately take responsibility for the way they live.

Choice continues to be the critical factor that practitioners must consider when recommending a transitional or permanent congregate housing arrangement. While many people enjoy congregate living and feel there are many benefits to gain living among peers, others do not. Residential communities have much to offer those who become increasingly anxious, symptomatic or isolated, when living alone or in less structured environments. A congregate setting may benefit those who need support for a co-occurring disorder such as substance abuse or HIV.

Competency 7

Facilitate problem solving and development of supportive relationships with roommates, other tenants or neighbors.

Living in a low rent and troubled neighborhood that is not near one's support system, or needing to share housing costs with a roommate when one's preference is to live alone, are some of the difficult decisions that individuals with mental illness often face (Goldman, Rachuba, & Van Tosh, 1994). The financial constraints of a fixed disability income, such as SSI, affects housing decisions. In a review of 26 studies on individual preferences in the areas of housing and support, the most frequently cited material supports that are needed include income, housing subsidies, transportation, money for housing deposits, and a telephone (Tanzman, 1993). Problem solving does not mean that all of these material supports can be accessed. Direct service workers can help individuals prioritize their preferences and needs, search out all alternatives, and reflect upon the kinds of housing and support services trade-offs that they will need to make. Richman (1992) suggests strategies to respond to the "challenges of crime, drugs, and affordability" of housing in urban areas such as: checking with police departments to avoid neighborhoods with high crime statistics and joining local community efforts like block associations to fight drugs, crime and other destructive elements in a community.

While there can be many conflicts and tensions to resolve related to roommates who are not truly desired, there are also stressors and problems that arise when intentionally sharing one's living quarters with friends, romantic partners, and family members. Relationship building and problem solving with housemates, other tenants in a building, and businesses in the neighborhood, etc. are important practitioner tasks which rely upon listening, communication, and other counseling skills. Living alone does not preclude the necessity to develop supportive relationships with others in the community. When there are problems, it is important to not assume that negative or positive symptoms of a severe mental illness are the reasons for relationship friction. Being shy, a poor communicator, verbally overbearing, insensitive to the needs of others, awkward in a romantic relationship, etc. are not pathological traits, but common impediments to relationships and characteristics shared by many people not diagnosed with a mental illness.

Gambrill (1983) identifies the following elements to be included in a framework for competency-based approaches for social work practitioners to address problems:

- Practitioners must clearly describe assessment and intervention procedures.

- The outcomes pursued must be important to the person and his significant others.

- The consideration of relevant ethical issues and legal constraints must be examined.

- Direct service workers must consider the situational and environmental context as well as any individual characteristic, paying attention to ethnicity, cultural, gender, and age factors.

- Conclusions about factors that influence the behaviors of an individual with mental illness should come from a systematic exploration of events that are presently occurring in the physical and emotional environment.

- Practitioners enable individuals to use already existing competencies and environmental resources.

- There is an educational aim of the intervention with an emphasis upon helping the individual with mental illness learn cognitive and behavioral skills that will not only address the current situation but create a nurturing environment in the future.

- Naturally occurring life-transitions, maturational changes, and crises are viewed as opportunities for individuals with mental illness to achieve desired outcomes.

These competencies embody the principles of psychosocial rehabilitation and promote person-centered practice.

Competency 8

Have general knowledge about all classifications of psychotropic medications. Know medication and treatment protocols for persons in the program.

Psychopharmacological treatments are an integral component in the treatment of serious mental illnesses. There are many benefits associated with the use of psychotropic medications but there are also risks that are generated from their usage. Their effectiveness can range from substantial relief from symptoms, partial relief, intermittent relief, non responsiveness to medications, or hypersensitivity to medication side effects which can outweigh benefits. The acceptance or rejection of medication are matters of individual choice (IAPSRS, 1995). Practitioners help people make informed choices about medications and other intervention strategies, but ultimately must respect the self-determination of each person. The importance of medications and the practitioner skills related to medications have been outlined in previous chapters.

Competency 9

Respond to psychiatric, medical and nonmedical emergency situations.

It is important that every individual with a mental illness has available a 24 hour emergency response system. Crisis services are one of the essential components of a comprehensive community support system and must be coordinated and linked with the full array of ongoing services and supports (Stroul, 1987). Practitioners providing direct services comprise one facet of a comprehensive emergency response system that is integrated with a person's needs and preferences, an agency's structure, the regional mental health system, and the broader community emergency response system. In some agencies, direct service workers rotate 24-hour on-call responsibilities, while other agencies require practitioners to always be available to the individuals they serve. Agencies typically establish protocols for crisis intervention services that provide guidelines to handle various kinds of emergencies such as: laboratory reports showing irregularities, medication overdoses, roommates reporting unexplained absences, interactions with the police, etc.

Competency 10

Employ advocacy skills to develop, retain, or access housing.

Housing discrimination by public and private housing providers directed toward people with a psychiatric disability continues to be a problem in many communities and impedes access to safe and affordable housing (Alisky & Iczkowski, 1990). Fear of personal harm or concern that property values will plummet when someone with a mental illness moves into a neighborhood precipitates the not-in-my-backyard attitude (Beggs, 1993). Advocacy work by practitioners entails an educational process to help communities and providers of public and private housing learn how to discern facts about mental illness from the fictional picture that is generated by the media. Some programs have found that preliminary educational work with community groups before locating individuals with mental illness in generic housing or congregate housing sites can facilitate community acceptance.

The South Carolina Department of Mental Health (1992) found that the current body of research demonstrates that group homes simply "make good neighbors." They looked at over 20 studies on the impact of group homes in a neighborhood that determined these residences were "nearly always the best maintained properties on the street," their existence did not lower property values, and group homes were not associated with noise, traffic, or parking problems. Two of the studies suggested that more than 50% of the residents within one block of a group home did not know it existed. Practitioners can also engage in constructive neighborhood improvement activities such as clean-up-the-litter campaigns, helping schools paint playground equipment, planting shrubs at the senior center, etc. Educational and hands-on proactive measures can diminish irrational prejudices while simultaneously increasing opportunities for integration and community inclusion.

People with a mental or physical disability are not required to seek neighborhood approval in order to secure or retain community housing. The Fair Housing Act, Section 504 of the Rehabilitation Act, and the Americans with Disabilities Act are federal statutes that prohibit discrimination in a variety of contexts. The Fair Housing Act of 1988 amends the Civil Rights Act of 1968. It prohibits any actions that obstruct, discourage or deny housing to people because they have a mental or physical handicap (NMHA, 1989; MHLP, 1991; The Housing Center, 1994). These protections do not extend to people who are illegally using drugs. Discrimination through zoning laws, safety regulations, land prohibitions, restrictive covenants, and health laws are prohibited. The Fair Housing Act requires housing providers to make "reasonable accommodations" in their rules, policies, practices, or services that would enable a person with a disability equal opportunity to use and enjoy the residence or the facility's common space. Examples of reasonable accommodations for persons with psychiatric disabilities may include substituting a reference requirement from the most recent employer to a representative from a human service agency because the applicant does not have a current work history, sending a monthly written reminder notice when rent is due, or having the housing manager give a verbal reminder to the tenant to compensate for memory deficits. There are some notable exceptions where these federal statutes do not preclude disparate treatment for individuals with disabilities: public housing authorities can designate sections of a public housing project for tenants with disabilities only and restrict other housing units as elderly only (O'Hara, 1995). Private housing providers using federal funds can also restrict units to only elderly tenants. These exclusions do not apply to elderly tenants with psychiatric disabilities.

PSR practitioners and individuals with mental illness have a vital advocacy role to increase the stock and access to safe and affordable housing. These efforts include informing local bureaucrats of the unmet housing needs for people with psychiatric disabilities in their communities, many of whom are homeless. Advocacy can take many forms and is particularly appropriate in the planning and program design of housing, services implementation, evaluation and policy development (Van Tosh, 1994).

Housing advocacy interventions extend to accessing a range of supports that are available from public and private entities such as food stamps, disability or retirement income, transportation subsidies, meals-on-wheels, visiting health care workers, etc. There are often obstacles or "hoops to jump through" to obtain these supports that can appear insurmountable to the individual. Practitioner advocacy can entail joint problem solving with the individual and an agency, mediating disputes, requesting appeals to review or overturn ineligibility decisions, or mobilizing family or other members in the natural support network to engage in advocacy activities. While advocacy interventions can be time consuming, they are strategies that empower people, their support system, and direct practitioners to be active agents of positive change in an individual's personal life and in the community.

References

Alisky, J.M. & Iczkowski, K.A. (1990). Barriers for deinstitutionalized psychiatric patients. *Hospital and Community Psychiatry, 41*(1): 93-95.

Bachrach, L.I. (1994). Residential planning: Concepts and themes. *Hospital and Community Psychiatry, 45*(3): 202-03.

Beggs, M. (1993). *OK in My Backyard.* San Francisco: San Francisco Study Center

Blanch, A.K. (1988). *Final report of the Vermont task force on community crisis options.* Center for Community Change Through Housing and Support, University of Vermont.

Bliss, S.M. (1993). In practice. *In Community, 3*(2). Burlington, VT: Center for Community Change Through Housing and Support, University of Vermont.

Bliss, S.M. & Curtis, L. (1993). Crisis services systems: Beyond the emergency room. *In Community, 3* (2). Burlington, VT: Center for Community Change Through Housing and Support, University of Vermont.

Bloom, M. & Fischer, J. (1982). *Evaluating Practice: Guidelines For the Accountable Professional.* Englewood Cliffs, NJ: Prentice Hall, Inc.

Cambell, J., Schraiber, R., Temkin, T., & Ten Tusscher, T. (1989). *The well-being project: Mental health clients speak for themselves.* Sacramento, CA: The California Network of Mental Health Clients.

Carling, P.J., Randolph, F.J., Blanch, A.K., & Ridgway, P. (1988). A review of the research on housing and community integration for people with psychiatric disabilities. *NARIC Quarterly, 1*(3).

Center for Mental Health Services (CMHS). (1993). Blueprint for a cooperative agreement between public housing agencies and local mental health authorities. Rockville, MD: Center for Mental Health Services.

Chen, Alfonso. (1991). Noncompliance in community psychiatry: A review of clinical interventions. *Hospital and Community Psychiatry 42*(3).

Cook, J.A. & Hoffschmidt, S.J. (1993). Comprehensive models of psychosocial rehabilitation. In P.L. Solomon & R.W. Flexer (eds.), *Psychosocial rehabilitation in practice.* Stoneham, MA: Butterworth-Heinemann Press.

Curtis, L. (1993). Crisis Prevention: The cornerstone of crisis response. *In Community, 3*(2). Burlington, VT: Center for Community Change Through Housing and Support, University of Vermont.

Curtis, L.C., Tanzman, B.H., & McCabe, S.S. (1992). Orientation manual for local level supported housing staff. Burlington, Vermont: Center for Community Change.

Finkle, M., Van Tosh, L., Chamberlin, J., Posey, T., Crafts, J. & Howie the Harp. (1990). Coming home: Consumer voices on supported housing. *Psychosocial Rehabilitation Journal, 13*(4): 5-8. Excerpted from P. Ridgway. (Ed.) (1988). *Coming Home: Expatients View Housing Options and Needs.* Burlington, VT: Center for Community Change Through Housing and Support, University of Vermont.

Ellsworth, R.B. Characteristics of effective treatment settings: A research review. In J.G. Gunderson, O.A. Will & L.R. Mosher (Eds.) *The Therapeutic Milieu.* Jason Aronson, 1978.

Gambrill, E.D. *Casework: A Competency-Based Approach*: 1-9. Englewood Cliffs, NJ: Prentice-Hall Inc.

Gardner, E.K. Community as Therapy. In: *Using Psychodynamic Principles in Public Mental Health.*

Harris, M. (1994). Modifications in service delivery and clinical treatment for women diagnosed with severe mental illness who are also the survivors of sexual abuse trauma. *The Journal of Mental Health Administration, 21*(4): 398-406.

Hatfield, A.B. (1987). Families as caregivers: A historical perspective. In A.B. Hatfield & H.P. Lefley (eds.) *Families of the Mentally Ill: Coping And Adaptation.* New York: Guilford Press.

_____ (1987). Coping and adaption: A conceptual framework for understanding families. In A.B. Hatfield & H.P. Lefley (eds.) *Families of the Mentally Ill: Coping and Adaptation.* New York: Guilford Press.

Hatfield, A.B. & Lefley, H.B. (1987). (eds.) *Families of the Mentally Ill: Coping and Adaptation.* New York: Guilford Press.

Hawthorne, W.B. & Fals-Stewart, W. (1994). A treatment outcome study of community-based residential care. *Hospital and Community Psychiatry, 45* (2): 152-55.

International Association of Psychosocial Rehabilitation Services (IAPSRS). (1992). Position statement on housing. International Association of Psychosocial Rehabilitation Services: Columbia, MD.

_____ (1995). Position statement on medication. Columbia, MD: International Association of Psychosocial Rehabilitation Services.

Jones, M. (1953/1956). Therapeutic community as a system for change. New York Basic books. *American Journal of Psychology,* 112-647.

Jonikas, J.A. & Zeitz, M.A. (In press). Responding to the needs of mothers with psychiatric disabilities: Thresholds' mothers project's family support program and parenting wards program. *Community Support Network News.* Boston, MA: Center for Psychosocial rehabilitation.

Kennedy, C. & Manderscheid. R.W. SSDI and SSDI beneficiaries with mental disorders. In R.W. Manderscheid & M.A. Sonnenschein (eds.) Mental Health, United States, 1992. Rockville, MD: U.S. Department of Public Health and Human (SAMHSA, CMHS, NIH & NIMH).

Lefley, H.P. (1987). Culture and mental illness: The family role. In A.B. Hatfield & H.P. Lefley (eds.) *Families of the Mentally Ill: Coping and Adaption.* New York: Guilford Press.

McCabe, S.S., Edgar, E.R., Ding, D.A., Ross, E.C., Mancuso, L.L., & Emery, B.D. (1991). Holes in the housing safety net...why SSI is not enough: A national comparison study of Supplemental Security Income and HUD fair market rents. Burlington, VT: Center for Community Change through Housing and Support, University of Vermont.

McCabe, S. & Tanzman, B. (1993). Rent subsidies: A key to community housing. *In Community, 3*(1). Burlington VT: Center for Community Change Through Housing Support, University of Vermont.

Mental Health Law Project (MHLP). (1991). *What does fair housing mean to people with disabilities? A guide for advocates, consumers, and landlords.* Washington DC: Mental Health Law Project.

National Alliance for the Mentally Ill (NAMI). (1992). Survey of members in 1992. National Alliance for the Mentally Ill: Arlington, VA.

National Law Center on Homelessness and Poverty (NLCHP). (1992). Beyond McKinney: Policies to end homelessness. Washington DC: National Law Center on Homelessness and Poverty.

National Low Income Housing Coalition (NLIHC). (1992). *1992 Advocate's Resource Book.* Washington, DC: National Low Income Housing Coalition.

Newman, S.J. (1995). The accuracy of reports on housing and neighborhood conditions by persons with severe mental illness. *Psychosocial Rehabilitation Journal, 18*(3): 129-36.

National Mental Health Association (NMHA). (1989). *Your rights to housing: A consumer's guide to the Fair Housing Act of 1988.* Alexandria, VA: National Mental Health Association.

Nicholson, J. & Blanch, A. (1994). Rehabilitation for parenting roles for people with serious mental illness. *Psychosocial Rehabilitation Journal, 18* (1). 109-19.

O'Hara, A. (1995). "Mixing": HUD'S implementation of Title VI...The PHA allocation plan. The Housing Center Bulletin.

Physicians' Desk Reference (PDR). (1982). Charles E. Baker, Jr. (ed.). Oradell, NJ: Medical Economics Company Inc.

Posey, T. (1990). Guest editorial: A home, not housing. *Psychosocial Rehabilitation Journal, 13*(4): 3-4.

Randolph, F.L., Ridgway, P., Carling, P.J. (1991). Residential programs for persons with severe mental illness: A nationwide survey of state-affiliated agencies. *Hospital and Community Psychiatry 42*(11): 1111-15.

Razzano, L. Common psychotropic medications and their side effects for women and men. Chicago: Thresholds National Research and Training Center.

Richman, E. (1992). Supported housing in urban areas. *In Community, 2*(1). Burlington VT: Center for Community Change Through Housing Support, University of Vermont.

Scallet, L.J. (1994). A message from the executive director. *Policy in Perspective, October 1994.* Mental Health Policy Resource Center: Washington, D.C.

South Carolina Department of Mental Health. (1992). Real homes for real people: Fair housing questions & Answers. South Carolina Department of Mental Health.

Spaniol, L., Jung, H., Zipple, A.M., & Fitzgerald, S. (1987). Families as a resource in the rehabilitation of the severely psychiatrically disabled. In A.B. Hatfield & H.P. Lefley (eds.) *Families of the Mentally Ill: Coping and Adaptation.* New York: Guilford Press.

Spaniol, L., Zipple, A.M. & Lockwood, D. (1994). The role of the family in psychosocial rehabilitation. In: *Introduction To Psychosocial Rehabilitation.* Columbia MD: International Association of Psychosocial Rehabilitation. Reprinted from the *Schizophrenia Bulletin, 18*(3): 341-348, 1992.

Stroul, B.A. (1987). *Crisis Residential Services in a Community Support System.* National Institute of Mental Health, Community Support Program: Rockville MD.

_____ (1993). *Psychiatric Crisis Response Systems: A Descriptive Study.* National Institute of Mental Health, Community Support Program: Rockville MD.

Test, M.A. & Stein, L.F. (1977). Special living arrangements: A model for decision-making. *Hospital and Community Psychiatry, 28*: 608-10.

Thresholds. (1994). Thresholds celebrates 35 years of innovation. *Thresholds Open Door,* (summer issue): 6-8.

Townsend, S. (1994). Federal perspectives: Housing policy for persons with mental illness. *Policy in Perspective, October 1994.* Mental Health Policy Resource Center: Washington, D.C.

Van Tosh, L. (1994). Consumer/survivor involvement in supportive housing and mental health services. *The Housing Center Bulletin, 3* (1). Baltimore MD: University of Maryland School of Medicine.

Wolfe, S.M., Fugate, L., Hulstrand, E.P., & Kamimoto, L.E. (1988). *Worst Pills Best Pills.* Washington, DC: Public Citizen Health Research Group

Zipple, A. & Anzer, T.C. (1994). Building code enforcements: New obstacles in siting community residences. *Psychosocial Rehabilitation Journal, 18*(1): 5-11.

12

Multiple Disabilities

Laura Blankertz

Introduction

Today it is a common occurrence for PSR providers to serve individuals who have a major disability in addition to a major mental health disorder. A recent nationwide survey of PSR workers revealed that 89% of PSR agencies work with individuals with mental health and substance abuse disabilities; 57% of the agencies work with individuals who have mental health and developmental disabilities; 27% of all agencies work with persons who have mental health disabilities and AIDS; and 42% of the agencies work with persons that have mental health and physical disabilities. Such combinations are often called *dual diagnosis*. However, to use this term is often confusing because of the variety of disorders that can be simultaneously co-occurring. In recent years, *dual diagnosis* has been applied frequently to individuals with mental health and substance abuse disorders and to individuals with mental health and mental retardation disorders. Although it is clear to providers within a specific field what the term means, it is often confusing when the term is used in referring to individuals with mental illness in a context where the disabilities are not clearly defined. In this chapter we will be looking at substance abuse, mental retardation, HIV and deafness as disabilities that can co-occur with a major mental health disorder. Despite the fact that approximately one half of all individuals with mental illness will have multiple disabilities, only in the last five years have these disabilities have been concurrently addressed. The comorbidities of mental health and substance abuse and mental health and mental retardation have received the most attention in research and in the literature.

Individuals with dual disorders provide a unique challenge to providers. *First*, they often have behaviors that differ from those persons with only a psychiatric disability. These behaviors may be the result of the interaction of the two disabilities (Parrens, et al, 1984) and may include a range of disruptive or emotional manifestations that are new for the practitioner. *Second*, both disorders need to be treated simultaneously. If one disorder (i.e., the non mental health disorder) is ignored, than this disorder will *bleed through* and in interacting with the mental health disorder cause behaviors that prevent the individual from being effectively treated in the mental health system. Treatment requires knowledge and skills in two sets of disabilities—and most often two different service systems—so that both disorders can be treated concurrently. ***Third*** the practitioner must work cooperatively with two different service systems. These systems (such as mental health and substance abuse, mental health and mental retardation, mental health and deaf community, and mental health and physical health care) may have different values, philosophies of treatment, interventions and entry requirements and may raise barriers to anyone who is different from those persons they have traditionally serviced. Without special care and attention, individuals with mental illness easily fall through the cracks between the systems and receive no help for either set of problems. ***Fourth***, the practitioner must be willing to be creative and flexible. Because people with dual disorders are heterogeneous and because attention to these fields is relatively new, there often are no set interventions or procedures. Staff must be willing to create a range of interventions that both empower the individual and are effective. At some points in the rehabilitation process the provider can offer service which pulls skills from one area or the other. At other times, the provider must create independent, hybridized interventions to meet the needs of the individual with mental illness. ***Fifth***, over time the disorders may change with or without treatment. Staff must be attuned to such changes and be ready to change rehabilitation interventions.

When a practitioner attends to the non-mental health disabilities of an individual with non-traditional interventions, the question can arise: Is this still PSR? As the material in this chapter attempts to illustrate, the underlying principle, attitudes, values, and skill competencies used by PSR workers in the mental health areas can be transferred to other disability areas. As will be pointed out in the material below, the key points in successful rehabilitation of these individuals with multiple diagnoses are:

Competencies 1–6

Understand the reality of the person with dual disabilities through observation and empathy.

Develop rehabilitation plans that meet the current goals of the person.

Assess their behaviors to discover the strengths that can be built upon, and the deficits that need to be addressed by learning new skills or providing the appropriate supports.

Create an empowering environment by maximizing the decision making skill of the individual and supporting their decisions.

Individualize the interventions by presenting a range of services from which the person can choose.

Maximize the flexibility of the rehabilitation process by helping the individual with mental illness to choose new goals over time and constantly trying to create new interventions and supports to meet individual needs.

All of these points are integral to PSR.

For each pair of co-occurring disabilities, this chapter will include:

- Descriptions of the behaviors associated with the various combinations of dual disorders;

- An examination of how these behaviors present a barrier to treatment in each relevant system of care;

- The principles of care that are needed to meet the needs of these individuals with mental illness; and

- PSR direct service workforce competencies that must be integrated into the successful provision of services for individuals with mental illness who have multiple needs.

This chapter is not intended to offer a comprehensive array of interventions for each special population (That would require the comprehensiveness of six different volumes!) Instead its purpose is to offer a good indication of the type and array of interventions that are needed to meet the needs of each population and suggest how the basic principles of PSR can be used in each specialized population. This chapter also does not cover the entire range of multiple disabilities that providers may face. Specifically, it does not include individuals with mental health problems and traumatic brain injury, individuals with mental health disorders and severe physical disabilities, and individuals with mental health problems who face disabilities caused by advancing age. However, it is hoped that the framework developed in this chapter could be extended to these disabilities. To work successfully with person(s) with multiple disabilities, staff must be knowledgeable about the relevant disability and service systems, must be able to appreciate individual strengths and not focus solely on dysfunctional or disruptive behaviors, and must be able to create interventions that have the potential to maximize positive behavioral change.

Individuals with Severe Mental Illness and Substance Abuse/Dependence

Although there are a variety of mental disorders that can occur in combination with some amount of substance use, the term "dually diagnosed" (or "substance abusing mentally ill," "chemically abusing mentally ill," "mentally ill chemical abuser") is usually reserved in the literature for those individuals with a major mental disorder (Axis I or borderline personality), whose use of substances has a negative impact on their functioning in areas such as socialization, work, and family. An individual does not necessarily have to be drug dependent to have a substance abuse problem. Some individuals are *exquisitely sensitive* and can have severe negative behaviors and mental problems occur after the ingestion of even minute amounts of substances.

Prevalence

Recent reviews of the mental health and substance abuse literature indicate that the problem of multiple illnesses and disabilities is the rule rather than the exception among persons seeking mental health and substance abuse treatment in the public sector (Ridgely, 1991). In a large scale epidemiological study, Reigier et al (1990) documented the magnitude of this problem. From a sample of 20,000 people in one community, (including people who were institutionalized, on the streets, and regular residents), it was found that, among those with a mental disorder, the odds ratio of having some addictive behavior was 2.7, with a lifetime prevalence of 29%. Among those with an alcohol disorder, 37% had a comorbidity of mental disorder. Those with drug disorders manifested the highest mental addictive comorbidity rate, with 53% having a mental disorder.

Rates may vary with the nature and setting of the sample. Rates are higher for those individuals in treatment. "Over a third of patients in general psychiatric settings and half or more of those in settings that provide more intensive treatment, such as psychiatric emergency rooms or in patient psychiatry programs, have problems substantially affected by substance abuse or dependence" (Galante, Castaneda, & Ferman, 1988). Rates of dual diagnosis also seem to be higher for younger individuals (Toner, 1992).

Characteristics

People who abuse drugs and also have a mental illness pose a severe challenge to service providers because of their behaviors. They have been described as non-compliant, disruptive, prone to relapse. "Such patients....usually identify themselves immediately to treatment staff by a demand for attention or other extreme behaviors." (Wallen). They are prone to become homeless, HIV positive, incarcerated or die (Drake, Teague & Warren, 1990). Clark and Drake (1992) note that substance abuse contributes to unstable social and marital relationships, including relations with families that have provided them with a social margin and housing. Thus, they are often very isolated from community and family networks, socializing with others who use substances and evolving a life style revolving around the use of substances. The combination of drug abuse and mental illness also exacerbates the person's inability to manage finances. Individuals with a dual diagnosis may be at a high risk of contracting HIV because of cognitive impairment, poor judgment, affective instability, and impulsivity. High proportions of this group have been reported in the prison population. For example, 88% of sentenced prisoners in the State of Washington met criteria for a substantial emotional or psychiatric disorder. Of that group, a full 92% also met criteria for alcohol/substance abuse or dependence.

People with a substance abuse disorder and a mental illness often are difficult to engage (Cooper, Brown & Anglin, 1989), reject treatment offered, and enter into rehabilitative centers only in crisis. Jails, emergency rooms, and streets become the providers of service (Cooper et al, 1989; Schutt & Garret, 1988; Meisler, Blankertz, McCay, and Santos, 1997). They are also very heterogeneous. They may vary by: diagnosis, drug of use, level of functioning, motivation, and psychosocial stressors. Each of these characteristics has implications for the interventions needed to address their disorders. Thus, treatment must be individualized.

Barriers to accessing service systems

The mental health and substance abuse systems have traditionally had different philosophies, assumptions, interventions, and entry requirements based on the profile and experiences of the population they have traditionally served. Mental health providers have traditionally expected service recipients to take psychotropic medication and have stressed the process of engagement, a bonding relationship with a mental health worker and a minimization of stress. There has been a traditional belief in the mental health system that drug abuse is a secondary problem to a psychiatric disorder and that effective mental health treatment will result in cessation of the drug abuse. Traditional drug rehabilitation programs have required total abstinence from all drugs and medication, compliance with a very regimented schedule and reliance upon high levels of confrontation to produce individual change. In addition, many in the drug rehabilitation community have trouble with the concept of ongoing, chronic impairment.

Thus, the two systems often form parallel systems of care. At best, people with substance abuse disorders and mental illness are supposed to integrate the services on their own, or to shuttle back and forth between services. At worst, the disruptive behaviors of the dually diagnosed individual threatens the mental health system. Persons evidencing psychotic behaviors are not suitable in the substance abuse system. Thus, the person with a dual diagnosis is excluded from each type of program and falls between the cracks of the systems often receiving no services except emergency hospitalizations.

Competency 1

Provide assertive outreach.

Principles of Care
Often individuals with a dual diagnosis are difficult to engage and have a low motivation to confront their disabilities. Providers must take the time to learn what their world is like, so that they can offer the person what they want in order to get them to begin to accept services and to come to see the provider in a positive light. Often this world is chaotic and may involve behaviors that the practitioner would not tolerate for himself, such as IV drug use, forensic experience, and episodes of homelessness. This requires that outreach take place in the community, at the time and place of the individual's choosing. Practitioners must recognize that it may take a long time to gain the trust of the person being served. They must make repeated overtures consistently attempting to offer something that the person wants. Because of the

difficulty in getting people with a dual diagnosis engaged in the treatment system, and the high rates of mortality, if positive offers are rebuffed, some clinicians have suggested using negative reinforces (i.e., having treatment as part of a probation or parole or sentence) to bring them into contact with the service system.

Competency 2

Develop accurate assessments.

It is important to determine if there are indeed two concurrent disabilities. This process can be very difficult because the symptoms of each disorder can mimic, hide, and exacerbate each other. However, if a substance abuse diagnosis is missed, then an individual may continue to abuse until their behaviors produce negative outcomes and they leave treatment. If someone is incorrectly given a mental health label, then they may unnecessarily be given medications.

Competency 3

Provide holistic treatment.

Many life stressors may contribute to mental health and substance abuse disabilities. Both mental health providers and substance abuse providers have found that if there is to be a strong chance for recovery in either disorder, then psychosocial stressors must be dealt with. For people with a dual diagnosis, these unmet needs are not only housing, financial, clothing, medical but also family issues, and treatment for past childhood abuse.

Competency 4

Provide structure and opportunities to develop responsibility.

Structure can be an important part of the treatment of people with mental health and substance abuse disorders. Substance abuse involves a lifestyle of immediate gratification and impulsivity. It is a life that often rotates only around the attainment of drugs. They must learn to control their impulses and delay gratification if they are to meet the demands of community living. One way to help a person with a dual diagnosis to do this is by developing a structure in daily life. An external structure provides security, as well as a sense of purpose in life until they develop internal structure. Drake et al (1990) found that sometimes the most gains are made during periods in which structure is provided.

Concurrent with the development of an internal sense of structure is the development of responsibility for actions (i.e., the acceptance of consequences for one's own behaviors). Because of the early onset of mental illness and substance abuse disorders, many dually diagnosed individuals have missed this important step of psychosocial development. Providers can help them develop a sense of responsibility by not protecting them from the natural consequences of their behaviors and by the utilization of contingency contracts for violations of program rules.

Competency 5

Provide opportunities to develop self esteem.

Because of the stigma and dysfunctional behaviors associated with dual disor-

ders, people with substance abuse and mental health disorders often have very low self images and do not feel that it is possible to change. Many have already suffered so many hurts that negative reinforcement does not change their behaviors. Positive reinforcement for appropriate behaviors, whether verbal praise or material rewards, can help develop positive attitudes towards change and increase feelings of self-efficacy. From 1988-91 Horizon House in Philadelphia, Pennsylvania, operated a residential program for dually diagnosed, homeless individuals under funding for a research and demonstration grant from National Institute of Alcoholism and Alcohol Abuse. Positive reinforcement was an important part of the program and was in fact the only programmatic factor that was significant in the final data analysis. Positive reinforcements included verbal praise for behavioral changes on a daily basis as well as symbolic and material rewards (e.g., poster, earrings, coffee mugs) for the completion of program levels.

Competency 6

Provide interventions tailored to individualization of care.

Because of the heterogeneity of the population with dual disorders and the chronic nature of the two disorders, each individual will have specialized needs over different periods of time. Staff should provide interventions that meet each person's needs at a particular time. Interventions may include: group therapy, individual counseling, peer group meetings, individualized contingency contracts, and clinical drug screens. Each practitioner should make a range of services available from which persons participating in services may choose. Empowering people to make choices will begin to empower them to take control of their lives again.

Understand and demonstrate the stages of care.

Engagement

Engagement is the key component in the care of people with substance abuse disorders and mental illness. Without successful engagement, none of the other stages can occur. The end goal of engagement is to form a trusting relationship or working alliance with the person. (Engagement with this population differs from engagement with persons with serious mental illness. Because of drug abusing behaviors, trust can not be automatically given, but rather is the outcome of the relationship.)

An ongoing process, engagement necessarily varies according to the needs and strengths of the individual. Letting each person know that someone cares about the individual helps to motivate him or her to form a relationship with the practitioner. To do this, the practitioner needs to recognize the validity of the person's own world view. This means listening carefully to determine what they are relating, reflecting back the person's view, expressing empathy for problems and past trauma and respect for their strength in surviving. The practitioner needs to demonstrate that they can help to achieve goals that the person deems important. This demonstrates that the practitioner is sincere in trying to help and that the relationship will have positive benefits. The result of the care and respect shown by the worker is that the person comes to see *self* as someone who is worthy.

Engagement should lead not only to the development of a respectful relationship between the individual and the provider but also to the development of empowerment. The provider must respect strengths of the person and let him be an active participant in the rehabilitation process. For example, clients have the ultimate power to decide if the bond is going to form with the practitioner. The Dual Diagnosis Community Treatment Teams that operate in the state of New Hampshire as the keynote of their dual diagnosis treatment systems have stressed the importance of engagement as the first step in the rehabilitation process. These teams, consisting of mental health workers, substance abuse workers, and a part time psychiatrist, offer individualized, concomitant, and coordinated treatment to the individual in the community. Case workers are in the community, talking to the people in the program, family, landlords and police. They stress meeting the immediate needs of the person (e.g., housing problem, medical care) so that the person served will look at the worker in a positive light and be more receptive to listening to them. Substance abuse is not a strong focus of the engagement process although an attempt is made to get everyone to attend substance education groups in the community mental health center.

Persuasion

This stage can only begin once the working alliance is formed. The purpose of this stage is to get the individual with a dual diagnosis to see abstinence as a positive goal that the person wants to attain. In order for each person to begin to work towards abstinence, the individual must want to change and must feel capable of change. Thus, two things must occur. First, the individual must see abstinence as a valued outcome. For this to happen, cognitive dissonance must be established, with all of the person's problems associated with the substance abusing behaviors seen as conflicting with a desired life style. One technique to develop this disequilibrium is motivational interviewing. Another is peer group discussions in which peers help each other to recognize the negative consequences of substance abuse.

Second, the individual must develop a sense of self-efficacy. He or she must see that they are capable of change and thus, capable of attaining abstinence. Several concrete steps can help this process. First, teaching new skills can give the individual the feeling that he or she can accomplish something. Many people view their lives as a series of failures. Second, positive feedback for any small progress helps the person feel capable of changes and also strengthens the bond between the participant and the practitioner. Third, the person can learn to control mental health problems through compliance with medication and counseling. Not only does this increase self-efficacy but it also reduces a major stressor for the substance abuse.

Active treatment
The practitioner must provide a range of interventions that fit with the biopsychosocial stressors that have caused the substance abuse and then let the individual choose the one that he or she feels is most appropriate. Such interventions may include: peer groups, NA or AA, medication (i.e., antebuse), and individual therapy.

Relapse prevention
Relapse must be seen as a learning experience rather than as a behavior to be punished. Because of the chronic nature of the dual disorder, a relapse that occurs in one problem area may stimulate a relapse in the second area. The practitioner should review the supports and skills of the person to see what additional ones can be added.

Competency 8

Understand the longitudinal nature of treatment.

Successful treatment often takes a long period of time because of the chronic nature of the two co-occurring disorders. Staff need to maintain a sense of optimism so that they can maintain a positive spirit of motivation for themselves and encourage it in the individual with mental illness with whom they work.

Staff competencies
Staff members must learn the philosophies and interventions of each system so that they have a wide range of service interventions to draw upon at each stage and the understanding of each disorder necessary to create innovative, hybridized intervention. Practitioners must be flexible and must be willing to continually learn. Practitioners must be willing to work with people who have behaviors that are incongruent with their own personal standards (e.g., drug abuse, prostitution) and must respect their strengths in the rehabilitation relationship. It is also extremely important for staff to be able to avoid burnout because of the difficult behaviors of the people with substance abuse disorders and mental illness and the long process of rehabilitation.

Mental Health and Mental Retardation

Introduction

If the goals of normalization and successful community living for individuals with mental retardation are to be met, then it is necessary for providers to be able to work with people with the comorbidities of mental health and mental retardation (Ruedrich & Menolascino, 1984). Mental illness (and disruptive behaviors) have been cited as factors leading to institutionalization and/or failure in community adjustment (Parens, May & Menolascino, et al, 1984). In providing interventions to those with this particular combination of dual diagnoses, providers must be able to offer services which meet the needs of individuals with mental retardation (defined as both intellectual retardation and deficits in social adaptation that are apparent before adulthood) as well as mental disturbances (Parens, May & Menolascino, et al, 1984).

Prevalence

Of individuals with mental retardation, 20% to 60% have a psychiatric disorder, with the estimates of major mental health disabilities (Axis I) ranging from 20% to 40% (Parsons, et. al, 1984). The prevailing professional opinion is that individuals with mental retardation are more prone to mental disorders than are their peers who do not have mental retardation (Parens, May & Menolascino et al, 1984). Although the exact reason is not known, it is conjectured that individuals with mental retardation face more frustrations and conflicts than do other individuals because of their handicaps or cognitive abilities (Ruedrich & Menolascinl, 1984). In addition, individuals with mental retardation may have a limited capacity to cope with the pressures of day to day life—for example, the frustration in recognizing that one never will be able to be "just like others."

It can be difficult to determine if a psychiatric disturbance coincides with mental retardation. The DSM III-R and DSM IV, similar to earlier versions, were created to assess psychiatric problems for those with normal intelligence. They can be applied with only minor modifications when the individual with mental illness has mild mental retardation but for persons with the severe retardation, the utility of these criteria is doubtful (Parens, May & Menolascino et al, 1984; Dosen, 1993). Through the process of *diagnostic shadowing,* the characteristics of mental retardation decrease the diagnostic significance of the accompanying mental health diagnoses. For example, the lack of ability to think abstractly becomes interpreted as "intellectual distortion," the content of psychiatric symptoms often differs, and the individual with mental retardation often cannot handle the stress of the testing situation, which becomes interpreted as "cognitive disintegration"(Fletcher, 1993).When individuals have severe mental retardation as well as a major psychiatric disorder, it is often difficult to distinguish a true psychiatric disorder from an unmanageable behavior (Gold et al, 1989).

Characteristics

There are many degrees of mental retardation. The more severe the retardation the less ability the individual has to verbally communicate with providers. The less able a person is to communicate, the more tempting it is for the practitioner to assume that he or she knows what the person wants and to make decisions on his or her behalf, in effect depriving him of power. Thus, it is the responsibility of the practitioner to seek out the dimensions of the world of the individual and to determine his or her likes and dislikes. If a person is not able to express preferences, then the provider must use behavioral observations and the observations of others close to the person to determine needs and preferences.

People with mental illness and mental retardation may present behavioral management problems. Some develop *severe reputations*. However, providers need to recognize that the negative behavior is often a form of communicating. The cycle of increased control being met by increased negative behaviors can become a vicious one (Small & Harrison, 1992).

Systems barriers

Both the mental health and the mental retardation systems have tended not to service people with both mental illness and mental retardation because of the "assessment difficulties and behavioral issues" (Gold et al, 1989). Often they are shuffled from institutions for the mentally retarded to institutions for the mentally ill in a lifelong cycle of nontreatment (Menolascino & Fleisher, 1993). What has happened, mostly by default, is that many people have fallen through the cracks. Currently, the best approach is to treat the acute psychiatric needs in psychiatric settings and to meet the long-term needs in community programs with secondary support provided by the mental health system (Fletcher, 1993; Menolascino & Fleisher, 1993). An innovative program, the MATCH in Canada brought together front line case managers from both the mental health system and the mental retardation system. Within a time limited series of meetings the case managers came to understand more fully the needs of those persons with a dual diagnosis, to develop an appreciation for how

case management differed between the two systems and what was shared in common and to develop a needs assessment and planning form that could be used in both systems as a starting place for rehabilitation planning and resource development. Participants in the group also discussed barriers and methods of addressing them between the two systems.

Competency I

Understand the individual is the essential core of the service plan.

Principals of care

The practitioner must start with the individual as the central core of the service plan and build the services around the needs of the person. The first step in the process is to determine whether the problem lies with the identified individual or with the systems in which the individual is involved. All too often persons in environments that are difficult for them, express their frustrations through nonconforming behaviors. The behaviors often cause them to be referred for mental health care (Fletcher, 1993). Programs should be developed for the individual rather than trying to fit the individual into pre-existing programs (Small & Harrison, 1992).

Establishing a bond with a the person is

Competency 2

Establish a working alliance.

the first step in the treatment process. "The relationship should be based on mutual trust and respect. The staff member needs to communicate such qualities as concern, acceptance, empathy and genuineness as a basis for their relationship" (Monsila & Menolascino, 1984, p, 155). To do this, the staff member needs empathetic understanding—understanding the inner world of the individual from his or her perspective and the perceived reality experienced by the person. This relationship may take time to develop because of the lack of previous experience in establishing trusting relationships on the part of the person with dual disabilities.

Competency 3

Conduct a careful behavioral assessment.

As previously noted, the usual diagnostic parameters may be clouded or inappropriate and self reported symptomatology may be inaccurate or absent (Ruedrich & Menolascino, 1989). Thus, the practitioner should use behavioral data acquired through observation or from information provided by the family or other care-givers (Ruedrich & Menolascino, 1984). Attention to the social, psychological, and biological factors contributing to the dysfunction is important and should be the key to the assessment. Also, there should be periodic reevaluation. Behavioral assessment is the key to determining the strengths and needs of the person and for determining the rehabilitation plan regardless of the degree of disability. For example, even for individuals who can not communicate verbally and who have destructive behaviors, acute observation and graphic monitoring of behavior can help to determine what stimuli create equilibrium and a better quality of life and what stimuli create disturbing behaviors (Bradley & Davey, 1994).

Medication should not be prescribed unless there is clear behavioral evidence that it improves the quality of life of the person. Too often psychotropic medications are used as a method of control.

Competency 4

Empower the person served.

Early in the treatment process the practitioner and the person served should establish goals on which they mutually agree, rather than relying on the workers' unilateral perception of the needs (Fletcher, 1993). All too often individuals with mental retardation are denied this opportunity. Thus, "a mutually agreed-upon treatment plan that articulates goals and objectives may be therapeutic in itself, as it provides an opportunity for the client to take an active role in the goal-planning process. Client input from the beginning state of goal setting empowers the client"(Fletcher, 1993).

There are many creative ways that can be used to empower a person. Positive reinforcement (as opposed to negative reinforcement) can be used to empower the most severely disabled persons so that they can learn behaviors that improve the quality of life. The goal is not to eliminate destructive behaviors but to teach new ones (Dosen, 1993). In providing this type of intervention for an individual, the practitioner must make sure that: 1) the reinforcers address the likes and dislikes of the person, 2) the individual can actually perform the behavior, 3) the person knows why the behavior is being reinforced, and 4) social reinforcements are used concurrently so that the positive reinforcements can eventually be *faded*.

Provide individualized rehabilitation interventions.

Many of the techniques used in PSR for individuals with mental health disabilities can also be very effective with people who have both mental retardation and mental health disabilities. These include:

- **Individual Therapy**

  Individual work can be psychodynamic, supportive, or counseling (Fletcher, 1993). It does not matter what type of individual work is used, as long as it is person-centered and focused on the goal of enhancing self-esteem, meaningful relationships with others and self empowerment. Although many people have felt that psychodynamic interventions would not be appropriate for individuals with mental illness and mental retardation, such techniques have more recently gained acceptance as a viable form of treatment. Psychotherapeutic approaches that stress warmth and acceptance and that are keyed to differing developmental levels of personality functioning can work very well with individuals with dual diagnoses (Fletcher, 1993). It is the quality of the working alliance and not the level of intellectual or cognitive functioning that is the key to successful psychotherapy (Fletcher, 1993).

  The idea of establishing a mutually valued relationship has been termed "Gentle Teaching" (McGee, 1993). This specific intervention involves unconditional regard for the other, displaying positive valuation even when the individual is rejecting, and eliciting valuation from them. The end goal is to be engaged, to feel that it is good to be with the other, to interact, to share, and to give and receive human valuing. It means displaying an appreciation of the other for just being, not for the positive behaviors that they perform (McGee, 1993).

- **Group Therapy**

  Group therapy can also have positive results. Several different functions can be performed by group therapy. First, because the group members have an opportunity to discuss, listen, and observe others who have similar circumstances, feelings, and goals, feelings of isolation, defeat, and inadequacy may be reduced. Second, the participation may create a sense of security, trust and a feeling of belonging. It may give the supports necessary to develop a strong and healthy sense of self. Third, the groups may provide experience and exposure in problem solving. Fourth, members learn to offer others encouragement in groups. This process of being needed and wanted by others increases self-esteem and decreases self absorption (Fletcher & Duffy, 1993).

Competency 6

Interventions should be empirically proven.

When the goals of the person are clearly defined, then several possible alternatives of interventions should be generated. One should be selected and implemented with definable outcomes observed. If, after a period of time, the intervention is not successful, then another one should be chosen (Parsen, et al, 1984).

A number of treatments should be offered concomitantly, such as medication, therapy (which depends upon motivation, verbalization, and insight and not on degree of intelligence) and a modification of the environment (Ruedrich & Menolascino, 1984).

Practitioner competencies

Practitioners should accept people with mental illness and mental retardation and have positive attitudes toward each person's potential. It is important for practitioners to have a strong commitment to the dignity and value of each individual if they are to work with people that have co-occurring mental retardation and mental health disabilities. Persons with mental retardation are "often denied adequate services because of negative staff attitudes which impede the development of a therapeutic relationship" (Fletcher, 1993, p. 330).

Practitioners must have basic information on mental illness, mental retardation, and medication. Staff must work to engage the person with mental retardation, interacting with them in ways that they understand. They must be cognizant of all the different ways/methods that people use to communicate, specifically that behavior in itself is a major form of communication. Thus, staff should be careful not to personalize inappropriate behaviors. Practitioners must realize that they themselves are models of appropriate behavior. And finally, providers of care must be patient and have a tolerance for frustration. They should also be warm and flexible.

Mental Health and HIV

Prevalence and vulnerability

Nationwide data are not available, but HIV infection rates among various populations of the mentally ill in New York range from 4% to as high as 19.4% (Shover, 1994). People with mental illness have been identified as one of the populations most threatened by HIV/AIDS (Shover, 1994). Having either mental illness or HIV increases the incidence of the other disorder. Because of these serious consequences, in this section we will be concerned not only about those with HIV but also those greatly at risk for becoming infected.

Characteristics

Individuals with major mental illnesses are very vulnerable to AIDS because they may engage in a range of sexual behaviors that put them at risk for HIV and because many are involved in IV drug use (Shover, 1994). These sexual behaviors include male homosexual contact and heterosexual contact with person considered to be at high risk, such as intravenous drug users (who may share needles) and prostitutes. Persons with mental illness are as knowledgeable as the general public about AIDS, but this knowledge may not be sufficient to bring about behavior change, especially during times of psychiatric crisis (Sacks, et al, 1994). Because of their mental illness, these individuals may have cognitive impairments, poor judgments, affective instability, or poor impulse control—all characteristics which may affect decision making. With an early onset of the mental illness, a person may have had a limited psychosocial development and lack a sense of sexual self efficacy. They may also lack self esteem (Carmen & Brady, 1991).

Individuals who are HIV positive may have a range of psychiatric problems. Some can come from the HIV virus (which attacks the central nervous system), some (such as depression, social isolation and personal fear of pain, weakness, and disfigurement) can come from the severity and stigma of the AIDS related illness, and some can come from the interaction of both these stressors with the previously existing mental disorders (Penner, 1994). Suicide may be the only way that some feel that they have control over their own destiny.

System barriers
Individuals with mental illness who are either at high risk of HIV or already have it need specialized services. These services must integrate mental health issues with knowledge about AIDS and must provide the necessary emotional supports. The locus of the treatment is currently in the mental health system. Because of cognitive impairments, low self esteem and low self-efficacy that often characterize persons with severe mental illness, the content of AIDS education must be specifically adapted to meet their needs (Goldman et al, 1991). But these practitioners must receive training from the physical health care system as well, to know what resources are available (Harvey & Triveli, 1990).

Competency I

Provide AIDS education and risk assessment.

Principles of care
At this point in our medical knowledge, given the absence of a vaccine, AIDS can only be controlled by behavior change, specifically getting people to either control or eliminate their high risk behaviors. Both sexual and drug abuse behaviors are difficult to change because they are strongly motivated, pleasurable, complex and poorly understood (Shover, 1994). To get people to change these at-risk behaviors, they have to see AIDS as a threat to themselves and feel that they have the ability (self-efficacy) to change their behavior (Cates, Bond & Graham, 1994).

The best way to get someone to admit vulnerability is by conducting a personal risk assessment (Carmen & Brady, 1991). Similar to other PSR assessments, this assessment is based upon the behavior of the person. The risk assessment is a series of questions about sexual activities (i.e., number and characteristics of partners) and substance abuse activities. Many agencies have now instituted it as a part of their intake process. The goal is to get people who are high risk to recognize their risk and then to agree to be tested for HIV. The completion of a risk assessment instrument is also a check to make sure that counselors, who may not be comfortable discussing sexual activities and AIDS, have covered these areas (Cook et al, 1994).

Individuals must also be able to see themselves as capable of change. Self-efficacy has been defined as confidence in the ability to organize and emit courses of action and to be in control in a particular situation. Some mental health programs have particularly targeted the development of sexual self-efficacy as part of their AIDS prevention work. They use role modeling, concrete rewards, and role playing in situations that are sensitive for persons with mental illness, such as delicate negotiations with intimate partners (Susser, Valencia & Torres, 1994). To communicate effectively practitioners utilize methods of interaction that are meaningful to the specific population. (e.g., in homeless shelters, where verbal competition and interplay is popular, workers make up games about AIDS and other sexual practices and have mock quiz shows). Effective programs to develop self-efficacy also build on strengths of the person. In the case of people who are homeless, workers use role playing, story telling, and an ability to entertain. Such programs also must provide a new set of behaviors, such as condom use, assertiveness, reasoning and decision making (Susser, Valencia & Torres, 1994).

Counselors must also be aware that some people may have their psychiatric problems aggravated by fears and concerns about AIDS. Indeed such fears may feed into delusional systems.

Competency 2

Understand the care of individuals with AIDS.

In this area "few specific therapeutic approaches have been suggested"(Lauer-Listhaus & Walterson, 1989). Basic services needed include crisis intervention, communication, and support. Staff have two goals in working with people with AIDS and mental illness. The first is to encourage prevention of contagion, and the second is to address the psychological needs and concerns of the person. Practitioners must be aware that they need to help each person handle concerns of physical and psychological deterioration, as well as death and the uncertainty of exactly when it will occur. They also need support to work through guilt feelings, anxiety, and depression (Knox, 1994). People with mental illness and AIDS need to be able to discuss fears and feelings about dying so that can go

through the stages of grief, mourning, and acceptance. Groups are an important mode of intervention. Groups can address the issues of isolation as well as provide a supportive atmosphere to bring up fears and concerns (Cook, et al, 1994).

Special needs of practitioners

Staff members may face a number of barriers to working with high risk and HIV populations. First, they must deal with a fear of contagion (Knox et al, 1994). Second, they may need to overcome feelings of blame: that individuals with mental illness are responsible for becoming HIV positive and see it as a result of their own behaviors. Third, practitioners may need to deal with reluctance to work with the terminally ill or may over-identify with those persons being served because they are so young. Fourth, practitioners need to develop patience with the person at risk because changing the targeted behaviors is a slow and complex process. Some of the best training programs for staff are experiential in nature. These involve observing others working with AIDS and talking to individuals with AIDS. Staff need on-going support so that do not experience burn out from their work with these very needy individuals.

Mental Illness and Deafness

Prevalence

Deafness is the single most common chronic physical disability in the United States. Individuals may be deaf from an early age or may acquire this disability through disease, accident or as a result of aging. Exactly when they became deaf and the degree of deafness that they have can make a large difference in the type and mode of communication that they utilize and in their patterns of social interaction.

Characteristics

Similar to people with other disabilities, the central focus of the practitioner is to understand the world experienced by the deaf individual with mental illness. To do this, staff must understand the importance of spoken language to the creation of reality for non-deaf individuals. It is not just the words themselves, but often the context and the tone of the words that are used to communicate ideas. Through our language, we express abstract ideas and emotions. Individuals who are deaf may learn to lip read (which places its own physical limitations on communication) or may use American Sign Language (or some other *home-grown* sign language) to communicate. Both miss the non-verbal aspects of the spoken language and thus some of the content of communication with the hearing world. Because of this difficulty in understanding and expressing thoughts in the "normal world," many individuals with deafness have immersed themselves in the deaf culture, with its own modes of interaction. For example, sign language often requires different physical actions in the communication process than are used with spoken communication (i.e. standing close, methods of attracting other person's attention and facial expressions). Based upon the need to have comfortable patterns of interaction, people with deafness have sponsored their own newspapers, sports teams, etc. This world thus becomes a place of social interaction where communication is entirely in a mode that can be comprehended by the person with deafness. It is a place where the person with deafness can have total acceptance and where its own standards for status and success can be established. A sense of empowerment comes from participating in the deaf community, which is deaf-centered and focuses on a positive deaf self-definition.

Because our psychiatric assessments are so tightly tied in with language, a provider can often not get an accurate assessment of a deaf person unless they are very familiar with the differences in communication patterns (Steinberg, 1991). For example, behavior that might be termed *flat affect* in the spoken world may in fact be a normal mode of communication for the deaf person.

Barriers to systems

The mental health system is not easily accessible to deaf individuals. Deaf persons with mental illness who seek help from programs designed for hearing patients risk being ignored, misunderstood, misdiagnosed or inappropriately treated. All too often there are not interpreters available and the individual is isolated rather than given treatment. The deaf need access to specific deaf services with deaf staff so that they have appropriate role models and they have the opportunity to identify with the deaf world. Identification with the deaf community does not mean that a deaf individual can not live out in the hearing community and use some of the same services such as supported employment, but the person needs to approach the hearing world from a position of strength rather than isolation.

Currently there are very few specialized programs for deaf individuals with mental illness. The need for such programs was not apparent until deinstitutionalization was well under way. The programs that do exist are in large urban areas where it is cost effective to devise such a program. Some of the best programs are part of a total system of care, where there are deaf inpatient units linked to deaf day programs and deaf residences and halfway houses and where staff themselves are deaf or deaf individuals recovering from mental illness who can serve as role models. It is much more difficult, however, to implement such programs in rural areas. Those in rural areas should be given a choice of either moving to where there are specialized services or accepting the services of translators and mobile support workers in their current community mental health facility. At the very least, deaf individuals with mental illness should be evaluated by psychiatrists who are experienced with the deaf culture and in working with this subpopulation. It would be best if the psychiatrist is able to communicate with sign language because even the presence of a deaf interpreter may affect the therapeutic alliance.

Competency I

Develop knowledge of the deaf community.

Principles of care

If a provider is not himself deaf, then he must have a thorough knowledge of the deaf community in addition to a knowl-edge of sign language. The practitioner must see deafness as a strength which allows integration into the deaf community rather than as a weakness.

Competency 2

Develop adequate supports and services.

If specialized deaf services are not readily available, then a practitioner must search as widely as possible to find the best services, starting with an adequate psychiatric diagnosis. The practitioner must be ready to find interpreters and supports so that the individual does not have to face the hearing community alone.

Competency 3

Listen to the values of the individual being served.

Some may want integration into the deaf community while others may identify with the hearing community.

Thresholds-Bridge Program for the Deaf

One example of a comprehensive PSR program for individuals with severe mental disabilities and deafness is the range of services offered by the Thresholds-Bridge Program for the Deaf in Chicago, which has received awards from organizations such as the American Psychiatric Association. Services include: assertive community treatment (ACT) model of case management, three levels of residential care, day programs, and vocational rehabilitation. Staff include mental health practitioners and persons with deafness (65%). All of the staff are fluent in sign language. In combining PSR and deafness, the goal is integration into the deaf community as an end in itself. The ACT project staff have been willing to take on many different roles such as coaching births, interpreting funerals, and acting as a witness for weddings to support program participants in the community. The three residences, each of which is especially equipped for persons with deafness, provide needed support to prepare for residence in commercial housing. The program has a psychiatrist who is knowledgeable about deaf culture, is skilled in American Sign Language and has close relations with a state hospital that operates an inpatient unit for patients who are deaf.

References

Bradley, E. A. & Davey, K. I. (1994). A procedure to assist in the assessment & treatment of behavioral, emotional & psychiatric disturbance in individuals with developmental disabilities. *The NADD Newsletter, 11*(5).

Carmen, E. & Brady, S. (1990). AIDs risk & prevention for the chronically mentally ill. *Hospital & Community Psychiatry, 41*(6), 652-657.

Cates, J., Bond, G. R. & Graham, L. L. (1994). AIDS knowledge, attitudes & risk behavior among people with serious mental illness. *PSR Journal 17*(4).

Clark, R.E., & Drake, R.E. (1992). Substance Abuse and Mental Illness: What Families Need To Know. *Innovations and Research, 1*(4), 3-8.

Cook, J. A., Kozlowski, K. K & Razzano, L. (1993). Psychosocial rehabilitation of deaf persons with severe mental illness: A multivariate model of residential outcomes. *Rehabilitation Psychology, 38*(4), 261-274.

Cook, J. A., Razzano, L., Jayara, A., Myers, M., Nathanson, F., Scott, M. A. & Stein, M. (1994). HIV risk assessment for psychosocial rehabilitation clientele: Implications for community based services. *PSR Journal , 17*(4).

Cooper, L., Brown, V., & Anglin, M.D. Multiple diagnoses: Aspects and issues in substance abuse. Sacramento, CA: Drug Abuse Information & Monitoring Project.

Dosen, A. (1993). Mental health & mental illness in persons with retardation: What are we talking about? In *Mental Health Aspects of Mental Retardation.* New York: Lexington Books.

Drake, R. E., Bartels, S. J., Teague, G. B., Noordsy, D. L. & Clark, R. Treatment of substance abuse in severely mentally ill patients. *Journal of Nervous & Mental Disease, 181*(10), 606-611.

Drake, R. E. & Noordsy, D. L. (1994). Case management for people with coexisting severe mental disorder & substance use disorder. *Psychiatric Annals, 24*(8), 427-431.

Drake, R. E., Teague, G. B. & Warren, S. R. (1990). Dual diagnosis: The new hampshire program. *Addiction & Recovery,* 35-39.

Editors. (1991). Gold award: Comprehensive mental health services for deaf people with major mental illness. 42 (10), 1057-8.

Fletcher, R. J. (1993). Individual psychotherapy for persons with mental retardation. In *Mental Health Aspects of Mental Retardation.* New York: Lexington Books.

_____. (1993). Mental illness—mental retardation in the U.S.: Policy & treatment challenges. *Journal of Intellectual Disability Research, 37*(1).

Fletcher, R. J. & Dosen, A. (1993). *Mental Health Aspects of Mental Retardation.* New York: Lexington Books.

Fletcher, R. J. & Dubly, T. (1993). Group therapy for persons with mental retardation. In *Mental Health Aspects of Mental Retardation.* New York: Lexington Books.

Gold, I.M.,Wolfson, E. S., Lester, C. M., Ratey, J. J., & Chmielinski, H.G. (1989). Developing a unit for mentally retarded: Mentally ill patients on the grounds of a state hospital. *Hospital & Community Psychiatry, 4*(8), 836-840.

Goldman, R.M., Kent, A.B., Montgomery, E.C., Cheevers, M.M., & Goldfinger, S.M. (1991). AIDS education for patients with chronic mental illness. *Community Mental Health Journal, 27*(3), 49-197.

Harvey, D.C. & Trivelli, L. (1990). HIV education for persons with mental disabilities. AIDS Technical Report. *NAPAJ, 1.*

Knox, M.D., Davis, M., & Friedrich, M. (1994). The hiv mental health services. *Community Mental Health, 30*(1).

Knox, M.D., Friedrren, M.A., Gares, J.J., & Achenbach, K. (1994). Training HIV specialists for community mental health. *Community Mental Health Journal, 30*(4), 405-413.

_____. (1981). Training HIV specialists for community mental health. *Community Mental Health Journal, 30*(14).

Lauer-Listheus, B. & Watterson, J. (1988). A psychoeducational group for HIV-positive patients on a psychiatric service. *Hospital & Community Psychiatry, 39*(7), 776-777.

McGee, J. (1993). Gentle teaching for persons with mental retardation: The expression of a psychology of interdependence. In *Mental Health Aspects of Mental Retardation.* New York: Lexington Books.

Menolascino, F. & Fleisher, M. (1984). Mental health care in persons with mental retardation: Past, present & future. In Menolascino, F. J., & Stark, J.A. (Eds.) *Handbook of Mental Illness in the Mentally Retarded.* New York: Plenum Press.

Meisler, N., Blankertz, L., Santos, A. & McKay, C. (1997). Impact of assertive community treatment on homeless persons with co-occurring severe psychiatric and substance use disorders. *Community Mental Health Journal, 33* (2).

Monsila, M. & Menolascimo, F. (1984). Modified individual & group treatment approaches for the mentally retarded —mentally ill. In Menolascino, F.J., & Stark, J.A. (Eds.) *Handbook of Mental Illness in the Mentally Retarded.* New York: Plenum Press.

Moran, S.F., Budd, R. & Shulk, B. (1994). Balancing the power: consumer-centered systems. *The NADD Newsletter, 11*(4).

Parsons, J.A., May, J.G., & Menolascino, F.J. (1984). The nature & incidence of mental illness in mentally retarded individuals. In Menolascino, F.J., & Stark, J.A. *Handbook of Mental Illness in the Mentally Retarded.* New York: Plenum Press.

Penner, S. (1994). HIV/AIDS & mental illness: The case for community health planning. *PSR Journal, 17*(4).

Regier, D.A, Farmer, M.E., Rai, D., Locke, B., Deith, S. J., Judd, L.L., & Goodwin, F.R. (1990) Comorbidity of mental disorders with alcohol and other drug abuse: Results from the Epidemiological Catchment Area (ECA) Study. *Journal of American Medical Association, 21*, 2511-2518.

Ruedrich, S. & Menolascino, F. (1984). Dual diagnosis of MR & MI. In Menolascino, F.J. & Stark, J.A. *Handbook of Mental Illness in the Mentally Retarded.* New York: Plenum Press.

Sacks, M., Dermatis, H. B., William-Hall, J. & Perry, S. (1994). Acute psychiatric illness: Effects on HIV-risk behavior. *PSR Journal, 17*(4).

Schutt, R. & Garrett, G. (1988) Social background, residential experience and health problems of the homeless. *PSR Journal, 12* (3), 67-70.

Smull, M. & Harrison, S.B. (1992). *Supporting people with service representatives in the community.* National Annotated State Directors of Developmental Disabilities Services, Inc. Alee.

Steinberg, A. (1991). Issues in providing mental health services to hearing-impaired persons. *Hospital & Community Psychiatry, 42*(4), 320.

Stover, E. & Pequegnat, W. (1994). Introduction. *PSR Journal, 17*(4), 3-4.

Susser, E., Valencia, E. & Torres, J. (1994) Sex, games & videotapes: An HIV-prevention intervention for men who are homeless & mentally ill." *PSR Journal,* 17(4).

Toner, B.B., Gilies, L.A., Prendergast, P., Cote, F., & Browne, C. (1992). Pattern of substance use disorder in the chronically mentally ill. *Hospital and Community Psychiatry, 43*, 251-254.

13

Resources

Ruth Hughes

As the field of psychosocial rehabilitation has grown, the number of organizations involved in training and research has skyrocketed. The following organizations can provide resource information and materials regarding mental illness, psychosocial rehabilitation, and advocacy for persons with mental illness. It is not an exhaustive listing. Many of the sources come from the *1995: Psychosocial Rehabilitation Training Resources*, a joint publication of IAPSRS and the Center for Psychosocial Rehabilitation at Boston University, by Marianne Farkas and Kathleen Furlong-Norman.

International, National, and Regional Associations

Bazelon Center for Mental Health Law
1101 15th St., NW, #1212
Washington, DC 20005
Phone (202) 467-5730
FAX (202) 223-6198

California Association of Social Rehabilitation Agencies
PO Box 388
Martinez, CA 94553-0038
Phone (510) 229-2300

International Association of Psychosocial Rehabilitation Services
10025 Governor Warfield Parkway
Columbia, MD 21045-3357
Phone (410) 730-7190
TDD (410) 730-1723
FAX (410) 730-5965

Maryland Association of Psychiatric Support Services
109 Melrose Avenue, #C
Catonsville, MD 21228
Phone (410) 788-1865

National Alliance for the Mentally Ill
200 N. Glebe Rd., #1015
Arlington, VA 22203-3728
Phone (703) 524-7600
FAX (703) 524-9094

National Community Mental Healthcare Council
12300 Twinbrook Parkway, #320
Rockville, MD 20852
Phone (301) 984-6200
FAX (301) 881-7159

National Mental Health Association
1021 Prince St.
Alexandria, VA 22314
Phone (703) 684-7722

New York Association of Psychosocial Rehabilitation Services
23 Elk Street
Albany, NY 12207
Phone (518) 436-0008

Training Programs

Boston Center for Psychosocial Rehabilitation
930 Commonwealth Ave.
Boston, MA 02215
Phone (617) 353-3549
FAX (617) 353-7700

Center for Community Change through Housing and Support
Trinity College Vermont
208 Colchester Ave.
Burlington, VT 05405
Phone (802) 658-000
FAX (802) 863-6110

Center for Continuing Education in Rehabilitation
Western Washington University
14110 NE 21st St.
Bellevue, WA 98007-3719
Phone (206) 957-4522
FAX (206) 747-5360

Center for Improving Mental Health Systems
Human Interaction Research Institute (HIRI)
1849 Sawtelle Boulevard, Suite 102
Los Angeles, CA 90025
Beth Howard, Project Coordinator
Phone (310) 479-3028
FAX (310) 479-4650

Center for Human Services Development
University of Maryland
3229 J.M. Paterson Building
College Park, MD 20742
Phone (301) 405-4573
FAX (301) 405-4576

Fountain House
Colleague Training
425 West 47th St.
New York, NY 10036
Phone (212) 582-0340
FAX (212) 397-1694

Hamilton Psychiatric Hospital
Rehabilitation Services Department
PO Box 585
Hamilton, ONT L8N 3K7
CANADA
Phone (905) 388-2511
FAX (905) 575-6035

Human Resource Association of the Northeast
187 High Street, Suite 302
Holyoke, MA 01040
Phone (413) 536-2405
FAX (413) 536-4166

Humber College, Ontario Chapter, IAPSRS Psychosocial Rehabilitation, Continuing Education Dept.
PO Box 19004/Sussex PO
720 Spadina Ave., #100A
Toronto, ONT M5S 3C9
CANADA
Phone (416) 481-5652
FAX (416) 481-5653

Independence Center
Colleague Training Program
4380 West Pine Boulevard
St. Louis, MO 63108
Phone (314) 533-4380
FAX (314) 531-7372

Matrix Research Institute
6008 Wayne Dr.
Philadelphia, PA 19144
Phone (215) 438-8200
FAX (215) 438-8337

Mid-Atlantic Center for Human Resource Development
University of Pennsylvania
Dept. of Psychiatry
3600 Market Street, Room 719
Philadelphia, PA 19104
Phone (215) 662-2886
FAX (215) 349-8715

Middlesex County College Psychosocial Rehabilitation and Treatment Associate of Science Program
University of Medicine
155 Mill Rd., Rm. LH2303
Edison, NJ 08818-3050
Phone (908) 906-4177
FAX (908) 906-4685

National Empowerment Center
20 Ballard Rd.
Lawrence, MA 01843-1018
Phone (800) 769-3728
FAX (508) 681-6426

National Mental Health Consumers' Self-Help Clearing House
311 South Juniper St., #1000
Philadelphia, PA 19107
Phone (800) 553-4539
FAX (215) 636-6310

Program for Executive Leadership in State Mental Health Administration
Harvard Medical School, Dept. of
Psychiatry/NASMHPD
74 Fenwood Road
Boston, MA 02115
Phone (617) 742-5657
FAX (617) 742-0509

Recovery, Inc.
802 N Dearborn St.
Chicago, IL 60610-3364
Phone (312) 337-5661

Regional HRD Systems Approach to 13 Southern States
The Southern HRD Consortium for
Mental Health
2414 Bull Street, P O Box 485
Columbia, SC 29202
Phone (803) 734-7893
FAX (803) 734-7897

Western Psychiatric Institute and Clinic Psychosocial Rehabilitation and Assessment Services
204 Iroquois Building
3600 Forbes Ave.
Pittsburgh, PA 15213
Phone (412) 624-2842
FAX (412) 624-0672

WICKE Mental Health Program
Western Interstate Commission for
Higher Education
PO Drawer P
Boulder, CO 80302
Phone (303) 541-0250
FAX (303) 541-0291

UCLA Clinical Research Center for Schizophrenic Psychosocial Rehabilitation
Box 6022
Camarillo, CA 93011-6022
Phone (805) 484-5607
FAX (805) 389-2700